PRIME MOVERS

THE MAKERS OF MODERN DANCE IN AMERICA

SECOND EDITION

PRINCETON BOOK COMPANY, *Publishers*

The second edition of *Prime Movers* includes the entire text
of the first edition, reprinted by arrangement with William
Morrow & Company, Inc., and additional material by
Joseph Mazo.

Published by Princeton Book Company, Publishers
P.O. Box 831, Hightstown, New Jersey 08520

ISBN 0-87127-211-3

Cover photo by Susan Cook of *Runes* by Paul Taylor

Printed in Canada

HISTORY IS WRITTEN
FOR THE FUTURE,
AND THIS BOOK WAS WRITTEN
FOR JENNIFER

ILLUSTRATIONS

Grateful acknowledgment is made to the following for permission to use their photographs in this book:

The Dance Collection, The New York Public Library at Lincoln Center, Astor, Lenox and Tilden Foundations, for use of the photographs which appear on pages 19, 25, 33, 39, 45, 51, 57, 63, 73, 77, 81, 87, 95, 101, 105, 111, 115, 141, 149, and 159, as well as for the use of the drawings of Isadora Duncan by Abraham Walkowitz which appear on the title page and at the beginning of each chapter. Thanks also to Susan Cook for reproducing these photographs.

Barbara Morgan, for use of her photographs which appear on pages 10, 119, 131, 139, 145, 155, 165, 169, 173, 192, and 203. All of these appeared in the *Barbara Morgan Monograph*, published by Morgan & Morgan, 1972. The photographs on pages 155, 165, 169, 173 and 192 also appeared in *Martha Graham: Sixteen Dances in Photographs* by Barbara Morgan, 1941.

Sotheby's Belgravia: 29; Soichi Sunami: 125, 135; Martha Swope: 177, 181, 187, 193, 319, 331; James Klosty: 209, 217, 228; Susan Cook: 261, 265, 269, 277, 281, 285; Jack Mitchell: 231, 275; William Pierce: 310; Herbert Migdoll: 311; Susan Schiff-Faludi: 245, 249; Abdul-Rahman: 267; Tony Russell: 315; Gjon Mili: 321; The Twyla Tharp Dance Foundation, Inc.: 307; The Nikolais Dance Theatre (David Berlin): 251; and The Merce Cunningham Dance Foundation (Oscar Bailey): 213, 221.

ACKNOWLEDGMENTS

A SECOND BOOK is considered an author's most difficult job. The first one is done in a burst of naïve exuberance; by the time you reach the third, you supposedly know what you are about. The second is nasty because you are never quite sure that finishing the first was not something of a miracle or that you will be able to do it again. This is a second book, and it was accomplished with the help of friends. It would have been quite difficult —if it had been completed at all—without the work of Paula Meinetz Shapiro, perhaps the only researcher in the world who also reads manuscripts, makes suggestions and invites the author over for homemade ravioli. The exacting research she devoted to this project could serve as a definition of tenacity. Thanks are also due to Harvey Shapiro, who typed some of the notes and provided conversation while the ravioli were cooking. It is also necessary to note the contribution of Samantha Shapiro, who considerately waited to be born until the project was finished.

The Dance Collection of the New York Public Library is an indispensable source for anyone doing research in the field, and anyone who has used it owes a debt to the staff, which is led by Genevieve Oswald. In this case, special thanks must go to Marta Lucyshyn who served as a guide through the labyrinth of books, articles, films, tapes, and pictures.

Pamela Hatch, my editor, managed to remain encouraging even when the work went slowly. Her interest in the field, her enthusiasm for the project, and her knowledge of the presentation of visual materials were intensely valuable, and her friendship was even more of a help.

Finally, in tribute to a much-maligned species, I should like to thank for his advice, assistance, and encouragement, John Cushman, literary agent.

INTRODUCTION TO
PRIME MOVERS, SECOND EDITION

PRIME MOVERS BY Joseph Mazo, first published in 1977, found immediate success with readers hungry for cogent, accessible dance history. Mazo's entertaining, journalistic style that placed choreographers within the political, artistic, and cultural context of their times proved popular to a wide audience and secured the book's demand during the sixteen years of its life.

In 1998, responding to requests for information about *Prime Movers,* Princeton Book Company owner Charles Woodford decided to explore the feasibility of republication. He concluded that the original was badly out-of-date and would be difficult to update: Mazo had died in 1995 and his distinctive style would be nearly impossible to match. The author needed to edit his own work.

Joseph Mazo had written for *The New York Times, Women's Wear Daily, Town and Country,* and *Dance Magazine*—but most prolifically for *The Record,* published in Hackensack, New Jersey. As a dance critic and feature writer for the newspaper, he had written hundreds of performance previews and reviews right up until the day he died, July 26, 1995. These articles became the basis of the second edition of Mazo's book.

To update *Prime Movers* some new material was added to the end of existing chapters and the concluding chapter was expanded to include choreographers who had earned Mazo's attention and praise since the original publication. In addition, the Bibliography was updated to include references which the author might have used since 1977, and an entirely new Videography was created.

Because Mazo integrated his own past work into his current writing, reviews often included his previous observations, many of which had already been stated in *Prime Movers*. As a result, reviews and previews are excerpted here. Each source is noted in parenthesis at the end of the selected section.

It becomes clear from these articles that the author retained and deepened his original judgement of everyone included in *Prime Movers*. Mazo revised his opinion of Martha Graham's later capabilities, and praised Erick Hawkins, who barely received a mention as a choreographer in the original publication of *Prime Movers*, with increasing passion. He remained entranced by Twyla Tharp and followed her development (impossible to have predicted in 1977) through the close of her own company, her position as resident choreographer for American Ballet Theater, and her creation of the first dance choreographed by an "outside" choreographer for the Martha Graham Dance Company.

It is impossible to state with certainty whom Joseph Mazo would call a genius today—or even if he would consider there to be any at all. Only Erick Hawkins seemed to have earned the title of "genius" in the author's articles. But during the period between the publication of the original *Prime Movers* and Mazo's death, his interest in a choreographer could be measured by the amount of coverage he gave in previews and reviews in *The Record*.

In addition, judging from his articles in *The Record*, it is likely that Mazo would have included additional choreographers in the second edition of his book. Those people—Judith Jamison, Garth Fagan, Trisha Brown, Laura Dean, Ulysses Dove, Jawole Willa Jo Zollar, Ralph Lemon, Mark Morris and Bill T. Jones—are included in the expanded *Epilogue*.

Readers of *Prime Movers, Second Edition*, need to read the material from the original edition with some caution. Information written in the present tense may no longer be true for the simplest of reasons: Martha Graham, John Cage (long associated with Merce Cunningham), Alwin Nikolais, and Alvin Ailey are no longer alive. Conclusions which Mazo makes in the first edition are, on occasion, revised in his later writing. Because of the unique quality of Mazo's writing and his seamless weaving of relevant fact and evocative description, it was decided not to tamper with the original text or interrupt it with awkward footnotes.

In the obituary which appeared in *The Record*, Joseph Mazo was "remembered by colleagues as a kindly, enthusiastic, knowledgeable critic, gifted at painting verbal pictures of a non-verbal art form." With an eye for seeing dance and a clear voice for translating those images into words, Mazo allowed readers to envision the dances he described.

"'He was a great enthusiast—he really loved what he was doing,' said friend and colleague Clive Barnes of the *New York Post*, who . . . may have been the last person to see him alive." They had both attended a performance the night of Mazo's death. The author was found in his apartment two days later with his review for *The Record* nearby. He was 56-years-old. (*The Record*, August 1, 1995)

* * *

Prime Movers, Second Edition would not have been possible without the help and permission of William Morrow and Company, Inc., publishers of the first hardback edition of *Prime Movers*, and Maggie Hutchinson and Paul Schulman of *The Record*. In addition, we would like to thank the research staff of the Hackensack (New Jersey) Library and and New Jersey State Library (Trenton, New Jersey).

—Naomi Mindlin, editor
Prime Movers, Second Edition

CONTENTS

The torso of Merce Cunningham as symbol of the dynamism and strength of American dance. From Root of the Unfocus, *1944.* DETAIL OF A PHOTOGRAPH BY BARBABA MORGAN.

PROLOGUE

THIS IS A BOOK about a group of geniuses who developed a new kind of art.

It is quite possible to be an unsuccessful genius. During the middle of the nineteenth century, an English mathematician, George Babbage, determined to build a machine that would perform complicated calculations without making mistakes. Unfortunately, the metalworking shops were incapable of manufacturing the necessary parts. Babbage, being a genius, built a better machine shop and tried to produce the components himself, but the technology of his time was simply too unsophisticated to manufacture what his mind had conceived. The inventor of the computer died, disappointed, in 1871.

A successful genius understands the ways of thinking, the needs and the rhythms that dominate his era. If he is an artistic genius, he demonstrates them to the rest of us, helping us to understand why we act as we do. When an artistic genius successfully rebels against the conventions of his culture, it is because he understands that processes are at work that demand a change. The successful genius works with the tools at hand and communicates in symbols which at least some of his contemporaries can understand. His work encompasses the spirit of his time.

A genius, according to my dictionary, is someone with an extraordinary capacity for imaginative creation, original thought, invention, or discovery. An artist is someone who takes human experiences out of context and sets them within an organized form. There are good artists and bad artists, just as there are good plumbers and bad plumbers, but all of them deal with perception and emotion. The good ones help us perceive more clearly and feel more keenly than we did before they showed up.

An unfortunate belief, which has not yet been eradicated, holds that art is meant to be appreciated, not enjoyed ("If I like it, it can't be good") and that artists are required by their profession to suffer ("I have to suffer to watch this stuff, so she had to suffer to invent it"). There are kinds of art which large segments of the public are not able to enjoy, but they are not the only kinds available. Artists suffer personally, not professionally—a glance at the extent of Bach's output convinces you that he did not agonize over each cantata—and they produce art because that is what they want to do.

Less than one hundred years ago, several people decided that they wanted to dance and realized that the kinds of theatrical dance being performed were academic, empty-headed, or both. So they changed them. In 1889—to accept the most probable date—a former temperance lecturer named Loie Fuller invented *The Serpentine* and started something that eventually became known as modern dance. Modern dance is not an exact term. It was invented as a name for "serious-theatrical-dance-that-is-not-ballet." American modern dance meant "Serious-theatrical-dance-that-is-neither-ballet-nor-German-modern-dance."

Ballet, despite the changes it has undergone in this century, is relatively easy to define. It is a form of dancing that employs five specified positions of the feet. There are more complex definitions, since ballet is a form of dancing based on a rigorous and specific set of techniques, but a work that is based on the five positions can be classified as ballet. Modern dance is not so simple to define. It demands freedom of expression which some artists thought was not available in the structure of ballet. It (generally) makes the movement more important than the music. It (at least during the dominance of Martha Graham and Doris Humphrey) depended on the confrontation of opposites, such as fall and recovery or contraction and release. The parentheses make it clear that there is no one form of modern dance.

Ballet is based on one system, however it is modified by different teachers and choreographers; American modern dance embraces many systems and even includes, in some of its recent manifestations, tap dancing, ballet dancing, and nondancing—activities such as eating and reading while curled up in a carton. It has taken steps from social dancing—which is not surprising since ballet evolved from court and peasant dances—and from the dances of cultures other than the one that produced it. It is an art that changes rapidly, since it was developed by people whose perceptions were constantly being altered by new ideas, new machines, new methods of perception.

This book starts with the Art Nouveau style of Loie Fuller and works through to the soft shoulders on a ballet base favored by Twyla Tharp. In between it touches on the "Greek" dancing of Isadora Duncan, the Oriental dancing of Ruth St. Denis, the dances of Spaniards and American Indians used as sources by Ted Shawn, the codified systems of Martha Graham and Doris Humphrey, the multiplicity of movements employed by Merce Cunningham, the dancing of black Americans that underlies the work of Alvin Ailey, and several other styles. Strangely enough, there is a main line of development that unifies this huge anthology of movement—it is an attempt to make dance that will communicate something of importance to an audience of the choreographer's contemporaries. American modern dance has always been more concerned with the present than with posterity.

This book is an attempt to contribute to an understanding of that development. It does not try to explore every aspect of the subject or to discuss every figure of importance. The book that sought to do this would have to be a scholarly tome, and I am not in the scholarly tome business. Instead, I have concentrated on a few figures who were of major importance to the development of the art—or who continue to be—and who were, or are, significant because of some specific contribution they have made that has helped the art to grow. Certain important dancers and choreographers have been excluded because their work does not contribute to the main line of development explored in this book, or because it was amplified and given more importance by artists whose endeavors *are* discussed. The work of the German Expressionist dancers, for instance, is mentioned but not detailed.

A great deal of scholarly work remains to be done in the field of dance. Genevieve Oswald, curator of the Dance Collection of the New York Public Library, has compiled a long list (and only a partial list, mind you) of topics awaiting scholarly research. If this book prompts anyone to continue his studies of dance, it will have done part of its job. The people who made this art were an astonishing, courageous, eccentric lot, and more should be known about them. However, works written by scholars too often are designed to be read by other scholars, and this book is for people who prefer to take their dance in the theater rather than in the library. I hope it will give them some idea of how methods originated, how they were passed from artist to artist, and how they changed in the process. I have been more concerned with ideas of dance than with techniques, since technique is usually more interesting to technicians than to bystanders.

This is not so much the story of modern dance as the story of modern dancers, who have proven to be a remarkable group. They have tended to have a touch of the evangelist about them, whether they were atheists like Isadora Duncan or mystics like Ruth St. Denis. They have always been individualists—which may be one reason why they did not always particularly like one another. They have never been dull. Most of the important modern dancers, at least in the beginning, were women. Ballet was largely produced by men, but in the years when modern dance was born American men did not dance—it simply wasn't done—and for the first time in recorded history it was the job of women to make a new art. Twyla Tharp remarks that "the ego of the male ballet choreographer must have colored his consideration—why is there no male *corps de ballet*, a group of men arranged in abstract patterns?" Furthermore, she says, the role of the male in ballet is not particularly well defined; all the great Classical roles are for ballerinas. Certainly, once women learned to dance on pointe—between 1820 and 1830—they were relegated to the roles of fragile, airborne creatures who died of a broken heart or were awakened with a kiss. It is hard to picture one of Martha Graham's great heroines waiting around for her prince to come. The development of modern dance parallels in many ways the development of the idea that women are real human beings. The first artists of American modern dance were feminists in that they believed themselves to be independent, capable, functioning human beings. No one who did not believe that would have been willing to devote a life to an art that did not yet exist.

The women who began this new kind of dance had their first successes in Europe, but they were Americans and the styles of dance they created could have developed nowhere but in the United States. In no other country would it have seemed logical to draw on so many ethnic sources. In no other country has technological change been accepted as quickly. Furthermore, no country or era has sustained as large and continuous an influx of people and ideas as twentieth-century America. This is a nation of continual motion. Americans change their residence as casually as other people change clothes. The history of the country is one of movement, of expansion and contraction, and of changes of direction. Americans are a people who do not like to stand still, and that accounts for many of our failures, as well as for our triumphs.

However, this book is not a celebration of a nation, or of a sex, or even of dance. It is merely the history of a group of individuals gifted with the greatest of human virtues: genius, passion, skill, and moral courage. In the cases of these particular people, those traits manifested themselves in dances, which is reason enough to care about the art.

LOIE FULLER

THE EVANGELIST OF LIGHT

BALLET WAS DEAD, to begin with. There is no doubt whatever about that. At least, it was dead in America.

At the turn of the century almost the only serious dance in the United States was the ballet at the Metropolitan Opera House, which had opened in 1883, and the Met imported its dancers (the most celebrated came from Italy) and did not even establish a school until 1909. The scraps of ballet served to Americans were lukewarm leftovers, academic, unimaginative, boring, and virtually the only kind of artistic dancing to be seen.

It is important to remember—and easy to forget—when reading the denunciations of ballet issued by the pioneer modern dancers, that they were not talking about the kind of ballet that holds the stage today. Russian ballet, stringent and ripe for change as much of it was, was a living art served by great performers. Even Isadora Duncan, who insisted that ballet was "a false and preposterous art," lauded the great ballerinas Kschessinska and Pavlova when she saw them perform in St. Petersburg. She had never seen their like elsewhere in Europe, and certainly not in America.

The United States had, in earlier years, developed a liking for ballet. The first season of the art seems to have been presented in New York in 1792, by a dancer from Paris. The great Romantic ballets were shown here shortly after their creation, often by important European artists who toured the country. The nation's affair with Romantic ballet reached its height between 1840 and 1842, while the great Fanny Elssler was dancing here, and the United States produced several notable dancers of its own. Mary Ann Lee (1823–1899) danced in Paris and became a prima ballerina in Milan before coming home to give America its first *Giselle* at the Howard Atheneum in Boston on January 1, 1846. She was partnered in that performance by another American, George Washington Smith. Augusta Maywood (1825–1876) was the first American ballerina to achieve wide international acclaim; she danced in Paris, Vienna, Milan, and Lisbon.

The Black Crook, an extravaganza that inspired music hall, variety, vaudeville, and musical comedy, opened in New York on September 12, 1866, featuring a celebrated Italian ballerina, Maria Bonfanti, and dishing up quite a bit of ballet along with its spectacle. In the later years of the century, though, ballet declined in much of Europe, tours to the United States became less frequent, and the work that was produced here was unoriginal and academic. Technique failed to advance, and the art was reined in by foolish conventions, such as having men's roles performed by women *en travesti.* Russian ballet was revitalized by the great choreographer Michel Fokine and the magnifico of producers, Serge Diaghilev, but they at least had a continuing tradition to reform. In America, ballet had gone beyond rigor mortis into decay, and it was an imported art to begin with, lacking tradition, continuity, and innovation. To produce great dance here, it was necessary to start from the beginning.

Aside from ballet, America had show dancing—what Ted Shawn described as "chorus girls kicking sixteen to the right, sixteen to the left, turning a cartwheel and kicking the backs of their heads." There were pageants, of course, and a very few artistic dancers who toured the theaters. And that was that.

The pioneers of modern dance were rebels, and rebels, by definition, must have antagonists. They found theirs in emptiness, the empty conventions of ballet and the simulated revels of show dancing. As far as most of the country was concerned, there was no such thing as serious dance, and the little that did exist clearly was less than exhilarating. The

One of the many posters designed by Jules Cherét for Loie Fuller, who made her debut at the Folies Bergère in 1893. Cherét gives realistic movement to Loie's draperies, and an unrealistic slenderness to Loie.

PHOTOGRAPH COURTESY OF THE DANCE COLLECTION
OF THE NEW YORK PUBLIC LIBRARY.

only thing contemporary ballet and theater dancing could inspire the originators of modern dance to say was, "I want to dance, and that isn't dancing." They did not call themselves modern dancers, by the way. That term came later, when the new art was being established and had to be differentiated from ballet. The pioneers just thought of themselves as dancers.

The logical starting place for a history of modern dance in twentieth-century America is the last year of the nineteenth century in France. An international exposition was held in 1900 at Paris. Exhibits demonstrated the triumphs of science, displayed the history of costume, and proclaimed the achievements and virtues of various nations. A small theater housed the performances of a Japanese actress-dancer, Sadi Yaco, and an American, Loie Fuller. Tourist services offered special excursions for Americans who wanted to see the exposition; wealthy citizens could travel on their own, and some Americans, artists and performers, were already living and working abroad. One of the people who visited the little theater to watch Loie Fuller was a twenty-two-year-old dancer named Isadora Duncan. Another, also twenty-two, was an actress who had just finished an engagement in England. Her name was Ruth St. Denis. Fuller, Duncan, and St. Denis were the founding goddesses of American dance. As any classicist can tell you, when three goddesses appear to Paris, something is bound to happen.

Thanks to motion pictures, books, television, and other forms of legend, everybody knows about Isadora Duncan. A good deal of what they know may be highly romanticized, but at least they've heard of her. Thanks to her longevity, artistry, and dedication, everyone who follows dance knows about Ruth St. Denis. But because of the quirks of history and the line of development followed by modern dance, few people know anything at all about Loie Fuller, which is a pity. She was quite a girl.

To begin with, Fuller managed—albeit indirectly—to scare the daylights out of Isadora Duncan, a feat the Russian Revolution was unable to accomplish. She once became involved in training some wolves, owned by one Prince Troubetzkoy, to dance—as a pack, of course—to the music of shepherds' pipes. She was married, by contract and unsuccessfully, to a nephew of President Rutherford B. Hayes. She was a hypochondriac. She was a homosexual. She presided over her own scientific laboratory, knew the discoverers of radium, and was considered "marvellously intelligent" by Anatole France, who wrote a preface to her autobiography.

Marie Louise Fuller, like many celebrated people, arranged to have herself born in several different years. Her autobiography, *Fifteen Years of a Dancer's Life,* asserts that the event occurred at a tavern in Fullersville, Illinois, in 1870. For the benefit of a French journalist who interviewed her in 1903, she made that 1869. *The Dictionary of American Biography* and *The Dance Encyclopedia,* less inclined to gallantry, list her birth year as 1862 and they are clearly correct, because the map of her career places her on the stump as a temperance lecturer in 1875, at the age of thirteen. (To be haranguing the populace at five would have been a bit too precocious even for Loie.) A passion for temperance was warming the Midwest. The Prohibition Party had been in existence since 1869; the Women's Christian Temperance Union had been formed. The WCTU endorsed women's suffrage in the 1880s, but mostly it stood square for motherhood, purity, and the home and square against whiskey and wickedness. One advantage of temperance, women understood, was that men who did not empty their pockets at the local tavern would be better able to feed their families.

Frances Willard, the second president of the WCTU and the woman responsible for joining it to the suffrage movement, was one of Fuller's idols. Another was Louisa May Alcott, who devoted some of her considerable energy to the women's movement after gaining fame as an author. Loie also expressed admiration for Carrie Nation, who managed to close some illicit bars in Kansas by public denunciation and prayer. Later, she found that a hatchet worked better. Carrie Nation apparently believed that she had been divinely entrusted with the job of closing saloons; Loie Fuller danced at the Folies Bergères, but both women were born in an era that admired intelligence, independence, and guts. The same Midwestern heritage drove them, although along different roads.

You can see something of the drive in photographs of Fuller, which show a stocky, full-bodied woman with a pug nose and a look of determination about the eyes. A thirteen-year-old temperance lecturer undoubtedly needed that, but then, Loie Fuller was always to be something of a missionary.

Except for a brief episode during her childhood, she had virtually no dancing lessons. She was on tour with Buffalo Bill in 1883, and by 1887 was established as an actress, playing leading roles at New York's Bijou Theater for actor-producer Nat Goodwin, who was as celebrated in his area of show business as the Wild West Show man was in his. However, even established actresses sometimes find themselves out of work. While making the rounds of auditions, and finding no roles, Fuller was asked by a manager if she could dance. She immediately decided that she could. "When you are starving," she said later, "you sometimes forget to be strictly truthful."

According to her story, Loie found some cheesecloth in a trunk, draped it around herself and pinned it in place. She discovered that by waving her arms she could make the cloth twist and sway. She told the stage manager that her act required dim lights, then moved her arms in the proper pattern and won applause and a contract, just the way it happened in the movies some years later. This, she said, occurred in London, and Loie Fuller did appear in *Caprice* at the Gaiety Theatre in 1889.

Fuller offered several versions of the story of her discovery during the course of her career. According to one, it happened while she was playing the Harlem Opera House, New York, in 1889 in *Quack, M.D.* In another account, given to a reporter in 1893, Loie said that she had been visited by inspiration two years before in Holyoke, Massachusetts, where the audience at the theater "was so small I didn't think it worthwhile to discard my skirts [she was to have changed to tights] for the second act."

The year 1889 makes the most sense, and the "inspired" dance made a sensation. Fuller called it *The Serpentine,* and it quickly achieved not merely popularity but the status of a fad. As soon as Loie went off to Europe, the United States was filled with Serpentine dancers, each claiming to be Loie Fuller. Ruth St. Denis pointed out that Loie "probably suffered more imitators than any woman alive." Frank Kermode's article, "Loie Fuller and the Dance Before Diaghilev," remarks that an English performer, Kate Vaughn, preceded Fuller as a skirt dancer. It doesn't matter. Nobody had ever done with cloth what Loie did.

It was fortunate for Loie's career that she learned to rely on her skirt rather than on her body. She was not much of a dancer. A film of her *Fire Dance* shows her doing little except turning round and round like an eggbeater. (Fuller was a pioneer in film as well as in dance. In 1905, she made movies for Pathé using slow motion, shadows, and negative printing.) Most of the dancing consists of her arms manipulating her dress. But the costume changes. Her gown becomes a kaleidoscope, changing from black to white to white with black patches. It changes shape, it floats, swirls and displays itself in drapes and in sections. Finally, the long sleeves, which Fuller controlled with sticks, rise over her head and the dancer turns into a tornado—a tall, whirling column of energy spiraling upward.

The rhythm of the dance is clear, but it is defined more by the movements of the costume than by the actions of her body. André Levinsohn, the great French dance critic who admired Loie's work, thought her dancing itself was "ordinary." However, as an innovator, as a maker of magic, he praised her. "She is a great imaginative creator of forms. Her drapes animate and organize space, give her dreamlike ambiance, abolish geometrical space . . ."

When she first performed *The Serpentine* in New York, members of the audiences gasped, "It's a butterfly—it's an orchid." Actually, it was just Loie's skirt, transformed by movement, by colorful dyes, and by contemporary technology. Loie Fuller had discovered light. When she was the featured act in a spectacle called *Uncle Celestin* at the Casino Theatre, she performed one dance under blue light, another under red, a third under yellow, and so on. She arranged lanterns of colored glass so that the light hit her swirling skirts and, as she moved, transformed them into natural objects and abstract patterns.

In her *Fire Dance,* she performed standing on a sheet of glass, lit from below. A contemporary French writer, after seeing the piece, called her "a nightmare in red clay. She smiled enigmatically in the flames; she stood and did not burn—she was flame . . ." Throughout her career, she looked at fabric and light, experimented, expanded her repertory of effects, and learned new techniques. Before she was done, she was traveling with her own crew of fifty electricians, and Sarah Bernhardt was asking her advice about lighting.

Fuller knew how to literally dazzle an audience. The *London Sketch* reported of a performance in 1900: "The orgy of color was so wonderful as to leave objection mute. Light came from every side. La Loie danced upon the glass, from which the vivid splendor of the headlights was reflected, while from the wings, stage, and orchestra, wonderful luminous streams seemed to flow toward her. With the rhythm of the music, the colors changed, and where white ruled before, there was a kaleidoscopic vision.

"Violet, orange, purple and mauve succeeded in rapid succession until a rich, deep red dominated the dancer, and she became, for one brief moment, a living rose with a palpitating heart and flying leaves. Then the hues of the rainbow came from all sides, and ranged themselves upon the ever-moving draperies. Every fold had its tint and scheme of color intensified by the surrounding darkness until the eye could scarcely bear to look . . ."

The critic's prose is at least as purple as Loie's lights, but you get the idea. Loie Fuller had made the discovery, to be repeated, in time, by Alwin Nikolais, that costumes and lights need not be only appurtenances to dance, they can be as much a part of it as human movement.

It is quite logical that Loie should have taken a liking to electricity—they were practically contemporaries. Her childhood years were not an exciting time for dance, but they were a whole amusement park for research and technology. Everybody in America was inventing something in his basement, and some of the inventions worked.

In Europe, William Clark Maxwell published his study of electromagnetic waves in 1865, three years after Fuller was born. During the 1870s and 1880s, Americans discovered the electric light, the telephone, and the sewing machine. (Moses Gerrish Farmer produced electric lights in glass tubes in 1858-1859, and in 1869 lighted a house in Cambridge, Massachusetts, but Edison's bulb of 1878 proved more practical.) Henry Ford produced his "gasoline buggy" in 1893, and the Model T came along in 1908.

It was a time of moving, of communicating despite distance, of increasing freedom from insularity. In time, people were to become as bound to machines as they once had been to places, but Loie Fuller was born to an age of movement and experimentation, to a time rejoicing in the increasing power of light. She employed the carbon arc lights and colored gels with which the theaters of her time were equipped, but she chose her own colors. She designed large projectors which used slides of frosted glass painted with liquefied gelatine. When the theaters at which she played were fitted out to use electricity, of course, she worked with that. (The Savoy in London, home of Gilbert and Sullivan, in 1882 became the first theater to employ incandescent bulbs. The next year, Steele MacKaye became the first manager to light an American stage with electricity. During the first decade of the twentieth century, reflectors and lenses increased the power of incandescent bulbs so that lights could be hung in the house as well as backstage.)

Fuller, posing for a souvenir photograph in 1896, is obviously not the sylph of Cherét's poster. She stands on a glass platform (camouflaged by vegetation) through which electric lights illuminate her costume from below, a device she used in her famous Fire Dance.

PHOTOGRAPH COURTESY OF THE DANCE COLLECTION
OF THE NEW YORK PUBLIC LIBRARY.

In 1892, Loie Fuller established herself in Paris. She did a forty-minute turn at the Folies Bergères; a picture shows her in a huge skirt painted with butterflies, a butterfly headdress and scarves ribboning her arms. Paris adopted her; it adored her, praised her and imitated her. The streets of the city sprouted a crop of women wearing full Fuller skirts. The talents and geniuses of the artistic capital of the world became her friends. The audiences called her La Loie, and everybody loved her.

At the same time that Loie Fuller was teaching light and color to dance, making of herself a butterfly, an orchid, and a lily, a new kind of art was developing in Europe. It was a reaction against the constant, academic reproductions of the styles of the past, and it demanded a return to the use of natural forms such as butterflies and lilies. It was an art that emphasized movement, enclosing floral forms within wavy, curlicued lines, an art that was almost rococo in its unrelenting activity. Any work, a poster, a lamp, or a piece of furniture, had to be an organic entity—and it had to be as busy as an eight-lane highway.

The formulators of this new art had a social conscience; they wanted to give to working people the carefully wrought furnishings and artifacts that had previously been the prerogatives of the nonworking people. In order to accomplish this, it was said, artists should use machines to produce their works in quantity, so they could be offered at reasonable prices. The machine, after all, was the central fact of the new era—why not use it? This idea, combined with the philosophy that the architecture of a building and its interior decoration should form a unity, eventually led the new art into a still newer school, the Bauhaus.

In 1895, Siegfried Bing opened a shop in Paris that was to give the new art of flowing lines and bright colors a name. He called the place, logically enough, "L'Art Nouveau."

Art Nouveau, with its curlicues and colors, its badge of a peacock's tail, its running glazes, and its irrepressible movement, learned from Loie Fuller, and she from it. Her *Serpentine* is part of the history of the style, as are dances in which she transformed herself into stylized impressions of natural objects. In one dance she worked with a large scarf of pure white silk and at the end lifted it high in the shape of a white lily. Émile Gallé, the most celebrated glassworker in France, sought her colors. She had an indirect influence on the design of furniture and on architecture. Her influence was not always indirect, either. Raoul Larche modeled her, scarves like storm clouds above her head, in an ormolu lamp. Jules Chéret and Toulouse-Lautrec made posters of her.

Poster art, made possible by the advances in lithography during the second half of the nineteenth century, seemed an ideal medium for Art Nouveau. Posters could convey emotion and information to an entire populace. You didn't have to go to a museum or gallery, or spend a great deal of money to buy intellectual and visual stimulation; it was only necessary to glance in passing at the walls and kiosks of the city. The ubiquitous reproductions of Alphonse Mucha's posters heralding the appearances of Sarah Bernhardt are examples of the style, and an examination of their colors, their sense of motion, their almost innocent combination of forthright statement and longing for an imagined medieval age will give you some idea of what Loie Fuller looked like when she danced. Except, of course, that Loie moved. Reading descriptions of her performance, you get an image of continuous action.

The poet Mallarmé, who saw her dance in 1893, wrote that the performance "is at once an artistic intoxication and an industrial achievement . . . She blends with the rapidly changing colors which vary their limelit phantasmagoria of twilight and grotto, their emotional changes— delight, mourning, anger . . ."

Her work was, indeed, an industrial achievement. Shortly after Pierre and Marie Curie discovered radium in 1898, Loie Fuller wrote to them. She wanted to dance in "butterfly wings of radium." The Curies explained this was impossible—it was too expensive, for one thing. But thoughts of radium and the light it emitted continued to shine in Loie's imagination, and eventually she did perform a "Radium Dance" on a darkened stage while the scenery and costumes glowed.

"In Paris," she said, "I have a laboratory in which I employ six men . . . I have had some success, for I have invented a process for treating cloth with phosphorescent salts . . . by stripping a fabric with such salts, I could produce a strong and beautiful glow at an expense of about $600 a pound. Part of my hair was blown off in an explosion while I was experimenting in my laboratory, and it made a great sensation in the neighborhood. People called me a witch, a *sorcière*. My hair will not all grow back again, but I do not care."

Her first "radium dance," though, seems to have been done by projecting iridescent colors onto her silks, using a multicolored slide, and then superimposing another upon it. In later years, she used slides printed with photographs of the moon. One of the attractions of the Paris exposition of 1900 was a great telescope through which one could see the moon, and although it is not certain that this is what gave Loie her idea, there is a fair chance that it was. She was fascinated by new gadgets.

By the time of the exposition of 1900, when automobiles were nudging horses off the great boulevards of Paris, Loie was sufficiently popular to have her own theater on the grounds of the fair, and sufficiently well off, generous, and imaginative to sponsor Sadi Yaco, the Japanese artist with whom she shared the theater. By then she was training a group of young women to perform as a dance company—Loie Fuller and Her Muses— and living in comfortable domesticity with Mlle. Bloch, known as Gab, who dressed in men's clothing and who kept the company going for a time after Loie died.

Ruth St. Denis was in London during the spring and summer of 1900, performing in David Belasco's production of *Zaza*. When the play closed, she crossed the channel for a look at the exposition, where she saw Loie dance and was impressed with "her astonishing and beautiful performance. She was not, in the strict sense of the word, a dancer. She had a heavy body and never a very polished technique, but she was an inventive genius and brought a wealth of richness to both the dance and the stage." It was at about the same time that Isadora Duncan saw Fuller dance and she, too, was impressed. St. Denis, Duncan, and everyone else were accustomed to seeing women billed as dancers appear on stage in tights and short muslin skirts to perform an assortment of leaps, bounds, pirouettes, and acrobatic feats. Instead, they saw Fuller, wrapped in a mass of drapery, making the gauze of her costume roll like waves and transform itself into fantastic shapes with the help of a play of lights.

Both Duncan and Fuller wrote accounts of their meeting and subsequent adventures in their autobiographies, and their versions of the events do not quite agree. For one thing, they seem to have unintentionally shocked one another. The manuscript of "An Experience," Chapter Twenty of *Fifteen Years of a Dancer's Life,* shows that Loie wrote in a clear hand, leaving wide spaces between the words, which march in straight lines across the page. The script is cursive but neat

---

An ormolu lamp by Raoul Larche shows Loie and her drapery. Art Nouveau began to develop before Fuller conquered Paris, but the style and her dancing gained importance at the same time, and influenced one another.

PHOTOGRAPH BY SOTHEBY'S BELGRAVIA.

and never extravagant, although initial capitals are sometimes very large and strong. She never mentions Isadora by name, but calls her "an unknown artist" or "my dancer."

Fuller described Duncan as "a young woman of twenty-three or twenty-four [whose] movements gave promise of great things." However, "She was always saying she intended to take nearly all her clothes off and dance in the streets." It is obvious from the tone that Loie herself would never have considered doing such a thing, and did not find the idea to be in the best of taste. Even so, she arranged for Isadora to dance for the wife of the American ambassador and other luminaries. Later, she suggested that the young American join Sadi Yaco in giving concerts under her management, and Duncan agreed to join her in Berlin.

At this point, Isadora's autobiography takes up the story. She reached Berlin and went to the Hotel Bristol, where, "in a magnificent apartment, I found Loie Fuller surrounded by her entourage. A dozen or so beautiful girls were grouped about her, alternately stroking her hands and kissing her." Isadora remarks that her "simple upbringing" had not prepared her for "this extreme attitude of expressed affection . . . Here was an atmosphere of such warmth as I had never met before." By the time Duncan came to write about the incident, she probably understood why all the pretty ladies were being so affectionate, but when it happened, she was in her early twenties and relatively naïve. Queen Victoria was still alive when Isadora first saw Loie dance (the queen died in January 1901), and during her reign certain knowledge was not considered the province of children or young ladies.

Later that evening, Isadora went to the theater where Loie was performing. "Before our very eyes she turned to many colored, shining orchids, to a wavering sea flower, and at length to a spiral-like lily, all the magic of Merlin, the sorcery of light, color, flowing form . . . Loie Fuller originated all the changing colors and floating Liberty scarves."

The tour moved on from Berlin and Isadora went along, under Loie's patronage. Unfortunately, Fuller's money was running short and she had to send one of her young ladies, a redhead called Nursey, on a nocturnal financial mission to Berlin. ". . . in the middle of the night," Isadora writes, "this redheaded girl approached me and kissed me passionately, saying in fervid tones, 'I am going away to Berlin'." Isadora began to wonder "what I was doing in this troupe of beautiful but demented ladies."

When the tour reached Vienna, she wound up sharing a room with her old acquaintance, Nursey, who, at about four o'clock one morning, marched over to Isadora's bed and announced, "God has told me to choke you." Isadora, with admirable presence of mind, asked for a reprieve until she could say her prayers—she was a devout atheist—and when Nursey backed off to allow her this grace, she slipped out of the room and ran. The doctors took Nursey away and Isadora sent a telegram to her mother and left Vienna, the "demented ladies," and Loie Fuller.

Fuller's autobiography recounts a meeting with some people who informed her that Isadora Duncan had said "She did not know Loie Fuller." Duncan's autobiography denies that she ever said any such thing. The two women admired one another as artists, but they seem to have had a conflict of personality. Loie could never understand why Duncan danced wearing so few clothes; Isadora could not face up to Loie's feminine ménage. Still, each knew genius when she saw it and Fuller, with typical generosity, helped give the younger dancer her start in Europe.

Jerome Doucet wrote in *Revue Illustré* in 1903 that Loie Fuller was "a charitable soul, the heart of a socialist, a being of goodness, dreams, imagination . . ." The charitable soul nearly went broke sponsoring the tour with Sadi Yaco and Isadora Duncan, but she recouped her losses and, in 1909, returned to the United States to give performances in New York and Boston. She traveled with her troupe of young dancers and fifty French electricians. Her brother, Bert, acted as their chief to ensure that her secret effects would not be stolen.

The company's performance caused the New York *Dramatic Mirror* to ask, "Is it necessary for Art's sake to make young girls appear without fleshings and in bare feet, with naught to shield their forms save a few folds of flimsy gauze?" Said Loie, "It is an American monopoly to combine stage dancing with self-respect." And she denounced the "hideous man-made lines of the corset." Fuller's dancers still were a good deal more thoroughly "shielded" than Isadora was, not merely by gauze but by the play of light. But America was easily shocked in 1909.

Duncan is usually given credit for disposing of the corset, but Fuller apparently shed it first. She also preceded Isadora in training a company of dancers in her style, and in using Classical music for her performances. Massenet gave her the rights to his scores, and she performed to the music of Gluck, Beethoven, Schumann, Schubert, Delibes, Chopin, Grieg, and Mendelssohn. The music for her *Fire Dance* was "The Ride of the Valkyries." (*Die Walküre* had its first performance in 1870, and many listeners still found the music unpleasantly modern when Fuller chose to use it.)

A brochure issued by M. H. Hanson, concert director, advertising Loie Fuller and Her Muses for the 1909–1910 season at the Metropolitan Opera House and the New Boston Opera House attempts to lure the public by assuring it that, "As Salomé, she dances with shimmering, flowing scarves, her fingers seeming to make pearls trickle all over her body." In Part VI ("The Storm") of the *Peer Gynt Suite,* the brochure proclaims, "The Soul of Woman . . . revolts against the tradition, the sensualism, the enslavements of the past. It fights against its chains." The Soul of Woman is the protagonist of the *Peer Gynt Suite* and, despite the election-poster language, the idea expressed is true to Loie.

Too often, she said, the dance is "a pretext for an exhibition of young girls, always smiling . . ." in very short costumes. Loie was not one for very short costumes, or for exhibiting young ladies. She believed, among other things, in human dignity. For her, dance resulted naturally from music, and was dedicated to expressing emotion. "The moment you attempt to give dancing a trained element," she said, "naturalness disappears. Nature is truth, and art is artificial. For example, a child will never dance of its own accord with the toes pointing out."

But her art was artificial. She called her dancers "instruments of light," and believed that light and cloth, pitchblende and dye, were as much a part of her dances as human bodies, provided that they, too, were used to interpret music and feeling.

In 1920 at the age of fifty-eight, inspired by developments in filmmaking, Loie returned to her laboratory to work out new techniques using shadows and silhouettes. One dance of this period veiled the performers in black, so that the audience saw only silver-sequined tassels being dipped into a narrow, horizontal beam of light. In 1923, her company performed her *Shadow Ballets* in London. One of the most impressive images was that of a huge, shadow hand grasping for cowering dancers. Loie brought the Shadow Dances to New York's Hippodrome two years later.

Fuller in her butterfly costume, the sleeves of which she controlled with sticks held inside the fabric. With the aid of costumes and light, the dancer transformed herself into a work of kinetic sculpture.
PHOTOGRAPH BY FARBER FROM REVUE ILLUSTRÉ, NOV. 1, 1903.

With her shadows, as with her lights, Loie Fuller subdued the human body to an environment. She cloaked it in masses of silk on which she projected patterns. She hid its arms in long sleeves, controlled from within by sticks, as manipulators control Eastern puppets. She surrounded it with shadow, inundated it with light, blazoned it with color, delineated it in monochrome. She never stopped; whenever she found a new idea, a new invention, a new effect, she sought a way to use it. Her art, like Art Nouveau, attempted both to return to natural forms and expressions, and to enjoy the excitement of developing technology.

She did not, like Isadora Duncan, bare her soul and body, nor did she glorify the body as Duncan did. Instead, she glorified the triumphs of her time; the ingenuity of the mind placed at the service of the body, the transcendence of daily concepts of time and darkness, the dignity of women, the power of the machine.

She died in Paris, of pneumonia, on January 1, 1928. The Associated Press obituary gave her age as fifty-eight. The AP was off by eight years, and Loie certainly would have been grateful.

II

ISADORA DUNCAN

THE RELIGION OF THE FOOT

ISADORA DUNCAN was a California girl. She wrote proudly that her grandparents had crossed the country in a covered wagon and of how, years later in San Francisco, her grandmother "used often to sing the Irish songs and dance the Irish jigs; only I fancy that into these Irish jigs had crept some of the heroic spirit of the Pioneer and the battles with the Redskins—probably some of the gestures of the Redskins themselves, and, again, a bit of Yankee Doodle when Grandfather Colonel Thomas Gray came marching home from the Civil War."

Isadora had a vision of a thousand children dancing to the Chorale of Beethoven's Ninth Symphony. She dreamed big, like an American. She was American in the scope of her imagination, in her self-righteousness, in her love of rural beauty and urban feasting, in her excesses, in her belief in the value of freedom and of the human spirit—and for Isadora, that belief was not convention but conviction. She was the right of the nation and the wrong of it; she embodied its strengths and its failings, and she discovered some secrets that the nation never managed to learn. Her "Greek" dances were American sensitivities dressed up in chitons, although they probed more deeply into personal emotion than most Americans—than most humans—care to go.

She helped liberate women from their corsets and dance from its academic restrictions; she had a distaste for conventional restraints. America in the early part of the century was not ready for Isadora. She shocked people.

"Isadora drank too much, she couldn't keep her hands off good-looking young men, she dyed her hair various shades of bright red, she never took the trouble to make up properly, was careless about her dress, couldn't bother to keep her figure in shape, never could keep track of money . . .

"but a great sense of health

"filled the hall

"when the pearshaped figure with the beautiful great arms tramped forward slowly from the back of the stage.

"She was afraid of nothing; she was a great dancer."

John Dos Passos wrote archly about Isadora, but he understood her dancing. The "great sense of health" was described differently by others, but was described so often that we can be certain it was there. She seemed to be transparent, a curtain through which music could glow. "Isadora," said Ruth St. Denis, "was dancing God right in front of you."

Isadora would not have used that word, of course. She was an atheist, raised by her mother on the lectures of Robert Ingersoll, the politician and orator who called James G. Blaine a "plumed knight" when he nominated him as the Republican candidate for President in 1876 (Rutherford B. Hayes won the nomination and, in a stolen election, the Presidency), but was more celebrated for his speeches about "The Mistakes of Moses" and "Why I Am an Agnostic." He was a hero to free-thinkers like Mary Dora Gray Duncan, who brought up her family on a diet of poverty, poetry, and piano music.

Isadora wrote in one of her essays, "I believe in the religion of the beauty of the human foot." What Ruth St. Denis called God and found outside herself, Duncan discovered in her own body and the breathing world. Her dancing was pagan. Max Eastman described her "running barefoot and half-naked, running and bending and pausing and floating in a stream of music, as though the music had formed out of its own passion a visible spirit to live for a moment and die when it died . . ."

The blue curtains that draped the stage when she danced, her bare feet, her revealing costumes, her devotion to Greek art, her use of the music of Chopin and other serious composers are famous, and were influential. Her first performances in St. Petersburg so thrilled young Michel Fokine that when preparing his ballet *Eunice,* he went to the Hermitage to study the Classical vases painted with depictions of dance. Isadora had little use for ballet, but her shadow falls forever on Fokine's *Les Sylphides* (originally performed in 1908 as *Chopiniana*), which is considered the dividing line between the old ballet and the new.

The less tangible aspects of her art, the transparency, the purity of movement, the inspiration of the rhythms of nature, the "religion of the beauty of the human foot," proved more difficult to emulate. Her dances were more concerned with feeling than with form; she improvised a great deal and never codified a set of steps into a formal system. She never succeeded in founding a style of dancing that could survive her. Had she performed in the 1960s, when the New Romanticism bloomed with back-to-nature movements and love-and-peace phraseology, she might have been more popular, if not more fully understood. Contemporary women—at least the younger ones—would be less upset (and some of the older ones less willing to admit they were upset) if Isadora danced before them pregnant but unmarried. But Isadora Duncan was born in 1878 and died in 1927; she shocked people.

Duncan was born in San Francisco and wherever she traveled, she remained a California girl. Her French never lost its American accent in all her years in Paris; the poet who most inspired her was Walt Whitman. Even her devotion to things Greek may well be traced to American lecture halls in which the congregations of democracy sat to be assured that they were the heirs of Athens. Fifteen years after Isadora was born, the planners of the World's Columbian Exposition in Chicago disregarded the genius of the country's greatest architect, Louis Sullivan, and erected "The White City on the Lake." The White City was Roman Classic, not Greek, but most of Chicago couldn't tell the difference—to them, anything white and stately was Classic, and they loved it. Sullivan insisted that The White City would retard the progress of American architecture by fifty years, and he was right. The popularity of the project, though, showed that more people than Isadora were classically inclined.

Isadora's childhood was mercifully free of ". . . the continual 'don'ts'," which, she understood, as too few have, ". . . make children's lives a misery." Mrs. Duncan played Chopin and Mendelssohn on the piano, and the children improvised movement to the music. Isadora indulged in amateur theatricals with other members of the family. She and her sister Elizabeth gave dancing lessons to the neighborhood's little girls, but as Isadora had never formally learned to dance, she simply taught what pleased her. She took three ballet lessons, decided that ballet was ugly, and stopped. She read the Oakland library dry. At the age of twelve, inspired by *Adam Bede,* her parents' separation and "the slavish condition of women," Isadora determined to "live to fight for the right of every woman to have a child or children as it pleased her, and to uphold her right and her virtue."

The Duncans moved frequently—they owed a lot of rent. There was a perennial lack of money and a perpetual abundance of bills. Mrs. Duncan gave piano lessons; Isadora and Elizabeth taught dancing in the wealthy homes of San Francisco, but the bills never seemed to diminish. As the sisters grew older, they began to teach "society dancing," and Isadora—who was eleven—fell desperately in love with one of her pupils. Falling desperately in love became a habit, one she never really wanted to break.

Isadora decided on a theatrical career, and began to make the rounds of managers in San Francisco. At her first audition, she wore a little white tunic and danced to some of Mendelssohn's "Songs Without Words." The manager told Mrs. Duncan to take her daughter home, this sort of dancing was suitable for a church, not for a theater—a remark that could hardly have pleased the disciple of Robert Ingersoll. Instead of going home, the Duncans went to Chicago where, in 1895, Isadora danced Mendelssohn's "Spring Song" for the manager of the Masonic Temple Roof Garden. He made no references to religion, but did suggest that the youngster try "something with more pep in it." She tried "The Washington Post March" and won a three-week engagement billed as "The California Faun."

The celebrated manager Augustin Daly was in Chicago with his company, and Isadora auditioned for him. According to her autobiography, she made a speech in which she said, among other things of the same tone, "I have discovered the dance." (Duncan's autobiography, *My Life,* was written because she needed money. It swelters in melodrama, and it seems inadvisable to believe that Isadora always said what she said she said. However, it would not be surprising if she offered Daly the thought, if not the words. One of the most shocking things about Isadora was her innocence.)

Daly offered her a role in a pantomime, *Miss Pygmalion,* and she played three weeks in New York and two months on tour. The produc-

Isadora Duncan in her late teens, dressed for dancing in her mother's curtains. The future barefoot dancer is wearing dancing slippers. The attitude of her head, the open arms, the relaxation of her fingers hint at the freedom she was to develop.

PHOTOGRAPH COURTESY OF THE DANCE COLLECTION
OF THE NEW YORK PUBLIC LIBRARY.

tion was not a success, but Daly hired her again, to dance in a production of *A Midsummer Night's Dream* starring the famous Ada Rehan. The production opened in New York in January 1896. Isadora was eighteen, and earning $25 a week, which was not bad, considering that some factory workers were earning $7. However, after the opening night, Daly had the lights turned down during the fairy scene in which she appeared because he objected to the applause that greeted her first performance. Daly took his Shakespeare seriously and he did not like to have the audience applauding anything as frivolous as dancing, especially if the applause were so prolonged that it interrupted the performance. If the spectators applauded a dancer, the dancer was obviously taking attention from the actors. For the rest of the run, Isadora danced on a darkened stage.

Some months earlier, Daly had produced *Dream* in London and, according to that era's finest critic, George Bernard Shaw, had finally taken advantage of the advent of electricity in theaters (some time after Loie Fuller began to show what could be done with light on stage) to fit up "all his fairies with portable batteries and incandescent lights, which they switch on and off from time to time, like children with a new toy." Commenting on Daly's casting of a woman as Oberon and on his treatment of Puck, Shaw wrote, "It must not be supposed that he does this solely because it is wrong, though there is no other reason apparent. He does it partly because he was brought up to do such things, and partly because they seem to him a tribute to Shakespeare's greatness, which, being uncommon, ought not to be interpreted according to the dictates of common sense."

No, Augustin Daly with his toy lights, his old-fashioned stagecraft and his adherence to a theatrical tradition that demanded the ritual butchering of Shakespearean texts, was not the man to appreciate Isadora Duncan, who had discovered the dance. Still, she lasted nearly two years before she quit. Victor Seroff, in his thorough and loving biography, *The Real Isadora,* points out that, courtesy of Daly, Duncan spent the spring and summer of 1897 in London, where she studied with Katti Lanner, ballet mistress of the Empire Theater, who had danced *Giselle* in New York in 1870.

Isadora returned to New York that fall, and a few months later resigned from Daly's company. By that time her mother and siblings had assembled in the city, and the family settled in a studio in Carnegie Hall, which they furnished with curtains and five spring mattresses. In March 1898, Isadora gave a concert to the music of Ethelbert Nevin, an

American composer, and another to the verses of Omar Khayyam. She went on to dance in the salons of society women; Mrs. Astor invited her to perform on the lawn of her villa in Newport in the presence of Vanderbilts, Belmonts, and Fishes. "These people seemed so enwrapped in snobbishness and the glory of being rich that they had no art sense whatever," Isadora wrote. Some things have not changed much since 1898.

Duncan continued to shock people. When she danced Omar's poetry, about forty women left the theater, stunned by the sight of her bare arms and legs. The corset and the body-covering bathing costume were in vogue; society was not ready for bare knees.

The family moved from Carnegie Hall to the Windsor Hotel on Fifth Avenue and, true to tradition, fell behind on the rent. Fortunately, the hotel burned down. The family joined in a benefit performance "Given in Aid of Miss Isadora Duncan and Other Sufferers from the Windsor Hotel Fire," and, with about $300 among them, left for London on a cattle boat.

Duncan danced in London as she had in New York, giving small, private concerts that were enthusiastically reviewed. The family slept in posh hotels and escaped without paying the bills. Brother Raymond sketched the Greek vases in the British Museum. Isadora worked out new dances in her studio, met the centerposts of artistic London and was visited by charming young men. In the summer of 1900, she and her mother packed their bags and went to join Raymond, who had moved on to Paris.

Raymond and Isadora got up at five in the morning to wander the city and worship the Greek rooms of the Louvre. The writer André Beaunier almost made love to Isadora, but at the last moment was appalled at the thought of polluting a virgin. Rodin, too, made advances, but that time Isadora was the one who demurred. (Isadora was part freedom-loving Bohemian and part Victorian lady; she rebelled against her age, but she was very much entwined in it.)

She danced in Paris, too. She found patrons wherever she went who would find her a studio or a salon, and an audience. The critics compared her to a painting by Botticelli. She was not yet fully into her Greek period, and some of her costumes were modeled on the Primavera, a reproduction of which had hung over the bookcase when she was a little girl in San Francisco. She embodied the sensual innocence the great Venetian had delineated and the Pre-Raphaelites had thought they understood. She went to the theater, met artists, fell in and out of love. Isadora was twenty-two, and learning.

The Greek vases in the Louvre were to influence her art, as were the great bronzes of Rodin with their muscular celebration of emotion, but in Paris she made another discovery that was to be at least as important, and far more difficult to understand. She had rejected the academic technique of ballet; she was seeking a way of dancing in which movement would be instituted by emotion and in which each part of the body would be related to the others. It is this concept, more than anything else, that Duncan contributed to the principles of modern dance: Motion is motivated by emotion, and must be expressed with the instrument of the entire human body.

She would stand in her studio with her hands covering her solar plexus, and she would stand like that for hours. ". . . I was seeking, and finally discovered the central spring of all movement, the creator of motor power, the unity from which all diversities of movements are born. . . . I . . . sought the source of the spiritual expression to flow into the channels of the body filling it with vibrating light . . ."

After months of such concentration, she found that when she listened to music the sound seemed to stream toward this center of her body. It was this concentration on the center, on the solar plexus, that she tried to teach her child pupils. Isadora, John Martin writes, "had, however crudely and in whatever inaccurate and unscientific terminology, discovered the soul to mean what less imaginative men have called the autonomic system."

She may have discovered more than that. She described herself as being "as if in a trance" and it seems likely that she was. From her writings, and from descriptions of her performances, it appears that Isadora experienced those peculiar sensations of energy that have been described by practitioners of yoga and masters of the Oriental martial arts. The energy is called *ki* by the Japanese, *chi* by the Chinese, *kundalini* in India and orgone by the followers of psychiatrist Wilhelm Reich. There are many explanations of the phenomenon, and many more explanations of why it does not exist. Nevertheless, descriptions of the sensations are remarkably similar—a tingling or a warmth flowing through the body. A karate master will tell his students that his *ki*, not his strength, allows him to break bricks, and the students will put it down to Oriental mysticism until they feel the tingling in their own arms.

An artist at the moment of creation focuses all his faculties on the work at hand, exactly as the karate master concentrates his entire being in two knuckles at the moment of impact. The barrier between the conscious and the subconscious is temporarily broken, allowing creation to occur, energy flows through the performer and "a great sense of health fills the hall."

It was in Paris that Duncan met Loie Fuller, and from there that she set out on tour with Fuller's company. She danced little, although Fuller, who was in financial difficulties, did arrange performances for her in Vienna. While she was dancing at the Künstler Haus there, Alexander Gross, a Hungarian impresario, saw her and offered to arrange her debut in Budapest. In April 1902, Isadora Duncan, alone on the stage of the Urania Theatre, danced "The Blue Danube," the "Rakoczy March" and other pieces to an audience that filled the theater. The "Rakoczy March" celebrates a Hungarian national hero, and Isadora's red costume made a further appeal to nationalist sympathies. The house was sold out for every one of her twenty-nine subsequent performances. Budapest was entranced.

Isadora became entranced by a young actor with the Hungarian National Theater, who has been identified as Oscar Beregi, but to whom she refers in her memoirs as "Romeo." In *My Life,* Duncan generally calls her lovers—with the exception of Gordon Craig—by fanciful pseudonyms. Paris Singer was "Lohengrin." Pianist Walter Rummel, whose name she does mention, was "The Archangel." The pseudonyms may have been used merely to conceal true names from her readers, but they have a ring of truth that surpasses any literary ruse. She probably never called Singer "Lohengrin" to his face, but she probably did expect him to live up to the knightly standard of the name.

She accepted each new love in the belief that he would be the ideal. Of course, he never was. Isadora embraced people, and philosophies, emotionally rather than intellectually. She saw the passion behind an idea rather than its practical workings, she endowed a man with a set of virtues, and she was hurt when neither the idea nor the man could live up to the assigned quality. The German philosophers, the Greeks, the Bolsheviks, Gordon Craig, Paris Singer, Oscar Beregi, none of them could match Duncan's image of them. She saw an idea or a man as it or he could have been—but what she had to live with was the reality.

The affair with Beregi was the first Isadora consummated. She was twenty-four. "Romeo" did not want a wife with her own career and Duncan was finally dancing, as she had always meant and needed to do, for a wide audience. No doubt her determination shocked the actor. After a tour of Hungary she moved on to Munich, where the young men unhitched the horses and drew her carriage themselves. She reached Berlin, and another triumph. Her dancing made use of simple movements—running, skipping, reaching—and pantomimic gestures such as beckoning and pointing. She got the idea of rippling her fingers from watching the wind ruffle palm leaves, and took other steps from other natural phenomena. She had no "technique" in the sense that a ballet dancer does, but her dancing did not make its impression with steps or intricate patterns. She simply moved to music, keeping her shoulders soft, her neck free, and holding a curve in her arms and legs. Her effects came from the emotional power of her dancing and from her peculiar ability to give herself up to the vision of an ideal.

Despite the acclaim she received in other cities, she could not conquer Paris. She gave several performances there in the spring of 1903, but the critics were not impressed and Isadora was tired. Her brother Raymond devised a vacation for them. They would travel through Italy and then, following in part the route of Ulysses, go to Athens, avoiding the comforts of the flesh and rejoicing in the comforts of the spirit. Isadora Duncan, the "Greek" dancer who had shown the world what she had seen revealed in the classical vases of the Louvre, finally got to Greece.

Duncan, by the way, was not interested in strictly reproducing the dances of the ancient Greeks: She hoped to take them as a model for a new form of dance. She knew that theatrical art in Greece had been religious ceremonial, and she wanted to free contemporary art from its commercial associations. She found that the dancers on Greek vases took poses that were natural to the body, not conventionalized as ballet positions are. Furthermore, she knew that the classical Greeks had found the human body beautiful, as she did. (The Victorian Era, especially in its silliest and most dangerous manifestations, thought the body shameful.) Duncan realized that Americans could not perform Greek dances, but she hoped that the ideal of the Greek art could shape the ideal of an American one.

In some ways, Isadora took a Victorian view of the Greeks. She had a tendency to write words such as Art, Nature and Beauty with capital

Duncan dancing in the ruins of a Greek Theater (1904). Her neck and shoulders display their characteristic soft curve, but the photograph also clearly indicates the strength and energy that animated her arms. PHOTOGRAPH BY RAYMOND DUNCAN.

letters, and to pen rhapsodic hymns to these qualities. She saw an idealized Athens, as she saw an idealized everything else, and she drew on that ideal for the material of her dance. She learned from the vases of the Greeks because there was no other teacher available. Ballet was formal and deforming; it forced dancers to turn out unnaturally from the hips and dressed them in whalebone corsets. Its movements were segmented, not flowing. Loie Fuller preceded her as a barefoot dancer, but Fuller's dancing, with its reliance on technology, did not celebrate the body as Duncan sought to do. Isadora fell back on the Greeks as a starting place.

During her sojourn in Greece, Duncan became fascinated by Byzantine music and decided to re-create the Greek chorus from boys who sang in the choirs of the Orthodox Church. She rounded up a priest, who was also a professor of Byzantine music, and ten boys who sang a chorus from Aeschylus' *The Suppliants* while she danced. The entourage took a train to Vienna, where they performed the chorus from *The Suppliants,* but the audience kept calling for Isadora to give them "The Blue Danube" instead. Audiences in Berlin and Munich wanted "The Blue Danube," too. Then the boys' voices began to change, and the little songsters started escaping from the hotel at night to pick up men at cheap cafés. The Duncans took the boys out of their tunics, bought them trousers, and put them on a train for Athens. Isadora decided to leave the Greeks alone for a while and get serious about the Germans.

She was invited by Cosima Wagner, the composer's widow, to dance the "Bacchanal" in *Tannhauser* in 1904 at the great theater at Bayreuth, the shrine of Wagnerian opera. She began reading Hegel, Nietzsche, Kant, and Goethe with the help of a dictionary. She studied the works of Ernst Haekel, the eminent zoologist who helped disseminate Darwin's theories in Germany, and became a devout evolutionist. She saw the passion behind the idea, as always, and reveled in it. Isadora invited Haekel to Bayreuth, much to the displeasure of Frau Wagner, a devout Catholic who took exception to the theory of evolution.

Cosima Wagner had not been reared on the lectures of Robert Ingersoll, nor did she believe in "the religion of the beauty of the human foot." She did believe in the religion of the music of Richard Wagner, and in that devotion Duncan joined her. She memorized the texts of the operas, immersed herself in the composer's mythic world and fell "into a constant state of intoxication from the music." Wagner's music was the culmination of Romanticism, rich in its orchestral texture, immense in its scope and overwhelming in its passion. It is also overwrought and monumentally self-important. Isadora realized that Wagner's operas encompassed the emotional content of an era of artistic revolt. She, who could envision a thousand children dancing in a new style, understood the composer who wrote operas that lasted for hours, and who needed to have new instruments made to execute his scores. In her idealism, and in her excesses, she shared Wagner's genius and his mistakes.

However, her state of intoxication did not cost her her ability to shock. One day at lunch she informed Frau Wagner that The Master had been wrong, despite his genius. There could be no such thing as music drama. Speech and rational thinking were born of the brain, music was conceived in emotion, and dancing "is the Dionysian ecstasy which carries away all. It is impossible to mix in any way, one with the other."

Isadora loved music and made it a motivating force in her art, but she found it constricting to dance to it, because not even music could give her the feeling of natural rhythms she sought to express. Later dancers were to try to free their art from dependence on music, most of them without much success. Duncan performed to scores by Gluck, Beethoven, Schubert, Wagner and, of course, Chopin, but she also made studies, not intended for performance, in which she tried to express emotion in dance alone, without the stimulation of music. Dance, she intended, was to be the expression of pure emotion by the body, the mad innocence of "Dionysian ecstasy."

However, descriptions of her dancing emphasize her understanding of the emotional content of a score. Music had been the catalyst she employed to release movement from her since her childhood, when she danced to her mother's piano playing. Despite what she told Frau Wagner, and no matter how much she may have wanted to make dance an independent art, music continued to be the inspiration for her dancing. She did not interpret a score note for note, of course; instead, she allowed the emotion of a piece and the flow of its rhythms and sounds to carry her through a dance, as if she were swimming in the music.

After a month of rehearsals, Duncan danced the leading Grace in *Tannhauser*. She wore a transparent tunic, although she was surrounded by a corps de ballet in conventional costumes. Cosima Wagner objected, but Isadora said, "You will see, before many years all your Bacchantes and flower maidens will dress as I do."

It was at this time that Duncan made her first major attempt to start a school. She found a villa at Gruenwald and selected twenty little girls as pupils. She did not, however, try to teach them a series of steps. Instead, she hoped that by heightening their sensibilities, she could turn them into dancers.

One of the pupils who studied at the school in the year it opened (1904) was a little girl named Irma, who later took the last name Duncan, danced with Isadora and eventually maintained a school started by Isadora in Russia for two years after the founder's death. In 1927, she published a short book, *The Technique of Isadora Duncan,* which gives some idea of what Isadora taught. Most of the lessons are devoted to simple movements such as walking, skipping, jumping, reclining, and rising. Isadora, wrote Irma Duncan, ". . . found that movement springs from an inner impulse . . . She fixed no style or form. . . ."

Isadora wanted to teach children to dance by making them feeling human beings who would express their emotions in movements natural to them. Each motion should be "of such a nature that the child feels the reason for it in every fiber." She wanted to teach children ". . . to breathe, to vibrate, to feel, and to become one with the general harmony and movement of nature." Obviously, she scorned the boned costumes, the box-fronted shoes, and the imposed steps of classical ballet. They limited freedom.

Her words are generalizations and almost mystical, but Duncan was not a mystic. She trusted, not in visions, but in her body. She wanted to teach Dionysian ecstasy by freeing other bodies but, as Joseph Campbell writes, "The best things cannot be told; the second best are misunderstood." Isadora could find no way to communicate what she knew; she never managed to found a school that would fully carry on her ideas. For one thing, she had no solid technique to teach.

Isadora was an intuitive genius, and she wanted to teach other people to be intuitive geniuses—which cannot be done. Irma Duncan writes that Isadora ". . . would demonstrate several times in succession a series of movements to her pupils, and if they did not immediately grasp her train of thought, she would give up impatiently." She apparently hoped that by doing the proper exercises, becoming sensitive human beings and thinking beautiful thoughts, her pupils would become great dancers. Isadora damned ballet for teaching form without content, but she tried to teach content without form, which does not work either. Had she remained long enough in one place, she might have transferred to at least a few pupils the spark that she had found. Her surrogates understood her methods, but could not partake of the purified frenzy that lit her dancing, and that frenzy was all she really had to teach.

Isadora had received an invitation to dance in Russia and was performing some last engagements in Berlin early in December 1904, when she met Gordon Craig. Craig, the son of the great actress Ellen Terry, was a designer, a director, a theater theoretician of genius and the father of seven illegitimate children—eight, if you count one conceived but not yet born. Francis Steegmuller has documented the affair through the couple's letters and diaries in *Your Isadora*. Some of Duncan's letters arrange themselves in patterns on the page, like the poems of e.e. cummings. Others are long, chatty missives; still others, punctuated with dashes, rush breathlessly along. The joy and passion of them communicate a bit of what Isadora's dancing must have been.

Steegmuller quotes a review of her first performance in St. Petersburg that appeared on December 14, 1904. The critic described her dancing to the music of Chopin: "Her body is as though bewitched by the music. It is as though you yourself were bathing in music." (This of a woman who never really found any music quite suited to her dancing, much as she loved it.) Duncan's bare legs were to have been the sensation of the evening but, the critic wrote, "Here *everything* dances; waist, arms, neck, head—*and* legs. Duncan's bare legs and bare feet are like those of a rustic vagabond; they are innocent; this is not a *nudité* that arouses sinful thoughts, but rather a kind of incorporeal nudity." The interesting point is the suspicion that, under less artistic circumstances, bare legs just might lead to sinful thoughts. The critic's remark that Duncan's entire body danced also is interesting, because it compares the soft bodyshapes she employed with the straight spine of ballet dancers and the organic style of her dancing with the more formalized, segmented technique of academic ballet.

These first performances in Russia constitute one of Duncan's greatest contributions to dance, and they influenced, not modern dance, but the ballet which she despised. She met the nation's greatest ballerinas, the designers Bakst and Benois and the impresario Serge Diaghilev. Her work was seen by the choreographer Fokine who, as noted, found a use for many of her ideas, including the notion of dancing to Chopin. The use of Greek themes and costumes, the insistence on a flow of movement and on symmetry, the realization of the beauty of simple movements and of Romantic music, all evidenced in the work of Fokine, are a legacy from Duncan.

On New Year's Eve of 1904, Isadora was on a train, bound for Germany and Gordon Craig. During the next several months they traveled together to St. Petersburg, Moscow, and various German cities, and Isadora danced. Her lover described her in movement as ". . . a figure growing at each moment more perfect—lavishing beauty on each side of her as a sower sows rich corn in a brown and ugly field . . ." She danced, taught, loved, and conceived. She had decided at twelve that women should have children as they choose, and Deirdre Duncan was born on September 24, 1906. Craig, who during the past months had been an infrequent visitor, was with her when their daughter was born. Isadora danced, taught, quarreled with Craig and, in 1907, returned to Russia.

Isadora quarreled not only with Craig, but with nearly all her lovers. She did not have particularly good taste in men. On more than one occasion, she fell in love with a man who insisted on a knight-and-lady relationship and refused to consummate the affair. In other instances, she found men who wanted her to surrender her work for marriage. Even Craig, who loved her passionately, seems to have preferred his women subservient. Besides, Craig had a constitutional incapacity for fidelity. Duncan, for her part, apparently did not fully trust men and, although she eventually did marry, she definitely distrusted matrimony. Her father had abandoned the family, reappeared when he made his fourth fortune, and faded out again when he lost it. She spent her life looking for the perfect cavalier—who, at the same time, would understand and encourage her need to fulfill herself. It is quite likely that her conscious and laudable determination to remain her own woman was coupled with a subconscious predilection for men who would demand that she give up her freedom, thus forcing her to break with them and enabling her to have in her life, as she had in her dancing, passion without form. The thing she most feared was constraint.

During her stay in Moscow in 1907 she met the stage director and teacher Konstantin Stanislavski and told him, "Before I go out on the stage, I must place a motor in my soul. When that begins to work, my legs and arms and my whole body will move independently of my own will." Stanislavski also was trying to start a motor. He was unsatisfied with the artificial style of acting that dominated his stage—as artificial as the conventional ballet of the time—but was too seasoned a professional

---

A woodcut of Duncan by Gordon Craig (1907) shows the famous Greek dress and bare feet, and gives an impression of the rooted security of her stance, the curving shape of her body, the dignity of her carriage.

COURTESY OF THE DANCE COLLECTION,
THE NEW YORK PUBLIC LIBRARY AT LINCOLN CENTER.

to believe that an actor could stand on stage and wait for revelation. He developed a technique of acting through which the performer could consciously reach for the subconscious to find inspiration.

The famous Stanislavski Method of acting is nothing more than a device for switching on at will what Isadora called the "motor in my soul." Stanislavski, armed with the discipline of the theater and his powers of ratiocination, was able to find a way to teach the unteachable; he developed a series of exercises through which an actor could learn how to hone his feelings, how to concentrate, and also how to move and speak effectively. Michel Fokine, raised in the strict discipline of ballet, was able to absorb and pass on Isadora's ideas, because he knew the importance of physical technique as a channel for emotional expression. Duncan, for all her genius, could never codify her ideas, nor find a way to transmit her passion to her pupils.

Despite his admiration for her, Stanislavski was unsuccessful in his attempt to establish a school of Duncan dancing attached to his Moscow Art Theater, so Isadora went out looking for money again. The only way she knew to raise money was to dance. She danced in Berlin, in Paris, in London. Paris, in the spring of 1908, was host to Serge Diaghilev's Russian concerts, including a presentation of *Boris Godunov* with Chaliapin in the title role, with whom Duncan could not compete for an audience. The London critics loved Duncan, but she still could not earn enough to maintain the school at Gruenwald. She found a home for her pupils and, for the first time since leaving New York on a cattle boat nine years earlier, set out to dance in America.

Her manager had arranged for her to dance on Broadway, which was a mistake. Her subsequent tour was even less successful. The America of Broadway and the provinces was not ripe for Isadora. In 1908, movements opposed to drinking and smoking began in earnest, and women wore sheath gowns, large hats, and high-button shoes. None of this was part of the America that danced in Duncan's dreams. Broadway accepted a certain amount of "serious" drama—much of it mawkish, melodramatic, or Daly-ized Shakespeare—but Shaw's *Mrs. Warren's Profession*, called "pervading poison" by *The Evening Post*, was closed by the police after one performance in 1905, and wits termed the work of a great Norwegian playwright "Ibscene." Dance as an art form was simply beyond the comprehension of most theater-goers.

Duncan rented a studio and began giving private performances, just as she had before leaving New York nine years before. These recitals attracted a distinguished audience, including the conductor of the New

York Symphony Orchestra, Walter Damrosch, who invited Duncan to perform with him at the Metropolitan Opera House.

In February 1908, a group of eight New York artists including John Sloan—realists known derisively as The Ashcan School—rebelled against the conservative National Academy of Design and mounted a private show. In the same year, Gustav Mahler and Arturo Toscanini conducted in the United States for the first time. (Toscanini made his debut at the Met only a few hours after Isadora's. She danced at a matinée on November 16; he conducted *Aida* that evening to open the opera season.) The Metropolitan Opera House was ripe for Isadora. Its patrons were more cultivated than those of Broadway houses, or at least wished to appear so, and they were accustomed to serious music. Isadora danced to the music of Gluck, Beethoven and Wagner conducted by Damrosch, and the house was sold out. Duncan's aim was to convey to her audience the spirit of the music. Theoretically she might have preferred to make dance an independent art, but in practice she responded to the emotion of music, and made her audience feel it along with her.

Duncan's dramatic dancing seems to have made extensive use of static poses and pantomime, clear gestures with her arms, and facial expressions conveyed further clarification of the emotion she was translating for the audience from the music. At times, she opened her mouth in unvoiced calls. A drawing by Grandjouan of her dancing Gluck's *Orphée* shows Duncan with her legs strongly apart, feet well planted, and legs bent so that a line runs upward and back from her knees to her head, which is so tilted that the chin points toward the roof, and her arms, which reach high with the palms of her hands open and facing out. She seems to be a goddess, reaching for a blessing and, at the same time, bestowing one.

Despite the ovations and the success, Duncan returned to Paris to be with her pupils, to be with her daughter, to dance, to found a school she did not have the money to sustain. Isadora decided that she would simply have to find herself a millionaire and, of course, she did. His name was Paris Singer, and he was one of the twenty-three children of Isaac Merrit Singer, whose name is still a virtual synonym for the sewing machine. The beginning of Duncan's affair with Singer coincided with yet another unsuccessful season in Paris. This time, Diaghilev had brought the Russian ballet to Western Europe, and it drew even larger crowds than the concerts had done the year before. The company included Tamara Karsavina, Anna Pavlova, and Vaslav Nijinsky. The repertory was composed largely of ballets by Michel Fokine, who had been so impressed by Duncan's performance in Russia five years earlier. One of his works, which had its première during the Paris season, was the revised version of *Chopiniana,* which had been given a new decor, including long, gauzy skirts, and a new name, *Les Sylphides.* In *Les Sylphides,* virtuosity was subordinated to mood, and the academic carriage of the dancers' arms was considerably softened. The ballet was, and is, an evocation of the emotional content of the music, and the superlative example of the debt of ballet to Duncan.

Since the Russians were in Paris, Isadora went to Russia. It was a short tour; she soon returned to France and to Paris Singer and their son, Patrick, was conceived. When Duncan arrived to dance in America again in October, her pregnancy was obvious, at least to those in the front rows. The audience at the Metropolitan Opera House was as cultured as ever, but unprepared for an Isadora who was pregnant but unmarried. The popular song of the year was "I Wonder Who's Kissing Her Now," but the ladies at the Met did not care to wonder about Isadora. Her tour was cancelled. She sailed for Europe and allowed Singer to take her on a yachting jaunt to Egypt. Patrick was born after their return to France.

The school in Germany, which had been supervised by sister Elizabeth, was moved from Gruenwald to Darmstadt under the administration of Max Merz, a musician who, according to Victor Seroff, was a proto-Nazi who had managed to take over not only the school, but Elizabeth. Isadora's life with Singer was degenerating into a series of quarrels—he was jealous, he wanted her to marry him, she wanted to go on dancing—and she decided that her own country was the place to raise funds for a school, which she would run herself. Even in their more peaceful days, Singer had not shown much interest in financing such an adventure. Duncan determined to try America again.

This was the beginning of her famous harangues of the audience. She was, Seroff writes, "One of the least gifted orators I have ever heard." Her speeches did the opposite of what she intended. Instead of inspiring the wealth of America to support her cause, she inspired the headline, "Isadora Insults the Rich." She said important things—"And this dancing, that has been called 'Greek.' It has sprung from America, it is the dance of the America of the future"—but she also said silly things.

Again, she returned to Europe, to her tours, her quarrels with Singer, her children. She began to teach her darlings to dance, or rather, she began to teach Deirdre. Patrick was an independent soul. "No," he told his mother, "Patrick will dance Patrick's own dance alone."

For once, Isadora was happy. Her audiences loved her, her children loved her, Singer had purchased land in Paris on which to build her a theater and a school. The plan was discussed at a family luncheon—Duncan, Singer, Deirdre, and Patrick. Isadora left for a rehearsal; the children were to return to her studio in a hired car. During the drive, the limousine stopped to avoid an accident and stalled. The chauffeur intended to leave the car in gear, but by accident shifted it into reverse. Then he got out to crank the engine, as was necessary in 1913. The crank turned, the motor started, the car backed away into the River Seine. The children were dead.

The rest was desperation. Her contributions had been made, the pattern of her life was established. There was nothing to do but continue. Singer did indeed buy a school for her, an estate at Bellevue outside Paris. She brought pupils from the German school and recruited more from Russia. When war came in 1914, she gave Bellevue to France as a hospital and came to dance at the Metropolitan Opera House again, this time with six of her pupils. She wrapped herself in a red shawl and danced "La Marseillaise," calling on "the boys of America to rise and protect the highest civilization of our epoch, that culture which had come to the world through France." Carl Van Vechten saw in the dance ". . . the majestic, flowing strength of the Victory of Samothrace . . ." Draped in her shawl, calm as ancient ivory, Isadora called for American soldiers and values to make the world safe for Art.

"La Marseillaise" was a revolutionary song in those days, and red was the radicals' color. However, for once Isadora was not identifying herself with a rebel cause; the American left opposed any consideration of the nation's entry into the war in Europe. Even so, the police forbade her to dance "La Marseillaise" again in New York. There was also trouble with the Fire Department, which evicted her students from the quarters she had improvised for them in the Century Theater, where Isadora and the girls were the chorus, and brother Augustin the protagonist, in a production of *Oedipus Rex*. Isadora thought it was a logical place for the girls to sleep; the Fire Department thought it was illegal. Isadora's revenge was to "Leave New York to Philistine darkness," and sail back to Europe.

She sold her possessions to raise money. She danced in South America, in London, in Paris, in the United States, in Greece. She was famous. She had imitators. She never had enough money. In 1917, she broke decisively with Singer. Two years later, in France, she gave a recital in the hopes of raising funds to reopen the school at Bellevue, but the attempt failed. It was in 1921 that Leonid Krasin, head of the Soviet Trade Commission in London, saw her dance "Marche Slav," in which she showed the suffering of the serfs and celebrated the Russian Revolution. Krasin was sufficiently impressed to report the performance to Moscow, and Duncan was invited to dance, and to teach, in the U.S.S.R., a nation scarcely four years old and, it seemed, devoted to freedom. In an open letter to the English press, Isadora wrote that she found in Russia "a new world, a newly created mankind, the destruction of the old world of class injustice, and the creation of the new world of equal opportunity."

It is almost certain that Duncan did not understand the politics or economics of her new world. Victor Seroff, who knew and loved her, writes, "I venture to say that at the time she was lecturing Paris Singer on 'a general reform of the world,' as she recounts in her memoirs, if she had been shown a photograph of Karl Marx, she would most probably have taken it for that of Giuseppe Verdi." Even Anatoly Lunacharsky, the Commissar of Education, wrote that Isadora's aim in going to Russia was "an emotional one." It was, as always, the passion behind the idea that moved her. Besides, the Russians had promised her a school, and she knew that under the Czars, the ballet school had been supported by the State. No other government had offered her assistance, and she had come to believe that only with the aid of a government could her school survive.

Isadora got her school, and she was invited to dance at the Bolshoi Theater on November 7, 1921, the fourth anniversary of the revolution. After "Marche Slav," Lenin himself rose from his seat crying, "Bravo, bravo Miss Duncan," but Lenin's cheers could not alter the situation in Russia. In the winter of 1921, Moscow had only half of its former inhabitants and the population subsisted on two ounces of bread a day and a few frozen potatoes. Others lived better: Early in her stay, Duncan was invited to a reception given by leading members of the Communist Party —she found them in evening clothes, gorging like members of the social

Isadora Duncan as she always should have been. A photograph taken in the garden of her school at Bellevue, outside Paris, in 1919 shows her with head high, arms outstretched, weight sure on the ground, body free.

FROM THE IRMA DUNCAN COLLECTION, DANCE COLLECTION OF THE NEW YORK PUBLIC LIBRARY.

set at Newport. For once, Isadora was the one who was shocked: Communists who had created a "new world" could not behave so crudely. Her politics, like her men, failed to live up to the image she had of them.

Then, Isadora married. After years of loving and lovers, of quarrels and holding to her freedom, after dancing pregnant and proud before a stunned America, she chose a man who had already been husband to two other women, a poet of brilliance who was as wild and as illogical as she. Perhaps she saw in him the children she had lost. When she left the Soviet Union in 1922 to dance in the United States again, Sergei Esenin went with her.

If there was one thing America feared in 1922, it was Bolsheviks. The great days of radicalism had ended with the nation's entrance into the World War; union leaders, pacifists and other malcontents were not suffered gladly. Skirts were rising, corsets were discarded, America was beginning to discover sex, but Warren Harding was President and the country wanted only to rest and enjoy "normalcy." And here was Isadora Duncan, who had gone of her own free will to the land of the Reds and brought back a Russian husband. The couple was taken to Ellis Island, they were investigated, their luggage was searched. The resultant publicity helped sell out three performances at Carnegie Hall, and Isadora's speech, asking America to extend its hand to Russia, did little damage.

Boston, though, was a disaster. Esenin, wanting a bit of attention for himself, sat in the audience dressed like a Cossack, but Isadora's oration caused the real trouble. She informed her audience that her art was "symbolic of the freedom of woman and her emancipation from the hidebound conventions that are the warp and woof of New England puritanism." She told them that she did not appeal to the "lower instincts of mankind as your half-clad chorus girls do." She denounced the women's costumes of the day, contrasting the beauty of her honest nudity with the vulgarity of other people's studied nakedness. Then, she tugged off her red scarf and waved it at the crowd crying, "This is red. So am I. It is the color of life and vigor . . ." and ripping her tunic to bare one breast, she informed Boston—prim, propriety-loving, bean-and-cod Boston—"This —this is beauty!"

It was great theater, but poor politics. What was beautiful to Isadora was not necessarily beautiful to Boston. Her innocence had defeated her again. The joke of it was, Isadora was something of a puritan herself. When she had a good opportunity to look at, and listen to, the Jazz Age of the 1920s, she did not like it at all. The teachings of Freud reached the country after the war, and were taken by young men and women as an antidote to their parents' teachings about the sinfulness of sex. Women took up smoking in public and drastically reduced the number of clothes they wore. The increase in the use of automobiles helped make the younger generation independent of chaperones, and jazz changed their dancing habits.

That kind of music, and that kind of dancing, displeased the Victorian in Isadora. Jazz, to her, expressed "the sensual convulsion of the South African Negro. It inspired movements which were indecent." "A seemingly modest young girl would not think of addressing a young man in lines or spoken phrases which were indecent, and yet the same girl will arise and dance those phrases with him in such dances as the Charleston and Black Bottom, while a Negro orchestra is playing *Shake that Thing!*" The bigotry of the statement is interesting, coming from one who praised Russia for creating "the new world of equal opportunity," but Isadora was as imbued with America's faults as with its virtues. Her comments on the immorality of jazz dancing were remarkably close to those of people she despised. (A group of socially prominent women in New York, including Mrs. J. Pierpont Morgan, proposed forming an organization to combat fashions that exposed too much flesh and "improper ways of dancing.")

That night in Boston demonstrated the paradox of Isadora Duncan. She bared her breast after denouncing "half-clad chorus girls." They were vulgar; she was Art. She may have been right, in a way. Her nudity was innocent; that of the 1920s tended to be naïve but deliberate. She may also have been fighting with Esenin again, or drinking more than was good for her. Still, like so many liberators, she was intolerant of any form of liberation other than her own. Like all great revolutionaries, she was a fanatic and had in her a strain of puritanism. She could see only one kind of beauty, only one end of art, only one road to freedom. And even if she truly saw through the sham of Harding's America that night, she was unable to share whatever vision she had. Her words lacked the clarity of her dancing; they finished her.

The newspapers and the guardians of morality had a party. "Red Dancer Shocks Boston," howled a headline. "The Bolshevik hussy doesn't wear enough clothes to pad a crutch," shrilled evangelist Billy Sunday. Isadora left for Europe again.

Her marriage to Esenin degenerated and ended. She left the Soviet Union to fulfill engagements in Berlin, but the contracts were fraudulent and she received no fees. American friends got together enough money to get her to Paris, and from there to Nice.

The last three years of her life were spent listening to music, running up bills, drinking, and searching for enough money to start a school again. The ones in Germany and Russia were lost to her. Her children were dead. Esenin had died. America had no use for her. She gave some recitals; she contracted to write her memoirs. When the book was published, in the year of her death, it was prefaced by a publisher's note explaining that Duncan had planned to write a second book about her years in Russia, "from which America would have learned that great as was her admiration and sympathy for this struggling country, she had no political interests or affiliations . . ." Even dead, Isadora might have shocked someone.

Her death is legend. She loved fast driving, and when she hinted that she might like to buy a low-slung Bugatti sports car, the garage sent a young mechanic to take her for a drive. Isadora settled herself in the low seat next to the driver. She called to her friends, "Adieu, mes amies, je vais a la gloire," and tossed her fringed shawl back around her neck and shoulders. The fringe caught in the spokes of the rear wheel on her side. The mechanic started the engine, spinning the wheel, jerking the scarf, breaking her neck.

Her use of great music, her bare feet, her free, flowing costumes, her performances on a bare stage were left as a legacy to be used and developed by other dancers. So was her belief that dance should be an expression of inner emotion, conveyed by the entire body. She never developed a system she could teach to others, and the cultists who virtually canonized her were unable to do more than imitate her simple steps; they could not invest them with her genius. She established no long-lasting line of succession; rather, she left dancers with a series of concepts and principles, which they developed in a variety of ways.

Her belief in the freedom of women became more than legacy, it turned to legend. She reached for the passion behind philosophies, for the heroes hidden in men, for the great visions that could free the world. The world was not ready for her freedom, nor was she; the attempt to encompass it destroyed her. She could not find a form to contain her passion; she could not resolve her own conflict between earth goddess and Victorian virgin. Even so, she envisioned great things—women free to live as they chose; children raised to love their bodies and their feelings; human beings living with gusto, unafraid. And, as she wrote, she saw America dancing.

III

RUTH ST. DENIS

SALVATION THROUGH SPECTACLE

IT IS APPROPRIATE that Ruth St. Denis' triumph as a dancer should have been inspired by an advertisement. She was the one founding goddess who built an American audience for the dance, made it popular outside the segregated arenas of higher culture and, at least for a time, made it pay.

St. Denis performed for more than seventy years, and during her great days inspired newspaper feature stories about dancing as an elixir for the attainment of health and beauty. During her late years, still beautiful and still dancing, she attained the status of a national monument: The name "Miss Ruth," by which the world called her, was more than a designation of respectful affection, it was an unofficial title, the democratic version of "Sir John" or "Dame Margot." St. Denis was not merely inspired by an advertisement—she was an advertisement; she loved her product and she knew how to sell it.

Miss Ruth decorated the stage with a series of sumptuous spectacles spiced with tang of the Orient. She draped herself in legend as she did in showy costumes; she teased the senses of her public with the incense of mystery. She did these things in the service of religion and art, but the spectators, leaning forward in their seats in the vaudeville houses, had their desire for flesh gratified too. There is little doubt that St. Denis' bare midriff sold as many tickets as her artistic vision.

Walter Terry, the dance critic who appeared with her in many lecture demonstrations, and who loved her, writes: "She adored sex, she served art with passion, she worshipped God, and she kept doing penance to one or the other for faithlessness." It is an apt comment, but a review of her life shows that sex ran third, while God and art used her subconscious as a trysting place for most of her more than ninety years. In addition to Terry's trinity, though, there was another force that drove St. Denis, and it was the power that helped her win American audiences for dance—a love, and an intuitive understanding, of spectacle.

Ruthie Dennis was less than ten years old when a friend of the family treated her to a trip from the family farm in Somerville, New Jersey, to upper Manhattan to see a performance of the Barnum & Bailey Circus. She enjoyed the sideshows and the elephants, but she was more impressed by the second half of the program, a pageant called *The Burning of Rome.* Houses burned, music played, Christians prayed, angels danced. In her autobiography, which was published fifty years after the performance, she recalled, "Nothing had ever been seen before like those houses going up in flames, with the Coliseum a black silhouette at one side. As a grand finale a ballet of a hundred angels floated about on the stage, dressed in costumes made of ribbons. . . . The first thing I did when I got to the farm was to go into the garret and slash up a pair of Mother's old curtains to create my first dancing costume . . ."

A few years later, another friend took her to the Palisades Amusement Park, where she became enthralled by another pageant, *Egypt Through the Centuries.* For months afterward she dreamed of it, even though the toe shoes of the dancers and other elements of the costuming were not proper to the period—an error St. Denis was to rectify when her turn came.

The Burning of Rome and *Egypt Through the Centuries* were popular entertainments, neither artistic nor historically accurate but carefully designed to pleased the relatively unsophisticated audiences of the 1880s and 1890s. Through their pageantry, they fired the imaginations of the spectators and, at least temporarily, altered reality for them

---

Miss Ruth, in her 80s, performs one of her famous Oriental dances draped in a sari. Age did not wither her sense of dramatic gesture nor stale the strength of her body.

PHOTOGRAPH COURTESY OF THE DANCE COLLECTION
OF THE NEW YORK PUBLIC LIBRARY.

and heightened their emotions. On the most basic level, that is the measure of success of all theatrical arts, and Ruthie Dennis never forgot it.

A third performance, quite different from the spectacles, was not forgotten either. She was about eleven when her mother was given tickets to a performance at which Genevieve Stebbens, whose style anticipated that of Isadora Duncan, was to dance. Ruthie went with Mother, and came home decided on a career. "The image of [Stebbens'] white, Grecian figure became so indelibly printed on my mind that everything I subsequently did stemmed from this revelation."

Genevieve Stebbens based her poses and plastiques on the technique of François Delsarte (1811–1871), who evolved a philosophy and method of pantomime designed to make motion honestly expressive of emotion. Isadora Duncan was exposed to it—Gordon Craig found a book of Delsarte's theories among her belongings—and undoubtedly based some of her poses and pantomimic gestures on it. St. Denis, too, was greatly influenced, as was her husband and partner, Ted Shawn, who found Delsarte's method of sufficient importance to pass it on in a book, remarking that the technique had been the basis of all the performing and teaching he had done since learning it. Thus, the work of a French pantomimist became an element common to the movement styles of three pioneers of American modern dance, and of immense importance to the development of the new art.

Delsarte observed people in public places—and even took lessons in anatomy and dissected corpses—in order to understand the correspondence between mood and movement. His work rings with overtones of mysticism, but is solidly based on the theory that grace is efficiency of movement—that is, movement which achieves its effect with the least amount of effort and the smallest possible shock to the organism. (In this, his kinship with Duncan is evident.)

Steele MacKaye who, as noted, brought electricity to the American stage, also brought the teachings of Delsarte. He studied with the French pantomimist in 1871 and came home to pass along the methods of the master. In a short time, Delsarte became a fad: His teachings were to the 1890s what the Hula Hoop was to the 1950s. Magazines carried advertisements for Delsarte gowns, Delsarte cosmetics, Delsarte corsets and a Delsarte wooden leg. (Advertisements for such products were the major source of revenue for American newspapers in those days. By 1900, the volume of business in patent medicines reached nearly $60 million.) A book designed to teach elocution to schoolchildren, *The*

Delsarte Speaker, was published in 1896 and widely used. There was even a popular song, "Since Birdie's Commenced Her Delsarte." The craze, of course, ruined the system, speeding its degeneration into stock poses of "Despair" and "Defiance."

Ruthie Dennis' mother had studied with "a seventh attenuation of a pupil of François Delsarte," and instructed her daughter in the method. She would read from the exercise book while Ruthie, grasping the brass bedstead, swung her legs back and forth. In 1893, when she appeared with her parents in an amateur performance of *The Old Homestead,* her dance was called "Lessons From Delsarte."

Ruthie Dennis was born into a naïve, rural environment of fads and dangerous patent medicines, of amateur theatricals and the occasional treat of a professional performance. The change in that environment was, to a small extent, her doing. Her birth year has been given by assorted authorities as 1877, 1878, 1879 and 1880. St. Denis herself opted for 1878, and it would be pleasant to accept this because it would make Miss Ruth an exact contemporary of Isadora Duncan.

She was born a continent away from Isadora, in Newark, New Jersey. Her mother had a degree in medicine and had practiced in a clinic in Philadelphia at a time when female physicians were not merely rarities, but oddities. Ruthie's father was an inventor and engineer, not particularly successful at either. He, like a few other men, dreamed of flying machines at a time when most of the learned were secure in the knowledge that such things were impossible. He passed his intellectual curiosity and independence on to his daughter.

Father, like Isadora's mother, trusted to the great agnostics, Robert Ingersoll and Tom Paine. Mother trusted the Bible, which she read aloud, especially as a salve for family quarrels and poverty. St. Denis was raised to a strange combination of scientific intellectualism and mysticism. Three books, read before adolescence, influenced the pattern of her life, however little she understood them on first acquaintance: Mary Baker Eddy's *Science and Health;* Kant's *Critique of Practical Reason;* and Dumas' *Camille.* She could not fully assimilate them, of course, any more than she could comprehend her mother's readings from St. John, but the emotional quality of words, and the emotional setting in which they are encountered, can take deeper root in a child's mind than the literal meanings of simpler sentences. Another book important to Ruthie combined mystical concepts with the pageantry she experienced in *Egypt Through the Centuries.* This was *The Idyll of the White Lotus,* and told the story of a boy in ancient Egypt who grew up to become a priest and experience illumination in a vision of The Lady of the White Lotus. That Lady, in other incarnations, was to have a starring role in St. Denis' dances.

Ruthie went to school, of course, and to a dancing school where children balanced their party manners as if they were trays of fragile china; little girls wore frilly dresses and little boys attended with a "smoldering resentment in their eyes." The dancing teacher was sufficiently impressed to suggest that Mother take Ruthie to study with the celebrated Swiss dancing master, Karl Marwig. Whatever Marwig, in his black knee breeches, thought of Ruthie in her homemade black lace dress, he was interested in her talent and offered to give her free lessons. The family, though, could not afford to send their daughter on trips to New York twice a week. St. Denis acknowledged that she had taken some lessons from Marwig, and later had some ballet classes with Maria Bonfanti. (Isadora also had a few lessons with the famous ballerina at about the same time—1896—but there is no evidence that the two young women met in the studio.) However, neither Marwig nor Bonfanti could teach Ruthie the kind of dancing she wanted to do—the dancing inspired by Genevieve Stebbens and *The Burning of Rome*.

She was about sixteen when she stepped forward to make her decision for dance. Before appearing in her "Lessons From Delsarte" in 1893, she had studied for a few months in the famous seminary of Dwight L. Moody; some relatives paid the bill in the hope that Ruthie would acquire more respectability than she seemed likely to learn from her parents. When the youngster informed the celebrated educator that she planned a career on the stage, Moody roared that it would be better if she threw herself into the nearby Connecticut River. Ruthie called the old bigot an old bigot, and left. Fortunately, her parents cared more for self-respect than for respectability, and in 1894 Ruthie and Mother crossed the river to Manhattan, settled into a small hotel on West Twenty-sixth Street, and set out to find Ruthie a job in the theater. On the corner of Thirtieth Street and Sixth Avenue, they found an institution common to the period, a combination variety hall and freak show. This was vaudeville.

American vaudeville was born in a long labor that began before the firing on Fort Sumter, but its most famous form can best be dated from October 24, 1881, when Tony Pastor's New Fourteenth Street Theater in New York offered a program of variety acts intended for family consumption. Previously, variety shows were stag affairs (that part of the business became burlesque) and although the jokes now seem not at all shocking and often not at all funny, they outraged people like Dwight Moody. Pastor, something of a puritan as well as a clever businessman, calculated that he could double his audience simply by inducing each man to bring his wife to the theater. He produced shows that brought no blushes, and he succeeded.

Pastor's methods, though, were not the only ones. One of the great impresarios of vaudeville, Benjamn Franklin Keith, began his career as a producer in 1893 by renting an empty candy store in Boston, calling it the Gaiety Museum, and exhibiting a midget and a stuffed mermaid. A bit later, he augmented the show with a chicken with a human face and a pair of comedians named Joe Weber and Lew Fields. The museums continued to be popular during the 1880s and 1890s. They were divided buildings, housing the freak show, which was what really drew the crowds, in one area, and variety acts in another. Worth's Museum, where Ruthie Dennis went seeking work, was this kind of enterprise.

Vaudeville in its great days was a major molder of American culture. Since acts did not change as they moved from theater to theater, the people in Pittsburgh learned the same jokes and heard the same songs as the folks in Kansas City. Film, radio, and television were to do the same job more thoroughly and more quickly later on, but vaudeville began it. Furthermore, vaudeville was not a limited form of entertainment; it was as likely to bring its audiences Sarah Bernhardt as to give them Fink's Mules or a juggling act. It was a training ground for great artists and entertainers: Keith may have started out with Jo-Jo, the Dog-Faced Boy, but he ended up booking W. C. Fields.

Ruth St. Denis did not really enjoy playing in vaudeville. She preferred touring legitimate theaters, playing in Broadway houses and performing with symphony orchestras. However, she did play vaudeville, and by doing so she brought dance to a wider audience than she could have reached any other way. She played the circuits and she played The Palace, and she did what Isadora Duncan had never been able to accomplish—she created a popular audience for dance in America. Miss Ruth, like Isadora, danced in the salons of society women and on the nation's great cultural stages, but those audiences were prepared to watch serious dance. It was during the exhausting rounds of theatrical touring, and the even more debilitating trouping of vaudeville stages, that St. Denis brought the art of dancing to people who had seldom seen it before, if they had ever seen it, and made them want to see more. It was a major achievement, and it started at Worth's Museum in 1896—the year Isadora danced in *A Midsummer Night's Dream.*

Ruthie auditioned for the manager, dancing to "Gavotte d'Amour" and throwing in a lot of cartwheels, backbends and her famous slow kicks—nearly everyone else did fast kicks. The manager puffed his cigar and looked bored, but he hired her to give eleven performances a day for $20 a week. It could have been worse; some museum performers had to give seventeen shows a day. There were no performers' unions in 1896.

Ruthie was booked into a few more vaudeville houses after her stint at Worth's, but was unable to establish herself as a performer. That old villain of melodrama, the foreclosed mortgage, deprived the family of its farm and they moved across to Brooklyn, which still was a separate city. It joined New York in 1898, the year Ruthie won a role in a play, *The Ballet Girl*. The play closed, still owing money to the cast, and Ruthie decided to audition for Augustin Daly, who hired her as he had hired Isadora Duncan two years earlier. She did so well in *The Runaway Girl* that Daly planned to make her a solo dancer in *The Greek Slave*, but he died before the play could be produced.

After suffering through four months of modeling evening gowns in a department store, she was informed by an agent that David Belasco needed a girl to dance in *Zaza*: Could Ruthie sail for England in two weeks? She got the job, caught the boat, and began an association with the great director that lasted for five years.

When *Zaza* closed in London, Ruthie crossed to Paris in the year of the Great Exposition, to be fascinated by the dancing of Loie Fuller. Equally impressive was the art of Sadi Yaco, the Japanese performer who shared Fuller's theater. St. Denis wrote about Yaco, "Her dancing (she was, of course, both actress and dancer) was the antithesis of the flamboyant, overblown exuberance of our American acrobatics. Here was a costuming in which the colors were vivid, yet so related to the mood that they seemed to emanate from a different pallet. Her performance haunted me for years." It has also haunted American modern dance. The concepts and techniques of Oriental theater—the use of costumes, props, and stage settings, as well as dance-acting—were incorporated into the art of Miss Ruth and form part of the theater of Martha Graham. Furthermore, Americans in the 1900s thought little of Orientals—plays made them into either villains or buffoons. Even Belasco's *Madame Butterfly,* though sympathetic, is not exactly realistic. St. Denis' dances gave America some idea that Orientals are cultured human beings.

Fuller's own performance, Miss Ruth found, was "astonishing and beautiful," and Walter Terry suggests that St. Denis' love affair with lighting effects may have started when she saw what Fuller accomplished. The swirling, flowing, and sometimes stage-filling costumes St. Denis used during her career also may have been influenced by Fuller.

St. Denis was beginning to have her own influence on people, especially men. She was astonishingly beautiful. Photographs show a tall, strong, slender young woman with fine eyes and the beautifully defined features she was to retain to the end of her life. Her thick black hair made as dramatic an effect as her costumes, and became even more striking when it turned pure white by the time she was forty. Stanford White, the celebrated American architect, was intrigued by her, as was Belasco, but Ruthie, like Isadora, was in no hurry for physical love. One of the legends about her is that Belasco called her "Saint" Dennis, which became St. Denis, because of her preference for purity. Whatever the reason, he did give her the name.

She was a determined woman, and although she toured with Belasco's plays, she did not forget that she had set out to be a dancer. She did not want to do acrobatic dancing, show dancing, or ballet dancing (which was all the dancing there was) but she wanted to be a dancer. Then, she saw the advertisement.

The vision occurred in 1903 in Buffalo, New York, while St. Denis was on tour with Belasco's production of *Du Barry*. The boarding house in which she and her roommate had been installed was dreary, and the two young women went across the street to a drugstore to comfort themselves with ice cream sodas. St. Denis happened to look up from her seat at the fountain, and saw an advertisement for Egyptian Deities cigarettes.

The poster, crowded and undramatic by modern standards of advertising, showed what purported to be an ancient Egyptian temple. Above the edifice floated the name of the product, and in the stonework was inscribed, "No Better Turkish Cigarette Can Be Made." A reproduction of the cigarette package seemed to grow at the foot of a niche, along with several lotus flowers—white lotus flowers, recalling *The Idyll of the White Lotus*. In a niche, bare-breasted (but without nipples—this was 1903), feet close together, hands on thighs, head high and proud, sat Isis, the mother goddess of Egypt. Her face and dress had been adapted to suit American taste, but she must have retained sufficient divinity to serve as inspiration.

Ruth St. Denis had to have that poster. She was even willing to pay for it, although she was earning only $25 a week. Her roommate brought it to her in the boarding house, and St. Denis hung it at the foot of her narrow bed, where she could stare at it whenever she was not on stage. From then on, wherever St. Denis and *Du Barry* went, the poster went also, and Miss Ruth dashed from the theater to the local library or museum in every town, to study up on Egypt.

The poster helped St. Denis' mind unravel a clump of events and emotions that had been tangled together for years. *Egypt Through the Ages, The Idyll of The White Lotus,* Genevieve Stebbens, Delsarte, Sadi Yaco, the Bible, Belasco's way of directing a scene, all came together around a central idea like cats converging on a dish of food. St. Denis was going to make a dance about Egypt.

The United States became interested in Egypt during the Chicago Exposition of 1893—the same enterprise that retarded American architecture—with the assistance of a belly dancer. The belly dance—known as the hootchy-kootchy—made its American debut in, of all places, Philadelphia, in 1876. It was a flop. Seventeen years later, the public, uninterested in educational exhibits and architecture, threatened to make the Chicago Exposition equally unsuccessful until a woman known as Little Egypt began to appear in *The Streets of Cairo* on the Midway, doing a belly dance. The public suddenly developed a remarkable interest in the fair. It took only a year for hundreds of imitation Little Egypts to show up, performing in museums and traveling shows at a charge of ten cents a dance. To the small-town American male of the early 1900s, Egypt was pretty hot stuff.

The big city also liked its fun. Little Egypt—the real one—appeared at a stag dinner given at Sherry's famous restaurant in New York by Herbert Barnum Seeley (nephew of Phineas T. Barnum, the circus man). She danced on the table, taking special care of her costume—she didn't put it on. Police and reporters crashed the party (they politely waited for the dancer to finish her number) and the episode became one of the juiciest scandals of the day.

However, when Ruth St. Denis became interested in Egypt, she had at her disposal more serious matter for study than *The Idyll of the White Lotus* or the imitators of Little Egypt. Napoleon's excursion to Egypt in 1798 had resulted in the discovery of the Rosetta Stone, and a great deal of scholarship, excavation, and grave-robbing had been carried on after that. St. Denis set out to study the history of Egypt. She knew that she would also have to learn stagecraft, costuming, lighting, archeology, and painting. By the time the company of *Du Barry* disbanded in California, she knew exactly what she intended to do: a dance-play portraying one day in ancient Egypt which, by extension, would show the lifespan of a nation. She also knew that such a production would cost $3,000.

On her return to New York, St. Denis made little progress in raising the money to stage *Egypta,* as she had decided to call the piece, but she kept up her studies in the city's libraries and museums. For diversion, she went with a friend to the amusement park at Coney Island, where she came upon an Indian village peopled by snake charmers, fakirs, and nautch dancers. *The Streets of Delhi,* which was probably a profitable descendent of Chicago's *Streets of Cairo,* switched St. Denis' train of thought from Egypt to India. She decided to create one or two nautch dances for herself, perform them in vaudeville, and use the money she earned to produce *Egypta.* Now she expanded her research in the libraries and museums beyond the Egyptian materials, and collected all the Orientals—of any nationality and description—she could find. From them she learned customs and dances, and from them she formed a company, which rehearsed scenes from her Indian dances in her mother's apartment.

St. Denis spent six months searching for an agent or manager willing to let her use his theater. Finally, Henry B. Harris took the time to look at the pictures she carried and listen as she described her dances. Then, he had his stagehands erect her set and sat out front to watch seventeen of the most important minutes in the history of dance.

St. Denis' Indian dance, *Radha,* convinced Harris to produce a matinée for her, and to invite the managers of New York's vaudeville theaters. However, the only engagements secured for the young dancer were one performance at a Sunday Night Smoking Concert at the New York Theater and a run of several weeks at Proctor's Twenty-third Street Theater. At Proctor's, the dancer's "act," as the managers called it, went on after Bob Fitzsimmons, who had lost the heavyweight championship to Jim Jeffries in 1899, and before a troupe of performing monkeys. St. Denis was billed as "Radha," and the program informed the audience that the entire dance would be performed in bare feet.

A strong hint that more than feet would be bared was dropped in the publicity preceding the next performance of *Radha.* St. Denis was also performing in the salons of society, as Isadora had, and a group of socially prominent women decided to sponsor a second matinée performance at the Hudson Theater. (The announcement of the performance concluded with the information that tea would be served in the theater foyer at five.) Newspaper editors, prompted by the eminent names of St. Denis' patrons, sent reporters to interview the dancer. Their stories convinced New York that the matinée would consist of an intensely sensual dance performed by a voluptuous young woman wearing very few clothes. They even insisted that the first performance was to be so daring that no men would be permitted to attend. The house was packed.

The Hudson Theater matinée was to include two dances in addition to *Radha,* which meant that Ruthie needed a new stage name. Mother Dennis suggested using the name "Belasco used to call you," and Ruth St. Denis it was.

The performance on March 22, 1906 was so successful that Henry Harris took over the management and presented a series of matinées, which played to sold-out houses. Three days after the first performance, *The New York Times* carried a long article—part interview, part review—under the headline, "Bringing Temple Dances from the Orient to Broadway/Hindu Types and Ceremonies in a New/Jersey Girl's Novel Exhibition."

"Society has discovered something new under the limelight. Out of the jaws of vaudeville a group of New York women who still keep a wary eye out for up-to-date novelties have snatched a turn which they hope to make more or less of an artistic sensation. A set of Hindu dances performed by a New Jersey girl with a rather convincingly clear notion of what she is doing, constitute this latest find . . . The fascination of the Orient is eternal. Women's clubs that have sipped tea over pretty much everything from Sun Worship to Mental Science generally fall back on Eastern lore for things to be enthusiastic about. The 'Road to Mandalay' is ankle deep with the papers of progressive reading societies."

The tone of the article, and the prejudices of the writer, gave a neat sketch of the tastes of the era. The performance was described as a "turn," a refugee from vaudeville, women were pictured as novelty-seekers who spent their time discussing foolish subjects, and America, it was noted, was fascinated by the East. The piece was illustrated with three large pictures; clear evidence that St. Denis had created a sensation.

Part of her vogue was explained by another anonymous reviewer in the *New York Globe and Commercial Advertiser,* whose report wore the headline, "A Bare-Legged Dancer," and noted that, "Wild stories of their shocking suggestiveness, coupled with society's O.K., drew a great crowd of curious folk to see the East Indian dances of Ruth St. Denis." The reporters were drawn to the theater by the irresistible com-

---

Ruth St. Denis as Radha *dances the delirium of the senses with feet and midriff bare, bells on her ankles and her gold skirt swirling about her.*

PHOTOGRAPH COURTESY OF THE DANCE COLLECTION
OF THE NEW YORK PUBLIC LIBRARY.

bination of sex and society, but once there, they gave up their fatuity for fascination. Like the audiences who filled the vaudeville theaters, they came not knowing what to expect of the new dancer, and went away impressed.

The representative of the *Globe and Commercial Advertiser,* like many of his colleagues, was particularly taken with the dance called *The Cobras,* because of "the peculiarly snake-like appearance and movements of the performer's hands and arms. Her body stained a Malaysian brown, her fingers tipped with blue and dressed with green stone rings, she put her upper limbs through a series of sinuous, snaky motions . . . and went through a slow serpentine which really made the audience see the snakes."

In *The Cobras,* St. Denis appeared in a brown, ragged costume, her arms crossed, her hands hanging unseen over her shoulders, the picture of Eastern malevolence. As she brought her hands into view, her green rings became the eyes of the cobras. Her hands transformed themselves into the snakes' heads, her arms became their bodies. St. Denis, the snake charmer, allowed her green-eyed pets to slither over her neck and body, then raised her hands high and darted her fingers at the audience in a striking attack which, according to the *Times,* "fairly makes one's scalp lift."

The Incense, which opened the program, and which St. Denis performed for nearly sixty years thereafter, was a more stately ritual. St. Denis, a high-caste woman in this incarnation, was dressed in a gray sari. She crumbled incense over a tray and followed the spiral of the smoke with a ripple of her arm. The kinesthetic echo of the rising smoke was the rhythmic theme of the dance. The motion that was generated in the performer's shoulders rode down her arms and into her fingers then, gently, possessed her entire body. In Walter Terry's words, "At one moment, she stands utterly still except that the hand bearing the tray moves slowly upward, almost hugging the body and head, until the dancer herself seems to have become a holy stele, a column of truth, or, perhaps, a stilled human receptacle for divine illumination." This moment of stillness, one arm raised toward heaven, was to become a thematic gesture in St. Denis' work.

Radha, though, was the most important work in the trilogy. St. Denis sat unmoving, the sculptured image of the goddess in her temple. Priests, "scantily clad," according to the *Times,* burned incense and performed their rituals before her. St. Denis had done her homework; an article in *The Theatre Magazine* for March 1906, notes that the worship of the priests is "an exact reproduction of the corresponding ceremony in the land of the blue lotus." Touched by the ceremony, the goddess Radha enters into her image, steps down from the dais and dances the lesson of the renunciation of the senses. The jewels she wore pleased the eyes; the bells on her fingers delighted the ears; she gathered garlands to her body to enjoy their scent; sipped from a bowl to experience the taste and power of wine, and, to know the beauty of touch, stroked her body and kissed her own hands. Radha spun her body through the Dance of the Delirium of the Senses and her golden skirt swirled about her as she gave herself up to ecstasy. As she turned she stretched into a deep backbend, filled with the joy of earthly experience.

Then, the goddess danced the pain of renunciation, twisting and writhing, and finally sinking to the ground in darkness. She rose again, discarded the skirt of gold and, moving on the balls of her feet, she showed the ecstasy that transcends that of the senses, the joy that may be obtained only by freedom from illusion. She held a lotus, and as she moved, her feet traced the pattern of an open lotus flower. She moved backward to her shrine, where she sat and withdrew herself from the temple, leaving only a statue and a lesson to be understood.

There it was—sex, art, religion, and spectacle. *The Theatre Magazine* reported: "Radha wears a bodice or jacket trimmed with lace, beaded with turquoise and coral. The bodice is cut short enough to expose several inches of bare skin between it and the start of the skirt." At the time, décolletage and tights were enough to make burlesque an entertainment unsuited to genteel tastes. The content of the dance, even more than the costume, was remarkably sensual for its time. So much for sex. Art was evident in the construction and execution of the dance, and religion was clearly evident in its lesson. As for spectacle—St. Denis had her brother, Buzz, develop a method of changing the color of the stage lights during a scene, a departure from the contemporary practice that allowed changes to be made only between episodes.

Obviously, St. Denis had learned something from her five years with Belasco, who was a master of stage effects, and from her glimpse of Loie Fuller. She did not dance, as Isadora Duncan did, on a stage draped with curtains, but used a full set. She did not costume herself, as Isadora did, in simple tunics, but wore clothing drab or resplendent, as demanded by the character or the dramatic content of the scene.

America could cope with St. Denis more easily than with Duncan. One reason, of course, was that Miss Ruth did not make speeches to the audience; newspaper headlines could concern themselves with her dress, but not with her tongue. Another is that Americans expected something a bit sinful of the East, and the religious connotations of St. Denis' dances (more obvious than those of Duncan's) took a bit of the sting off the sensuality. More important, St. Denis understood theater. "Isadora Duncan placed her reverential dances before the public as artistic products," stated *The Theatre Magazine* reporter, implying that St. Denis—"a new priestess of the cult"—did something more.

Indeed she did. Her work was filled with color—green cobra eyes, purple smoke, turquoise beads, and the golden skirt. She provided her audiences with something more theatrical and less threatening than Isadora's pure dance, something they were ready to see. The folks in the vaudeville houses went to see St. Denis and came away titillated, but preening themselves on their touch of culture. Duncan never tried vaudeville, or cared to. St. Denis did, and her audiences went home as thrilled as the artist had been as a young girl by *The Burning of Rome*. Duncan dressed her art in austere passion, and the popular audiences could accept neither the performer nor the dance. St. Denis let her Orientalia serve as a disguise. She cloaked the meaning of her dances in rich regalia; she danced stories, letting the secrets of the art creep up on the audience from behind the stagecraft, and she triumphed. Ruth St. Denis' dance, unlike that of Isadora Duncan, was show biz and show biz, as Aeschylus and Shakespeare knew very well, is what sells tickets.

After the series of matinées in New York, St. Denis performed in Boston and Washington and then, having dazzled at least the Eastern Seaboard of America, she was ready for Europe. Henry Harris arranged three matinées for her at the Aldwich Theatre in London in the late spring of 1906. Her work was admired by many, including Loie Fuller, but business at the box office was slow. She moved on to Paris where, after an encounter with an imitation Radha, she made her debut on September 1. The season succeeded.

Large rings on each hand form the eyes of the snakes as St. Denis performs The Cobras (1906). *Her sense of theater shows in her makeup and costume, the dinginess of which contrasts sharply with the glamorous decor of* Radha.

PHOTOGRAPH COURTESY OF THE DANCE COLLECTION
OF THE NEW YORK PUBLIC LIBRARY.

Ruth St. Denis left Paris for Germany, where she danced for nearly two years in various cities and studied Egyptian and Oriental lore in the libraries and museums of Berlin. The city was a center of Egyptology and St. Denis, who had not forgotten *Egypta*, talked with specialists, feeding her constant hunger to know everything about a subject that interested her. Her sojourn in Germany gave her two new dances, *Nautch* and *The Yogi*, both of which were first performed in Vienna.

Nautch was the dance she had started to create when she began work on *Radha*. It was the first of several nautch dances with which she was to captivate audiences for several generations. A nautch is a secular dance, intended to be seductive. In her first nautch, St. Denis wore a green costume and worked up to a series of rapid turns that swirled the fabric around her. She also made the fabric flow around her arms, a trick she may have learned from watching Loïe Fuller. Later on, she was to extend the sleeves of her costumes with rods, a technique she definitely culled from Fuller's methods. In *Nautch*, she wore ankle bells, walked with a slight backbend that brought her pelvis forward and made quite clear to the audience what she was doing. *Nautch* and its descendants helped her fill theaters for years.

The Yogi was an extension of St. Denis' private study of yoga, and a work very different in tone from its companion piece. The yogi was as clearly a spiritual figure as the nautch dancer was a physical one, and the piece showed him invoking the presence of Brahma and being, at least for a moment, united with the divine. Its gestures were measured, its balances precarious, its central image, meditation.

St. Denis danced her way across the Continent, then returned to England where she found the box office receipts considerably more satisfactory than on her first visit. A season at the Coliseum in London brought her 500 pounds a week. In 1909, still thinking about *Egypta*, she came home.

1909 brought a historic autumn to American dance. New York saw the three goddesses of the art perform within a few weeks of one another. St. Denis offered a series of matinées; Duncan appeared with Walter Damrosch; Fuller and her company played the Metropolitan Opera House. Modern dance was being performed in America to serious music, for a serious audience, as mystery, as artistry, and as theater. The stagecraft of Fuller, the purity of Duncan, and the esoteric rites of St. Denis came together. The birth had been accomplished.

After the series of matinées in New York, St. Denis set out on tour, performing in vaudeville houses and at society parties in order to earn a living. Vaudeville was in the middle of its greatest expansion. W. C. Fields, then known as a juggler who dressed up as a tramp and did funny tricks, was pulling down $500 a week. Eva Tanguay, whose act concentrated on sex and left out the art and religion, rescued audiences from the sentimentality of songs such as "You'll Be Sorry Just Too Late" to tease them with "It's All Been Done Before But Not the Way I Do It," and could command $2,500 a week.

St. Denis took a repertory composed of her Indian dances to theaters in the East and Midwest. She was in Cleveland when she received a letter from Henry Harris: He had decided to produce *Egypta*. Harris wanted a full production, not the solo she had planned six years earlier, and he wanted it in six weeks. Walter Meyrowitz provided a score. St. Denis' brother devised an elaborate lighting plan. St. Denis herself found that "An odd assortment of dancers, knowing nothing and caring less about Egyptian banquets than I care about the Chocktaws, had to be assembled and disciplined into an Egyptian ballet which used flat, two-dimensional movements." There were no dancers trained in St. Denis' style from whom she could form a company; such performers did not exist.

The years of study, of scurrying off to libraries and talking with learned Germans, were put to use. On December 10, 1910, Ruth St. Denis danced *Egypta* in New York. It was an expensive production: Even in this, her dream dance, St. Denis understood the need to offer a show.

In the first scene, the "Veil of Isis," St. Denis danced the goddess. The second scene showed a king and queen at a colorful feast, being entertained by a dancer. The next scene, "The Dance of Day," was the one that had been inspired by the poster and, before that, by Genevieve Stebbens. An Egyptian peasant was seen lying on a slab, asleep. She woke and moved through the actions of a day in a metaphor for the rise and decline of a kingdom. The last scene was the production number, the trial of Egypt before her gods. The set was huge, the lighting was Belasco and, at the end, a boat appeared to carry the soul of Egypt into the afterlife. *Egypta* was a full-length drama on a serious theme in a new style of dance. It was a remarkably ambitious production. It lost money.

Ambitious productions were not new to the American stage. In 1908, Florenz Ziegfeld had informed the press that in his production of *Miss Innocence,* Anna Held would wear a $25,000 sable coat and a $30,000 dress. Two years later, in the year of *Egypta,* Ziegfeld's *Follies* opened with a view of the Manhattan skyline and later offered an effect in which

Anna Held was seen on film as a comet with a smiling face until she burst through the screen mounted on a silver rocket. Ziegfeld was the master purveyor of sumptuous effects and beautiful women; he and his followers tied together on Broadway the entire American tradition of popular entertainment, and the public loved it. This type of theater helped make the country ripe for St. Denis' art, but not sufficiently ripe to keep *Egypta* on the boards. Certainly, the *Follies* cost more than *Egypta,* but just as certainly more people wanted to watch Anna Held, Fanny Brice and Bert Williams than to see Ruth St. Denis dance. The *Follies* had a long run; *Egypta* closed twenty days after its first performance. It went to Boston for a short run in January 1911, and then was broken into a series of separate dances suitable for taking on tour.

Harris arranged the bookings, and the circuit carried St. Denis past Chicago, through the Midwestern states and into California. The first time she toured, St. Denis had to create an audience for herself; the second time, it was waiting for her, but she refused to accept "too much credit, for in 1910 and 1911 any 'show' that looked at all promising was avidly seized upon by theater-loving people." America did not know much about dance, but it was ready to be entertained and Ruth St. Denis was ready to oblige.

The tour, like others before and after, was a trail-blazing expedition. St. Denis even had to instruct the reporters who came to review her work, because there was no such profession as dance criticism. Few things, good or ill, that Miss Ruth did for the dancers who followed her were as important as her early trouping, which trained an audience for her successors. The nation was learning that there were more forms of entertainment than reading the ads for wooden legs, and St. Denis, on the vaudeville stages she hated, was helping to teach them.

One member of the audience whom she had educated was her manager, Henry Harris. Despite the money he had lost on *Egypta,* he offered

"The Legend of the Sun Goddess" from O-Mika (1913). The diffusion favored by early photographers accents the softness of St. Denis' bodyline, but does not cloud her astounding beauty. (She was about 35 when this was taken.)

PHOTOGRAPH COURTESY OF THE DANCE COLLECTION OF THE NEW YORK PUBLIC LIBRARY.

to produce two new St. Denis dance-dramas, *O-Mika*, a work with a Japanese theme, and *Bakawali*, a Hindu love story. Both were inspired by the works of Lafcadio Hearn, expatriate and author, and *O-Mika* was born of the impression made on St. Denis by Sadi Yaco in Paris. Harris was sailing home from Europe to begin work when, on April 15, 1912, the liner *Titanic* struck an iceberg south of Newfoundland and east of New York. The producer was one of the 1,157 who died.

St. Denis managed to bring *O-Mika* before an audience at New York's Fulton Theater on March 11, 1913. She had been scrupulous in her research, as always. She used devices of the classical Japanese theater and she learned to speak Japanese words phonetically, because the dance-play contained spoken lines. *O-Mika*, like *Egypta*, was a lavish production and, unlike the turns of vaudeville dancers, it told a coherent story.

Bakawali also made use of spoken words and presented, as one of its episodes, "The Dance of the Black and Gold Sari," the ancestor of one of the most popular and enduring pieces in St. Denis' repertory. The two dance-plays were dismembered into pieces for touring as their predecessors had been, and St. Denis went back to the halls. She danced at the house that was to become the goal of all vaudeville performers; an agent told her, "You know, we're trying to put this new Palace Theater on its feet. We need to interest society in vaudeville. If you want a week, you can try it."

The Palace had opened on March 24, 1913, nine days after the première of *O-Mika*. Its first card gave top billing to a pantomimist and interpretive dancer, La Napierkowska who, *The New York Times* reported, "danced with feet and arms bare, and wore several veils which she gradually took off as she Duncanized and Saintdenised." Americans had learned enough about dance to make fun of it, and two names were sufficiently well-known to be subjects of parody. The dancer's veils, by the way, were part of a vogue that began when Mary Garden sang Richard Strauss' *Salomé* at Oscar Hammerstein's Manhattan Opera House in 1907. "The Dance of the Seven Veils" caused enough of a stir to make veils popular stage accessories for many years—in time, they worked their way into the dances of Ruth St. Denis.

After playing The Palace, St. Denis moved on to Chicago where, at Ravinia Park, she made her first appearance with a symphony orchestra. She kept moving, dancing in concerts, at soirées, in vaudeville, performing short segments from her major works, impressing her audiences with sex, art, religion, and spectacle.

The year after her first appearance at The Palace, St. Denis realized that the public's taste was changing; exhibition ballroom dancing had come into fashion, and her audiences wanted to see her performing with a partner. Miss Ruth sent out a call for male dancers and wound up with a husband. Together with Ted Shawn, she continued her tours, and even took Oriental dance to the Orient. Together they built a school that trained the next generation of modern dancers, establishing the line of succession that had been denied to Isadora Duncan. That, however, was largely Shawn's doing.

St. Denis continued to perform and to devise dances; she invented music visualization—her Synchoric Orchestra—a plotless dance in which each performer corresponded to an instrument and moved when it played. A similar style of dance was created in Germany at about the same time, but Miss Ruth's version came from her own head, and from her memories of Isadora dancing the Unfinished Symphony. Even so, by the time she met Shawn, her greatest contribution had been made; she had taken serious dance on the road and introduced it to the nation.

Years later, she told Walter Terry that her first vaudeville dances had been "very ordinary. I could copy anyone. Technique? Never heard of it. . . . I'd just look at some of the girls with acrobatic tricks, watch them twice, then do what they did." To be "very ordinary" was not enough for Miss Ruth; "acrobatic tricks" were not her way of dancing. She studied Oriental arts, she made story-dances, she took on the full regalia of theater, and from those ingredients she made a new style. She took it to "the despised vaudeville," the popular theaters of America, and taught audiences to like it.

St. Denis took what was handy—a contemporary interest in the exotic, the nation's delight in spectacle, its enjoyment of sideshow attractions, its growing appetite for theater of all kinds, even its periodic religious revivals—and made it serve her purpose. The mind that reveled in mysticism and understood dance as a religious experience also had a remarkable appreciation of popular taste. That taste, in the form of an advertising poster, triggered the idea that made her a dancer. She returned the compliment by inventing dances that delighted the spectators. Miss Ruth did not like dancing in vaudeville; she considered it an expedient for earning money to devote to more serious work—but often it was the only outlet available, and she used it. Fortunately for American dance, vaudeville liked Miss Ruth.

IV

TED SHAWN

MEN DO DANCE

THE DIVINITY STUDENT's fraternity brother was shocked; perhaps his friend's recent illness had affected his mind. "But Ted," he explained, "*men* don't dance."

He was right. In other societies, cultures in which dancing was integral to religious observance and the functioning of life, men danced as a matter of course, but in the United States, where dance was merely entertainment, males did not take the stage. During the closing years of the nineteenth century, men's roles in ballets at the Metropolitan Opera House were danced by women in tights. (In the 1870s, burlesque established itself in America by adopting the English custom of having the "principal boy"—a woman—perform in tights. The sight of women's legs brought sold-out houses.) Men did not appear in modern dance; Duncan and Fuller had trained only women to dance with them; St. Denis had used men, but had no partner of stature. The young man who startled his fellow-student with the remark that he was going to quit the University of Denver for a career in dance changed everything. He not only became a dancer, he taught other men to dance, and eventually led a company of men through the country, proving to audiences that male dancers were not merely acceptable, but necessary. His name was Ted Shawn.

Shawn was lucky; he fell in love with dance when the art was mature enough to need a man, if there was one with sufficient courage to embrace it. When Diaghilev's Russian ballet had electrified Paris in 1909, much of the current was generated by Vaslav Nijinsky and Mikhail

Mordkin. The next year Mordkin and his ballerina, the great Anna Pavlova, made their American debut. The full Diaghilev company did not reach the United States until 1916, but by then, three of the ballets in its repertory had been staged in unauthorized versions by Gertrude Hoffman, whose performances employed male dancers. (Hoffman had previously pinched some ideas from Ruth St. Denis to use in vaudeville. She had a good eye.)

Vernon and Irene Castle were wowing vaudeville with their exhibitions of ballroom dancing. Dozens of other couples copied their act and even their costumes (Irene started the headband habit), and society followed the fashion set by the stage and started to dance. In 1911, the year the American Suffragettes held their first big parade in New York, men wore high collars and women dressed in high-collared shirtwaists, lisle stockings and narrow skirts that swept the tops of their shoes. Dancing was a social duty, not a pleasure, and few couples bothered once they were married. By 1920, the year woman's suffrage was established by a Constitutional amendment, clothing was less restricting and the nation was relishing the dances that so shocked Isadora Duncan.

The Castle Walk, made popular by Vernon and Irene, was the fashion in 1913. A year later, the Argentine tango and the hesitation waltz were banned by the Federation of Women's Clubs. A bestiary of other dances —The Lame Duck, the Turkey Trot, the Fox Trot, and the Bunny Hug— pattered along while public officials denounced the orgies that were taking place in public dance halls. Fifteen young women were fired from their jobs at the Curtis Publishing Company in 1915 when it was discovered that they were doing the Turkey Trot during their lunch break.

In 1914, South American dances were the rage and Ruth St. Denis insisted that there no longer were any waiters in America; they had all transformed themselves into tango and maxixe dancers, who seemed to be the leading attraction at every vaudeville house and restaurant in

---

Shawn in a Spanish dance from O Libertad *(1936), a work he choreographed for his men's company. When Shawn and St. Denis toured with the* Follies, *his Flamenco number sometimes stopped the show, and he obviously enjoyed performing in the style.*

PHOTOGRAPH COURTESY OF THE DANCE COLLECTION
OF THE NEW YORK PUBLIC LIBRARY.

the country. (Some years later, an assistant gardener at New York's Central Park achieved a good deal of success after changing his profession to tango dancer and his name to Rudolph Valentino.) The vogue of ballroom dancing on stage helped prepare the way for more serious duets, and when the time came, Shawn was waiting to greet it.

Edwin Myers Shawn was born in Kansas City, Missouri, in 1891. His father was an editor with the *Kansas City Star;* his mother had been a high school principal, wrote book reviews, and was a distant relative of Edwin and John Wilkes Booth. She died when Ted was eleven, and the same year cost him his brother. Ted was a junior in high school when his father left Kansas City to take up duties on the *Rocky Mountain News* and the Denver *Times.* In Denver, Ted became friendly with the pastor of a Methodist church, and when he entered the University of Denver, he chose to study for the ministry, a calling which had attracted him since his childhood.

All the pioneers of American dance were evangelistically inclined. Loie Fuller had been a temperance lecturer; Duncan, the atheist, was driven by a need to preach her physical truths; St. Denis was raised on the Bible and came early to mysticism. A missionary intensity was required by those who chose to make a career in an art that did not yet exist, and a religious fervor was evident in the work of the early dance-makers. Shawn eventually choreographed a church service, and St. Denis tried to marry the stage and the altar in the later stages of her career. It was not a shotgun wedding. Religious ceremonies frequently are celebrated in dance, even, at times, in the Western tradition. A Chassidic folk-song bids the congregation be quiet, the rabbi is going to dance, and when the rabbi dances, the tables and chairs dance with him, and the Scrolls of Law in the Holy Ark dance with him, and Satan falls dead in the middle of the floor. There comes a moment of ecstasy in which voice and words are too weak to contain fervor; the entire body is enraptured and impelled to movement.

Ted Shawn's mission in dance was evangelical. He, not St. Denis, was the force which created the Denishawn school, the field in which American modern dance ripened. He brought men into the art, developed specialized techniques for them and proved their importance. He demonstrated to America that it had music and themes from which dances could grow. Finally, he turned his farm in Lee, Massachusetts, Jacob's Pillow, into a summer school and festival which has as its altar one of the most beautiful dance theaters in the nation. During the first twenty years of the festival, which began in 1942, Jacob's Pillow presented more than one hundred premières and, although Shawn was a modern dancer, the Pillow offers its stage to all forms of the art. Shawn did not lose his vocation when he turned away from the ministry, he simply transferred it to the stage and to the classroom.

The conversion was occasioned by an attack of diphtheria during his junior year at the University of Denver; an overdose of serum left him paralyzed below the hips. He spent more than a year in the hospital, and while his body could not move, his mind refused to be still. His thoughts led him away from the ministry. At the same time, he was forcing his leg muscles to function, willing each tension and extension until he could move again. He returned to school in 1911 and continued his therapy by appearing in plays, but friends informed him that he was too clumsy to act and suggested he study ballet. He began his lessons with Hazel Wallach, who had left a career with the Metropolitan Opera Ballet because illness in her family called her to Colorado. Shawn began to dance with the odds against him. He had been partly paralyzed; he was larger than is usual for a ballet dancer—more than six feet tall and weighing about 185 pounds—and he was twenty years old. Dancers, especially ballet dancers, generally begin training before adolescence. An artist of exceptional determination sometimes begins his studies as a young adult and succeeds in joining the profession, but it is not general practice. Also, Shawn was a man. There is no better measure of his religious zeal and calling than his triumph in becoming a dancer.

Ballet did not attract the young man, but Hazel Wallach did. She became the third woman to whom he had proposed, and his first official fiancée. The couple performed together, offering an exhibition of ballroom dancing at a benefit for charity. A newspaper photograph showed Hazel in a skirt slit to the knee, a pose which the university's chancellor found so lascivious that he regretted audibly that Shawn was no longer enrolled as a student, because it would have been such a joy to expel him. The chancellor undoubtedly would have been a staunch friend to Dwight Moody, who had suggested that Ruthie Dennis throw herself into the river rather than onto the stage. Shawn choreographed a solo to perform for his fraternity brothers before he had fully learned his art. He was exploring it. He was committed.

The commitment was sealed in March 1911, when Ruth St. Denis played Denver's Broadway Theater. She danced *The Incense,* and Shawn wept. For him, the performance was what St. Denis had intended it to be—a religious experience—and it completed his conversion. The next year, understanding that ballet was not his form, he left Denver and

Hazel Wallach for Los Angeles, where he hoped to find a teacher. He became one instead.

He took a job as stenographer to the auditor of the City Water Department of Los Angeles and rented a studio where he gave lessons in social dancing. He made his students the subjects of experiments in choreography, trying to create the dances he had seen in his head and on the stage of the Broadway Theater in Denver. He had known that he would be a dancer before he saw St. Denis, but her performance provided fuel for his determination. He was not the only dancer in the world.

He found a partner, a former ballet dancer named Norma Gould, who also ran a school, and together they gave a series of recitals in which the tango was always the most popular number. Shawn pounded his typewriter in the Water Department, then hurried out to perform at a tango tea with Gould, reached his studio in time to instruct his pupils, and then moved on to the Alexandria Hotel where he and his partner danced for the after-theater crowd. In his spare time, he worked on choreography.

Los Angeles already was transforming itself into America's Dreamland with the magic potion of the motion picture. Thomas Alva Edison had invented the peep-show (known by the more resounding name of *kinetoscope*) in 1889, and by 1896 the Edison Company was presenting films to the public in converted storerooms which charged an admission fee of five cents, thus earning the name of "nickelodeons." The first films were such a miracle of technology that they needed no plots to ensure themselves an audience—any action, even a man sneezing, would pack them in. The first film with a true plot is generally said to be *The Great Train Robbery* of 1903. Technology and content advanced, as did competition among producers and distributors. In 1908, a group of nine companies, which held the patents essential to the industry, set out to form a group that would, in effect, create a monopoly and limit the development of independent producers and distributors. The independents countered by moving from the East Coast to Los Angeles, where they found ways to circumvent the law. It was also in 1908 that the first of the great American directors, D. W. Griffith, joined the industry. His *Birth of a Nation* appeared in 1914, the year Ted Shawn arrived in New York to continue his career.

During Shawn's sojourn in Los Angeles, the film industry was busily searching for properties, and the young dancer created one of the first dances made for film, *Dance of the Ages*. It started with the dances of primitive men, as conceived by Shawn, and raced through history until it reached the apogee of choreographic civilization, the ballroom dances Shawn and Gould performed during their tango teas. Years later, Shawn used the same title for a major work made by his all-male company.

Shawn and Gould were developing a reputation, but neither was satisfied with dancing at teas. Shawn wanted to make dances, to give concerts, to continue his studies. Perhaps he could find a teacher in New York. The Santa Fe Railroad was hunting for performers who could entertain at employees' recreation centers along its route. Shawn and Gould gathered a company and, with two other dancers, a pianist, and a soprano who doubled on the violin, worked their passage east with Greek dances, Oriental dances, Hungarian dances, the dances of Henry VIII, the tango, and the hesitation waltz. They always ended the program with the tango and the waltz, the only sure hits in the repertory. The troupe gave its first performance on January 2, 1914, in Gallup, New Mexico. It was billed as The Shawn-Gould Company of Interpretive Dancers, and the program notes warned that "Some people may object to an entertainment of this character because it is dancing; but please do not commit an error here. It is a portrayal of perfect development by the most exacting labor and much self-denial." The words "labor" and "self-denial" were well chosen. "The stage on which we were to dance was simply a tiny platform at the end of a lounge where off-duty employees read or played checkers or shot pool," Shawn wrote. "The performance area was impossibly small for any of our dance numbers. No provision was made for theatrical lighting and there was no front curtain."

Having worked his passage across the country to New York, Shawn set out to study. He took lessons in ballet, in Spanish dance, in the latest ballroom steps. He also taught ballroom dancing, and he and Norma Gould joined the swarm of ballroom stylists who were crowding the vaudeville stage. He was not pleased. He already knew that he did not want to spend his life stepping through the tango. He intended to study Oriental dancing, and he intended to study with the leading artist in the field, Ruth St. Denis. He did not know whether or not St. Denis accepted pupils, but that was beside the point. One of his own pupils was on her way to a party at St. Denis' studio when Shawn asked her to tell her hostess that a young man wanted very much to study with her, and could afford to pay for the honor. St. Denis dispatched her brother to inspect the applicant and, having received a favorable report, decided to invite him to tea at her studio and home on West Eighty-ninth Street.

St. Denis had issued a call for young male dancers. She was engaged for a tour of the South, and the intensity of the craze for ballroom dancing had convinced her that if she were to sell tickets, she must insert some such entertainment into her programs. She was not quite sure how she would employ a male dancer, but she knew that the taste of the time demanded that she have one with her. However, she found the young men who auditioned for her "so superficial in their attitude and so inadequate in their dancing" that she nearly abandoned the idea. Then Shawn arrived. He came expecting a dancing lesson, and for years one of the family jokes was that he never got it. Instead of the lesson, they had a talk. They talked until dinner, they talked during dinner, they talked after dinner. Shawn left at midnight, after arranging to come back in the morning.

The next day he danced for her; he performed an Aztec dagger dance which St. Denis later described as "one of those rather crude and simple rhythmic dances which in after years one looks back upon with a kind of loving tolerance." Still, the young man who performed it was certainly not superficial in his attitude, nor was his technique inadequate. In fact, St. Denis was convinced she had discovered "the best male dancing material in America." The suppliant who had come hoping for lessons was signed as St. Denis' partner. They first performed in Paducah, Kentucky, on April 13, 1914. When they were not dancing, they were talking. In her autobiography, Miss Ruth recalled the romance in simple, loving sentences: "We talked on the trains, in the theaters, in the hotels . . . our idyll began to bloom. . . . In Knoxville he sent me my first gladioli. In Norfolk he proposed."

St. Denis was in love, but marriage frightened her. She had seen a childhood friend dwarfed and cloistered by an early marriage and there were other, deeper reasons for her fear. Her mother, who had been her closest companion, complicated matters further with her opposition to the match. The prospective bride was fourteen years older than her wooer. They separated briefly, and wrote letters passionately; Shawn spent a wracking three hours with Mother Dennis, and the couple was married on August 13, 1914. Ruth refused to say "obey" during the ceremony, which was most radical in 1914, and she never would wear a ring, which she considered a symbol of bondage. They set off on a six months' honeymoon of one-night stands, keeping the marriage a secret at Ruth's insistence. She gave the game away in Kansas City.

The couple gave one of their customary interviews to a local reporter. After Shawn had left the room, St. Denis, under the impression that the on-the-record interview was over and that she and the reporter were simply having a woman-to-woman chat, confidentially remarked that she and her handsome young partner were married. No reporter in her right mind was going to keep that item off the record. The news got on the wires, and was picked up by newspapers throughout the country, which quoted St. Denis as saying that she had married "the most beautiful man in the world." Shawn was handsome enough, but not quite that pulchritudinous. A well-known vaudeville performer, Paul Swan, billed himself as "the most beautiful man in the world," and both Shawn and St. Denis insisted that a journalist or telegrapher confused "Shawn" and "Swan." On the other hand, St. Denis just might have said it in the throes of a romantic tête-à-tête. She had a talent for self-dramatization.

The Call, New York's famous socialist paper, ran the story on November 8, using the "most beautiful man in the world" remark and asking readers to send in a picture of any man they considered more beautiful than Shawn. Four days earlier, the Peoria *Journal* had carried the story, quoting St. Denis as having said, not only that her Ted was the most beautiful man in the world but that "We shall be happy because we love the same thing—our art. Temperament cannot come between us. I do not believe in temperament, anyway, nor does he."

It didn't work out that way. Shawn's autobiography avoids the subject—St. Denis appears and disappears from its pages like a character in an animated cartoon. Miss Ruth's book is more analytical and discusses the subject thoroughly, but generally in mystical, convoluted phrases. The difficulties began shortly after the marriage: Shawn believed that as St. Denis' partner, he deserved equal billing; she insisted that he had yet to earn it, which was probably true at the time, although his name was subordinated to hers long after he had attained a fame of his own. The matter culminated in 1927, thirteen years after that first tour, when St. Denis, standing on the stage of Carnegie Hall, announced to the audience a plan to build a school and studio in New York—a plan conceived by Shawn—giving the impression that she alone had instigated the enterprise. The fissure widened and four years later, after a final concert in New York's Lewisohn Stadium, they separated. They never divorced; in their later years they danced together again, were friends to one another again, and continued their epic conversations, but the marriage effectively ended in 1931.

The school, which had bound them, also came between them, since it was Shawn's dream, not St. Denis'. Their styles of dance began to differ, also, and their needs were not the same. Walter Terry, who knew them both, believes their constant proximity was part of the problem, and also quotes St. Denis' remark, "I was a very bad wife to a very good husband." In her own writing, St. Denis did blame herself for the rift, in highly colored prose, rather as if she were enjoying it. Psychoanalysis at a distance is, in the terminology of mountain climbing, difficult and dangerous, but a study of St. Denis makes one suspect she was one of those people who lived in dread of love. The classical explanation involves an unresolved fear of incest; those who suffer from it often are, like St. Denis, intensely attractive, vibrant, intelligent people but, the moment they begin to love deeply, they become emotionally paralyzed, and drag themselves away. St. Denis' tendency to mysticism helps sustain the hypothesis. As for Shawn, a man who made a habit of proposing to his teachers could well have been seeking a mother, and a man who was himself an incurable teacher could well have been seeking a protégé. In either case, he needed assurance, praise, and a center on which to balance himself. St. Denis, as great as she was, did not fit those requirements.

The outlines of the problem became visible in 1914, but there were more obvious difficulties that needed attention then. Shawn's description of the tour is hilarious, as many traumas are when regarded from a safe distance. He reports the filthy theaters, the unpalatable food, the cacophonous trombone player who could not be dismissed from the orchestra because he was also mayor of the town—"Either I play or there won't be any show"—the trains that left small-town depots at five A.M. "I sometimes marvel that we ever built a dance audience," he wrote. "The general public didn't know what to make of us . . . Those people accustomed to the stereotyped entertainment of melodrama and comedy were disappointed by our numbers designed for neither the sob nor the guffaw. Bigtime-Charlies who misinterpreted the pictures of our ad-

---

Ted Shawn and Ruth St. Denis do The St. Denis Mazurka *at a private home in California. Exhibition ballroom dancing had been made popular by Vernon and Irene Castle, and the costumes of Shawn and St. Denis hint at vaudeville. Performances at private homes were not unusual.*

PHOTOGRAPH COURTESY OF THE DANCE COLLECTION
OF THE NEW YORK PUBLIC LIBRARY.

vance posters booed when they realized we weren't putting on a hootchy-kootchy, Little Egypt sort of show. The front-row boys paid to see legs in action not legends unfold." Nevertheless, they moved.

In Portland, Oregon, the manager of the theater at which they played decided publicity could be arranged by offering eight box seats to the person who could come up with the best name for one of the couple's ballroom dances, the *St. Denis Mazurka*. It would be nice if the name made some reference to Portland, too. Margaret Ayer, otherwise unknown to history, suggested *The Denishawn Rose Mazurka*: Portland was the City of Roses, Denishawn was an obvious contraction, and the Mazurka was there to begin with. The elision baptized a school, a company, and a style. Margaret Ayer never came backstage, and nobody knows if she even used the free tickets.

The school was planned in Pullman cars during long rides between engagements; it was definitely Ted's idea. It was to be in California, where he had already conducted classes, it was to stage its lessons outdoors, and it was to offer instruction in all styles of dancing. Shawn's passion for teaching and for organization found expression in the plans for Denishawn; the system of instruction was largely his work. St. Denis' task was to teach Oriental dance, to act as a spiritual influence on the students, and to give instruction in music visualization, which she had derived and adapted from the work of Isadora Duncan. In this way, some of the ideas of Duncan, as translated by Ruth St. Denis, were built into the foundation of American dance.

In a similar manner, the methods of François Delsarte were incorporated. After a performance in Los Angeles, the same year the school opened, Shawn was approached by an elderly woman who informed him that one moment of his dancing had been superb, and "all the rest . . . was rot." The self-appointed critic was Mrs. Richard Hovey, who had studied for eight years with Delsarte's son. Shawn took private lessons from Mrs. Hovey for five years, and the Delsarte theories became an integral part of his dancing and teaching techniques. The disparate elements that influenced the first dancers in the American style were, in one form or another, codified and passed on to a new generation of performers, at Denishawn.

Denishawn opened in Los Angeles in 1915. Each student dropped a dollar into a cigar box, and received in return three hours of class, the use of the swimming pool, and lunch. Classes were conducted on the lawn, but the greensward was covered with a well-sanded floor, since both Ruth and Ted had learned through experience that dancing barefoot on a lawn was more pleasant to think about than to do. The methods of teaching were to remain basically the same throughout the school's existence. Shawn began the day by supervising the students' exercises in stretching and breathing, then led them through a ballet *barre* and into free movement. In the middle of the morning, St. Denis took over and taught Oriental dance and the special techniques which she had evolved. In the evening, she led the group in yoga meditation. This was the beginning of the Denishawn style.

Denishawn offered private lessons, at higher rates, and celebrated performers came to study and have dances made for them. The school did not merely teach technique; it equipped its students with material for performance. Gertrude Shurr, the eminent dancer and teacher, was a member of the company from 1925 to 1927, and her recollections of training at the school—a *barre,* then a free style of ballet in the center of the room, then improvisation—show that the school maintained its methods of instruction as it grew and matured. She also recalled that students left, even after a summer course, with dances they could perform. "Miss Ruth . . . chose one or two girls and made a dance on them. The rest imitated it." Shawn came to the studio early in the morning and made a dance. When the students arrived, he taught technique from nine-thirty to eleven, and then from eleven to twelve, they learned the dance he had invented earlier. "After six weeks, they had technique, a whole répertoire, dances, they had notes, they even had their picture in the costumes—and Mr. Shawn sold everything." The sales of dances, lessons, and pictures helped keep the school alive.

The original school grew into a company when Shawn and St. Denis selected eight young women to tour with them, and designed a program of dances for the troupe. The first tour, starting in the fall of 1915, took them from Los Angeles to New York, and left them in debt. St. Denis' brother, who was to become an immensely successful businessman, took them back to vaudeville to recoup their losses, and he started them at the top; they played The Palace. They signed for one week, the box office turned away more than five thousand ticket-seekers, and the act was held over for another week. They trimmed their concert program, selecting individual numbers to please the vaudeville audiences, as St. Denis had done a few years earlier. They pleased the audiences so well that brother Buzz wangled a contract that gave the new company fifty-six weeks of vaudeville bookings, divided into two segments of sixteen and forty weeks. The summer was to be devoted to teaching, and the proceeds of the tour were to support the school.

During the summer of 1916, Ruth St. Denis was honored with the first invitation extended to a dancer to perform in the University of California's Greek Theater. She and her husband conceived a large and lavish production, *A Dance Pageant of Egypt, Greece, and India,* based on the customs and religious beliefs of the three civilizations. The production required a cast of 170 and the services of the San Francisco Symphony Orchestra and the University's chorus. Shawn and St. Denis rehearsed the dancers, designed the costumes, and, in between times, taught their classes. Individual dances were rehearsed at the school, but the two principals had to share the expense of moving the entire crew to the theater for final rehearsals.

The pageant was presented on July 29, 1916, before an audience of ten thousand, and was repeated in an outdoors performance in San Diego and at the Shrine Auditorium in Los Angeles. It contained revised versions of dances from *Egypta,* Greek dances, and Indian dances, and began with a piece that was to become celebrated, "Tillers of the Soil." "Tillers" was an austere work that paid homage to the elementary labors of human beings: plowing, reaping, spearing fish, tending sheep. A branch served as a primitive plow which Shawn guided and St. Denis pulled, harnessed to it by a rope of fabric riding over one shoulder.

The pageant also contained an episode called "Pyrrhic Dance," the first piece Shawn made for an all-male ensemble. It used sixteen dancers and displayed them in muscular, virile leaps and jumps. The newspaper critics had never seen anything like it, and praised it lavishly. Shawn had attempted to interpret the spirit, if not the precise form, of the men's dances of Attic Greece, and the reception accorded the performance led him to think about devising other works for male dancers, and about a company which could perform them.

A Dance Pageant of Egypt, Greece, and India was the most ambitious work St. Denis and Shawn had attempted. It involved the theatricality and scope of ballet, but set them in a different form. The two artists were not trying to invent a completely new technique or a purely American style as their successors were to do. They drew on other nations and other forms of dance and interpreted them in their own fashion. Their attempts at authenticity separated them from ballet, in which "ethnic" interludes were performed with classical technique, and from vaudeville dancing, in which Irish jigs and American Indian numbers were staged in steps as stereotyped as the dialects employed by comedians. Furthermore, Denishawn demonstrated that dance could have a serious purpose, as spoken drama did.

Though artistically important, the pageant was not a financial success, and Shawn and St. Denis found themselves in debt, as usual. They edited the pageant into touring-sized dances and went back to vaudeville to play out their contract. Shawn, according to St. Denis, disliked vaudeville even more than she did, because he believed that the commercial aspects of two-a-day detracted from the artistic prestige of the company. Vaudeville also removed Shawn from his school, which may have seemed a far more important loss than prestige. St. Denis' religiosity expressed itself in mysticism; his found a missionary outlet.

Denishawn flowered. It had acquired a musical director during the company's 1915–1916 tour, when a young conductor and pianist was taken on for a two-week engagement and stayed for ten years. His name was Louis Horst and, in conjunction with a student who came to the school in the summer of 1916, he was to affect the shape of American dance. The student was Martha Graham. She was older than most of the aspirants who were arriving to study, and Shawn remembered her as "shy and plumpish." Shawn wanted the school to continue its sessions throughout the year, and hired a faculty to teach classes and manage the enterprise. He hoped that a string of schools could be threaded through the major cities of the country, each using a curriculum approved by Shawn and St. Denis, and each helping to disseminate the Denishawn style.

In 1917, the United States entered the World War, an action which interred the Progressive Era, which had actually died two years earlier. Shawn, in turn, entered the United States Army. He enlisted for service in an ambulance unit, but spent the war in Camp Kearney, near Los Angeles. Shortly before he joined the service, he formed into a program works he had been constructing for several years and performed, at the First Interdenominational Church of San Francisco, a church service in dance. "The Doxology" became an integral part of his performances in later years.

Shawn's war was fought with other soldiers, to whom he determined to prove that a man who danced was, nevertheless, a man. He accepted a nomination to Officers Training School simply because it was assumed that no light-footed dancer could last the course. He won his commission. While he fought for his profession, Doris Humphrey, a young dancer from Oak Park, Illinois, took her first lesson at Denishawn; St. Denis' father died, and St. Denis herself played four shows a day on the Pantages vaudeville circuit and sold Liberty Bonds—her triumph was the sale of $68,000 worth.

The armistice was signed on November 11, 1918. As soon as Shawn was quit of the army, he boarded a train for Detroit, where St. Denis was performing, and traveled with her for several weeks while they argued the future of Denishawn. St. Denis "had become possessed with the idea that I must come out from under the burden of the school"; she believed it was stealing time from her work. Money was scarce, Shawn could not support the enterprise alone, and the school was closed. Shawn operated a small studio, where Martha Graham acted as his assistant teacher. In 1919, he signed to tour the Pantages circuit, and constructed as his vehicle a three-act dance, *Julnar of the Sea,* based on a story in the *Arabian Nights.* The work employed a cast of seventeen, one of whom was the first narrator ever used by a professional dance company.

The next year, hoping to repeat the success of *Julnar,* Shawn made a dance, *Xochitl,* for vaudeville using an Aztec theme. Xochitl (The Flower) was a stunning young woman who served an Aztec emperor with a bowl of *pulque.* The liquor heated the emperor's passions as well as his throat, and he chased the maiden around the room. At the climax of some heartily realistic struggles, Xochitl's father appeared, ready to save his daughter by stabbing his king. Xochitl averted the assassination, married the emperor and, no doubt, lived happily ever after. The audiences loved it, and the *Pacific Coast Musical Review* of October 1, 1920, found it "unique, artistic, dramatic, musically well worked out . . ." The title role in *Xochitl* was created on and danced by Martha Graham. The performer who played the emperor broke his foot during the tour and was succeeded by another Denishawn student, Charles Weidman.

Shawn signed for a tour which would use *Xochitl* as the finale of the program, but a dishonest manager and contractual difficulties turned the venture into disaster. St. Denis, meanwhile, was touring with a company of her own, which included Doris Humphrey. While Shawn was choreographing *Xochitl,* Miss Ruth and Humphrey together were making *Soaring,* a work to Schumann for five women, and *Sonata Pathetique,* to

---

St. Denis and Shawn in "Tillers of the Soil" from their Dance Pageant of Egypt, Greece and India *(1916). The costumes are as authentic as research could make them, and are obviously designed to facilitate movement.*

PHOTOGRAPH COURTESY OF THE DANCE COLLECTION
OF THE NEW YORK PUBLIC LIBRARY.

Beethoven, for eleven women. These pieces were called music visualizations, a term St. Denis and Shawn preferred to "interpretive dancing." They were completely removed from the ethnic and theatrical dances for which Denishawn was famous. The costumes were neutral in color and simple in design; they had no purpose other than to display the bodies of the dancers. The dancers themselves were told, "in no uncertain terms," according to St. Denis, that "their personalities were of no account. They were members of a group that had no purpose except to reflect the rhythm and structure of the music and "to see that the patterns, space coverings, and groupings were as beautiful as possible." Shawn and conductor Louis Horst helped furnish an understanding of the music; St. Denis and Humphrey devised the choreography; the inspiration came from Miss Ruth's recollections of Isadora Duncan.

Music visualization led to the Synchoric Orchestra—a name invented by Shawn—which used a company of fifty or sixty dancers and attempted to echo in movement all the values of symphonic music. Late in 1975, Martha Graham recalled for a theater-full of listeners that she had not been allowed to dance in Miss Ruth's version of the *Unfinished Symphony,* "because I wasn't a blonde." She did make the second company of the *Unfinished,* though: "I was the oboe; whenever it played, I moved."

As Shawn and St. Denis led their separate companies, with their different styles, on the road, the Boston *Post* of September 12, 1920, reported rumors of a divorce. Both principals denied them. In the same year, a branch of Denishawn opened in St. Paul. Until Denishawn ended, strangled by the Depression, branches were constantly being started by former pupils, who paid $500 for the privilege of using the curriculum and the name. Shawn opened the Denishawn studio in New York in 1922, the same year he gave his first solo concert in the city. The pamphlet announcing the school's season for 1923 noted that Denishawn schools were functioning in Boston, Rochester, Minneapolis, Wichita, San Francisco, and Berkeley, as well as in Los Angeles and New York. The announcement assured prospective students that "The wholesome standard of the school attracts the best character of artistic and beauty-loving boys who desire to make dancing as a fine art their life work," and noted that Charles Weidman was a Denishawn dancer.

While the work of the school went on, Shawn toured, sometimes with his own company, sometimes with his wife, continuing his choreographic mission to the Americans. It was getting a bit easier. The earlier tours, the Broadway spectaculars that made their way across country, vaudeville, and films were making audiences more sophisticated about movement.

The early film comedies, being silent, relied on action and gesture for their effects, and the antics of the great comedians helped prepare people to respond to dance. The finest comic artists of silent films were very nearly dancers themselves. One of the classic definitions of the art of Charlie Chaplin was laid down by W. C. Fields, who refused to watch Chaplin's films because the genius of the other master unnerved him. Toward the end of Fields' life, according to Robert Lewis Taylor, a friend managed to drag the Great Man to a screening of an early Chaplin movie. Fields fidgeted through part of the film, then left the theater and waited in his car. After the screening, his friend asked what he thought of Chaplin. "The-son-of-a-bitch is a ballet dancer." Yes, but wasn't he funny, too? "He's the best ballet dancer that ever lived, and if I get a good chance I'll kill him with my bare hands." Fields relied greatly on physical humor and dexterity; he had been a celebrated comic juggler before his verbal humor was discovered. He understood the dimensions of Chaplin's art. Films helped kill vaudeville, but they also helped to make the country ready to enjoy "ballet dancers," whether in Chaplin's style or in Shawn's.

Shawn estimated that he traveled fifty thousand miles a year, giving performances, lectures, and lessons. The pace was exhausting, as he and his company gave eight or nine performances, in six cities, within a week. When not dancing, he was teaching. When not teaching, he was learning. He went to Spain, studied, and came back to choreograph *Cuadro Flamenco*. He went on to Algiers, and returned to make *The Vision of Asissoua*. Wherever he traveled, throughout his life, he took lessons in the local style of dancing and spent whatever money he had on authentic clothing in which to dress his dances. Then he came back to teach and to tour.

The tours were artistic successes and financial flops. Part of the difficulty was the size of the productions; in the true St. Denis tradition, they were elaborate, theatrical pieces, and Shawn was no less a trouper than his wife. The black velvet backdrop for *Cuadro Flamenco* cost him $1,800; the score he commissioned for *Feather of the Dawn,* a work inspired by Hopi dances, took $1,200. Shawn computed a balance sheet, which showed that during three years of touring, he and Miss Ruth had achieved an average income of $200,000 a year. Then he added up the debit side of the ledger for their third (1925) tour: Commission to their manager, $40,000; railroads and Pullmans, $54,000 (consider the mileage implicit in that figure); salaries to the company, $46,000; production expenses, $30,000; billboards, circulars, photographs, and other artifacts of publicity, $20,000; transportation of baggage, postage, telegrams, music, and miscellaneous expenses, $10,000. They had managed to break even, which was an achievement; the first two tours had left them in debt. But there were compensating satisfactions. They realized that America was becoming conscious of dance, that Americans wanted to study dance, and that audiences were prepared to welcome them.

In the summer of 1925, Shawn, St. Denis, and the Denishawn dancers began their famous tour of the Orient. In each nation they visited, Shawn took dancing lessons and bought costumes. India gave him his famous "Cosmic Dance of Shiva." To prepare it he read, talked with scholars and mystics, and bought a drum made of two human skulls They performed their Oriental dances for Orientals, and were cheered. India applauded Miss Ruth's *Nautch* and "Dance of the Black and Gold Sari." On trains, they discussed his plan for building Denishawn House, where they would have their home and a studio. St. Denis, for some reason she herself could not understand, did not want to build. She was always a performer, a producer, and a mystic rather than a teacher; the idea of being tied to something as solid as a Greater Denishawn, with its walls, its schedules and its requisite thorough organization frightened her.

They returned to the United States with a group of new Oriental dances, which they mixed with older works to make a program for their next tour. They tested the new repertory on friendly ground, in Southern California. By this time, their names and methods were familiar to newspaper editors, and the notices lacked the tongue-in-cheek style that had greeted them in the early years. There were headlines such as "Dazzling Oriental/Beauties Mirrored/In Stage Splendor" and "Rich Raiment/ And Beauty/In New Show." The Los Angeles *Evening Express* noted that the program was presented "In a series of the most brilliant and colorful settings ever seen on an American stage." On January 7, 1927, John C. Wilcox in the Denver *Morning Post* proclaimed, "So sparingly do Ruth St. Denis and Ted Shawn employ the technical devices of conventional dance forms that their offerings call for the coinage of some new term

---

The Denishawn Company in Cuadro Flamenco, *one of its production numbers. St. Denis is center, Shawn at lower right. Large, flashy works like this helped the company win vaudeville audiences for dance.*

PHOTOGRAPH COURTESY OF THE DANCE COLLECTION
OF THE NEW YORK PUBLIC LIBRARY.

to classify their diversified stage presentations. Dances they are, to be sure, in the sense that they almost constantly employ grace of motion; but pantomime and pictorial groupings contribute equally to their stunning effects . . . The Denishawns exploit no toe dancers, nor do they present a phalanx of 'pony' girls to kick in unison for the delectation of the tired business man." This gives a hint of what other dance companies were offering.

Most of the reviews were naïve by our standards but then, so were the dances. There was a remarkable innocence to the "wickedness" of Miss Ruth's *Nautch,* as films demonstrate. Her seductiveness displays the same sort of charm as a little girl practicing flirting. A *Hoop Dance* performed by a group of young women is so gauzy in its flowing drapes and light in its steps that it might have been painted by Watteau. Shawn's celebrated *Death of Adonis* starts out resembling the silly "Greek Posing" into which Delsarte's pantomime degenerated, but his movements are flowing, his waist is flexible, his arms curve beautifully and his full weight is solidly planted in the ground. His *Cuadro Flamenco,* although he studied the original sources, looks a bit like an early Hollywood version of *Carmen*—passionate Spaniards teasing and flirting—and displays the same, peculiar innocence as Miss Ruth's Oriental naughtiness. However, even the old films show what a powerful, sinuous dancer he was. He holds his poses tightly, his heel-taps are aggressive and demanding, and the sense of pride demanded by Flamenco dancing dominates his carriage. His arms have a ripe curve and bend sharply at the wrists, his head is high, his knees free and supple.

It was characteristic of Denishawn dancing that the waist was fluid, and that there was a clearly defined curve to the performers' bodies. It is evident in St. Denis' Oriental pieces and equally clear in Shawn's movements. This curvature is evident in photographs and sketches of Duncan, and a lack of rigidity is demanded by Delsarte. The Oriental influence, of course, came from Miss Ruth. This soft quality seems to add to the naïveté of the Denishawn plots and style: They made no excursions into psychology or sociology; they portrayed the visual beauty of myths— whether ancient tales of the Orient or contemporary visions of gypsies —rather than seeking the darker meanings of the visions.

After concluding their tour in the spring of 1927, Shawn and St. Denis gave four performances at Carnegie Hall. As a result of these performances, petitions were drawn up requesting New York newspapers to appoint professional dance critics to their staffs. St. Denis and Shawn led the list of several hundred signatories, and the *Herald Tribune* responded by creating a new position, dance critic, and appointing Mary

Watkins to the beat. A few weeks later, the *Times* named its own critic, John Martin. It was during the Carnegie Hall series that St. Denis announced to the audience the plan to build, near Van Cortland Park, a headquarters for the movement to be called Denishawn House. This was the venture she had not wanted to enter, and this was the venture she announced without mentioning the name of Ted Shawn.

The plan demanded a great deal of money, and to find it Shawn and St. Denis joined the touring company of the Ziegfeld *Follies*. In New York, the *Follies* starred such artists as Fanny Brice, Bert Williams, and W. C. Fields. George Wintz, who had purchased the right to create a touring *Follies,* knew that in the smaller cities, St. Denis and Shawn had a larger following than those performers because they had built an audience with their own tours. He induced them to sign by offering them $3,500 a week. In the *Follies,* each of the stars had two solos and an ensemble number; Shawn's solos were Flamenco dances and the *Cosmic Dance of Shiva.* The Topeka *Capital* of November 19, 1927, reported that the audience insisted that he give an encore of his Flamenco solo, and the Wichita *Eagle* of November 16 noted that about 38,000 persons had attended the two local performances of the *Follies.* George Wintz had been right in picking his drawing cards.

The end of the *Follies* tour led to another ending for Denishawn. By then, Doris Humphrey and Charles Weidman had each achieved critical acclaim and public approval; they were the most celebrated members of Denishawn except for the name stars. The two had been entrusted with minding the school in New York while Shawn and Miss Ruth were on tour, and they were beginning to discover, in their separate ways, styles of dancing that differed from the gospel according to Ted. In the summer of 1928, they were summoned to a meeting to discuss the future of Greater Denishawn. According to Humphrey, Miss Ruth had decided that it would be best to limit the number of Jewish students to ten percent of the group; Shawn delivered a lecture on the immorality of various students who were conducting affairs that did not end in marriage. Then he announced that he and St. Denis had toured with the *Follies* to raise money for Greater Denishawn, and it now was the turn of Humphrey and Weidman to take to the road.

Humphrey objected; she was beginning to find her own way of working and did not want her experiments interrupted. Furthermore, she disliked the way the Denishawn numbers in the *Follies* had been altered to suit popular taste. Shawn defended the changes, asking if Jesus Christ had been less great because he addressed the common people. "No," said Humphrey, "but you're not Jesus Christ."

"I am the Jesus Christ of the dance," he told her, and there was really no answer to that. Humphrey was being priggish and Shawn pompous, but determination and defensiveness does that to people. She wanted to continue her own work, he saw only the greater good of Greater Denishawn. Humphrey and Weidman left the company.

A few days later, Miss Ruth wrote to Humphrey, regretting the scene that had taken place and giving assurance of her faith in the younger woman's artistry and potential. "As far as I am concerned," she wrote, "the old Denishawn is dead. We have had a house divided against itself." St. Denis believed that the "reactionary attitudes" held by Shawn and by herself were limiting the progress of their students, and even of themselves. It was time, she felt, to start again.

Shawn and St. Denis began to move in different directions. He built a Japanese studio in Westport, Connecticut; she spent much time in California and taught at Denishawn House, New York. In 1929, Shawn gave his first solo performance at Carnegie Hall, and the next year brought his first solo recital to Europe, where he studied with Margarete Wallman of the Mary Wigman School; Wigman herself had studied with two theorists of movement and rhythms, Emile Jaques-Dalcroze and Rudolf von Laban, and in 1914 she became the latter's assistant. Von Laban, with German thoroughness, studied every aspect of motion and devised a sort of shorthand for writing dances as music is noted. Wigman transferred the theories of Dalcroze and von Laban to performance and became the fountainhead of modern dance.

Wigman's method of training dancers, which employed gymnastic exercises, was not designed to produce a specific technique or vocabulary but to make the body an instrument capable of performing any movement demanded of it and of expressing emotion. She evolved a technique of alternating tension and relaxation, and she trained her dancers to work without music, building phrases from body rhythms. After that, they combined dance with simple accompaniment that made much use of percussion.

The style and themes of her work were related to the Expressionist movement, which arose in a Germany devastated by World War I. In drama, Expressionism became a theater of revolt, as well as an attempt to present subjective, emotional truths. Kurt Jooss, another pupil of von Laban, made ballets in the Expressionist mode. The most famous is *The Green Table*, which uses symbolism and didactic methods to demonstrate the causes and horrors of war. *The Green Table* is in the repertory of the City Center Joffrey Ballet, allowing modern audiences to find out for themselves what Expressionist ballet tried to do. The piece was made in 1932, after the peak of the style, but it is relevant to it.

Wigman's style did not appeal to Shawn; the tense, somber mood of defeated Germany was at odds with the optimism of America in the 1920s and created a different style of dance. The Depression was to teach America a new style, too, but for Shawn, at least, it would be a style of heroic striving and hope. Still, he believed that he should study all the dance he could find, and he was sufficiently impressed with his teacher, Margarete Wallman, to persuade her to spend the following year teaching at Denishawn. That year also saw the fifth and last in an annual series of performances by The Denishawn Dancers at Lewisohn Stadium in New York. Shawn's *Job: A Masque for Dancing* was on the program, along with a mystical work by Miss Ruth, *The Prophetess.* Then, they parted. It was 1931, and the end of Denishawn. Doris Humphrey and Charles Weidman had left the company in 1928; Martha Graham and Louis Horst had broken away even earlier. The Depression was in power, the change of style was happening. The opulence and mysticism of St. Denis gave way to social comment, to psychological probing, to more stringent movement befitting a harsher reality and a new mythology. Shawn made his new headquarters at Jacob's Pillow; St. Denis managed to keep Denishawn House operating for a time after the company itself ended, but the foundations were eaten away by swarms of debts. The mortgage was foreclosed in 1933.

The Depression also crushed Shawn's work. In the fall of 1931, he began a tour with a company named *Ted Shawn and His Dancers,* but the hard times brought cancellations, not bookings. The tour was cut short, leaving Shawn $5,000 in debt. He did manage to salvage something of value. He still believed, as he had since the making of *Pyrrhic Dances,* in choreography designed especially for men, and for his tour he had made three works, *Brahms Rhapsody, Workers' Songs of Middle Europe* and *Coolie Dance,* to be performed by five men. He offered the new works at several small colleges and one of them was sufficiently impressed to ask Shawn to join its faculty and teach its young men to dance.

Shawn became associated with the International Young Men's Christian Association College (Springfield College in Massachusetts) in 1932. Springfield was the leading school in the field of physical education; it turned out coaches, playground directors, and teachers. Shawn had five hundred young athletes at his disposal, and he insisted that every one of them study dance, so that those who did not want to take the course could not toss unpleasant epithets at those who did.

He drew the best of his Springfield College students into a coeducational company he had gathered to give ten performances at the Boston Repertory Theater after two trial runs in Springfield. It opened in the face of disaster. The United States' banking system had been severely disrupted, and on March 6, 1933, the new President, Franklin D. Roosevelt, declared a bank holiday, which suspended all banking operations and transactions in gold. On March 9, the Congress passed the Emergency Banking Act, reopening banks in sound condition, but for three days the ordinary citizen had no spare cash with which to buy theater tickets. In 1933, the ordinary citizen did not have much spare cash at any time, yet Shawn gave his season in Boston and ended it with only a minuscule deficit.

The second program in the series was of major importance. It was billed as *Ted Shawn with his Ensemble of Male Dancers*, and it offered thirteen works danced by fourteen men. The only female listed on the program was Mary Cambell, the pianist. The works presented on that first program show the kind of pieces the men's company offered throughout its seven-year history. The first half of the program consisted of *Osage-Pawnee Dance of Greeting; Invocation to the Thunderbird; Cutting the Sugar Cane; Charlie's Dance; Workers' Songs of Middle Europe; Flamenco Dances; Los Embozados.* Intermission was followed by *Japanese Rickshaw Coolies; Spear Dance-Japonesque; Camel Boy; Gnossienne (Satie); Rhapsody (Brahms); Four Dances Based on American Folk Music,* and *Negro Spirituals.*

The program summarizes the thematic material of Shawn's later creative period—ethnic dance, music visualization, dances of labor, religious dances, and dances on American themes. The nation was packing together a new bundle of myths. Franklin D. Roosevelt had pieced together the coalition of ethnic groups, labor, and the intelligentsia which, together with its penchant for running against Herbert Hoover, was to keep the Democratic Party in the White House until 1952. Labor unions were respectable again, the heroes of the proletariat and the dignity of labor

---

Shawn and his men dancers (1938) in the "Earth" section of Dance of the Ages *show the athletic poses and sculptured, formal groupings favored by the choreographer.*

took on epic proportions, the downtrodden were lifted up, at least by artists and intellectuals, and the heritage of America was packed as ammunition against adversity. In 1924, Shawn had choreographed *Five American Sketches,* including a cowboy duet and *Crapshooter* (danced by Weidman) for one of his tours with St. Denis. He had made *Invocation to the Thunderbird* early on, in 1917. Now, in the Depression, he came back to American themes, and the public was more interested in them than in exotic dances.

Shawn and St. Denis had followed Loie Fuller and Isadora in dancing to Classical music. Shawn used the music of Scriabin, Bach, Beethoven, and Mozart, among others, but he also commissioned scores from American composers, and used American folk songs in his work. The men's company was important, not merely because it demonstrated the dignity of men who dance, but because it brought dances based on native themes to a wide audience which was ready to receive them.

Shawn and his group of male dancers lived at Jacob's Pillow during the summer, preparing and rehearsing for their winter tours. Every Friday, Shawn led the company in a lecture-demonstration-tea, and the nominal fee paid by the spectators helped pay for the groceries. Mary Cambell, believing that a men's dance troupe should have a male pianist, bowed out to make a place on the piano bench for Jess Meeker, who remained at Shawn's side, as accompanist and composer, for years. The company lived as a commune, sharing expenses and profits, if any. Summers also brought students to the Pillow to work with Shawn, and a British journalist who visited the company in the summer of 1934 noted that he had never seen "a higher degree of morale, nor better physical condition" than was displayed by the group at Jacob's Pillow.

Some members of the company came to Shawn from dance, some from athletics. Barton Mumaw, a superlative artist, had studied piano before he joined Shawn as a pupil in 1931. Wilbur McCormack had been captain of the Springfield College wrestling team; Frank Overlees had been a competition swimmer; George Horn had danced in musical comedy. In 1933–1934, the company, now composed of Shawn, seven other dancers and Jess Meeker, played 109 performances in one hundred communities. That first season it appeared, among other places, at Amherst College, the Kiwanis Club of Oswego, New York, the high school audiorium in Asheville, North Carolina, the Florida State College for Women at Tallahassee, the community theater in Hershey, Pennsylvania, and the Shubert-Belasco Theater in Washington, D.C. In later years, it was to cover even more ground.

Shawn had added several works to the repertory, including *O Brother*

Sun and Sister Moon, a consideration of St. Francis, and *John Brown Sees the Glory,* which was not welcomed in the South. Both works, which were highly praised, dealt with men called, in one way or another, by evangelical missions. The success of the company was recorded by the visiting British journalist: "No one not intimately acquainted with the hinterlands of the States can conceive of the intense prejudice against a programme entirely masculine—yet Shawn has been asked to return this season to almost every one of the one hundred and fifty stops of last winter." The writer called the company "one of the most signal and constructive advances that the dance world has seen for a decade." The one hundred and fifty stops included places at which Shawn lectured even if the company did not dance.

For the second tour, Shawn made *Labor Symphony* of which the final section represented, he wrote, "the spirit of metals and the machine itself." He continued to make ethnic dances which he offered, not as examples of authenticity, but as derivations from original sources. Reviews everywhere stressed the power of his performances and the muscular virility of the dancers. Probably the most famous work performed by the company, *Kinetic Molpai,* was choreographed for the tour of 1935–1936. It is a dynamic piece which rejoices in a sense of flowing motion. Some of its sculptured poses look like posters urging the workers of the world to discard their chains, making the piece seem dated in revivals, but its power and dignity is still apparent.

Kinetic Molpai formed the third section of a three-act dance, *O Libertad,* with which the company toured in 1936 and 1937. The first section, *The Past,* led the audience through a history of California that began with the Aztecs and culminated in the Gold Rush, and made use of Shawn's familiar themes. *The Present* described the decadence of the Jazz Age in a masked dance, led young men to war, and offered a note of hope with a section depicting the Olympics, and, incidentally, the relationship of dance and sports. The Olympics passages were choreographed by members of the company. Act III was *Kinetic Molpai.* When, in 1938, the company finally reached Broadway, a reviewer found that *Kinetic Molpai* illustrated "the athletic art of the dance as a field of creative endeavor for the American man . . . an excellent example of the abstract in dancing, yet is usually quite clear in meaning . . . There is abundant example of ballistic style in the group, which at times suggests birds in flight by their beauty of design."

Shawn knew in 1940 that the men's group had achieved its goal by establishing male dancers in the art and bringing them the respect that was due them. On May 7, 1940, the company gave its last program, ending where it had started, in Boston. Shawn owed $25,000 from the early years, but the job he had set out to do was accomplished. He not only had raised men to their rightful place in dance, but he had changed the style of the art. The author of a 1934 article in *The Dancing Times* was convinced that he had "succeeded in hitting upon a trail-blazing style of dancing for men which is both artistically important and entirely free from the purple tints which usually hover about his own solos." The reviewer remembered Denishawn dancing "as a whirling of colored scarfs and impressions from the Orient," and pointed out that while Shawn had carried on many of the Denishawn traditions, he also had moved away from many others. The new choreography was as proud of its muscles as a lifeguard, and rejoined in big movements and strong poses. The movement of his 1938 epic, *Dance of Ages* seems kinesthetic sloganeering, as unsophisticated as its politics, but that is because we look at the film from an era of dance which has different myths and methods and which, in addition, has incorporated Shawn's teachings so thoroughly that they no longer seem revolutionary. In his time, he was a rebel and a prophet.

The demobilization of the men's troupe signed the end of Shawn's great creative period, as the termination of the Denishawn company nine years earlier had marked the end of St. Denis'. There was war in Europe, the Depression was reined in, the times asked for new styles and new heroes. In 1941, the choreographer solved his financial difficulties and ensured a future for his art by selling Jacob's Pillow to a corporation, which hired him to direct a summer dance school and festival. On July 8, 1942, he personally dedicated the Ted Shawn Theater, and he remained active as teacher, lecturer, impresario, and performer until his death in 1972.

Miss Ruth, who was fourteen years his senior, founded the dance department at Adelphi College in 1938; she organized her Rhythmic Choir and staged masques and pageants for churches. In 1940, she and

---

Shawn, at 50, in one of his Four Dances Based on America Folk Music. *The line of his body and the solidity with which his weight rests on the ground rebut those who deny his skill as a dancer.*

PHOTOGRAPH COURTESY OF THE DANCE COLLECTION
OF THE NEW YORK PUBLIC LIBRARY.

La Meri, an important performer of authentic ethnic dance, founded the School of Natya in New York, where they taught and offered recitals. The next year, ten years after her separation from Shawn, St. Denis danced at Jacob's Pillow, performing the work that had launched her career, *Radha*. After that, her dancing again gained recognition and as time went on, she acquired the stature of a national shrine. In 1964, she and Shawn celebrated their fiftieth anniversary by dancing (at Jacob's Pillow) a new duet, *Siddhas of the Upper Air,* based on a poem by Miss Ruth and using a score by Jess Meeker. St. Denis died on July 21, 1969. *The New York Times* paid her the homage of a front page obituary. It was accompanied by an appraisal of her work by the paper's leading critic, Clive Barnes, who wrote: "Of all the American dance pioneers of this century . . . no one has had the influence of Ruth St. Denis . . . When she and her husband, Ted Shawn, founded the Denishawn School in Los Angeles in 1915, they were in effect laying the foundation for American modern dance."

Miss Ruth and Papa Shawn lived long enough to see their conceptions of dance become dated, to watch the times move to new rhythms that demanded new ways of dancing. Luckily, they also lived to see their pupils create the new styles, and to be honored for their inspiration. In 1963, nine years before he died, Shawn wrote an article, "The Changes I've Seen" for *Dance Magazine*. Parts of it sound as if Papa Shawn were telling the kiddies how lucky they were, and how tough things were back when he was a boy, but there are other words that still ring clearly: "I believe dance is a language—a means of communication. Why sacrifice discipline and work without end, unless the result is the communicaiton of *something?* Too many dancers today are satisfied with technical accomplishments and feel that just to dance is enough . . . I will always give my accolades to those dancers who, having mastered the language, *say* something. For, that indescribable something is the life-enhancing element of the art of dance."

In contemporary terms, probably neither Shawn nor St. Denis was a great choreographer, if one measures their choreography by the way they carved and served time and space, or by the inventiveness of their methods of movement. The miracle of it is that they were able to become choreographers at all, that they were able to assemble the few building stones available into a foundation for dance. That foundation has enabled other Americans to become great choreographers, and the faith of their successors is a fitting monument for missionaries.

V

DORIS HUMPHREY

THE ELOQUENCE OF BALANCE

"UNLESS YOU BELIEVE in yourself, no one else will." The voice uncurling from the tape has a flat, Midwestern flavor, a heritage from Oak Park, Illinois. Doris Humphrey was delivering a lecture to a group of students in 1956, two years before she died. Arthritis in her left hip had forced her off the stage in 1944, but had not ended her work; she choreographed, she taught, she wrote.

A bit later in the lecture she told of her days at Denishawn, about the "magnetic and stimulating personalities of the two leaders" and the "vision" that was Miss Ruth's bequest to her students. But Denishawn did "any kind of dance that they could lay their hands on . . . I felt as if I were dancing as everyone but myself. I knew something about how the Japanese moved, how the Chinese or Spanish moved, but I didn't know how I moved." Humphrey began to feel a need to discover how she moved as an American and as a contemporary dancer.

In order to find out, she entrusted herself to that most dangerous of companions, a mirror. She stood in front of it, watching her body as well as feeling it in motion. She concluded that dance happens in the frightening moment between falling and recovering, during the arc swept by a body moving between equilibrium and uncontrol. On that balancing rock, she built her method. It was a logical choice. She believed that emotion must guide one's life, yet she declined impulsive action. She taught that a dance must be rooted in a specific situation and concerned with feeling, yet she cast much of her work in an abstract mode, allowing an immediate situation to serve as metaphor, or even working with pure motion and rhythm. She left detailed notes about many of her dances, she wrote letters about them, she planned them with intense concentration. She was devoted to individual creativity, yet among her greatest contributions was the development of formal structure, and many of her most important dances were concerned with social commentary. Humphrey walled her emotions with her intellect, and made dances of the arc of unbalance.

Her career epitomizes the ephemeral quality of dance. She was revered by many as the greatest choreographer of her time; twenty years after her death she is merely a name to many who follow her art. The performing arts evaporate more quickly than their more static cousins, painting, sculpture, and literature. Time will mutate a painting or a piece of sculpture, but the quality and structure remain as the artist formed them. Written words hold off the ages, although a dictionary and a sense of history may be required of readers a century or so younger than the book. Plays survive in altered context; those great enough to be revived as something other than curiosities offer emotional information sufficiently universal to survive a transplanting in time. Each age filters Shakespeare through its own sensibilities, but the life in his lines is so rich that no age can fail to profit from it.

We do not hear the scores of Bach exactly as the composer did, because our instruments are different and we are uncertain about certain techniques of ornamentation and playing. Mozart's tempi were certainly slower than those of contemporary conductors; what we consider a moderate pace would probably seem to him an unconscionable rush.

Dance is even more difficult to reconstruct. Videotape, sound-on-film and modern techniques of notation are recent inventions; we often have no more knowledge of exactly what Doris Humphrey meant by a phrase than of the precise intentions of Bach. Furthermore, dance is made for specific performers, often for the choreographer. Sometimes the choreographer designs a movement and the dancer tries it on as though it

---

Doris Humphrey in Passaglia *(1938) demonstrates the purity of her line and shows the working of the arc—her weight moves to the left, her torso curves to the right against the fall.*

PHOTOGRAPH BY BARBARA MORGAN.

were a pair of trousers; if it does not fit, it may have to be altered. When a new dancer succeeds to the role, the movement will look different.

Ballet fans seem to watch an endless parade of *Giselles* and *Swan Lakes* not merely because they adore them, but because fewer than a dozen ballets of the Classical and Romantic periods remain in the standard repertory and many of those have been reworked by contemporary choreographers. There were many more—Marius Petipa, the father of Classical ballet, alone made more than sixty—but they have fallen out of the march because their choreography was insufficiently inspired or because our tastes have changed. (It often seems that a plot was suitable for ballet only if it was too silly for opera.)

Ballets are kept on stage by the beauty of their steps and patterns and the emotional power of their mythic content. Styles of movement change quickly, and what is fresh today may appear either mannered or foolish next month. Ballet, with its canon of steps, operates within an accepted convention; modern dance is often less academic, lacks such specific references, employs a number of different styles and consequently erodes more rapidly. Methods of movement change along with the guidebooks we use to interpret events; some psychological and sociological thinking that made dances of the 1930s seem advanced appears naïve forty years later. Even emotional intensity cannot prevent a work from seeming stale a few years after its making if the fashion in movement has changed or a dominant way of thinking has altered: Many of Doris Humphrey's works now seem more pretty than powerful. A great dancer becomes a ghost shortly after retiring; a great choreographer may be only an interesting study to the succeeding decade. Dance is an art to be elected only by the courageous. It suited Doris Humphrey.

When she could no longer perform, she made dances for the company of her protegé, José Limón, and for the Juilliard Dance Theater, which gave the première of her final work five months after her death. She also furnished a testament unrivaled by any of her contemporaries—a written record of her works, her theories, and her methods. Should all her dances disappear, her writings would maintain her stature. Her major statements about choreography are contained in *The Art of Making Dances,* a book which gives you everything you need to be a choreographer except dancers and genius. Chapter Eighteen is devoted to a check list of choreographic mistakes, and includes such cautions as: "Symmetry is lifeless; two-dimensional design is lifeless; All dances are too long; A good ending is forty percent of the dance; Don't be a slave to, or a mutilator of, the music."

The book, along with her other writings, offers a method of work and a guide to her successors, and Humphrey was a great believer in method. She was concerned with theory from the beginning; she completely altered her ideas about dance after leaving Denishawn, and within three years (in 1931) she had determined a series of principles on which she was to rely thereafter: All patterns of movement consist of opposition, succession, and unison; all qualities of movement may be trisected into sharp accents, sustained flow, and rest; a balanced dance must use at least two elements from each division. She used these principles as Denishawn had used methods derived from Delsarte and Oriental dance, but Humphrey did not borrow theories but worked out her own, in her effort to learn how she danced.

Despite her passion for codification, she wrote in *The Art of Making Dances* that she "never believed in teaching with a set vocabulary of movements, hardened into technical sequences. I always thought students should learn principles of movement and be encouraged to expand and embroider on these in their own way." In practice, her choreographic principles triumphed over her dancers' originality, but the striving for equilibrium was always present.

Doris Humphrey was born October 17, 1895, to a father who had been educated at Beloit and worked for Chicago newspapers and a mother who had graduated from Mount Holyoke and the Boston Conservatory of Music. She was three when her father gave up journalism to become the manager of Chicago's Palace Hotel, which catered to theatrical transients who generally owed rent and maintained the good will of the establishment by teaching the manager's daughter to turn cartwheels. Her parents sent her to the most progressive educational institution they could find, the Francis W. Parker School, where she had her first lessons in dance. Her mother had tried to teach her to play the piano, an experiment which did not succeed, and decided that perhaps her daughter could learn to do something of value "even if it's only dancing."

Doris was eight when she began classes with Mary Wood Hinman, a gifted instructor who was teaching twice a week at the Parker School. Hinman encouraged the child to study with others, too, and she learned some ballet, some ballroom steps, and a smack of clog dancing. In 1913, she spent her senior year on what her mother described to the high school authorities as "a trip West." The trip consisted of playing the same Santa Fe Railroad circuit that Ted Shawn was to follow a year later in the opposite direction. Her graduation present was a trip to

New York, where she watched Vernon and Irene Castle teach the latest fads in ballroom dancing to a group of instructors while a Victrola ground out popular melodies. Doris had one turn around the floor with Vernon.

She returned home to find the Palace Hotel sold, her parents living with relatives in nearby Oak Park and her father short of cash. Her mother took over; she organized a dancing school at which Doris taught children on Saturday mornings and adults two nights a week. She was a good teacher, but she wanted to dance. She was in Oak Park, and dying of dullness. Her first teacher rescued her, suggesting that Doris go to Los Angeles to study with Ruth St. Denis and Ted Shawn. "It will be different for you, at least," Hinman said. "And something may happen." Something did. The course at Denishawn included a private lesson with St. Denis, who agreed that Doris' future was in dancing, not in teaching, and invited her into the company. That was in the summer of 1917 and, as Humphrey was fond of pointing out, she never went back to Oak Park.

Doris was rehearsing for her first tour with Miss Ruth when two young people joined the school. One was Charles Weidman, who was to become famous for having a sense of humor when dance needed it; the other was Pauline Lawrence, pianist, conductor, composer, designer, manager, and Jewish-Mother-in-Residence to a major sector of the modern dance movement. Weidman had seen Ruth St. Denis and Ted Shawn dance in his home town, Lincoln, Nebraska, at the age of twelve. (He was six years younger than Humphrey, having been born in 1901.) He was good at drawing, particularly good at caricatures, and was supposed to develop into an architect or a cartoonist. However, five years after seeing Shawn and St. Denis, and after study with a local dance teacher, he left Lincoln and high school for Los Angeles and Denishawn.

Doris Humphrey was one of his teachers; she had been promoted from student to faculty during her second year at Denishawn. She was a member of the company and on her way to becoming a choreographer. Her first dances were clearly in the Denishawn style; they relied a great deal on scarves. *Soaring* used five women and a scarf; it had been preceded by *Valse Caprice,* which used Doris Humphrey and a scarf and became known, logically enough, as *Scarf Dance.* In the same year (1920) Humphrey made a solo to a Bach bourrée—Bach was to become a major source of music for her—and collaborated with St. Denis on *Sonata Pathétique. Scarf Dance* was a filmy, pretty work; the St. Denis-Humphrey collaborations, *Soaring* and the *Sonata,* were far more important. They not only inaugurated the style of music visualization, they indicated the direction Humphrey's work would take by being choreographed for groups of dancers. St. Denis wrote that even then, Humphrey was capable of finer and more complicated choreography than she.

Between 1918 and 1923, the second generation of modern dancers worked among the first. Humphrey, Charles Weidman, and Martha Graham toured as members of the Denishawn companies. St. Denis had formed a concert troupe while Shawn continued to play vaudeville, and Denishawn toured sometimes as a unit, sometimes as two companies, and sometimes as several. Humphrey was most often associated with St. Denis; Weidman achieved his fame working with Shawn. He made his debut in *Xochitl,* standing in for an injured dancer; reviews praised his regal bearing, his passion, and his solo dancing. Graham spent most of her Denishawn career in the Shawn camp, separated from Humphrey; they were set on different roads from the beginning, and the differences between them—and between them and Weidman—helped create the diversity of modern dance. Graham left Denishawn before the company made its tour of the Orient, but Humphrey and Weidman went along on the excursion. During the season St. Denis and Shawn spent in the *Follies,* they taught classes at the New York school while Pauline Lawrence played the piano.

Gertrude Shurr recalls that Doris was "a tremendous teacher—very strict," while Charles taught dances rather than technique. Each was searching for a more basic style of movement than the one sanctified by Denishawn, and was going about it in a characteristic way. Weidman's work was flavored with theatricality and concerned with presenting character and situation, as he had done as a dancer when Shawn made *Crapshooter* on him. Humphrey, the strict teacher, was trying to devise a technique, and drew her inspiration from Miss Ruth's music visualizations. She was finding Denishawn nearly as constricting as Oak Park had been, could not abide the thought of another tour, and knew that as far as her own work was concerned, her time was being wasted.

In 1927 she wrote that she was "tired of darling little dances and I long for a good thick juicy beef-dance-steak that I can chew on hard." She was developing a new way of dancing, "of working from the inside out . . . It's the dominant expression of our generation, if not of the age." The generation of the 1920s was inspecting its drives, desires, and motivations. It was a generation of rebels, although Humphrey understood that the concept of a dance originating in emotion had been developed by Isadora Duncan, and by Miss Ruth. She was convinced that St. Denis had been wrong to allow Shawn, with his work at the *barre* and his kind of technique, to dictate the form of training used at Denishawn, probably not realizing that Miss Ruth had not really wanted the school at all. It is a paradox of modern dance that St. Denis was the inspiration of young dancers—both Humphrey and Graham praised her—while it was Shawn who created the environment in which they could be inspired.

Humphrey's rebellion was directed more at Shawn than St. Denis: She believed that with his tours, his superschool, and his technique he was demeaning the art, and that he was "about ten years behind in his theories of movement." She was ready for her own style and she meant to have it. She, Weidman, and their students from Denishawn began to give concerts. On March 24, 1928, the Brooklyn Little Theatre offered the premiere of her setting of Bach's *Air for the G String* for five dancers, her choreography of Grieg's *Concerto in a minor* for seventeen, *Color Harmony* for Weidman and a group of thirteen, and seven other works.

Fourteen dances by Doris Humphrey reached the stage in 1928. She had wanted to make dances that were "absolutely my own," for which she would need to rely on no one, not even a composer, for inspiration. She wanted her choreography to be "a symbolic or ritualistic thing— with some direct communication with our own human emotions and desires." In *Color Harmony* she tried to demonstrate her theory that any abstract idea can be danced, an assumption challenged by some of her later writings. The works she invented were not devoid of the tradition of Denishawn in that they relied on music visualization, but they avoided Oriental, Spanish, and Indian motifs. Humphrey was beginning to dance as a contemporary American, and she and Denishawn separated in June 1928.

Weidman left with her. They took over the lease of the Denishawn studio and set to work, with Pauline Lawrence to play piano, make

---

Humphrey represents the color violet in Color Harmony, *one of her first plotless dances, which was first presented in March 1928, shortly before the break with Denishawn. The formality and tension of her group choreography is evident.*

PHOTOGRAPH BY SOICHI SUNAMI.

schedules, design costumes, and keep track of the finances. The last job was fairly simple, since there was almost no money. They intended to give only as many classes as were needed to keep them in groceries and devote the rest of their time to choreography, but both Humphrey and Weidman spent much of their lives in the classroom, paying for groceries. In the early days, students presented their fees to Pauline Lawrence, and the triumvirate lived on a three-way split of the proceeds. They were in debt, they were competing for students with the dozens of schools that had opened in New York because of the success of Denishawn, and they had too little time for their real work, developing themselves as choreographers. The task was complex, since they were developing not one method, but two.

Weidman was pursuing, at first with much despair and little success, his unique blend of pantomime and dance. He was not trying to invent a codified technique, as Humphrey was, and he was uncertain of how to express his ideas. After finding himself standing in the studio, literally unable to move, he was ready to seek lessons even from Denishawn. He thought of studying with Ronny Johansson, a German modern dancer imported as a teacher by Shawn, but Humphrey stopped him. His first pieces showed more than a touch of Denishawn and had such titles as *Singhalese Drum Dance* and *Japanese Actor* (both 1928), but slowly he developed an individual style. While Humphrey devoted herself to ordering space and time in a logical manner, Weidman was concerned with action and character. Much of his finest work was pantomimic—Humphrey was occupied with pure dance—and many of his great pieces were funny, which Humphrey's most certainly were not. The Humphrey-Weidman company was divided into separate styles in a more obvious way than was Denishawn, and the two systems—one structured, one investigative—complemented one another over the years.

Humphrey was hunting for a style in which dance would stand on its own, independent of and equal to the other arts. Other choreographers were concerned with what to say and why it should be said, Humphrey's genius was perplexed by how it should be said. The quest for method made the years following the break with Denishawn the most creative of her life; she made forty-four dances, nearly half her life's work, between 1928 and 1931.

Her great achievements of this period resulted from her attempts to make dance an independent art and her fascination with the ensemble. Other choreographers, including Weidman, were concentrating on solos, but to Humphrey, the group was "the flowering of the dance." Shawn and St. Denis had made group dances, but Humphrey developed the form and made it one of her chief concerns. She was convinced that ensemble choreography would bring dance "to its full stature, just as music flowered through the symphony. A group of bodies is as varied and colorful a medium as the orchestra, and gives the composer equally rich material to fulfill the range of his vision. The new ensemble also has the architectural and impersonal attributes of the orchestra, as distinguished from the personal and expressionistic." Her concept, with its comparison of a group of dancers to a company of musicians, is a development of her work with St. Denis on music visualization, which, in its turn, had been inspired by Isadora Duncan. Each generation was building on stones laid down by the previous one, no matter how differently it shaped them. However, neither Duncan nor St. Denis was as logical, coherent, or thorough a theoretician as Humphrey. Isadora relied on inspiration, Miss Ruth on inspiration plus the study of various sources. Doris Humphrey believed in method.

Air for the G String has been reconstructed and revived by the José Limón Dance Company, allowing us to see an early Humphrey dance on the three dimensions of a stage instead of on the flat plane of a movie screen. The work is so thoroughly formal and restrained that it seems more a *plastique* than a dance. Five young women wearing long blue cloaks step slowly around the stage in a pace so measured that the dancers seem to have been hired by a teacher of geometry to illustrate a problem. The patterns of the dance are as carefully weighed out and balanced against one another as the ingredients of a recipe.

As the dancers move, their cloaks intertwine, further defining the patterns of the exercise. The performers are aloof; they betray no strong emotion. The dance is concerned only with classical beauty of form, and the conscious intention to create such a form is rather too obvious. The effect of the dance is that of watching five Renaissance Madonnas, or five pieces of Classical sculpture, which have been endowed by a magician with the power of motion, but with neither passion nor will. Isadora Duncan had concerned herself with the emotional as well as the formal ideals of Greek sculpture and Renaissance painting. In Humphrey's cool evocation of Bach, only the form remains.

As she worked, she analyzed her progress. *Water Study* (1928), gave her independence from the composer. (A dance without music, *The Queen Walks in the Garden,* had been choreographed the previous year by Tamiris, another young rebel against the dependent status of dance, but the idea was still novel.) Humphrey determined that the measured beating of time is the feature that distinguishes musical rhythms from others, and constructed *Water Study* so that the rhythm developed in natural phrases. There was no set of counts to weld together the sixteen dancers; instead, they were to feel a wave that curved their backs and made them move from its force and rhythm, an example of "working from the inside out," and similar to exercises for actors invented by Stanislavski. The waves gained force, bending the dancers, pulling them to their feet, sweeping them over the stage, then diminished to leave them still again.

The Life of the Bee, contemporaneous with *Water Study,* also used no musical score. An off-stage chorus hummed in rhythmic phrases and on occasion broke the drone with an open vocal sound. After making a thorough study of bees, the choreographer set out to find a dramatic story which would lend itself to dance and state a universal truth. She developed her drama from the struggle of the old queen and the young, and from the visual contrast between the groups of workers and the solitary queen. She insisted, though, that the drama was merely a structure from which the form and movement could hang, then went on to contradict herself: "The theory is never of primary importance except as inspiration . . . Form is much, but feeling is much more . . . I shall never, I hope, become identified with a dance or with a set style. I want to change!" Again, there is the conflict between her obsession with form and her desire for personal expression, a set of opposites for which her concept of dance as the movement between balance and imbalance might well serve as a metaphor. Most of the time, form was to dominate.

The Humphrey-Weidman company could not come to a truce with Denishawn. Doris wrote that St. Denis and Shawn "have convinced a number of people that I am most unethical in every way . . . and no loyal Denishawner is allowed to take lessons from me on pain of dismissal." Five years later, when Humphrey and Weidman were appearing in a Broadway show, they received an affectionate note from Miss Ruth congratulating them on their work, and part of the breach was eventually healed. Humphrey, the puritan of dance, was convinced that the vaudeville circuits and the *Follies* had cheapened the art, and she determined to make her dances without catering to a demeaning public. Perhaps her determination to invent works in which costumes, music, setting, and properties, if they were used at all, were to be subordinate to dance was in some degree a reaction to the Denishawn style.

The program notes for *Drama of Motion* (1930) called the piece an attempt to establish dance as an independent art. "This experiment has no program, no music, almost no costumes . . . It has three contrasting qualities expressed both in movement and design." The first quality was slow, sustained, and curving, the second depended mostly on quick movements and surprising accents, the third developed a contrast between a power that surged through the bodies of the dancers and a more delicate feeling that was finally overwhelmed by the powerful movement. By the time the piece had its première, the stock market had crashed, the nation had been shocked out of its joyous irrationality of the 1920s and Denishawn extravaganzas were outmoded. Furthermore, reversion to simplicity, tension, and a stark vision were the logical reactions of the second generation of modern dancers to the first.

Humphrey made fewer dances with no music or with unconventional scores in later years; there was no longer a need to prove the artistic value of dance. However, she continued to believe that the absence of music increases spectators' attention to movement. Duncan had made private studies, and Wigman exercises, which used no music; contemporary choreographers sometimes perform to the accompaniment of sounds, or to no score at all. Jerome Robbins has even made a work in the ballet vocabulary, *Moves,* which is performed in silence. Humphrey, more than anyone, developed the idea.

Humphrey was determined that nothing should stand between the audience and the emotions of the dance. She insisted, despite all her theorizing, that young dancers should find their private ways of moving. Her desire to develop independence and individuality in her students, of course, conflicted with her devotion to ensemble dancing. The ensemble came out on top, partly because few students were brave enough to move in a special way, and partly because Humphrey's works were carefully planned and demanded coordination. "Miss Humphrey," wrote *New York Times* critic John Martin, "has built up an ensemble which is unquestionably the peer of any similar organization which has been seen in America . . . It responds to her direction with equal completeness whether the demand upon muscular control seems almost inordinate, as in certain movements of *The Life of the Bee,* or whether the necessity is for such subtle mental feats as memorizing the space and its rhythmic counterpart for *Water Study.*"

The use of the ensemble, of unconventional scores and emotional power united in 1930, in *The Shakers.* The Shakers, officially The United Society of Believers in Christ's Second Appearing, were members of a religious sect that grew out of the English Society of Friends and established its first American community in 1787. They received their popular name because of the ecstatic movements that sometimes overtook them during worship. They danced during their services, lived in communal societies, and left a heritage of furniture, beautiful in its cool, pure functionalism, to the museums and antique collectors of America. Since they practiced celibacy, they left little else.

The Shakers' austerity, the discipline of their lives, and the clean lines of their design fascinated Humphrey. The suppression engendered by celibacy gave her an element of tension. The dance is performed to the accompaniment of voice, drum, and accordion; the dancers move, for the most part, in straight lines. They advance in little hops, they sway, fall forward, pull back, freeze in stillness, and move through their hard-edged ritual. Now and again, one will be moved to trembling. A man and a woman, approaching one another within the chains of their separate lines, reach out with quivering hands, but may not touch. The Mother of the community, stricken with ecstasy, cries out, "Ye shall be free when ye are shaken free of sin." Shawn had used a narrator in *Julnar,* but Humphrey made words an interior part of the dance, and their unexpected sound still startles an audience. The choreographer experimented further with the use of words in later years, but in many ways *The Shakers* still stands as her monument.

It takes less than ten minutes to perform, in accordance with Humphrey's belief that "All dances are too long." It sets out a carefully balanced stage, in which each group stands in opposition to the others. A semicircle of kneeling women is played against a group of men rising from their knees, and the seated figure of the Mother, upstage center, serves as the fulcrum to balance them. The tension in the movement results not only from the arc between balance and unbalance, but from the conflict between earthly and religious passion. The will to salvation through work, to self-denial, to purity of form, to individual ecstasy within the bounds of an accepted discipline were qualities that Humphrey understood. Her puritanism welcomed the fervor of the Shakers; her artistry gave her knowledge of why the sect was doomed. She stood

---

The Shakers *(1931), a supreme example of balancing form and emotional tension in dance. Humphrey is center, Weidman is farthest right.* PHOTOGRAPH BY BARBARA MORGAN (1938).

always balanced between the desire for order and the wish for passion, and the lurching and trembling of *The Shakers* is a magnificent metaphor for tension which cannot be resolved.

The winter of 1929–1930 gathered together the second generation of American modern dance. Shawn had not yet started his men's company; St. Denis had faded from importance; Denishawn was over for all practical purposes. A new movement was coming together in a spirit of mutual distrust. The Dance Repertory Theater was designed to allow several groups to rent a theater for a week—most of their performances in New York were relegated to Sundays—to hire a manager and to bring in larger audiences than each could attract alone. It was a financial cooperative, not a joint artistic venture. Humphrey distrusted the idea; she thought that overorganization had sapped Denishawn, and that such endeavors were dangerous. She also had little trust for the other participants. In 1927, when she was getting ready to break with Denishawn, she wrote sympathetically about Martha Graham, who was already working on her own. Now, she remarked that Graham "is a snake if there ever was one." Humphrey was a bit paranoid about her contemporaries; modern dance in the 1930s was not a friendly profession. Nevertheless, Humphrey, Weidman, and their company participated in the project.

The Dance Repertory Theater was conceived by Helen Becker, who took the name Tamiris from a poem and her sense of social mission from her family of Russian Jewish immigrants. Her brother Maurice was a painter, her brother Samuel a sculptor and musician. She studied dance at the Neighborhood Playhouse as a child, danced with the Metropolitan Opera, studied with Michel Fokine and in a Duncan studio (though not with Isadora) played in night clubs, and appeared in musical reviews. Between 1927 and 1929 she performed twenty-seven different solos and gave seven different programs, four in New York and three in Europe. Like Humphrey, Tamiris was certain that costumes and music were appurtenances of the dance, not essentials; that a dance should maintain its identity even if performed in the nude and that movement should be clear even without music. She made a scoreless dance a year before Humphrey tried it. In 1928, she offered pieces choreographed to spirituals and her *Prize Fight Studies*. Two years later, she made a solo, *Dance of the City,* to the sound of a siren.

Tamiris found her subjects in speakeasies and skyscrapers. She maintained that, "The dance of today in America has been the melting pot of all superficialities, sentimentalism, and affectations of the theater of foreign countries . . . some of these shouting one hundred percent Americans should emphasize the need for one hundred percent Americanism in American art. My aim is to define the vigor and intensity of contemporary life."

In her first recital, in 1927, she danced to the music of Gershwin in a tribute to that vigor, intensity, and Americanism. She liked to show her legs, to wear a flower in her red hair, and to exult in her beauty when other dancers seemed to be doing their best to hide theirs. Her technique let movement begin in the torso and extend into the head, arms, and legs. She was hardly a contained dancer; she was not a logician like Humphrey, and she did not evolve and codify a vocabulary of movement as Graham did.

Her work was characterized in her early years by a passion for social justice—one section of *How Long Brethren?* (1937) dealt with the Scottsboro rape case—and later, by her love of theatricality. From 1945 to 1955 she devoted herself to Broadway musicals. She started by demanding the independence of dance; she eventually demanded that dance become an integral part of musical theater, augmenting and even replacing songs and scenes. In 1946, reviewing her dances for *Park Avenue,* John Martin wrote in the *Times* that what Tamiris did was to "steep herself in the style, the dramatic and musical content, the theatrical material she is working on, and evolve movement to heighten them where they need heightening," and he praised her for the rare ability "to see a show whole."

That year Tamiris also staged the dances for *Showboat* and *Annie Get Your Gun. Touch and Go* earned her the Antoinette Perry award in 1949, and she continued to distinguish herself until the end of her Broadway career in 1955, when she choreographed *Fanny* and *Plain and Fancy.* Two years later, she returned to modern dance as a performer and choreographer. She and her husband, Daniel Nagrin, formed a company and a workshop, and she continued to choreograph and teach until she died of cancer in New York in 1966, at the age of fifty-nine.

She was always an individual. She was concerned with society when other dancers were looking inward; she was theatrical when they were lean and spare; her techniques were eclectic when others' were strict, and vibrant when theirs were cool. Her vision was didactic, passionate, and personal, and her concern was with the immediate rather than the universal. She based her early pieces on the credo, "The validity of modern dance is rooted in its ability to express modern problems (and some of these are social problems), and to touch the modern audiences into sympathetic awareness of social conditions, even to excite them into wanting to do something about them." Dancers such as Doris Humphrey did not expect their works to excite people into trying to change the world; only to make them aware of it.

Tamiris' theories about show dancing were expounded in an interview in 1951: "In the concert field, the artist creates a work because he has something to say which he thinks will be interesting to others. The audience comes with the premise that they want to listen to that statement. In musical comedy, however, the choreographer comes prepared with his experience in the craft which is used toward enhancing what the author of the book has to say, which has, in turn, been dictated by the demands of the show audience." She told another reporter, "As a concert artist you starve, but on a very high plane."

In her time, psychological modern dance supplanted the sociological, and Tamiris' work had only a small influence on the development of concert dance. Her lack of an institutional, codified technique made it difficult for her work to be transferred to another generation. In the field of musical comedy, however, her influence, along with that of Charles Weidman and of Agnes de Mille (*Oklahoma!* was staged in 1943) was of great importance. The integration of choreography with the play—even the domination of the play by choreography—is commonplace now, and part of the reason is the passion of Helen Tamiris.

In the years of the Dance Repertory Theater, Tamiris tried to draw the new companies together for a common fiduciary benefit. The project was financially sound—as sound as any dance project could be, that is—but there were too many differences of ideology and technique among the participating companies to allow it to survive for more than three years. Its second season, though, brought Weidman his first major work, *The Happy Hypocrite,* based on a story by Max Beerbohm. John Martin found that it encompassed "the most genial ridicule of human foibles,

Tamiris, skirt short, elbows sharp, eyes bright, demonstrates the vigor of urban America and the vibrance of jazz in dance.

PHOTOGRAPHY BY SOICHI SUNAMI.

ranging from finely edged satire to unctuous horseplay, and all set forth by entirely choreographic means."

After their first season with the Dance Repertory Theater, Humphrey and Weidman signed on as the choreographers for Norman Bel Geddes' production of *Lysistrata*. Humphrey was to choreograph several theatrical works during her career but, unlike Weidman and Tamiris, she never enjoyed the task or found it artistically rewarding. When a member of her company asked for a leave of absence to appear in a musical she thought she might enjoy, Humphrey snapped, "You're not supposed to enjoy it." Ironically, *The Shakers* achieved much of its fame when it, along with other works by Humphrey and by Weidman, was included in *Americana*, a musical review, in 1932.

The coming together of the second generation of American modern dance that began with the Dance Repertory Theater was continued in a number of schools and educational programs. In January 1931, The New School for Social Research organized the first series of lecture-demonstrations of modern dance. The New School, which had recently opened, was sensitive to the avant garde. Doris was one of the first to appear in the program, which was successful enough to be held over for a run of eight years. Humphrey found the lecture-demonstrations a valuable method of building an audience and, with her group, offered similar sessions at other schools. Three years later, Bennington College, a new women's school in Vermont, created the nation's first center for modern dance. The summer program consisted of a school and a series of concerts given by the faculty. Martha Hill, director of Bennington's dance department, and Mary Josephine Shelly, of the University of Chicago, organized the program and attempted to constitute the faculty of the finest dancers in the country. Humphrey, Weidman, Martha Graham, Hanya Holm (a disciple of Mary Wigman), Louis Horst, and John Martin, who, as a critic, championed the new ways of dancing, were the teachers. The concert series offered a showcase to the performing members of the staff.

Doris was not pleased with all the results of her first summer at Bennington. She insisted that the young women, "Ninety physical education teachers in the rain all frustrated and yearning for something," were all in love with Weidman and resented her for being his partner. Furthermore, the permanent staff was made up of "Martha's votaries, so anybody else is at a decided disadvantage." Humphrey was right to some extent: Louis Horst had been Graham's co-worker and guardian since she set out on her own; Martha Hill, one of the program's organizers, had been a Graham student. Furthermore, although John Martin, and even Graham herself, acknowledged that in those days Humphrey was the best of the modern choreographers, Graham was the greatest of the dancers and her passionate style and personal magnetism attracted many of the students.

Humphrey was not proof against jealousy, and the dance movement certainly was not armored against internecine warfare. There was no one style, no single theory, no dominant method—and nobody fully trusted anybody else. The Bennington Years (1934–1938 and 1940–1942) gave the modern dancers a chance to work under excellent conditions, to develop themselves, and to inspect one another's work and learn from it, even if they did so reluctantly. Bennington served the same function as Denishawn had done—it was a training ground—but it provided a vastly expanded spectrum of ideas.

Fortunately for Doris Humphrey, she had found one person whom she could trust completely. In 1931, after the official première of *The Shakers* and several months of strenuous work, she had taken a cruise to the West Indies and made the acquaintance of one of the ship's officers, Charles Francis Woodford. Woodford, who was eight years younger than she, became her lover and wanted to become her husband. Humphrey did not want a husband. Like most of the women who founded modern dance, she was afraid of marriage. In Isadora's time, or Miss Ruth's, or Doris Humphrey's, a wife was somebody who washed socks. It was generally expected that a woman would leave her work, assuming she had any, in order to marry, and be happy to do it. Duncan, St. Denis, and Humphrey were not about to give up the art they were building, nor were they prepared to become something less than individuals, as contemporary marriage mores assumed they would. They considered themselves figures outside society and beyond convention, and they liked it that way.

Charles Woodford understood the problem. He told Doris that, in marrying, "We might use convention and not be used by it," and won his case. They married in 1932; their son, Charles Humphrey Woodford, was born in July 1933; in August, Doris began dancing again.

In the same year, Charles Weidman produced his second major work, an evening-long version of *Candide*. John Martin wrote that Weidman "was obviously ideal for the role of Voltaire's hero, and his brilliant style of composition with its understatements, its assumption of blandness and of naïveté, made him equally ideal as Voltaire's choreographer . . . [The choreography] was built, indeed, with the most meticulous attention to formal considerations; each of its acts ended with a fugue based on characteristic themes from the preceding action and contained any number of ingenious inventions and intricately devised phrases."

Weidman had encountered more difficulties than Humphrey in learning how he moved. He was not as formal in his thinking as she, and in many ways his idiom was more closely related to that of Tamiris. He, too, had used the music of Gershwin and had made a work, *Ringside*, based on boxing, which, however used dance movement instead of the realistic pantomime with which he had constructed some of the pieces he devised immediately after leaving Denishawn. After his first major piece, *The Happy Hypocrite*, he made pieces such as *Dance of Work*, in which he abstracted realistic movement, and *Studies in Conflict*, in which he dealt with abstract ideas of human conflicts and interpreted them in realistic terms. In 1932 he made dances for the musical review *Americana*, and continued to occupy himself on Broadway. His dances for *As Thousands Cheer* (1934) were widely praised: A critic for *The Dancing Times* called the production "the outstanding review in New York," noting that it contained "three brilliant dance scenes" and that " 'Heat Wave Hits New York' has Mr. Weidman's characteristic wit."

Weidman's wit was the most frequently noted characteristic of his dances. His *Kinetic Pantomime* alternated passages of music with episodes of movement executed in silence. "Its pantomime is pure nonsense," John Martin wrote, "though it has qualities which identify it with human experience. In content it is light as air . . . but it shows a mastery of possibly the most difficult of all techniques, that of comedy." There was little dance comedy in those days—it was a period in which choreographers were devoted to the grim business of self-searching—but Weidman had shown a precocious talent for caricature and it did not leave him when he left the page for the stage. His interest in satire was an indication that his technique was immediate, rather than universal. There is no "Weidman style" of modern dance, as there is a Humphrey style or a

---

This celebrated photograph of On My Mother's Side *(1940) is quintessential Charles Weidman—insouciant, theatrical, completely original. Despite Weidman's self-assurance, the pose is not an easy one to maintain.*

PHOTOGRAPH BY BARBARA MORGAN (1944).

Graham style. His major technical contribution was to expand the technique of male dancers. However, Gertrude Shurr, who knew and worked with all three choreographers, has said that Weidman was the greatest artist of the three, and the most intuitive. "He had such great love that it came across the footlights . . . [he was] an actor more than a technical mover."

Although his bent was for didactic theater, he did not confine himself to comedy. He shared with Tamiris a sense of social concern that was to manifest itself in works such as *Atavisms: Bargain Counter, Stock Exchange, Lynch Town* (1935). The "Lynch Town" episode, Walter Terry writes, ". . . strikes the very being of the American, for the trembling evil of the lookers-on who share vicariously in the thrill seems to reverberate across the footlights and attack the complacency of those who sit in the safety of the theater. The dancers move with racing frenzy, halting to look at death with lust and, perhaps, with fear. A figure stretches forward to get a better view of murder . . ."

Didactic theater pieces generally have short lives; the specific evils against which they campaign become less common, or at least less noticeable, and occasionally even are conquered; the general evils costume themselves for new roles. Satire and specific comedy also pass quickly. One of Weidman's most celebrated works, *Flickers* (1936), mocked silent movies. It is not very funny to a generation without memories of the genre. Weidman, with his specific targets and personal way of moving, which for motivation relied more on specific situations than on a formal method, made pieces that had even less chance of surviving into the next generation than Humphrey's. His methods and her more abstracted style exemplify some of the divisions of modern dance as it developed beyond the roofs of the Denishawn studios. The Humphrey-Weidman company

---

Humphrey and Weidman in "The Dream of Sganarelle" interlude which they choreographed for the Theatre Guild's production of The School for Husbands *(1933). Humphrey considered working in the theater a fiscal necessity; Weidman did some of his finest work on Broadway. His face and body offer a complete description of character, period, and attitude.*

PHOTOGRAPH COURTESY OF THE DANCE COLLECTION
OF THE NEW YORK PUBLIC LIBRARY.

was unusual in that it staged dances in two distinct, but complementary, styles. The two choreographers worked together, but they also worked separately. They toured together because both were committed to the new dance and because they relied on one another. Economics also contributed to the alliance. They left Denishawn together and maintained a joint studio, even when one or the other went off to work on his own, until Humphrey retired from the stage in 1944. The following year, she turned the studio over to Weidman, who formed his own company. In 1948, he made his most famous work, *Fables for Our Time,* based on some of the whimsies of James Thurber. He made a second Thurber piece, *The War Between Men and Women,* in 1954. In the late 1950s, he and artist Mikhail Santaro shared a studio in which they produced works that blended dance, painting, and sculpture. Weidman made no major pieces during the last years of his life, but he taught master classes in colleges and gave occasional performances with a small company. He died in 1975.

In 1935, the Humphrey-Weidman company set off on tour to bring a new version of modern dance to America. St. Denis and Shawn had opened the way, but Denishawn dancing was neither as deep as Humphrey's pieces nor as biting as Weidman's. Humphrey invented a modern, effective method of setting the stage; she used boxes of various sizes, which could be arranged as imaginatively as children stack orange crates, to mark off the spaces and levels required by each dance. Pauline Lawrence designed costumes, but the choreography continued to be all-important to Humphrey's work.

Touring continued into the next decade; as with Denishawn, the general rule was artistic acclaim and financial cliff-hanging. The Cleveland *News* of February 5, 1938, called their work "the next great successor to ballet," citing its "illimitable wealth of vocabulary and of matter to communicate therein, couched in superb formal design." The critic went on to remark that "If their performance last night at Severance Hall failed to elicit the box office approval of society, it is because their art is running several years ahead of society's invertebrate consciousness."

The lack of box office approval was alleviated to some extent by teaching. In 1935, the New School and Bennington were joined as centers of study by the 92nd Street YM-YWHA in New York. John Martin was head of the committee, and Doris, Charles, and Martha Graham took part in the program. The steady salary was welcome, since modern dancers were generally behind on the rent. Those who are not leading performers often still are.

The same year and the following one brought Humphrey's major creative period to its peak with the invention and mounting of a trilogy: *New Dance, Theater Piece* (Weidman made one section of each) and *With My Red Fires*. The first piece showed the world as Humphrey thought it should be; it was an abstract work, showing harmonious human relationships through form, motion, and rhythm. *Theater Piece* presented the competition of contemporary life in a realistic succession of mundane struggles, grim but touched with comedy. *With My Red Fires* dealt with love in a dramatic work; the plot concerned the betrothal of a young couple and their revolt against the Matriarch of her family. In Humphrey's vision, the foibles and pains of the race could be shown in terms of satire and dramatic ritual, but the ideal could be presented only in abstract terms. The pieces were conceived as a triptych, but received separate premieres before being presented as a unit during one, long evening.

The trilogy was received with enthusiasm by many critics, though not by all, and continued to win praise after its first performances. John Martin asserted that the trilogy, ". . . because of the grandeur of its conception and the masterliness of its realization constitutes the crowning achievement of American dance thus far." He admired the way in which, in *With My Red Fires*, ". . . the opening group dances maintain the abstract note and gradually materialize into specific characterizations and dramatic theme."

The trilogy was notable for its length and scope, and for its full employment of the choreographer's theories. Humphrey had abandoned the Denishawn system of music visualization, finding it redundant to have the movement exactly follow the score, and also noting that the need to fit each gesture and step to a specific phrase or beat limited the scope of the dancing. Instead, she attempted to relate the dance to the music, while allowing each component to maintain its individuality. She had learned to make use of rhythms in all their complex beauties. Selma Jeanne Cohen, in her book, points out that in *New Dance*, "the oppositions of the soloists' phrases of seven, seven and ten against the ensembles' steady four, four . . . resolved at the end of each twenty-four counts (the individual in harmony with the group). In *With My Red Fires*, dancers moved in, contrasted phrase units to underline their frenzy and confusion, building the dramatic tension of the pursuit of the lovers."

The three natural rhythms of Humphrey's method—motor, pulse, and breath—the three divisions of movement patterns and movement qualities, the arc between balance and imbalance, the play of dance phrases against musical phrases, and the play of the soloist against the group, all were evidenced in the trilogy. Even still photographs show the power of the compositions, and give an impression now of severity, now of lightness and happy imbalance.

Red Fires had its première in 1936, the same year Humphrey taught class at the Federal Dance Project of the Works Progress Administration. The WPA was a Federal agency designed to create jobs. It produced a good deal of theater during the Depression, giving employment to actors and helping to develop a style of didactic theater. It was a voice of the New Deal, and a podium for ideas considered even more radical. The Living Newspaper and other techniques of didactic drama were used as methods of educating and agitating the populace, as theater is used today in China. Similar methods were employed in the commercial theater: Clifford Odets' *Waiting for Lefty* had its première off-Broadway on January 5, 1935, and the ending brought the audience to its feet crying "Strike" in empathy with the characters on stage. A reading of the script will leave you wondering what all the fuss was about, just as a look at some of that period's dances will leave you with the feeling that they were remarkably unsophisticated, but *Lefty* had the same impact on its audiences that the early songs of Bob Dylan had on theirs; it said what they wanted to hear better than they could say it themselves.

Tamiris, as might be expected, was instrumental in bringing a Dance Project under the aegis of the WPA's Federal Theater Project, and she devoted all her time to the job. In 1937, the Project offered a forty-one-performance season of Tamiris' *How Long Brethren?* and a revised version of Weidman's *Candide.* Although Humphrey taught at the Dance Project, she was not as deeply involved as Tamiris or Weidman. She did not share their interest in theatrical dance, and although her work dealt in social commentary, it did so in abstract terms. The two most influential systems of thought in America between the two World Wars derived from Freud and Marx. The art of Weidman and of Tamiris was most influenced by the historian of economics; that of Martha

Doris Humphrey in her most celebrated dramatic role, "The Matriarch" in With My Red Fires.
PHOTOGRAPH BY BARBARA MORGAN (1938).

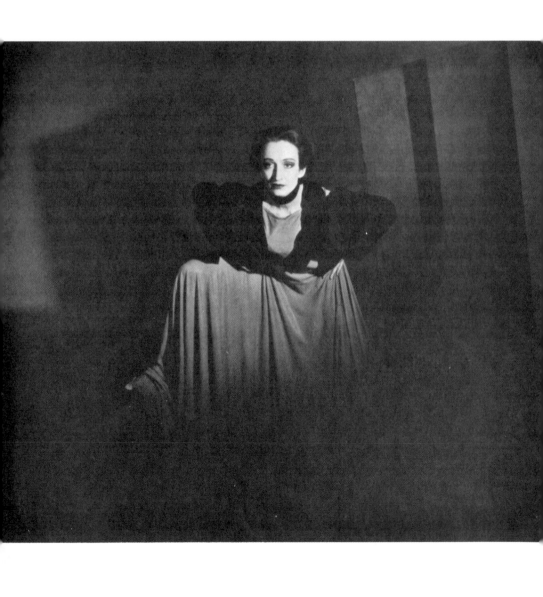

Graham by the psychiatrist. Humphrey cared about individuals, but she was far more interested in society. She was inspired by causes, but she interpreted them in generalized, intellectual ways. She was no fire-eater avid to join the artistic picket line.

After 1936, Humphrey continued to tour, to teach, and to make important works, but her output diminished. In 1940, she fell down a flight of stairs and began to suffer from pains in her left hip. The arthritic condition ended her career as a performer four years later, and in 1945 she turned the studio theater over to Charles. The Humphrey-Weidman era was over.

It is a peculiarity of American dance that companies almost invariably carry the name of their choreographer or leading dancer, and the two are frequently the same. Humphrey-Weidman, a group of dancers with two leaders, each with a distinct style, split the honors between them. In the 1940s, Humphrey, pained even more by her inability to work than by the physical ruin of her hip, declined into despondence. She needed a vehicle for choreography; Pauline Lawrence, the protector of her early years in the studio, provided it. She convinced Doris to make dances for another artist, and Humphrey became not only a choreographer, but the artistic director of a company that carried the name of José Limón.

Limón was born in Mexico in 1908, and came to the United States at the age of seven. Like Weidman, he came to dance from the graphic arts (he had started out to become a painter) and like Shawn, he turned to dance at an advanced age. He was twenty when he saw a dance recital and enrolled in the Humphrey-Weidman school. Male dancers were still rare; good male dancers were almost unheard of. Limón, with his tall, powerful body, proud carriage, and instinct for the art proved to be a find. In 1930, Humphrey put him in the back row of dancers in *Lysistrata* only two years after his first lesson. He danced with the Humphrey-Weidman company between 1930 and 1940, gaining larger and more important roles in works made by both choreographers. As he developed a taste for choreography, however, he began to follow Doris' style, rather than Charles'. The intense, dramatic quality of his finest dances, though, demonstrates the influence Weidman had on him.

He already had two short pieces in the Humphrey-Weidman repertory in 1936, when he won a fellowship in choreography at Bennington. The work he produced that summer was *Danza de la Muerte,* a symbolic piece about the Spanish Civil War. Weidman or Tamiris probably would have dealt with the subject in precise terms, making a specific comment in either raw anger and Dionysian power or in satire. Limón's choice of a symbolic approach was his heritage from Humphrey; his choice of subject was, at least to some degree, his heritage from Weidman. Three years later, when the summer program had been transferred from Bennington to Mills College, Limón created what some consider his first major effort, *Danzas Mexicanas*. He offered portraits of five kinds of Mexicans: the Indian, the Conquistador, the Peon, the Landlord, and the Revolutionary. As Humphrey remarked, he had "bitten off a huge hunk of his native land to exhibit . . . He always scorns the dancers he knows for wanting to be dramatic—but he invariably goes for it himself. Now this is not a natural talent with him. Consequently, Charles and I try to help when he is obviously looking stunning but not saying anything."

Humphrey, who had helped him to develop as a dancer, continued to coach his choreography; he welcomed her criticism and learned. Then, in 1940, Limón left the company because of personal tensions between Weidman and himself. The next year, Doris, her husband, and her son, now eight years old, moved to their own apartment, quitting the extended family of the studio and offending Pauline Lawrence, who had been caring for the entire ménage since its formation. Lawrence went to California, where Limón was living and, on October 13, 1941, she married him. Now Pauline guided José's tours, leaving Humphrey-Weidman to take care of itself. But the artistic links were not so easily broken. In 1942, Limón choreographed Bach's *Chaconne in D minor* while Humphrey, on the opposite coast, worked to the composer's *Four Choral Preludes* and his *Partita in G minor*. The pure, formal structure of Bach had always appealed to her, and she had passed her love of his music on to Limón.

In April 1943, Limón was drafted. Pauline, temper cooled, returned to New York to get Humphrey-Weidman properly organized and on schedule again and, when Doris was forced to stop dancing, convinced her to start making dances for José. She had choreographed Aaron Copland's *El Salon Mexico* on Limón before the army took him, but how could she devise dances when she could not move, could not create the action in her own body or demonstrate it to other dancers? Pauline Lawrence had the answer, as usual. Humphrey was to give José a hint of what she wanted, using words or rhythms, a curve of her arms or any of the other systems of signals that choreographers have evolved. It is not always necessary to demonstrate; one can merely sketch the outline of a step and allow a sensitive dancer, aware of the choreographer's style and needs, to provide the color. (Martha Graham says that she never demonstrated steps for a male dancer in all her years of choreography.) Limón was a sensitive dancer, and he had been trained in Humphrey's style.

Her first major work for him was *Lament for Ignacio Sánchez Mejías*, a dance based on a poem by Federico Garcia Lorca. Pauline Lawrence, of course, designed the costumes. The dance was made on Limón and two women; the text was read as part of the performance. Humphrey sought to use words and dance as she used music and dance; the two methods of communication were to remain separate, but to comment on and support one another. "I see words as a means of conveying facts, and the dance as the means of expressing emotion. . . . I believe the feeling should be the function of the dance and the words should convey whatever we need to know about place, time, stage of being, or any fact which the dance, by its nature, cannot express." The *Lament* is an epitaph for a bullfighter who stands as a personification of all men of courage who fight the forces to which destiny has tied them, and who go to die alone, yet somehow victorious.

The dance stated the theme of the collaboration. Humphrey made a work to suit Limón's heritage, physique, and pride. She analyzed every movement with him, questioning him about his feelings, intensifying his imagination. The other work she did on him at the same time, *The Story of Mankind*, suited him less well. It was based on a series of cartoons, and showed a woman who pushed her mate toward refinement as they moved from cave through castle to penthouse. Stately José did not think much of comedy in dance.

The works had their first performances at Bennington in July 1946. Limón formed a small company: Betty Jones, Lucas Hoving, Ruth Currier, Letitia Ide, who had been with Humphrey-Weidman, and Pauline Koner, who appeared that first season as guest artist. The troupe

José Limón shows the dramatic power of his best-known work, The Moor's Pavane. *Strength and emotion seem to flow from his torso into his sharply pointed feet.*

remained small and cohesive until the mid-1950s, when Limón began to invent dances calling for larger ensembles. Although the *Lament* and *Story of Mankind* were given their premières at Bennington, the war had effectively ended the dance program there. In 1948, the winter classes at the YM-YWHA were carried over into a summer program at Connecticut College, New London, where the Bennington plan was revived and where it continues to operate.

By 1949 John Martin could write of Limón, "There is no other male dancer within even comparing distance of him . . . He is handsomely built and moves with the easy command of a fierce animal; his gesture is simple and broad, his dynamics and phrasing are beautifully controlled, his responses are extremely musical, there is a complete honesty of feeling behind his movement, as well as an emotional intensity that projects itself eloquently."

Humphrey and Limón worked at Connecticut College. In the summer of 1949, José told his mentor that he wanted to make a dance based on *Othello*. She suggested as music Thomas Beecham's arrangement of Henry Purcell's *The Moor's Revenge*. To that score, Limón made his most famous piece, *The Moor's Pavane*, a dance without which, it seems, few ballet companies consider their repertories complete. American Ballet Theater, The City Center Joffrey Ballet and The Royal Danish Ballet have all staged *The Moor*, although it is a work that grew out of a movement sharply antagonistic to their style of dance. *The Moor's Pavane* is an intensely dramatic work, made by a choreographer for whom drama was not a natural talent," and it is a superlative example of its genre.

Limón used only four dancers, stripping all the panoply of war from Shakespeare's play and reducing it to its essence of domestic tragedy. He did not attempt to give his dance the scope of *Othello*, but rather, to comment on the play. The Moor, His Friend, and their wives step toward tragedy at a stately pace, which is relieved by huge swings of the body from the waist, strong lunges and kicks, and small but intense contractions from the shoulder as the passion grows. Certainly, the formal construction, taut lines, and repressed power of the dance are derived from Humphrey. The more placid style of some of Limón's other pieces, such as *There Is a Time*, shows the influence of her concepts of music visualization, and his *Choreographic Offering*, to Bach's score, was deliberately made in her style, as a tribute. His most celebrated works, however, were dramatic pieces which show in their composition the trained eye of Limón, the young painter, as well as the body tensions of Limón, the mature dancer. His failures as a choreographer, the cool, static quality of some work, also seem to be a legacy from Humphrey.

Humphrey made thirteen works for the José Limón Company. In 1951 she was invited to join the faculty of the new dance department at the Juilliard School of Music as teacher of choreography and repertory. The repertory class, in which dancers were prepared for performance, gave her the opportunity to revive some of her famous works. Four years later, she and the department's director, Martha Hill, founded the Juilliard Dance Theater, a company that allowed students and young professional dancers a chance to perform. Among the participants in Humphrey premieres for that company were Jeff Duncan, Deborah Jowitt, Baird Searles, and Joyce Trisler, all of whom have gone on to make contributions to contemporary dance, taking with them some of what they learned from Humphrey.

Doris Humphrey died before she could see her last dance completed and performed, but her writings, her students, and the students of her students have carried her ideas and quiet passions into the flow of dance. Ruth Currier and others managed to keep the José Limón Dance Company in operation after Limón's death in 1972, and the troupe has revived *The Shakers* and other Humphrey works.

Some of her dances seem too trite, too simple, too limited in scope for the contemporary stage; a few retain their power. Even if only one or two survive, she will have fared better than most choreographers. More important, perhaps, are the systems and theories she developed and codified; they remain part of the current of American dance. It is appropriate that her greatest weakness as a choreographer should be her greatest contribution to dance: The arc between two poles is again justified as a conception. She was a formalist, always intellectualizing passion, always making sure that space and time were precisely marked out upon her stage. Her dances seldom make us feel strongly as we watch them. However, that very quality led her to her theorizing and to her writing, and to evolving a system of dance. The more immediate works that Weidman and Tamiris wrought from their feelings will have less influence, in the long run, because neither of those artists fully defined a method of movement. Humphrey did, and her principles of composition continue to influence choreographers, especially those who work in abstract patterns.

Martha Graham was the other dancer of the second generation who devised a system; it stems from the Oriental theater of Ruth St. Denis, and has the floor as a base. Humphrey developed the aspect of Denishawn dancing that led to music visualization, setting it in the arc between imbalance and security. She organized her vision and wrote it down in precise terms, so others may learn from it. American modern dance continues to swing in the arc between introspection and didacticism, between cool and hot, between emotion filtered through the mind, and intellect communicated through emotion. Now, it seems, we are moving through the cooler regions of the arc, and the choreographers who investigate that territory received their maps from Doris Humphrey.

* * *

The following excerpt suggests Mazo's more recent thoughts:

In an age of hype, when superlatives have become a form of assault . . . what is one to say when confronted with greatness? Doris Humphrey's *Day on Earth* is an authentic masterpiece; a dance so beautiful and so touching, so pure in form and so expertly made that it demands to be experienced, not described.

Day on Earth, choreographed to Aaron Copland's *Piano Sonata*, is as spare and pure as a Shaker table. The dance reduces the life of a man . . . to its essential factors: work, love, procreation, and death. He encounters three women—his youthful love . . ., his wife . . ., and his daughter . . .—each of whom leaves him.

At the beginning, the mature woman is seated center stage, a long cloak draping her shoulders; the young girl, crowned with a garland, stands nearby; under the woman's cloak, which spreads over the floor in front of her, we can see, if we look carefully, the sleeping, unborn child. The man, who stands upstage right, advances with long, weighted lunges, as if sowing a field.

During their duet, the girl is all swirling, airborne lightness; the man is weighted and direct. Her feet are playfully pointed; his, seriously flexed. She flees into the wings like a fawn. The woman rises from her seat, moving with a mature weight, and a supple power, and a warm, open honesty that makes her the man's true partner. The child, drawn out from under the cloak to be born, dances with loose legs, fascinated by the game of life.

The child leaves; the parents twist and stretch in grief. Finally, the adults tuck themselves under the cloak while sunset illuminates the returned child, seated where the woman was at the beginning." (*The Record*, April 25, 1991)

VI

ℳ𝒜ℛ𝒯ℋ𝒜 𝒢ℛ𝒜ℋ𝒜ℳ

CASTA DIVA

ONE DEFINITION OF "CHASTE," according to the dictionary, is "restrained from all excess." That is the art of Martha Graham.

When the list of those who devised and organized our century's modes of perception—Darwin, Marx, and Freud, the forerunners, Lenin, Einstein, Picasso, Stravinsky, Joyce, and the rest—is compiled for the benefit of next century's college freshman, the name of Martha Graham will be enrolled. She is the greatest artist of American modern dance and one of the molders of the age.

Graham is not only a great choreographer, she has been a consummate dancer and, within her chosen form, one of our finest actresses. She is a costume designer of genius and an innovator of theatrical lighting. She has influenced music through commissions to such composers as Aaron Copland, Norman Dello Joio, Ned Rorem and Alan Hovhaness. She has furthered scenic design, working with artists of the stature of Alexander Calder and Isamu Noguchi and insisting that the setting be integral to the performance.

To the average bystander, the words "modern dance" bring a picture of a group of young women in black leotards and footless tights sitting square-hipped and spread-legged on the floor, bending sharply from the middle. That is Graham technique, one of the pylons of modern dance. Her influence on theatrical performance is nearly as great and, although she works with movement instead of words, she is a major poetic dramatist, a deviser of high tragedy.

The list of those who have danced in her company is a history in itself: Merce Cunningham, Erick Hawkins, Paul Taylor, Pearl Lang, Jean Erdman, Anna Sokolow, Sophie Maslow, Gertrude Shurr—and they only begin the roll. Graham is to modern dance what Queen Victoria was to the royalty of Europe: Everybody's grandma. Even those who trace their descent to Humphrey, Hanya Holm, or the founders of other houses find somewhere in their pedigree a droplet of Graham blood.

The artistic revolt in dance that was heralded by Merce Cunningham in the late 1940s and reached its height in the diversity of the 1960s was a reaction against theatricality, obviously strenuous technique, mythic content, emotionalism, the psychoanalytic viewpoint, and solemnity. It was, therefore, a rebellion against the art devised by Martha Graham.

She invented and evolved a technique as rigorous and complex as the one that ballet required centuries to develop. She devised it for herself, as a method of expressing her own ideas and emotions, but it has been so assimilated into the American style of theatrical movement that young people cannot understand why it ever seemed unusual or shocking. Actors as well as dancers study Graham technique, and her personal conception has become part of the daily matter of our stage.

She is a choreographer who sets her dances in dramatic form and uses all the resources of the theater to move her audiences. It is because of her work that dramatic dances dominated the art for years, and that dance performances came to be accepted as theatrical productions rather than concerts.

She took dance away from the sociologists and gave it to the psychologists. She chose to make works that were introspective and concerned with human emotion and motivation, and that, too, became the fashion.

At its best, the dance of Martha Graham is pared to essentials; a taut, intense attempt to concentrate the full resources of body, intellect, and emotion on a moment of movement. The theatricality of her works is integral to their purpose; the strict technique of her style is demanded by her intentions. The major intellectual movements of the century—

"There is a pain so utter, it swallows being," wrote Emily Dickinson. In Letter *Graham's technique is a method of making motion evoke emotion; her art is theatrical as well as choreographic. The pose is classic Graham.* PHOTOGRAPH BY BARBARA MORGAN.

especially the exploration of the mind by Freud and Jung—are the ingredients of her art. Her way of dancing embodies the entire mythology of America: The ideal of progress, born of the Enlightenment of the eighteenth century, and the anguish of failure, born of the inability of progress to protect the powerless; the strict discipline of New England and the freedom of the West; the tiered crowding of cities and the flat spaces of the frontier; the command to be always doing and the desire to dally in idleness, and the terrible need to explore geography, technology, experience and, when all else is exhausted, ourselves.

She has danced our desires and our dissatisfactions. She has spun her dances of myth, ecstasy, and fear, and woven them from the depths of our minds and the luxury of our bodies. She has built them from political anger and self-searching satire, mapped them from her explorations of space and time, and created them from that peculiar process called the poetic vision. Her dances lunge for the jugular and kick at the gonads, because their power comes from an attempt to understand what happens in the caves beneath our minds.

Her inventions can be pompous, self-indulgent, abstruse, and bullying; her dances sometimes convolute themselves into arguments with herself that no outsider can untwist; her plot lines are not always clear; her earnestness and insistence on discovering and presenting the meaning of every action can become a bore. These qualities are as much a part of her heritage and era as the great ones; although a genius can transcend his time and self, he cannot escape them. Every artist makes bad art from time to time; many make good art fairly often; a few, like Graham, make masterpieces more frequently than the laws of probability would predict —and that is one definition of genius.

The racking dialectics of Puritanism and passion, desire and duty, rashness and restraint, that have formed the American character molded Graham also, and the major instrument of her art has been the succession of contraction and release. The dancer pulls his body in on itself, then opens by thrusting his chest forward and elevating his head. The spine and the pelvis are the axes of Graham technique; arms and legs do not function separately from the spine but move in concert with the rest of the body.

Graham, like Duncan and Humphrey, studied the functioning of her body; the changes in the organism produced by breathing led her to develop the sequence of contraction and release. She studied the relationship of the moving body to space, and began to use the dance floor not as a launching pad for balletic leaps but as a foundation for more earthy movement, understanding that a tree draws energy through its roots as well as through its leaves. Falls, which acknowledge the power of gravity rather than defying it, were incorporated into her method. "We teach the falls to the left," she has explained, "because, unless you are left-handed, the right side of the body is the motor side; the left hand is the unknown. You fall into the left hand—into the unknown." Over the years Graham technique has become as specialized as that of ballet, and as artificial, for only through the artificial can art comment on reality, but it was never intended to be an end in itself. Each movement has an emotional meaning as well as a physical one. As early as 1934, the choreographer said, "If you have no form, after a certain length of time you become inarticulate. Your training only gives you freedom." Her aim has always been to translate emotional experience into physical form.

Graham's dances have evolved with the perceptions of their maker and are constructed of personal materials. She was born in 1894 in a highly moral suburb of Pittsburgh. Her parents were Pennsylvania born, but had long roots tapping New England: Graham is a tenth-generation American, a direct descendant of Miles Standish.

Her father was a physician who specialized in the treatment of mental illness, born in the same year as Sigmund Freud. He was thirty-eight at the time of Martha's birth, and he must have engendered great respect as well as affection in his eldest daughter. There was warmth and a bit of awe in her voice even in 1973, when she told a press conference that her father had presided at her first dancing lesson. "It wasn't really a dancing lesson. He said, 'Martha, you must never lie to me, because movement never lies and when I see your body, I'll know you are lying.' This doesn't mean we always have to tell the absolute truth" —she made a wry moue—"but we have to be dedicated; you must be absolute in what you are doing."

Martha was eight when the family moved to Santa Barbara, California, leaving the Presbyterian preoccupation with sin and the middle-class preoccupation with social structure that were the major industries of Allegheny, Pennsylvania. The warmer meteorological and metaphysical climate of California caressed the girl; her childhood was divided between two Americas—cool and puritan, and warm and pagan. Dr. Graham maintained his practice in Pennsylvania, seeing his family only during vacations. Martha was seventeen when, during one of his visits, he took her to see a performance by Ruth St. Denis. Graham may already have been drawn to the theater, a profession unsuitable for Presbyterian ladies from Pennsylvania, but the Oriental gestures of St. Denis won her completely. From then on, she was among the chosen, although she attended an academic school as her parents wished and did not begin to study at Denishawn until after her father's death. It was 1916, the summer of the pageant at the Greek Theater, and St. Denis and Shawn, who needed all the dancers they could find, gave Martha a small role and her professional debut. She was twenty-two.

Shawn was her teacher (he made *Xochitl* for her) but Graham's life-long respect and admiration have been given to St. Denis, who was her first inspiration and whose Oriental techniques, religious expression, and theatrical presentations have been translated, greatly altered, into the Graham style.

She served seven years with Denishawn, touring and teaching. In 1920, when St. Denis and Shawn underwent one of their professional separations, she worked as a teacher in Shawn's studio. The company reunited, as usual, and Graham knew she would never replace Miss Ruth as the leading female dancer. Furthermore, she was growing restless. John Murray Anderson, producer of the *Greenwich Village Follies,* saw Denishawn perform in New York and offered Graham a contract. She did two numbers in that season's version of the show, which opened in September 1923. Sexy Spanish and Oriental specialties—the influence of Denishawn was prevalent—were not Graham's idea of dancing, and after a second season with the *Follies* she gave up show business to teach in New York City and at the Eastman School of Music in Rochester, New York, while looking for dancers to form into a company. Three of her students made the grade and, on April 18, 1926, they appeared with Graham at New York's Forty-eighth Street Theater in her first concert as an independent choreographer.

Her first dancers were pretty creatures, dressed seductively in kimonos and chiffon shifts; they resembled their parents in the Denishawn reper-tory. Graham offered eighteen dances at that first concert, including

---

The kind of dancing Martha Graham left Denishawn to escape. With Ted Shawn in Malagueña *(1921). Graham and Humphrey, in separate ways, led American dance away from the derivative forms and emotional naïveté of the Denishawn style.*

PHOTOGRAPH COURTESY OF THE DANCE COLLECTION OF THE NEW YORK PUBLIC LIBRARY.

Debussy's *Maid With the Flaxen Hair* (in which the choreographer wore a blonde wig), *The Three Gopi Maidens* (Cyril Scott), and *Deux Valses Sentimentales* (Ravel). As the titles demonstrate, it was not a revolutionary beginning. However, she presented twenty-eight dances that first year and sixty-eight by the end of 1930, and her style pulled further from Denishawn prettiness with every concert. Those who were absent from a single program missed a stage in her development.

A motivator of the changes, and of subsequent developments in Graham's conceptions and technique, was Louis Horst. Horst was something of a wandering minstrel, playing in cafés and theaters, when he was engaged for a two-week stand as conductor-pianist during Denishawn's tour in 1915. He did not leave for ten years. He was the pianist when Graham took her first class at Denishawn, and he stayed with her, too. They became acquaintances, lovers, and friends. Horst went to Vienna to study composition in 1925, found the school too conservative for his taste and, after seven months, came home to continue the work that excited him most, making music for dancers. He encouraged Graham to set out on her own, became her music director and was for twenty years her adviser, her guide and her goad. He was ten years older than she, married to a woman who stayed in California when he moved to New York, analytical, affable, and erudite. He was a large, imposing man— a late photograph shows a face that might have belonged to a rabbinical scholar, with challenging eyes and a thoughtful mouth—who seems to have had an affection for dachshunds.

It was Horst who educated Graham in music, who encouraged her to dance to the works of contemporary composers and to commission scores. He taught her that music should be written to suit the design of the choreographer, and that it should be sublimated to the dance. In this, and in his use of reeds and percussion, he may have been influenced by the work of Mary Wigman, whom he saw in Europe. Horst brought Graham books to read; he influenced her taste in art; he became the companion of her travels. It is at least partly his doing that she became a reader of almost incredible scope, a connoisseur of art and a wide-ranging and sensitive voyager. For twenty years, Horst was Graham's composer, pianist, music director, organizer of concerts, and sounding board for ideas. He was there to rage at when things went wrong and to rejoice with when they went well. He called himself the wall against which she, the young artist, could grow. He was the one who, early on, knew she was a genius.

If Horst had done nothing more than assist Graham, he would have been important enough, but he worked with other dancers too. The dominance of Graham's style resulted from her brilliance, but it was advanced by the missionary work of Horst and John Martin. Horst was a musician, not a choreographer, yet he was perhaps the most influential teacher of choreography of the century, partly because he, like Doris Humphrey, believed that choreography could be taught. In 1928, at the Neighborhood Playhouse, he offered the first of his famous courses in Pre-Classic Dance Forms—the court dances that were stylized into ballet. He used these pavanes, sarabands, and gavottes to teach the formal structure and composition of dance and its relationship to music, and he stimulated the imagination of a generation of choreographers.

Alwin Nikolais still remembers a class in which Horst had each student devise a courante (a running dance) after instructing them "not to move unless it is absolutely necessary." Nikolais solved the problem: He "kept one foot on the ground and ran all over the place," but his solution was no more ingenious than the problem set by a gifted teacher. Horst also published *Dance Observer*, which first appeared in 1934, a magazine dedicated to the superiority of modern dance to all other forms, and to Graham's superiority to all other modern dancers. It died with its founder in January 1964.

In 1927 and 1928, Graham's style, influenced by Horst and her own perceptions, was changing; her dances became harsher, more angular, less balletic. Although she still made works like *Adagio* (Handel) and *Fragilité* (Scriabin), she also produced *Revolt* and *Immigrant: Steerage, Strike* during a brief period of social commentary. By 1928, like an adolescent revolting against the forced primpings of childhood, she had entered her "long woolens" period, creating stark, threatening movements to be performed in shapeless garments she ran up herself from materials purchased in the bargain houses of Fourteenth Street. "Life today is nervous, sharp and zigzag," she declared in 1929. "It often stops in midair. That is what I aim for in my dances."

That year, when the stock market stopped in midair and fell with a thud, Graham exchanged her trio for a larger group, still exclusively female, and presented a manifesto called *Heretic*. Graham cast herself in the role she was to maintain, as a dancer and as a theoretician of dance, for the next ten years: She became the rebel, the heretic, the outcast, the solitary evangelist, the iconoclast and, less consciously, the rebellious adolescent whose anger is watered a bit by self-pity. She became the self-appointed opponent of balletic beauty and Denishawn daintiness and derivation. Her first task when working with students, she said, "is to teach them to admire strength—the virile gestures that are evocative of the only true beauty. To try to show them that ugliness may actually be beautiful if it cries out with the voice of power."

In *Heretic*, she portrayed the outcast who tries to penetrate a disapproving society, personified by a phalanx of women. In the first two sections of the dance she succeeded momentarily, only to be repulsed. The third attempt failed and the heretic, bested and banished by the mob of her inferiors, folded to the floor. The dance was composed in harsh, sharp, angular actions. Graham avoided transitions between movements in order to intensify the impact of each cluster of shapes, forcing the audience to accept a dance in which it saw only the moments of highest pitch, and to link them in its own imagination. The choreographer put accent marks over her intentions by choosing for her music a revolutionary folk song, and by dressing herself in white and her opponents in black. She performed, as she was to do for years, in a strict makeup, blanching her face and aggressively coloring her mouth, eyes, and brows, imprisoning her exotic features in a mask that seemed to express contempt for the set, simpering smiles of ballet girls. It was not until ten years later that Graham made theatrical history by smiling on stage.

The following year, 1930, Graham was selected by the ballet choreographer Léonide Massine to perform the role of The Chosen in Stravinsky's *Le Sacre du Printemps*. To Graham, ballet was the enemy. It was artificial, aristocratic, and un-American. Her own work was assertively the opposite. She was convinced that "To be great, art must become indigenous, it must belong to the country in which it flourishes, not be a pale copy of some art form perfected by another culture and another people. The psyche of the land is to be found in its movement." Graham had spent four years developing a technique that rested in the floor, and in attempting to make a form of dance that would reflect the tensions and rhythms of America, yet she agreed to dance in the airborne style demanded by Massine. The performance enhanced her reputation, and it added a new direction—up—to her dancing.

That summer, she and Horst visited New Mexico, and Graham experienced a new expanse of space and discovered the cult of the Penitents, which resulted from an interweaving of the religion of the local Indians with Spanish Catholicism. The culture of the Indians and its symbiotic relationship with the land impressed her. In some Southwestern cultures, religion, daily life, nurture, and the passing of the seasons are inseparable; there is no division between ritual and reality. Graham could not be moved or intrigued without incorporating the experience into her work, and her "primitive period" began.

Shawn, Tamiris, and Weidman also made dances on indigenous themes during the 1930s, taking inspiration from Indian ritual, black music and history, and the demand for social justice. Graham, however, was not content to cite a specific instance of injustice, or to document a culture and extrapolate its movement; she needed to investigate the poetic machinery that propelled it. She was continuing her attempt to define the matter of America in movement, trying to invent dances that would be recognized as native either by their subjects or "through a tempo, rhythm, and attitude toward space which is peculiar to America and . . . unlike any country on earth."

Primitive Mysteries received its première on February 2, 1931, along with five other works by Graham, during the second season of the Dance Repertory Theater. The reviewer for the New York *Telegram* found that the choreographer's efforts resulted in "angular, cold, stylized movement . . . Mellowness is no part of her. The freshness that is newness consumes her." *Primitive Mysteries* evoked the hot expanses of the desert and the red and blue intensity of New Mexico, but besides exploring an aspect of the American land and character, it concerned itself with the experience of the numen—the essential, indefinable spirit—in any religion, anywhere. Twelve young women (there were still no men in the company) wearing long, blue, square-necked dresses stepped in a ceremonial procession, advancing one foot and drawing the other even with it before moving forward again. Graham, in the white, puff-sleeved dress of an initiate stood alone, fenced in on three sides by lines of dancers, and moved alone while the others moved in concert. They circled her, first to the right, then to the left.

The second section began in silence, like the first. The women again circled the virgin, but now they took long strides, leaning forward like bears. Then the music began and as its tempo increased the women were driven by it, as by some overwhelming force that was taking possession of them. Graham stood still, her hands pressed against her face, but at the end of the ceremony she had been accepted into the community of worshippers.

The final portion of the dance confirmed the initiate in sanctity. The outcast of *Heretic* had been accepted, and her superior virtue earned her honor, rather than exile. The "primitive" society of people secure in their relationships with their warm land and their spirits was freer than the puritan urban culture depicted in the earlier dance, and had no need of spite. The community of *Primitive Mysteries* was cemented by shared religious experience; the society of *Heretic* was embittered by an imposed ethic. The tension between these two American ethics has been a major subject of Graham's work throughout her life.

The choreography of a spiritual experience was inspired by the culture of the Southwest, but it also owed a debt to Ruth St. Denis. At Denishawn, Graham had learned methods of Oriental theater, including the organic use of properties, and she had been impressed with the importance of a dramatic presentation of dance. More important, she learned that dance can be about more than movement or stories; it can concern itself with the place of humans in the universe. That is the question posed by all religion, and although Miss Ruth sought the answer in mysticism and Graham in the psyche, both felt a need to dance the search.

Graham followed *Primitive Mysteries* with dances that evoked the "primitive" Greece that preceded the glory of the city-states. These works, like her dances of "primitive" America, investigated ceremony and the force of religion. Graham's search for the spirit is Bacchic; it does not involve the suppression of sexuality that provides the tension in Humphrey's *The Shakers*. Her early rituals provoked a free flow of emotion through the body as Isadora's did, but her carefully evolved technique gave her a control of her work, and of her audiences, that Duncan's lack of defined form had denied her.

John Martin noted that *Primitive Mysteries* had altered Graham's technique. "She has built her physical system upon the basis of percussive movement—a stroke of muscular effort and its consequent vibrations of recovery. In her earlier and more defensive compositions it was a stroke that assumed the chief importance, while the overtones were allowed to take care of themselves. Now, without having violated in the least the

Primitive Mysteries *(1931), a legacy of Graham's trip with Louis Horst to the American Southwest. Contractions prevent the formality of the composition from becoming rigid. Graham is in white.* PHOTOGRAPH BY BARBARA MORGAN (1938).

canons of the method, she has found the secret of striking without clangor . . .''

Martin's perceptions were of the utmost importance to the development of modern dance, and to the success of individual modern dancers. His notices in *The New York Times* lauded the style when balletomanes rejected it as arrogant, ugly, static, and dull. His books explained the new dance; his courses in history and criticism proselytized for it. His teachings at The New School and at Bennington were to shape the theory that dominated the art until the 1950s; he was one of those who intended dance to be an independent art, not secondary to music or to anything else. He defended and encouraged, in public, the performers and choreographers who made modern dance. He was a demanding critic, his standards were high, and he used his serious, unadorned style of writing as a weapon with which to fight for the art he championed. His teaching and his theories, like those of Louis Horst, helped form the ideas and movement styles of a long generation. His pieces in the *Times* were instrumental in building an audience for the works of that generation.

In 1931, the year of *Primitive Mysteries,* Mary Wigman made her American debut. Horst had brought back from Europe pictures of the choreographer in her despairing dances and somber costumes and had shared them with Graham. She learned more about the Expressionist style, and reinforced her belief in the importance of the floor, at recitals given in New York by Ronny Johansson, the German dancer who had been imported as a teacher by Ted Shawn. When Wigman herself appeared in New York, Graham, Humphrey, and Weidman went to examine the competition.

John Martin wrote that in Wigman's dance, "space assumed definite entity, almost as a tangible presence in every manifestation of movement." Graham was no disciple of the German dancer, but they shared a belief that movement must result from an emotional impulse. Graham's use of space as part of the emotional content of dance is not far removed from Wigman's use of her space as a symbol of the forces of the universe which exert themselves upon individuals. Wigman had developed a technique of contraction and release, as Graham was to do, but their methods had different purposes: Wigman tried to create a universal style of moving; Graham invented a technique to express her own emotions, then extended it to members of her company.

Hanya Holm, who remained in the United States after Wigman left, taught the style here and became a choreographer of importance in her own right. She altered the style she had studied, making it less somber, and in 1937 at Bennington she produced *Trend,* which won *The New York Times* award for the best dance composition of the year. However, she achieved her greatest fame as a choreographer of such un-Expressionistic productions as *Kiss Me Kate* and *My Fair Lady.* Her dances seek to convey ideas through form and her sense of form, both of the body and of stage space, have been passed on to generations of students. She is considered one of the greatest dance teachers in America.

Graham certainly learned from Wigman, as she had learned from St. Denis, Shawn, Léonide Massine, and from the Indians of the Southwest. Part of her genius, however, has been her ability to transform any movement that interests her into a gesture or step that is peculiarly her own; the influences on her style are less important than her personal conceptions, which have subdued all influences and unified them into a technique which could have been developed by nobody else, since it is a production of her mind as well as of her body.

A major influence was the thinking of Sigmund Freud. Freudian theory helped condition the ideas of the generation between the two world wars, and was used by artists to interpret their reality. During the 1920s, when Graham was maturing as an artist, Freud's teachings were being seriously discussed among the intelligentsia and absorbed by less scholarly sophisticates by a form of intellectual osmosis. Graham gained a solid understanding of the psychoanalytic conception of human motivation and, as her work developed, began to use the articulations of the body to explore the motions of the mind.

However, during the 1930s she was more concerned with continuing her essays in Americana. She, like Humphrey, was determined to create dances integral to her nation and her time. The United States is not an indigenous nation—even the Indians were immigrants—or an old or heterogeneous one. We have had to create culture heroes and a national mythology as we went along, making a pantheon of the framers of the Constitution, for example, or framing an Armageddon from the Civil War. Graham has drawn from that mythology, especially from the parts of it that are her personal heritage, material for her dances.

In 1934, she produced *American Provincials.* The first part, "Act of Piety," was a solo; the second, "Act of Judgement," a group dance. The work was a vitriolic attack on her old enemy, the Puritan tradition. The Puritan created by Graham was a dangerous opponent, who could never really be conquered. She was, in effect, a figure of mythological stature, as John Martin understood when he compared the character to Medea and defined her as a "regal New England Gorgon." In the next decade, when Graham did confront the archetypes of Classical mythology, including Medea, she was changing her viewpoint, not her emotional subject matter.

American Provincials showed how closely allied are the self-wounding piety of Puritanism and the Dionysian ritual of pagan religious observance. Both are frenzied, both are sexual, both require the surrender of individual thought to shared emotion. Religion in Graham dance can be a purifying, saving force, as in *Primitive Mysteries,* if it remains earthy. The religion of New England is seen as a force that twists the instincts into a cord that strangles freedom and emotion.

A more optimistic conception of the American legend received its première a few months later, in April 1935. *Frontier* has a score by Louis Horst and a setting, the first Graham had used, by Isamu Noguchi. The obvious theme is the conquest of the American frontier; the deeper subject is the mastery of all expanses. Graham, as always, worked in metaphor, concentrating on essence rather than immediacy. Noguchi's setting is a section of fence—two dark end posts supporting a pair of horizontal runners, one knee-high, the other level with the waist. Two heavy ropes, anchored to the ground behind the fence, form a V as they extend forward and up, hinting at a vast plain leading to a distant horizon. The costume Graham designed for herself stylized the homespun of the American pioneer woman into a heavy, long dress worn over a full-sleeved blouse. It is a tender, hopeful shade of pink. Colors, like everything else in a Graham dance, have a purpose.

Frontier was reconstructed in 1964, and in 1975 was presented in New York for the first time in thirty-one years. The dance is as superb in its economy as Noguchi's setting; it takes about six minutes to perform, and it does not include one extraneous step or gesture. The dance begins with the performer sitting on the fence, looking over the plain. With

---

Frontier *(1935). Choreography, costume, and performance, Martha Graham; setting, Isamu Noguchi; music, Louis Horst. Graham reaches up and out, measuring herself against space.*

PHOTOGRAPH BY BARBARA MORGAN.

small steps, she marks off an area as her domain, and then explores it. She reaches out with her forward leg and extends her arm directly over it, while her head leans forward and the other arm bends out from the shoulder and down from the elbow; a bound of joyous freedom. An arm beats through the air with the youthful jubilation of a drum majorette; both arms cradle and rock an infant as the dancer steps softly through her space. She investigates all directions, including up and down, then sits again on her fence, mistress of her territory.

Graham continued to concentrate on the heritage and mythology of America, although she interrupted herself to make two dances about the Spanish Civil War. They were not involved as specifically with events as a treatment of the subject by a choreographer such as Tamiris might have been. Graham chose to deal with individuals—with a woman's strength in adversity or her acceptance of a challenge. She has always used her subject matter of the moment as a way of examining her eternal subjects: All contests, even those between ideologies, are fought on the field of the human mind; all victories and defeats are those of individuals, but the individuals are often of such stature that they become archetypes and personal conflicts stand for universal agons.

Her dance was maturing; the changes in her technique and style became less frequent than they had been at the beginning of her career. In 1938, the form which she had been developing for twelve years crystallized in *American Document,* and she began her great period of theatrical dance. She became dedicated to bringing together decor, lighting, music (commissioned especially for her works), and dance to create organic dramas which, by their use of a complete theatrical apparatus, allowed the spectator no escape from her vision. Choreography for a group had made up a larger part of her output since 1929, but the personal solo had continued to be a major form of expression. She made three solos (out of four works) in 1937; she has made only five solos since then.

American Document used the spoken word more extensively than any of her previous dances. More important, it involved a male dancer. Previously, Graham had worked with a regiment of women; the sexual conflicts that are major events in her later work were absent. After 1938, men took increasingly important roles in her pieces, allowing her to develop new tensions and expand her investigations of human conduct and conflict.

The first male member of Graham's company was a refugee from ballet. Erick Hawkins had danced with Ballet Caravan when that company made its first appearance at Bennington in 1938; he admired Graham's work and she praised his. Two years later, he arrived at Graham's studio to take class. Four weeks after that, he had a major role in *American Document,* which Graham and her group had been preparing. Hawkins was to become Graham's leading dancer (second to her), assistant, lover and, for two years, husband, before the relationship tore and he set out on his own as a choreographer. During his tenure with Graham, he also concerned himself with organizational matters and publicity. A few months after he joined the company, Graham recruited a second man, Merce Cunningham, who eventually was to change American ideas about dance as drastically as Graham had.

American Document was a condensed history of the United States, treating of the Revolution, Puritanism, the exploitation of the original inhabitants of the land, and the end of slavery. Graham was continuing her personal version of the American tradition of translating history into mythology. As always, she saw history in terms of her own experience, and the dance-drama depicted the conflict between the individual and society. During one section the speaking character, The Interlocutor, read alternate lines from the Song of Songs and the scalding sermons of the most celebrated of New England's hellfire preachers, Jonathan Edwards. As the denunciations and glorifications of sexual pleasure succeeded one another, Graham held her upper body primly rigid and rocked her pelvis sensually.

From then on, theatricality dominated her work and sexuality was a major theme. She softened her technique, giving her body a less aggressive line and her phrasing a less staccato attack. She began to bring more curves into her work, and made the transitions between movements less abrupt. She continued to base her work on the pulse of contraction and release, to dance sitting, or lying, on the floor, and to make steps and gestures that flashed through the air, but she no longer needed to be defensive about movement that was beautiful. She had passed the rebellion of her artistic adolescence and could afford to unbend. She put off her long woolens, donned sensuous costumes, integrated settings and music into her work, and in *Every Soul Is a Circus* (1939), she smiled.

Graham had discovered the best vehicle for her genius and, during the next few years, she learned to drive it with increasing panache. The Freudian satire of *Every Soul Is a Circus,* the sense of loss and triumph of *Letter to the World* (1940), the nightmare passions of *Deaths and Entrances* (1943), are presented theatrically. Her theater is less realistic than that of conventional drama, but more concerned with the dramatic event. Its job is to make the internal, external, to delineate and liberate the poetic logic of the subconscious.

Graham seldom dealt specifically with World War II—she was no longer interested in social comment—but it is interesting to remark that at this time, she intensified her search for the causes of conflict, and began her investigations of time, forcing her characters to look into the past or shuttling them between past and present. There are moments in our lives that can never be escaped, patterns that recur forever. Freud taught that a re-experiencing—memory plus affect-memory—could break the pattern. Graham made the pattern into a play, forcing recollection of a decisive moment, as Hamlet did to trap the king. In *Every Soul Is a Circus,* the leading character, in the role of the Ideal Spectator, must watch her own flighty behavior as it is enacted by another dancer, The Empress of the Arena.

Letter to the World, which was inspired by the life and poetry of Emily Dickinson, has a cast list divided into Characters in the Real World and Characters in the World of Imagination. The poet recalls her joy in the man she loved, and sees herself threatened by The Ancestress, perhaps Graham's most hideous representation of the Puritan spirit. Love loses, defeated by duty and tradition. Graham again divided her protagonist between two dancers, one who speaks (the rememberer) and one who only moves (the memory). The lines were extracted from Dickinson's works, and the eminent theater critic, Stark Young, told his readers that, ". . . the reading of the poetry was imaginatively conceived, as if it were music calling out the movement's soul."

Graham did not adhere to the metrical line of the verse, and she deliberately altered its meaning. She chose lines and short poems that would contribute to the development of Dickinson's legend, and used

---

An episode of wit and fantasy in a dance of repression and loss. Merce Cunningham is "March," Graham the "One Who Dances" in Letter to the World *(1940). The dance blends reality and fantasy, past and present in one of Graham's early evocations of the poetry of the subconscious.*

PHOTOGRAPH BY BARBARA MORGAN.

them sometimes as accompaniments to the movement, sometimes as commentary, and sometimes almost as chapter headings. The lines from which the dance takes its title say wistfully, "This is my letter to the world/ that never wrote to me/." Graham took only the first phrase, and used it to finish the dance with a proclamation of triumph in despair. *Letter* is a portrait of unbearable grief and loss, but it lacks the dreadful solemnity of Graham's early works. There are moments of lightness, and even of humor, despite Emily's frenzied beating of fists and prostration in pain. The critics were aware of the change. Margaret Lloyd of *The Christian Science Monitor* noted the difference between an earlier dance, a "plastic monument of grief . . . aloof, detached . . ." and the dramatic cohesiveness of *Letter* in which, "It is Emily's inner life that holds the stage in an ordered, compact phantasmagoria that through the specific touches the universal."

In 1944, four years after Emily's defeat by her New England conscience, Graham brought her American saga to fulfillment with *Appalachian Spring*, the greatest national hymn of American dance. The work, with its promise of a taxing but rich life for the frontier Bride and her husband, found a synthesis for Graham's dialectic of Puritan America and joyful America. The wandering Revivalist is severe, but he is not a threat to the couple's happiness. The serenity of the old Pioneering Woman speaks of a life that has produced satisfaction. The themes of her early American dances are blended and softened. The rigors of frontier work will allow the young couple to enjoy their love without guilt; their freedom is not of the bacchanalian variety, but a freedom of serenity, that will continue in joy.

It is sometimes remarked that modern dance reached a peak in the 1930s, and declined during the next decade. The action was less a decline than a consolidation. By the early years of the 1940s modern dance was accepted by critics and public. There was no longer a need for it to demand attention; it was offered attention. There was no longer a necessity for it to proclaim its alienation from ballet; it was acknowledged that ballet was one form of theatrical dance, and that American modern was another.

For one thing, American ballet was coming to life. The appearance of Diaghilev's Russian company in 1916 began the revival, which was helped by the spectacular performances of Nijinsky. The tours of Anna Pavlova, who made her last appearance here in 1925, helped create a national audience for ballet as Denishawn built one for modern dance. A quiet time followed Pavlova's final tour, but the Ballets Russes de Monte Carlo arrived in 1933 and, that same year, Lincoln Kirstein invited George Balanchine to take up residence in America and found a school and company. The company, The American Ballet, gave its first performance in December 1934, and in the fall of the following year became the official company of The Metropolitan Opera. It changed names and affiliations several times, but never changed direction or leaders: Balanchine and Kirstein still guide the great company called The New York City Ballet.

In January 1940, Richard Pleasant and Lucia Chase presented the first season of their new company, Ballet Theater, which had grown to greatness long before it added the prefix, "American" to its name in 1957. By the middle of the 1940s, by the time of *Appalachian Spring*, American ballet was no longer an affair of overweight women performing ritual steps to slow music. It was an art that had regained its life and self-respect, proud of its European heritage but finding new ways of presenting it, an art served by great dancers, musicians and choreographers.

Modern dance, too, had established its roots and its pedigree. During the 1920s and 1930s, the radical dance, like radical politics, spent a good deal of time and energy in faction fights. It needed to discredit ballet, and it sometimes seemed as if each company needed to discredit the others. During the great period of the 1930s, though, certain styles became dominant. By the end of the decade, Weidman had decreased his productivity; Shawn had disbanded his men's company; Tamiris was concentrating largely on teaching and concerts until, in 1945, she found her way to Broadway. Hanya Holm had produced major works in the declining years of the 1930s, then established her Center of the Dance in the West in Colorado Springs and lost some of her importance until she, too, reached Broadway. Some choreographers, such as Agnes de Mille, were already trying to establish a rapprochement between the themes of modern dance and the style of ballet. Two major styles took upon themselves the leadership of the modern movement—that of Doris Humphrey, and that of Martha Graham.

In the year that Graham made *American Document*, Humphrey choreographed Bach's *Passacaglia and Fugue in C Minor*, which Horst's *Dance Observer* taxed with being overly abstract and formal. However, four years later the same publication praised the "sweet formality" of her dance to Bach's *Partita in G Major*. As modern dance established itself, the factions had less need to scramble for dominion, and the days of exciting anarchy and rebellion ended—for a while.

Appalachian Spring. Matt Turney (seated) is "The Pioneering Woman," Robert Cohan dances "The Husbandman," and Ethel Winter plays Graham's role of "The Bride" in this revival of the choreographer's great American hymn. Noguchi's setting is integral to the dance, as decor must always be in Graham's theater.
PHOTOGRAPH © MARTHA SWOPE.

Still, two separate streams were feeding the river. Humphrey stood at the center of her universe; she could create states of unbalance in order to restore them to equilibrium. She was able to stand apart from her emotions, and to define them with geometric precision and beauty. She consciously created conflict, knowing that it could be resolved.

Graham evolved her technique from a need to control intense emotional power; she required a more stringent physical method than Humphrey because her passion was more overwhelming. She has been driven by emotions that pull apart, rather than seeking equilibrium. The conflict in her works is generated by tensions that must be made manifest if the protagonist is to find peace. Humphrey's theory of the arc assumes that there is a point of balance; Graham's dramas start with the issue in doubt. Humphrey learned early to arrange her passions in patterns consisting of other people; Graham needed to dance hers personally. In Humphrey's art, a cool head prevailed; in Graham's, hot emotions are dominant. Humphrey's intellectualism, and some of her lyricism, have been reflected in the work of contemporary choreographers, and her sense of form and order is her great legacy. Graham's emotionalism and magnetism led many to study her methods, and the lesson that a technique can be devised to communicate intense feeling is a major part of her contribution. She danced Dionysus to Humphrey's Apollo, and the mood of the country will decide which god receives more abundant sacrifices during any particular era.

However, Graham developed from a great dancer into a great deviser of dances. She became a mistress of stage space, and of the ordering of time. Her insight into the material of myth and the tensions of the mind gave her material with which to work, and her sense of theater gave her a medium in which to present her ideas with intense impact. That theatricality is one of her greatest contributions to modern dance; her emotionalism is another. No great art is purely emotional or purely intellectual, but art in which intellectual information is conveyed through the emotions has tended to be greater than its counterpart. Ben Jonson was a Classicist, a clear thinker, a superb logician of theater. His plays are far more precisely constructed than those of his friend Shakespeare. Still, Shakespeare was the greater dramatist, because nearly every line of his plays is charged with emotional meaning, and because his characters are endowed with all the complexities of humanity. He could be careless and sloppy and make terrible blunders of which Jonson would never have been guilty, but Jonson, great as he was, lacked his friend's quality of daring passion, and therefore takes second place. Doris Humphrey was the Jonson of American modern dance; Graham, at her best and at her worst, is our Shakespeare.

After *Appalachian Spring,* Graham turned from her democratic inclinations; the dances she was making required figures of a more lonely constitution. She was engaged in tragedy, and left the secular religion of Americanism for that of psychoanalysis. In 1945 she consulted a Jungian psychotherapist, and those sessions must have influenced the course of her work. The next year she produced *Cave of the Heart,* the treatment of the Medea legend that John Martin had seen foreshadowed in *American Provincials* twelve years before. She was still dealing with myth, but she had turned to Classical sources, including the Bible, for her material. Her retellings of legends during the late 1940s and 1950s interpreted mythology through psychological theory. It was as if she had taken to heart Jung's dictum that one should trisect one's life and spend the last segment meditating on one's self and the world. Graham was in her early fifties.

The greatest achievement of her Classical cycle is the evening-long *Clytemnestra* of 1958. The dance begins in the underworld, where Clytemnestra reviews the events of her life. Those she loved, those she killed, the chain of revenge of which she was the strongest link appear to her again and again. In the end, she takes on herself the burdens of guilt and lust and, by accepting them, is freed. Graham's sense of theater and knowledge of Oriental theater contributed to one of her greatest episodes: She uses a red-purple drapery, first as a regal cloak for Clytemnestra, then as the carpet Agamemnon follows to his death, and finally as the curtain which opens to reveal the stabbing of the king and of his mistress, Cassandra. Graham knew that the walk on a carpet of purple, the royal color, told the Greeks that Agamemnon was guilty of *hubris* (equating himself with the gods) for which sin he died. She also knew that in the Greek theater acts of violence were not acted out, although their results, the wrecked bodies, might be revealed on a platform. In her dance, the audience does witness the stabbings, but the use of the curtain reminds spectators of the classical practice, and the visual image she creates produces a shock that echoes the effect Aeschylus' trilogy must have had on its first audience. The production is choreographed so that history looks over the shoulder of the present, a technique which accords with the theme of the dance and which makes it, despite the difficult complexities of plotting, one of the great theater pieces of our time.

By the time she reached *Clytemnestra,* Graham had broken with Horst and with Hawkins. She was sixty-four; her body had finally begun to falter. She had found help in psychotherapy, she began to seek it in alcohol. Still, she worked. *Acrobats of God,* a celebration of dancers made in 1960, seems in retrospect a salute to a long era she was forced to end. She began to make works in which she did not appear, or to cast herself as an observer of the action, rather than as a figure central to it. Few of the dances she made after *Acrobats* are major pieces. The change in her position on the stage, and the sense of weakness it had to engender, brought a new perspective to her choreography. The heroic quest had been intrinsic to her work from the beginning, but the quarry now was love and a hope of peace. Images of death were frequent.

Graham danced for the last time in the spring of 1969, and made no new works for four years. In 1973, after a series of tensions that changed the composition of her company, she announced a Broadway season and made her 154th dance, *Mendicants of Evening,* in which she used an electronic score and a painted, rather than a sculptural setting, both for the first time. The work, even in its revised form of 1974, *Chronique,* is not fully satisfactory, but it gives evidence that Graham still has new things to reveal to us. In it she seems to be reaching, uncertainly as yet, but with understanding, into mysticism and affirming the value of a lifetime of journeying through the mind toward a culminating period of poetic rest.

In 1975, she made several works including two, *Lucifer* and *The Scarlet Letter,* for Rudolph Nureyev. She had long planned to make Hawthorne's novel the base for a work and her notebooks contain the outline of a film on the theme. The dance employs her celebrated method of having a character look back over the events of his life, but is unusual in that it has a male figure, rather than a woman, at the center of the action, a choice Graham never would have made while she herself was still capable of dancing. A story making the rounds of the

Clytemnestra (1958) is the most complex of Graham's investigations of time and of the psychological meaning of myth. The queen must not only observe, but reexperience the crises of her life in order to win peace. Graham is at far left; Helen McGehee and Bertram Ross are center.

PHOTOGRAPH © MARTHA SWOPE.

dance world has it that at the first rehearsal of *Lucifer,* Graham told Nureyev, "If you want to work with me, you will do exactly as I say or I will destroy you." The man who has been hailed as the greatest male ballet dancer of the time looked down at her and said, "Yes, ma'am."

Nureyev brought new attention and a new audience to Graham's company, and the alliance has certainly been of financial benefit to the company. Graham not only began to work with a ballet dancer, but to speak of her works as "ballets," a term she certainly would not have used fifty years ago. "If you will look in the dictionary," she says (This is one of her favorite ways of beginning a statement) "you will learn that 'ballet' means 'dance.' " She goes on to discuss her respect for Classical dance, admitting that fifty years ago "I was more of an iconoclast" and had to be less accommodating.

When Graham answers a question, she holds the eyes of the questioner with her own, and her gaze has all the power of her person behind it. The same power is apparent when she addresses an audience. When she returned to choreography after her four-year pause, she began a practice of speaking to the audience during gala performances. She sits on stage in a high-backed chair, but her magnetism is as great as it was when she danced. The long face, with its high forehead, strong jaw, high cheekbones, and huge, deep-set eyes still rivets the attention of everyone in the theater. If she so much as flicks a hand, it is a gesture of command. You look at no one else as long as she is visible. It comes as something of a shock to realize that she is only five-feet two-inches tall, and small-boned at that.

Part of her power is an intense feminine sexuality, which is no less apparent merely because she has passed her eightieth birthday. Graham is a feminist, but she is also feminine, and there is no contradiction in terms. The exotic seductiveness that pervaded her dancing and still hangs about her like perfume is as much a part of her as her searching, independent mind. She has used all aspects of herself in her work, and their cumulative power is the reason for her strength. She speaks quietly, spacing her words carefully, now and then tossing off a line with the timing of a consummate comedian. Graham obviously knows the effect she has on people, and is not afraid to use it: She is not only a major artist, she is what show business calls "a professional"—even if she is only taking a curtain call, she gives you a show for your money.

Comparing Graham and Shakespeare implies more than mutual genius; they both are products of their times. Poetic drama was the dominant art form of Elizabethan-Jacobean England, and in return, the era was one of the greatest in the history of drama. Shakespeare was no anomaly, but the epitome of his time. Dance may eventually be judged the greatest art form of twentieth-century America because of its originality, its scope and the vitality and variety of its presentation. Film is certainly a more popular medium and has a strong claim to the honor. Both arts are expressed through moving images, both depend on complex rhythms and phrasing, both trick us into discarding our customary conventions for considering space and time—they take their material from the complexities of the age. However, film can no longer be considered unreservedly American. It is imported and exported everywhere, but modern dance remains as American as jazz, and we are the only major supplier to the world market.

American ballet alone has given us George Balanchine, Jerome Robbins and Antony Tudor. (Balanchine is Georgian by birth and Russian by training, but his ballets are native New Yorkers.) Musical comedy has benefited from the work of many of the choreographers already mentioned; the work of Tamiris and Agnes de Mille in making dance an integral part of the production has been furthered by such choreographers as Robbins and Gower Champion, who have consolidated the functions of choreographer and director. Productions such as Robbins' *West Side Story* and *Gypsy* proved how much dance has contributed to theater.

Modern dance is the province of an impressive array of major figures and an even larger group of secondary talents. One of the signs of a great age in any art is an abundance of talent in the second rank, those not enlisted in the elite corps of genius, but sufficiently brilliant to produce work of high value. Without such a group, the interchange of emotional and technical information that marks a time of creativity cannot occur. The charming composers of the Gallant era are overshadowed by Haydn and Mozart, but those two masters did not compose in a musical vacuum. Graham, like Shakespeare, stands as a deity in a pantheon. Both encapsulate in their works the tenets and perceptions of a prodigal era.

Throughout the Shakespearean canon, there is a concern with order, with the Great Chain of Being which the age believed began with the Godhead and linked all living things in an irrevocable hierarchy. There are other themes, too—the growing strength of England, the virtue of the heroic spirit, the power of time, and of love. Graham's work also is a canon. Themes of rebellion, repression, purification, the need for choice, and the search for fulfillment are always present. Her world, however, lacks the sequential logic of Shakespeare's. It is the chaotic world of desire brought to light by Freud; the rebellion against oppression written out by Marx; the need for choice dramatized by the Existentialists. Order, to Graham, is not in the nature of things; it must be wrested from the universe.

The central motif of Graham's work is the heroic quest. The theme is most obvious in the works of her mythological period, but the search is carried on even in earlier pieces. The outcast of *Heretic* seeks accommodation with society; the pioneer of *Frontier* searches out her own territory. Later, the object of the hunt is a reconciliation of the conflict between duty and desire. The choreographer-dramatist places her heroines at the critical moment of their lives, when they must make a choice and accept its consequences; when they must reconcile the actions of the past with the condition of the present in order to withstand the future. Her characters are positioned like Dante at the beginning of his great dream, midway in the journey of life and alone in a dark wood. In Graham's mythic dances, as in *The Inferno*, "memory gives shape to fear," but only when a fear is given a shape and made manifest can it be defeated. Clytemnestra finds rebirth by confronting her actions; Joan of Arc attains sainthood when she understands that her choices were correct. The quest is carried out not in space, but in time. A Graham heroine does not merely revisit the site of a decisive action; she makes a pilgrimage through time and experiences again the action itself. Time is the dominant dimension of Graham's dances, as space was in the works of Doris Humphrey.

The perception of time as a subjective phenomenon is the most striking aspect of her dramatic method, and the theme is reflected by her technique. Graham's theatrical dances are cinematic, not only in their rapid succession of episodes, but in their use of flashback, flash-forward, and merging events. Such sequences are not the inventions of the cinema; rather, film-makers have discovered the technical means to reproduce the universal imagery of dreams. Graham is among the most acute and sensitive students of the great unravellers of sleep, Freud and Jung. In her studies of the processes that move us, she has recreated on stage the vision of dreams and their daylight counterparts, fantasy and insight.

Even the colors of her costumes—the proud red-and-purple of Clytemnestra's cloak, the joyous green worn by March in *Letter*—are echoes of the dreamstuff. (The more vivid the color on the mind's screen, the deeper the meaning of the dream.) Events and people fade into one another onstage as they do in dreams, and symbols are prevalent. Graham uses her dream vision to consider humans as processes, rather than static beings to which things happen. Characters see themselves as they have acted, or might have acted, as we do in our nightly theater. The aged Abbess of *A Time of Snow* (1958) observes the actions that have brought her to the convent. Joan of Arc, in *Seraphic Dialogue* (1955), watches herself as she performs the separate roles of Maid, Warrior, and Martyr. She not only must choose, but must watch herself doing so, to justify her life to herself.

The dark world of *Deaths and Entrances,* which developed out of Graham's interest in the Brontës, seems to be entirely and terribly a dream. The leading character is attacked by memories of her sisters and her lovers that seem to whirl in and out of her consciousness, giving her little chance to focus on them clearly, and in the end it seems that her mind returns to clarity only by an immense effort of will. One purpose of dreams is to deal with fears too violent for daylight encounters. The dream will disguise the fear, but if on waking we can penetrate the mask the demon will be exorcised—the lurking danger that seemed so like a tiger will turn out to be a pussycat after all. Clive Barnes, writing in *Dance and Dancers,* quotes Graham as saying, "I really don't believe exactly in forgiveness. I believe in acceptance and trying to face the truth as much as possible, sorting it all out and then making a reconciliation with yourself." Her tragic heroines are not merely living a nightmare, but recounting it as one does in psychoanalysis, expounding on its meaning and learning to tame the tiger. The heroines, though, have no priest or analyst to help them; they must go alone into themselves.

Graham's dramatic method also uses the dream cinema in another way, shaping a story from a series of short, intense images. Barnes, reviewing a revival of *Appalachian Spring,* noted that "Graham shows us scenes of pioneer life, almost cinematic in their sharp speed, all adding up to a total picture of people, a place, and a time. The method has been one of evocation, and the resulting image is all the more powerful because we ourselves have been drawn to put so much of our own imagination into its eventual delineation." The method is much the same as the one she used early in her career, when she avoided transitional steps and forced the audience to fill in the outlines she had sketched.

The central figure of Graham's canon, then, is the voyager of the heroic quest, and the journey is dramatized by the methods used by the subconscious to fashion myths and dreams. However, Graham has added an important factor; her seeker is female. One reason for this is that for most of her career, Graham fashioned the leading roles in her dances on herself. Even so, a lesser artist might have seen herself and her characters as reflections of femininity as presented by the male poets and dramatists who have dominated literature. Graham does not. One of her great accomplishments is to look at patriarchal mythology from the feminine viewpoint. She calls her dance-drama *Clytemnestra,* not Orestes or Agamemnon.

In *A Time of Snow,* the character in whose memory the action passes is The Abbess, whose wrinkled body holds the glittering spirit of Heloise. The pity and terror of the legend (it is no less a legend for having happened) usually is seen only in the fate of Peter Abelard who, in point of fact, displayed far less courage than his mistress. We have been accustomed to thinking of Heloise as an accessory to the tale of Abelard. Graham makes it clear that a love story demands two participants, and that Heloise was not an incident in a history, but had a history of her own.

Cave of the Heart (1946) tells Medea's story as Medea, not Euripides, might have told it, and *Errand Into the Maze* makes the quest of the Minotauricide a woman's journey. Graham has made the point—one of those obvious insights it takes a genius to discover—that the term "hero" requires no specific gender. The possessor of excellence, the one armed in courage, may be male or female. Graham has said, "Modern dance isn't anything except one thing in my mind; the freedom of women in America—whether it is Isadora Duncan or Ruth St. Denis or Clara Barton. It comes in as a moment of emancipation . . . Modern dance is the moment when an emergence took place from behind the bustle . . . All the things I do are in every woman. Every woman is a Medea. Every woman is a Jocasta. There comes a time when a woman is a mother to her husband. Clytemnestra is every woman when she kills."

Takako Asakawa as "The Girl in Red" performs one of the balances that are a recurrent theme in Diversion of Angels *(1948). This performance was given during Graham's 50th anniversary season on Broadway in 1975–76. The costumes, which combined the attributes of culottes and skirts, are among Graham's finest.* PHOTOGRAPH © MARTHA SWOPE.

Fuller, Duncan, and St. Denis danced in an awareness of their sex. Duncan went further than any dancer before Graham in presenting women as people of power, passion, and dignity, but Duncan did not create dramatic dances; instead, she made of herself a work of art and conveyed her convictions through her person. Humphrey developed female figures of stature, but she seldom gave them the depth Graham offers her characters, nor did she deal with material of equal weight.

Bertram Ross, who was for years one of Graham's leading dancers, said that her Greek works symbolize first, the isolation of the creative artist from society and second, the aging choreographer's terror at the loss of her own physical and emotional powers. Citing *Legend of Judith* (1962) as an example, he went on to say that in Graham's work, coitus is an act of murder by the female. The female praying mantis chomps the male like a candy cane, from the head down, as he fertilizes her, and some of Graham's heroines have similar habits. Her words suggest that the murders are committed by mothers on their children, but her dances imply a murder done by daughter upon father. The cause of the hero journey in the mythology of every culture is the need of the hero to find his father, and by doing so to establish his own identity. Graham's heroes are women, but the quest could well be the same.

Her father was a major force in her life; she did not begin dancing until after his death; she still remarks on what she learned from him. Her first alliance was with Horst, a married man older than she who instructed and scolded her genius into maturity. The male dancers of her company, from Hawkins on, have often been tall men whom she, a tiny woman, could regard from the perspective of a child. Horst, too, was an imposing figure. In *Every Soul Is a Circus,* she sets herself between a whip-swishing Ringmaster and a flirtatious Acrobat, and she chooses the authoritarian who will protect her from her own instability. She has the reputation of being something of an authoritarian herself. Paul Taylor said, after leaving her company, "It was marvelous working with her, but I was damned if I was going to be dominated." Merce Cunningham used a Freudian metaphor: "Graham's great—but unless you move quickly she does tend to castrate people." The protagonists of Graham's dances may set out to find the beloved father, then mutilate or murder him to escape domination. However, the image is too limited: Electras abound in the walking world; *Clytemnestra*s are rare.

Graham has not always cast herself as the avenger, she has occasionally been the mythic victim. The Ancestress of *Letter,* who represents the entire force of the repressive superego, is a woman's role. (The Ancestress,

unlike Agamemnon, triumphs.) The woman who kills in Graham tragedy is a woman who has been supplanted or restricted. Going a step
beyond the desired death of the father, one can see in the dances the
killing of the enslaving male by the chained female. Yet even that is not
enough. In *Heretic,* long before there was a male to love or kill, Graham
built a wall of women to reject her and curtail her journey. She needed
no male dancer to make her first embodiments of New England conscience, or to pit herself against it. The one who rejects her, who limits
her, who thunders "Thou Shalt Not" is the enemy, regardless of sex,
and she is wise enough to know that the enemy is not only an external
force, but part of herself as well. She has used the Freudian ambivalence
toward the father as a metaphor for an even more catholic process—as
indeed it is.

Dreams, poetry, and myths are different forms of the same process, as
psychoanalytic theory, art, and religion are all methods of trying to learn
about ourselves and the world, and to reconcile the two. Graham has not
relied only on the Greeks for her sources, but has conned the Bible,
Shakespeare, and history, knowing that the lives of Emily Dickinson
and St. Joan have as much mytho-poetic content as the tales of Hecuba
and Jocasta. Her notebooks display the immense range of reading and
knowledge available to her. On one page, she can quote T. S. Eliot,
Democritus, and a work on Japanese drama, none of which have any
immediate relevance to her subject, but all of which are involved in her
vision of it. Graham's major works are no more subject to a single interpretation than is *Hamlet;* the veins are too rich for one mining. Individual moments have precise meanings; the full works demand more
of us.

"Dance," said Graham, "is another way of putting things. It isn't a
literal or literary thing, but everything that a dancer does, even in the
most lyrical thing, has a very definite and prescribed meaning. If it could
be said in words, it would be; but outside of words, outside of painting,
outside of sculpture, *inside* the body is an interior landscape which is
revealed in movement. Each person reads into it what he brings to it."

In Shakespeare's plays, poetic images are linked with specific states
of being throughout the writer's work. One cannot explain why specific
images recur, except to say that Shakespeare's mind functioned through
metaphor, and that he associated specific objects and happenings with
emotional states. Graham, too, has worked in images—kinesthetic ones.
A swirling of the leg, which is bent forward at the hip and down and
in at the knee, calls forth a swirling of the mind. A deep contraction at

the waist, simultaneous with an inward, upward pulling of the leg and a wrenching inward of the arm signals an anguish so intense it is physically painful. Large, sweeping kicks to the side are used in moments of overpowering emotion of either ecstasy or despair, as if the wells of feeling were overflowing and carrying the limbs into large, forceful movements. Rapid, springing jumps that scissor the legs, like those of the Archangel Michael in *Seraphic Dialogue* are associated with religious ecstasy. Slow, measured falls and recoveries can be combined with sharp jumps to expand the sense of vertical space, and the emotional drive that deprives humans of a resting place. Some of the steps and arm movements of *Frontier* are incorporated into the dancing of the Bride in *Appalachian Spring*, linking the two episodes of Graham's American cycle despite the years that passed between their making, and demonstrating the way in which particular images evoke specific responses in the mind and body of an artist.

In her early dances, Graham made little use of her hands, believing that they should come into play only when the emotion demanded it, and when the gesture would be telling. This reserve has helped her create hand movements that are among the most memorable things in her dances. The little clappings, a cross between prayer and applause, that are the theme gesture of the four young followers of The Revivalist are a major example. A peculiar fluttering of hands recurs in several dances—The Abbess uses it, as does Clytemnestra—and this gesture has the connotation of trying to sweep the past from the eyes and, at the same time, of attempting to bat away the mists that cloud vision. There is a sense of weeping and of helplessness, too. The Queen's arm stretching up with the short curved sword in Clytemnestra's irrevocable decision to murder is perhaps the most arresting gesture ever performed on an American stage. It is a statement as poetic as "night's candles are burned out"; as complete, as definitive and as impossible to restate without loss.

Graham has always concentrated on movement as a vehicle for meaning, rather than on movement as an end in itself and she has done the same with costumes, settings, and music. *Appalachian Spring*, named from a line in Hart Crane's poem, "The Bridge," is a famous example of her use of setting to define mood. ". . . if you have seen spring come, the first shimmer on one of those willow trees in the light, or when you have seen the ground break for the first moment—it is that moment that I hoped would come out of the words 'Appalachian Spring.' That's why the scenery for this dance is the framework of a house. It's not a house, it's just the outline, the uprights of a house. It's a structure on which the house is built and behind the structure is the emotion that builds the house, which is love."

A similar relationship between the decor, the emotional texture, and the physical action of a dance is evident in most of Graham's work. The set for *Seraphic Dialogue,* designed by Noguchi, as were those for *Appalachian Spring, Clytemnestra* and other major productions, is a fine example. The central object calls to mind a stained glass window or the frame of a medieval triptych. Heavy, shining wires are the material for the frame, and for the other elements of the design. A sort of sculptured bleachers provides seats for the three avatars of Joan. Sections of the large pieces, when detached, become objects needed in the dance—a sword and a cross. All are constructed of the same bright brass strands.

Noguchi made a magnificent machine for theater, a setting which serves all the needs of the performance and is as much a part of the event as the choreography. The brass shines like a halo. The audience sees through the sculptured shapes as Joan sees into herself. The elements of the setting, like those of *Appalachian Spring,* are outlines to be filled by motion. However, the setting of the American dance is less high and demanding; the Bride's future is yet to come and what is destined is domestic peace. Joan's past is history, her future glory, her dance the justification of her choices. Her peace must be reflected in lasting metal, not in transient wood.

Nothing is permitted to be on Graham's stage if it does not con-

---

(Page 192)
Fabric stretches across 45 years. In Lamentation *(1930) Graham encased herself in a tubular costume that amplified and abstracted the motions of grief.*
PHOTOGRAPH BY BARBARA MORGAN (1935).

(Page 193)
Rudolph Nureyev in Lucifer *(1975) reaches out from a cocoon of fabric. The costumes for the dance were designed by Halston, but Graham's influence is clear.* PHOTOGRAPH © MARTHA SWOPE.

tribute to the matter at hand; no bauble is up there merely because it is pretty. Her costumes are supremely functional, as garments to dance in and as appurtenances to the action. In *Lamentation* (1930), she enclosed herself in a sheath of stretch jersey that revealed only her feet, hands, and face. The upper part of the costume formed a triangle with the apex at her head and the base running across her forearms to each elbow. She performed almost the entire dance seated on a low platform, and as her body keened from side to side, the fabric pulled and stretched, making the dancer into a moving sculpture of grief.

". . . her entire approach to costume," wrote Agnes de Mille, "was to strip everything down to the essentials so that the body movement could be seen. And certain symbolic embellishments that she used most tastefully and meaningfully, the way Orientals do. She began to build up an entire decor for the theater which was hers, and I think she's been enormously influential." Her dresses are made to dance in; a skirt is designed to swirl around a leg or stretch as the leg develops out; arms often are uncovered, allowing the power of emotion and muscles to ripple visibly from shoulders to hands. Men are dressed to show the power of their bodies and to free them for energetic movement. Nothing is wasted.

She commissions the music for her dances, giving the composer a script which includes not only the action, but the mood and timing of each section. He is free to alter details as his work goes on, but he is always making music for a specific dance. Graham listens to sections of the score as it is being written, but does not begin choreographing until it is finished. As usual, she is the dominant figure in the collaboration, which may be why her theater has produced so much great dance and so little great music. Aaron Copland's score for *Appalachian Spring* won a Pulitzer Prize and was made into a popular concert suite, but most of the compositions are inseparable from the dances they accompany and limited in their inspiration.

"Music for the dance," Horst had said, "cannot be judged apart from the dance for which it is written, because it is an integral part of it . . . The question is not how great a dance composer is, but what he does for the dance. The composer-accompanist must expect to sacrifice some of his identity as a musician when he writes or plays for the dance . . ." Graham's first works were accompanied by a piano played by Horst. In scoring his music for *Primitive Mysteries,* he added a flute and an oboe, and for many year's Graham's music was performed by a small ensemble of woodwinds, brass, and percussion, because Horst had

thought strings too lyrical for modern dance; they reminded him too much of ballet. He considered that brass supplied brilliance and reeds gave primitive coloring. Horst's theories became Graham's theories, and she has admitted that Horst was responsible for much of her artistic upbringing.

Graham has said that her work stems "not from the interpretation of music, but from the drama of an idea." She, has, however, made a few dances that are not overtly dramatic, such as *Diversion of Angels* (1948) and *Canticle for Innocent Comedians* (1952). *Diversion of Angels* is very nearly "pure dance," like many of Balanchine's ballets. It is so beautiful in its movements and patterns that one needs nothing more. However, as in Balanchine's works, there is more. Graham uses symbolic gestures—a man standing behind a woman, his hand resting on her breast—to heighten the atmosphere of love and youthful pleasure. The difficulties of some of the steps comment on the proud strength of youth, the lyricism of others connote warmth and tenderness; they are bodily parallels to the soft, open faces one sees, on rare occasions, worn unselfconsciously by couples in love.

There is an emotional climate that envelops the audience in every one of Graham's dances. Her lighter pieces depend less than her dramatic works on specific events, and more on a general emotional tone, but there is always a substance holding the dance together. The jottings of her notebooks show how many emotional threads she weaves together, how many patches she pieces into every work. Then, if the dance is successful, it is more than the pattern of pieces; it is a physical record of a peculiar emotional process, the poetic vision, and is complete in itself.

In the end, despite the learning and feeling she brings to every dance, despite the complexity of interpretation and the wide use of theatrical methods and strong technique, it is all so very simple. We inhale and exhale, expand and contract. We choose an action and accept its consequences. We search, and we find. After all the complications and inner compulsions, we come to know ourselves, and the knowledge is not always pleasant. Graham's solemnity and earnestness result from an attempt to explain human conduct in the terms of her generation—the psychoanalytic method—and that does not offer much humor, or much hope. Her greatest dances are ringed with the aura of Freudian pessimism, but when all action and emotion have been stripped to their essentials and understood, complexities disappear and there is a hope of peace.

"You have to take life as it surges through you," she said in 1973. "Young dancers are afraid to reveal too much of the potential that is in them; there's a potential for evil as well as for good. Evil cannot be denied, any more than good can." Graham has the courage to feel the surge, to accept the vastness of human potential and to exist, not as an object, but as an active force.

The great tragedies of the English stage nearly always contain a single line—a simple sentence—in which the hero, confronted by forces beyond his power, affirms his responsibility, his position, and his humanity. By this action he accepts his place in the universe, and triumphs even in death—"I am Antony yet"; "I am Duchess of Malfi still"; "Aye, every inch a king." It is in that moment of affirmation that Graham's heroines live. Choreographing *Mendicants of Evening* at the age of seventy-nine, she could still hurl from her stage the challenge written by St. John Perse—"Great Age, behold us."

* * *

Joseph Mazo continued his examination of Martha Graham's genius until his own death in 1995.

. . . After her last appearance as a dancer—at New York's City Center in 1969—Graham began to revive pieces she had made in the Thirties and early Forties. Many of these came as revelations to audiences who knew the choreographer largely from the monumental works, many of them based on Greek mythology, that she created in the mid-Forties. . . .
(*The Record*, April 7, 1991)

Deep Song (1937): *A reconstruction/excavation:*

The reconstruction of Deep Song was . . . difficult; neither tape nor film is available. [Terese] Capucilli was given 200 stills photographer Barbara Morgan made of Graham dancing the solo. She began by studying the photos and by researching the Spanish Civil War. She listened to Henry Cowell's music. . . .

The dancer spread the photographs on the floor of the Graham school's huge Manhattan rehearsal room and studied them some more. "I began putting them in some form of order," she explains, "because you could start seeing the phrases after you looked carefully enough. Then I would show Martha what I had done, and we went on. She created the bridges between the steps and the phrasing, and she talked about her own experiences in doing the piece and gave me images to work from. Martha remembers some movements, but not all of the sequences, so she has had to rebuild them while working with me."

Obviously, the *Deep Song* [of 1988] . . . will not be identical with the one that was produced in 1937. "Even if Martha remembered it perfectly," says Capucilli, "it couldn't be the same. I'm not Martha and this isn't 1937.

"Nor is the audience the same. For us, the war in Spain is history; for them it was immediate—a cause of pain, of suffering, and of intensely partisan feelings and disputes. . . .

"Reconstructing something old is always very difficult," says Graham . . . "You think you remember it, then come away and see that it wasn't like that at all. And as you work, it becomes something new."
(The Record, September 29, 1988)

Errand Into the Maze (1947): *The artist's vision fully realized:*

Errand . . . is an ideal example of the choreographer's mature work. The concise dance makes an ancient myth into a contemporary metaphor and then goes further, making physical action a metaphor for emotional upheaval.

Graham gave a psychological reading to a Greek legend: Theseus' journey into the Labyrinth of Crete to kill the Minotaur. The maze becomes the unconscious; the devouring monster represents the undefined fear that lurks in the basement of everyone's mind, and the hero is transformed into a heroine who dares to face her fear and destroy it.

. . . The delicate quivering of the dancer's abdominal muscles translate into physical action that feeling we call *butterflies in the stomach.* The high, tiny steps with which the heroine follows the path are at once determined and tentative, and when the woman lashes the rope across the entranceway, locking herself inside, her arms are frantic with fear.
(The Record, October 7, 1994)

Appalachian Spring (1944): *Hymn to America:*

Since the United States already has a national anthem, a national bird, a national pastime, National Guard, National League, and national debt, it seems only logical that we also should have a national dance. I nominate *Appalachian Spring.* . . .

Appalachian Spring is a danced hymn to the ideal America. Its hints of zealous violence (in the revivalist) are offset by its suggestions of honest self-sufficiency (the pioneering woman) and mutual trust and love (the husbandman and the bride). It is a very great dance.
(The Record, April 5, 1985)

Martha Graham: On choreographing, feeling, and genius

Visiting Martha Graham is like calling on Helen of Troy, or taking tea with the Lady of the Lake. Approaching her 91st birthday, Graham has taken on nearly mythical stature as possibly the world's greatest living artist, the woman who completely altered the world's conception of dance. It is almost impossible not to expect her to work at least a little miracle during the course of conversation. . . .

Graham does not think of herself as a goddess, or even as a genius. "I don't really like the word," she explains. "I'm not sure what a genius is. Edvard Varese, the composer, once told me, 'Everyone is born with genius, Martha; the sad thing is that most people only keep it for a few minutes.' I never think of myself as a holier-than-thou thing. When I'm making a piece, I deal with the meat-and-potatoes of dance. . . .

At the moment, Graham is more concerned with the meat-and-potatoes than with miracles. She is choreographing a new dance, [*Song*], the most recent of nearly 170 she has created since making *Chorale*, her first independent work, in 1926.

Song probably will be reworked after its opening as so many of Graham's dances—including last year's *Rite of Spring*—have been. "I keep thinking about a dance even after it reaches the stage. . . . I'm never satisfied—nobody is. . . ."

A dance, Graham says, is "one instant of life—a vibratory piece of energy. A great piece of sculpture is never self-contained; it reaches out to affect the space around it. We exist in space—that is the energy of the world, and each of us is a recipient of that energy, if he so wills. Some people get old and sit on the porch [in their minds] at 16, and other people are willing to seek out the energy of the world at 60 and beyond. There has to be about you a transparency to receive the energy around you—maybe that's what genius is; I don't really know. Talent is the ability to experience life and to communicate the experience to others. . . .
(*The Record*, April 5, 1985)

"Many people don't want the responsibility of deep feeling. . . . You have to go very deep into the heart and the emotions, and you have to respect the ancestor. People want merely to mimic daily life in the arts, and the arts are a glorification of life, not a mimicry. . . . Think of how many thousands of people have gone into making you."
(*The Record*, April 7, 1991)

One method she has used to communicate is the mythological theme. Before *Song* she made several works drawn from biblical sources and many more based on Greek mythology. "The myths came to me as nursery rhymes." she says. "They were read to me when I was a child. They contain truths, the constancy of return to the essentials of life.

"When you make a dance—or any kind of art—you're talking about experience, whether it is present experience or that of 2,000 years ago. The Chinese say that there is only one permanency—and that permanency is change. You can't step twice in the same stream. . . ."

To Graham's way of thinking, dance demands the cultivation of two seemingly contradictory qualities: instinct and discipline. "If you lose instinct," she says, "it will never come back. A child's instinct, an animal's instinct, are present in our bodies—in the pores of our skins. It is instinct that lets us feel the common pulse of humanity and of history."

As for discipline, she likes to think of it in St. Augustine's words, as "the regality of order." Technique, she says, "is a joy and a terror, a bore at times and a necessity always. Those who do not have order and discipline can never be dancers. . . ."

In her use of movement and of words, Graham is constantly aware of meaning, and constantly seeking to refine that meaning and to define the truth.

"My father was a doctor," she says, "and I remember being a little girl in his office, standing on books to look through a microscope. I must have been about 4. My father showed me a drop of water and asked me if it were clear. 'Yes,' I said. 'it is.' Then he put the water on a slide and let me look at it through the microscope and I said, 'It has wrigglies in it.' 'Martha,' my father told me, 'you must always look for the truth.' I think that was my first real lesson.

"You have to look for the truth. You eat the truth in your mouth. Sometimes it is bitter and sometimes sweet, but you have to eat life.

"Everyone needs to discover the hidden room inside himself. There are some things you cannot teach—either they are there or not. . . ."

In the end the small, elegant, dedicated woman who does not use the word *genius* because she cannot define it precisely does, perhaps perform miracles. It is not merely that she re-created dance, or that, at nearly 91, she continues to create, fearfully and joyously. It is that she forces her audiences (in the theater and in her home) to reconsider the universe and their places in it. In this humdrum, self-satisfied world, that is indeed a miracle. *(The Record,* April 5, 1985)

Tangled Night (1986): *The best of Graham—old and new:*
Martha Graham . . . has personified in her newest dance humanity's oldest and greatest heroine: the sea.

It is the sea as seductress that Graham has personified in *Tangled Night,* her 176th work. . . . [It] is a masterpiece that combines the best of the old Graham style and the new. Its design is rich but uncluttered, its drama tense and universal. It is relentless in its energy, compelling in its imagery, and at once violent and seductive in its movement—like the sea itself.

The dance is choreographed to the Piano Concerto No. 2 of the contemporary Norwegian composer Klaus Egge, and has been greatly enhanced by Halston's costumes and by Ming Cho Lee's striking set. (*The Record*, June 5, 1986)

Maple Leaf Rag (1990): *Graham outdoes herself:*

Wisdom includes the ability to poke gentle, perceptive fun at one's civilization; supreme wisdom permits aiming the fun at one's self. . . .

Maple Leaf Rag, the 96-year-old choreographer's 180th work [and her last work], has Graham parodying Graham. Well-known postures from her dramatic dances—palms pressed to forehead as elbow angles forward, for example—are taken out of context and teased. The choreographer's own intense stage persona, familiar to all those who saw her dance, provides another focus for the good-natured self-mockery.

The piece [is] set to music by Scott Joplin, with costumes by Calvin Klein. . . .

. . . During the 1920s, when Graham was frustrated or depressed she would turn to her mentor and musical director Louis Horst and say, "Oh Louis, play me the *Maple Leaf Rag*." Her new dance starts by suggesting a mood of dramatic—indeed, melodramatic—depression, then sweeps it away in the rhythms of Joplin's ragtime. A ballet barre supported by rockers provides the decor and the metaphor of the dance. . . .

The company circles the barre with percussive jumps, the dancers holding their arms and bodies in tense, almost anguished poses. One of the women falls to the ground and then, as the company leaves the stage, hoists herself up to pose on the barre. It bounces. That bouncing, and [dancer] Terese Capucilli's slightly perplexed expression when it happens, set the tone for the rest of the piece. . . .

. . . At the end, Capucilli is left alone, sitting on the barre, still looking puzzled. The dancer's strong physical resemblance to the young Graham heightens the self-parody, and those familiar with the great choreographer's canon will have fun picking out references to earlier works. . . . Graham is looking back, not in anger but in amusement. (*The Record*, October 4, 1990)

Martha Graham's next work was to be Eyes of the Goddess, *a commission by the Spain '92 Foundation as part of a celebration of the 500th anniversary of Columbus' voyage of discovery. Graham died on April 1, 1991—six weeks before her 97th birthday.*

VII

MERCE CUNNINGHAM

MULTIPLE CHOICE

THE EXPLOSION THAT EXTINGUISHED Hiroshima on August 6, 1945, slashed an exclamation point after the sentence painted by the war on every wall: "Nobody lives forever!"

Virtually every artistic accomplishment since then may be seen as an attempt either to erase the words or to come to terms with them. The generation that survived the Depression and World War II turned to materialism, trusting that the goods would make them free. Their children tried self-searching, mysticism, communalism—almost anything that might help them dissociate themselves from the past. During the 1960s, using hallucinogens was known as taking a trip, and a trip is an escape as well as an exploration. Faith in technology during the 1950s was succeeded, with the logic of reaction, by reliance on astrology during the 1960s. Freud lost followers; seekers turned to Jung, to General Motors, and eventually to the disciplines of the Orient which generally teach concern for one's inner being and involvement with the sum of the universe, rather than a deep emotional commitment to other individual human beings. Composer John Cage wrote that artists had "moved away from simply private human concerns towards the world of nature and society of which all of us are a part."

Ernest Becker, in the book he precisely titled *The Denial of Death,* insists that "guilt is not a result of infantile fantasy but of self-conscious adult reality," and asks if it is advantageous to destroy our defenses with psychotherapy when, after the ramparts have been razed, we will only be more terribly aware of our impending personal ends. Since the day of the mushroom cloud, we have tried to obviate the existence of the future, which means that we must negate the existence of the past. The only time of importance is now.

Hiroshima proved that Einstein was right: Energy can be liberated from matter. It has even been said that if you take the long view, you can't tell the energy from the matter without a cosmic scorecard. The Theory of Relativity suggests further that time is a dimension, intertwined with space, and that time and space cannot be defined independently of one another. Time may be considered a structure, and space a process. Engineering took this knowledge from the physicists and metaphysicians and forced everyone to accept it, if not to understand it. The jet engine did not reduce the size of the Atlantic Ocean, but it achieved the same effect by cutting the flying time between New York and Paris.

Artists began to investigate relativity while facing up to the same news that was worrying everyone else: Nobody is going to live forever. The urgency of the immediate became utterly important; what matters in art, or in anything else, is what is happening at this moment. The events of last week are meaningless because they no longer exist; tomorrow, we may all be dead. This urgency developed into a sense that, if this moment is all-important, then every moment is all-important, since every moment becomes this moment as it occurs. If every moment is all-important, then each moment is as important as any other and no more so. The same may be said of every point of space and every living thing. The ultimate democracy had been reached.

The individual is instructed to consider himself as a cell within an organism, and to restrict his attention to the present. He is not expected, as Martha Graham's tragic figures are, to confront the pattern of his life and act heroically. World War II had given the world a sufficiency of heroism; those who had it, like Falstaff's man of honor, died o' Wednesday.

The change may be part of a longer, slower process, a tilt of the balance from Romanticism, exemplified in modern dance by Martha

Merce Cunningham in 1940: The body defines itself in space and time. PHOTOGRAPH BY BARBARA MORGAN.

Graham, to Classicism, personified by Doris Humphrey. Romanticism as a system of thought and creation is concerned with the individual, exalts emotion, disputes the dictatorship of form, incites rebellion, and is dedicated to a belief in the possibility of progress. Classicism deals with structured groups, praises the intellectual, seeks to refine form, instills order, and devotes itself to the preservation of balance. Darwin, Marx, and Freud, codifiers though they were, were produced by a Romantic age. That epoch reached its epitome in the music of Wagner, music that was enshrined by the Third Reich, a government that was a metaphor for Romanticism gone insane. The line between Classicism and Romanticism is never sharply drawn, and neither style can exist without its complement. New syntheses continually arise, but the insanity of World War II may well have been the climax of the latest Romantic age. This traumatic ending brought about a wish for more measured thought, which is reflected by the cooler, more intellectual style of recent art, and notably of recent dance.

In dance, this art devoted to immediacy, relativity, and logic demanded a performance without narrative, without dramatic characterization or theatrical trappings, without a central figure or climactic event, and without projected emotion. Since it denied Freudian and Newtonian notions of cause and effect, it also asked that dance, music, and decor operate independently of one another. All events were to be important, all figures equally interesting, all areas of the dancing space equally challenging to the audience. Movement became important not for what it meant, but for what it was. The ego and the id were of less consequence than the arm and the leg. The subject of dance became dancing.

Paradoxically, this dance in which nothing is more important than anything else produced an artist of more importance than any since Martha Graham: Merce Cunningham. Furthermore, in the words of Carolyn Brown, a great dancer who worked with Cunningham for twenty years, his dance ". . . is no place for democracy; we do not have equal gifts; we are not equally driven to success or failure; we are not equally capable or in need to create or perform." When a space is filled with dancers, each involved in a private task, your eye sooner or later finds Cunningham and settles on him. He is one of the great dancers of the world, because he invests each movement and moment with its full value and meaning. By doing so, he brings elitism into the dance democracy.

You notice him immediately—a man so angular you are conscious of his bones. The long body leads up to a sad face sharpened by a strong nose and a high forehead and topped by tense, curly hair. When he stands still, he seems to grow from the stage like a tree. When he moves, he can change direction as quickly as a cat fight. His body flips from stillness to motion in seconds; he can accelerate as smoothly as an expensive automobile. Even when he is dancing quickly he never seems to hurry, and each step is shaped with photographic clarity. When Cunningham runs with his arms outstretched you feel the wind; when he executes one of his low, strong *jetés* you sense the ground flashing between your own legs; when he makes an elementary movement, such as pulling his knee to point his toes directly at the floor, you feel the articulation in your own joints.

Cunningham's dancing and his choreography seem more balletic than those of any modern choreographer before him, partly because of his rapid shifts of weight and direction, and partly because of the clear rhythm that is marked out by each phrase. Carolyn Brown says his teaching involves ". . . training the body to move with speed, flexibility, and control; to move with the sustained control of slow motion; to move free of any particular style." Freedom from idiosyncratic style is a hallmark of Classicism.

Further recollections of ballet are called up by the clean line of the spine that characterizes the Cunningham style. The spine, however, is not rigid. Cunningham teaches that the body operates from a point of balance in the lower spine, and has written that the spine "acts not just as a source for the arms and legs, but in itself can coil and explode like a spring, can grow taut or loose, can turn on its own axis . . ." Graham's technique requires two axes—the spine and the pelvis—but Cunningham depends upon the vertical line of the spine. As a result, his dancing seems more buoyant, and even when he uses the floor or sweeps horizontally through space you are aware of the line between ground and sky. Speed in dance, he told Walter Sorell, "is not a case of the feet or arms twiddling at some fantastic tempo, but speed comes from the diligence with which the spine allows the legs and arms to go."

His choreography makes use of pedestrian actions—walking, running, skipping—and of the awkward motions with which most humans propel their bodies, but it also demands that dancers move with an intense degree of virtuosity and a sure sense of balance. His dances are based on the division of time into segments, but he is also concerned with penetrating space with long horizontal leaps, deep reachings, and bouncing jumps. He shapes bodies into curves, sharp angles, and combinations of the two, and has dancers fall or lean against one another without bending from the waist. His style involves the entire body and is one of consummate elegance, which, again, relates it to ballet. In fact, his choreography might be more accessible if spectators would regard it as a dance less akin to Martha Graham modern than to George Balanchine ballet.

Balanchine is most celebrated for his "abstract," plotless, ballets in which he has dispensed with narrative, with story-telling mime, and with the characters of drama. Many of these dances are performed on a bare stage in costumes that are merely cleaned and pressed rehearsal clothes partly because the company has not always had money for trappings, but also because Balanchine wants nothing to stand between the audience and the dance. Balanchine also has altered the traditional structure of ballet to some extent. His *corps de ballet* does not merely do simple steps while forming a pretty frame for the leading dancers; it covers the stage in intricate patterns, often becoming an environment through which the principals move. Dancers may emerge from the corps to perform brief, personal turns before melting back into the anonymity of the group.

Cunningham, too, has dispensed with narrative and character. His works have often been performed in rehearsal clothes and when he uses decor it is independent of the content of the dance. He goes further than Balanchine in decentralizing the stage; his dancing space is filled with different actions and has no central focus. He does not use a hierarchy of performers—corps, soloists, ballerina, and cavalier—but makes every dancer at once a soloist and a member of the ensemble.

Some of Balanchine's greatest works have needed years to achieve popularity, and some still appeal only to a limited portion of the audience because of their method of projecting emotion. The choreographer's great *pas de deux* are, as he has admitted, love songs, but the passion must be understood from the movement; there is no plot to inform the audience of the relationship between the dancers. Cunningham's dances encounter similar difficulties. He has made duets of great tenderness, group dances of violence and bewilderment, solos of intensity and anguish, but the audience must discover the emotion from the movement, and from nothing else.

In Balanchine's ballets, the emotion also is present in the music. Balanchine is a master musician who sees music as the foundation of his art. He is fond of saying that "the composer is the architect of time," and he erects his edifice according to the architect's plan. He does not follow the music note for note and phrase for phrase, but his dances are inseparable from the scores to which they are made. The music and steps together create the atmosphere of a work.

Cunningham is quite different. He has brought to a logical conclusion the attempt to make dance independent of music. Humphrey and Tamiris made dances without a score; Graham has her music tailored to fit the dancing; Cunningham has made works that have no relationship at all to their music, except to occupy the same theater at the same time. The dancers may not have heard the score before the first performance of a piece. Cunningham, like Balanchine, is occupied with questions of time, but his phrasing and rhythm are not imposed by a composer but develop out of the movements he invents. The shape and duration of a phrase are determined only by the phrase. However, his dances demonstrate how choreography and music can complement one another, each affecting the audience in a different way. In his theater, the two arts live together as symbiotes.

Cunningham was the subject of a profile in *The New Yorker* in May 1968, and he told the reporter that the audience at one of his earliest recitals, in 1944, had liked a particular piece "because it seemed to them to be tied to an emotional meaning. They thought it had to do with fear. It had nothing directly to do with fear . . . The main thing about it—and the thing everybody missed—was that its structure was based on time . . . it was divided into time units . . ." In that dance, *Root of an Unfocus,* the steps and the music started together and ended together in each unit of choreography, but developed independently of one another in the middle. "That was the beginning of the idea that music and dance could be dissociated," and the gap between them widened as Cunningham continued his work.

He is concerned with Einsteinian, not Newtonian, physics. He times segments of his dances with a stopwatch when he rehearses them, "from the belief," Carolyn Brown writes, "that rhythm comes out of the nature of the movement and the movement nature of the individual dancer . . . Accuracy of time is necessary to maintain the desired space. Change the space and the time changes, unless the speed of the particular phrase changes in order to keep the time the same. Change the time and the space and the movement changes." If time is a dimension, you cannot measure space without taking it into account.

Cunningham begins working out his dances on his own body as he works alone in his studio every morning. He starts by making a movement, from which other movements develop. Later, working with his company, he will discover relationships among the dancers, between the dancers and space, between space and time, and he will use those relationships to further the development of the dance. His dancing is intensely physical, predicated on his personal rhythms and emotions at the moment of creation. It is not based on music, but on human rhythm.

"You don't need a meter to walk in the street," Cunningham explains. "You stop and go and slow down and speed up, and I take my premise of a human moving from walking. We all walk with the same mechanism, but we all walk differently. We all use the same technique, so to speak, but we all express ourselves differently just by walking. Dancing is simply an extension, in a big way, of walking; if we don't need a metric beat for walking, we don't need it for dancing." In rehearsing some sections of a dance he has to count it for the company; other sections, he does not.

Cunningham has an intense intellectual curiosity, and many of his conceptions have their beginnings in the discoveries of science or the inventions of engineering—in short, in the world he finds around him. When he begins to work, though, he does not involve intellectual concepts or images, but concerns himself only with movement. He opposes the schools of choreography that dictate that every step must have a specific meaning. "I don't even want a dancer to start thinking that a movement means something," he told *The New Yorker*. "That was what I really didn't like about working with Martha Graham—the idea that was always being given to you that a particular movement meant something specific. I thought that was nonsense."

The meaning of a movement, to Cunningham, is intrinsic in the movement and in the person doing it—it is not imposed by an external convention. Emotion is always present in dance, "because it's a human being doing it. A human being is not an abstract. I never considered my dancing abstract—everyone else did, but I don't. I think that everything a human being does is expressive in some way of that person." Furthermore, the emotion of a movement "will appear when that movement is danced, because that's where the life is. The life does not lie outside the dancing, however strange or non-strange, conventional or non-conventional the dancing is, the life of a dance lies there."

The subject matter of Cunningham's dances is vastly different from that of ballet or earlier modern dance. The central theme of classical

Classic Cunningham and classic Brown in Place, *1966.*
PHOTOGRAPH BY JAMES KLOSTY.

ballet is that peculiar conceit of Western civilization, romantic love. Heroines of ballet may go mad after having been betrayed, may be transformed into swans, or awakened with a kiss. Romantic love and its ultimate expression, the *liebestod,* provide them with a reason to exist. Nearly all great ballet choreographers have been male and, despite the perceptive remark of the late critic Greer Johnson that *Sleeping Beauty* is a universal metaphor—"We're all asleep until someone kisses us awake"—the classics take a masculine view of relationships. Modern dance brought changes because many of its inventors were women of strength who realized that they had individual reasons to exist, and functions other than being transformed, in one way or another, by a man. Loie Fuller ignored the subject. Isadora Duncan danced passion, but she danced it alone or with a group of young girls. Denishawn brought love back to the stage, only to have it transformed by Humphrey into sociological terms, and by Graham into Freudian combat. Cunningham banished the subject, at least in literal terms.

Despite his lovely duets and passionate encounters, his most celebrated works are more concerned with the interaction of individuals in groups than with the tensions and attractions experienced by a couple. He considers dancers as people in social situations and as individuals. This "is why I don't have a *corps de ballet,* I don't have a chorus," says Cunningham. "We dance together sometimes, but people do things together like go on picnics, but still, people are separate and at any moment they could do things separately." This sense of separation gives some of his works an air of painful loneliness, although others exhibit wit, tenderness, and joy.

The popular arts continue to propagate sentimentality and romantic love, but the serious arts do not. This century has changed the content of painting and sculpture; they may be concerned with form and material, or they may express emotion which is either personal or avowedly polemic, but not romantic. Botticelli's *Venus* may personify feminine desirability, but no man is likely to be set mooning by one of Picasso's *Demoiselles d'Avignon,* and certainly nobody will form a passionate attachment for the vertical lines of Barnett Newman. Art that induces the viewer to desire or adore the subject is a manifestation of Romanticism; art that removes the subject from such consideration is Classical. Since World War II, Americans and American art have behaved as if shared emotion were futile, dangerous, or both; subjects are presented as matters for study, not as inducements to love.

Cunningham's dancing contains emotion, but unlike earlier choreographers, he does not theatrically heighten feeling. He has said that he does not aim at producing a specific emotional result, but rather at presenting an event and allowing the audience to "make up their own minds about how they think about what they are looking at." He does not say ". . . how they *feel* . . ." The emotion of his dances is neither specified, personalized, nor intensified. It is presented through movements, through the relationships of dancers in space and time, and through form. It is more closely allied to what one might feel during a walk through the park than during a night of making love.

His art is not concerned with discrete, intense sensations but rather with a multiplicity—one of his favorite words—of experiences. That is why his dances do not force the spectators' attention to a single event, but present a number of things to watch. That also is why his dances do not rely on Freudian concepts of searching the past. "My work is not a matter of reference," he says, "but of direct action. One draws from one's own experience, and what someone sees in the dance is something that refers to his experience, but it's not necessarily my experience. That doesn't make it invalid; the dance offers a multiplicity of meanings to a number of different people."

In a Graham work, and in the dances of other American choreographers, the costumes, music, choreography, and stage setting are integrated to reinforce the audience's reaction to a single experience. The Spanish inn of Denishawn's *Cuadro Flamenco,* designed in the tradition of Belasco realism and the framework house of *Appalachian Spring* serve the same purpose; they contribute to the theatrical convention employed by the choreographer and help focus the emotion of the dance. Cunningham's convention makes each element of the work a separate experience, a discrete performance in itself. There is no reason why his *Rainforest* (1968) should be danced amid Andy Warhol's helium-filled silver Mylar pillows. Then again, there is no reason why it should not be. When the dancers encounter the pillows during performance, they gently and unconcernedly brush them aside. If the movements and the pillows link themselves in the spectators' minds as two distinct ideas, gathered from different sources to help clarify the meaning of one another, so much the better. If they do not, the audience may enjoy the pillows and the dancing separately, or they may ignore one and concentrate on the other. Cunningham issues no orders on the subject. Certainly, the pillows do not contribute to the creation of an emotional impact, as Noguchi's setting for *Seraphic Dialogue* does, although they cannot help contributing to a general mood.

Cunningham, when he makes dances with decors, does not collaborate with the designer or specify his requirements as other choreographers do. The first time he decided to use a setting, he asked painter Robert Rauschenberg if he "would make something for *Minutiae* that could be put in the middle of the stage and around which we could move." Frank Stella, who did the decor for *Scramble* (1967), received a similar request and produced a simple frame made up of two uprights, between which stretched, at the very top, a horizontal band. Sometimes it framed the dancers, sometimes it simply waited in the background in case anybody cared to look at it. Cunningham believes that all the arts and disciplines that come together in the theater should function independently of one another. Each artist should be free to make his own work without considering the other components of the event.

However, in the theater, each component influences the audience's experience of the others. Bruce Nauman's design for *Tread* (1970), is a hedge of electric fans on poles, spaced fairly far apart at regular intervals across the foot of the stage. The breeze from the fans reaches the spectators in the front row, and the poles interrupt the line of the dance as it is seen by anyone in the orchestra. At times, a dancer's head might be on one side of a fanpost and the rest of his body on the other. Cunningham's progress across the stage is interrupted every few feet by a shank of metal. After a time, the interruptions stop being an annoyance and become a game. If you want to follow Cunningham across the stage, you have to watch carefully and pick him up each time he passes behind a fan, as you might watch a friend walking across the street between cars. Then again, you can elect to watch the space marked out by one pair of fans and concentrate only on the dancing in that area, as you might watch people coming and going in one small area of a park. You can also try to see the entire stage, fans and all. Cunningham made the dance, Nauman presented a choice of ways in which to watch it. His setting may be considered a distraction or an augmentation. However, it may not be considered completely as an independent entity, simply because it occupies

Barbara Lloyd and Cunningham amidst the helium-filled silver Mylar pillows of Andy Warhol's setting for Rainforest *(1968). Cunningham's intense concentration and rooted stance are hallmarks of his dancing.*

PHOTOGRAPH BY OSCAR BAILEY.

the same space and time as the choreography. The two arts were not independent, but symbiotic.

The score that accompanies a Cunningham dance is even further removed from the movement than is the setting. During *How to Pass, Kick, Fall and Run* (1965), composer John Cage and a colleague or two sat on the sidelines and read one-minute-long stories. *Canfield* (1970) had an accompaniment engineered by Pauline Oliveros, in which Cage, David Tudor, and Gordon Mumma communicated with one another by walkie-talkie throughout most of the dance. Their radio gave out static, squeals, and other electronic noises, and critic Marcia B. Siegel reported that Cunningham later decided that the sounds of the landing on the moon, specifically the astronauts' conversations with ground control, were just the thing he had wanted to accompany *Canfield*. Cunningham does not collaborate with composers any more than he does with designers. He tells them how long the dance is going to be, and very little else. The sound, like the decor, is intended to be an entity in itself.

There is a logic to this form of presentation, as there is to everything that Cunningham does. The making of a dance may be a purely physical act, but many of his works are based on ideas, on an article he has read, a concept he has encountered, an advance in technology, or a change that he has noticed in our reaction to the world. Like a good scientist, he has the courage of his curiosity; he likes to try things. A laboratory experiment may end up proving the opposite of what its originator thought it would, but that does not mean the experiment was wasted. "I do these things because the ideas are available and interesting to try out," says Cunningham. "The ideas themselves are valid. Sometimes, in some of the ways I've worked them out they don't quite appear. Other times, they do."

The use of electronic music or, in the case of *Canfield*, electronic communication, brings contemporary technology into the theater and makes it part of the performance, as it is part of the world outside the theater. Cage's story-telling during *How to Pass* is distracting, but so is much of life. *Winterbranch* (1964) is accompanied by La Monte Young's two recorded sounds, blasted at the audience through loudspeakers. Robert Rauschenberg's lighting for the piece leaves much of the stage in darkness. White lights, sharply focused, rarely hit the dancers except by chance. The stage is bare. The lighting and sound combine to help create an intimation of unconquerable chaos, which is appropriate to the tense angles and slow falls of the choreography.

Although the choreography, the lighting, and the score of *Winter-*

branch were discrete creations, they affected one another because they happened in the same place at the same time. On the street, Cunningham says, one may see an action and hear a sound that have nothing to do with one another but affect the way in which each is perceived because they coexist. Again, the spectator is confronted with a multiplicity of events that affect one another but do not effect one another. During a performance of *How to Pass* members of the audience may concentrate on Cunningham, or on Cage, switch back and forth between the two, or allow themselves to be affected by both at once. Everything is important, or rather, each spectator must decide for himself what is important and what is not. Neither Cunningham nor Cage is going to help.

This logic sometimes is more effective in the theory than in the theater. Most of the people who attend Cunningham's performances are there to see the dancing, and a score such as the one used in *Canfield* or *Winterbranch* is not merely a distraction but an assault. It is a bit like trying to listen to a friend playing Bach while a jackhammer breaks up the sidewalk outside your window. However, that conjunction probably would not upset John Cage.

Cage has been associated with Cunningham since 1937, when he played the piano for a dance class in Seattle, Washington, and Cunningham was among the students. It was the most important meeting of its kind since Louis Horst played for Graham's first class at Denishawn. When Cunningham began to choreograph solos for himself, he asked Cage to write the music, and the composer has been his accompanist, music director, helper, and friend ever since. In many ways, Cage has been even more influential than Horst, because his students and followers include painters and sculptors along with dancers and musicians. In 1952, Cage taught at Black Mountain College in North Carolina, and his lectures enjoined artists to eradicate the boundary between life and art. He called for an art without dramatic climaxes, in which each moment would be valued for itself. Cunningham danced at the college that year, and the next year he organized a company (he had been doing mostly solo work and recitals with Cage) and began a second phase in his career as choreographer.

Cage is a musician, a pianist, and a composer, but he is not especially interested in entertaining an audience. His art is polemic; it is dedicated to a purpose. Part of that purpose is the glorification of noise. As long ago as 1937, he wrote: "Wherever we are, what we hear is mostly noise. When we ignore it, it disturbs us. When we listen to it, we find it fascinating." He contends that music should not exclude any kind of sound, as

Cunningham maintains that dance should not ban any kind of movement. Cage, though, goes further, saying that music should be constructed with holes in it, to allow outside sounds to find their way in. Since we cannot avoid extraneous sound, which we call noise, we should listen to it. If the sound of the jackhammer coincides with the sound of Bach in life, a composer should allow it to do the same thing in the theater. In fact, he should arrange for it. Cage has been known to perform a piece called *Butterflies,* which consists of releasing butterflies into the audience, and to announce that at a concert, he will offer a piece lasting for twenty-two minutes, then sit at the piano for twenty-two minutes without playing. He is attempting, it seems, to alter our conceptions of what a concert is, to force us to listen to commonplace sounds, and simply to *épater les bourgeoises.* To date, he has not been lynched.

His lectures, some of which are collected in his book, *Silence,* give an understanding of his principles. He is interested in experiencing the environment, rather than in investigating a selective piece of it, and in experiencing every moment rather than existing in a continuum. "There is a tendency in my composition away from ideas of order to ideas of no order . . ." he said in 1958, and he is fond of quoting Kafka's remark, "Psychology—never again." Cage is a student of Zen, which teaches its disciples to live without reference to past or future. ("I eat when I'm hungry; I sleep when I'm tired," said the master asked to define Zen.) The religion enjoyed a vogue during the 1960s when young Americans wanted to sever themselves from the values of their parents and, especially after the Cuban missile crisis of 1963, to forget that they were not going to live forever.

One instrument used in teaching Zen is the *koan,* a riddle that has no logical answer. A *koan* is designed to convince students to abandon logic as a guide and to alter their methods of perceiving the world. It often is

Tread *(1970): Choreography, Merce Cunningham; decor, Bruce Nauman; score, Christian Wolff. The placement of the fans segments the dance and the dancers, demanding that the spectator choose which action to follow and creating a sculptural rhythm by playing against the arms of the dancers. (From left: Merce Cunningham, Meg Harper, Mel Wong, Carolyn Brown.)* PHOTOGRAPH BY JAMES KLOSTY.

couched in tones of smug superiority, quite close to those exuded by Cage's lectures. You sometimes get the impression that the teacher, or lecturer, is conveying the idea that he is smart enough to understand these things and you are not.

Cage's theories lead him to support the superiority of the twelve-tone row to the older system of harmony, because in Schoenberg's twelve-tone system each note is equal and functions as a member of the group. In harmony, each tone functions with respect to the most important tone in the group. From there, Cage goes on to determine that even twelve-tone music is too thoroughly organized, because it is a method, and "A method is a control of each single note. Their development, the climax, the recapitulation . . . there is not enough of nothing in it."

When each note is equally important, no note is particularly important, which leads Cage on to the complete equality of everything. The preface to one of his lecture-performances notes, "This view makes us all equals—even if among us are some unfortunates: Whether lame, blind, stupid, schizoid, or poverty-stricken." Whether Cage seriously considers the stupid to be his equals is an interesting question—and just whom he considers stupid is another—but his theory certainly terminates the concept of the heroic individual as the center of a work of art.

The ultimate democracy is the ultimate despair. We are all equal since we are all going to die. Eventually, the sun will go nova and that will be an end to art, to thinking, to pleasure, to heroism, and to the compelling past. Unless, of course, by the time the sun goes nova, art, thinking, heroism, fabrication, and the compelling past have led us to other worlds, to perpetuate the race among the stars.

Cunningham's theories often are similar to Cage's, but in the choreographer's case, the art seems to transcend the theory, while in the composer's, the theory—and the preaching of it—seems far more important than the art. Cunningham's dance democracy demands that performers work to the extreme limits of their abilities, and his theory of multiplicity allows the possibility that, at any moment, something exciting may happen to somebody, or to everybody.

One of the things he dislikes about older forms of dancing is that they set and force relationships between the dancers. He thinks the Rockettes at Radio City Musical Hall "were the loneliest people in the world, because they were in their little pigeonholes," while performing their celebrated high kicks with inexorably linked arms. The multifaceted stage set by Cunningham, with many dancers going their separate ways, sometimes seems symptomatic of big-city loneliness, but Cunningham insists it is merely a kind of separation, engendered by the speed at which we move and act. His dancers may act separately, "but at the next moment they can turn around and do things together."

Cunningham is a private person. Interviews with him and articles about him contain information about his dancing, his ways of work, his theories, but little about his own affairs. Carolyn Brown writes, ". . . few of the people I've known have grown so profoundly as Merce, despite his unchanging need for seclusion and his refusal to reveal any more about himself than that which he willingly offers. One must always meet him on *his* terms; anything else is an encroachment on his territorial rights to privacy. Psychology doesn't interest him. Anthropology and zoology do."

He is a stunningly gentle man, serene and not severe. He seems to have made his choices long ago, and to be willing to let you take as much time as necessary to make yours. His voice is quiet, his speech is clear, his eyes are clearer still. Any violence in him was buried deep long ago, yet he seems immune to attack. An hour with him induces a sense of emotional peace and intellectual excitement. If Cunningham wanted to set up shop as a guru he could make a fortune, but he seems to believe with the Buddha that one should teach with silent speakers.

Cunningham was born in Centralia, Washington, where he studied folk, tap, and exhibition ballroom dancing, and served as an altar boy in the Roman Catholic Church. He has said that the experience prepared him for his five years with Martha Graham's company, since it accustomed him to spending a good deal of time on his knees.

In 1937 he entered the Cornish School of Fine and Applied Arts in Seattle, where he studied dance with Bonnie Bird, who had performed with Graham, and met John Cage. Since he had completed high school, he must have been seventeen or eighteen, which would put his year of birth, about which he is reticent, at 1919 or 1920. He did a brief vaudeville and nightclub tour in Oregon and California, studied at Mills College and at Bennington, and joined Graham's company with which he danced from 1940 through 1945. He created the roles of the Acrobat in *Every Soul Is a Circus* and the Revivalist in *Appalachian Spring,* among others. While performing with Graham, Cunningham took the unusual step of studying at The School of American Ballet, the academy founded by Lincoln Kirstein and George Balanchine which became the official training camp for The New York City Ballet. Ballet was not popular with modern dancers at the time, but Cunningham has never wanted to exclude any form of movement from his investigations.

Four or five years after Cunningham was recruited by Graham, Cage recalls, the composer arrived in New York and encouraged his friend to give his own recitals. In 1942 Cunningham co-choreographed three works with Jean Erdman and made two on his own, both with music by Cage. The following year he began making solos for himself. His first recital of solos in New York, on April 4, 1944, with Cage at the piano, pleased the critics. The reviewer for Horst's *Dance Observer* praised him for putting everything he had to say into "clear, beautifully timed and executed movement which was a joy to watch. He is a classicist." The critic, following the Horst party line, commended the young artist for obviously believing that dance is an independent medium, but chided him for a lack of humanity and warmth. "When he has put more 'theater' and more warmth and variety into his work, he will have the same attraction for a less specialized audience."

The country's most perceptive and poetic dance critic, Edwin Denby, wrote in the *New York Herald Tribune* that Cunningham's performance "was of the greatest esthetic elegance." As usual, Denby found the key element of the choreographer's work: "His dances are built on the rhythm of a body in movement and on its irregular phrase lengths." The following year, Denby reviewed another recital by Cunningham. "He is a virtuoso, relaxed, lyrical, elastic like a playing animal. He has an instinct for form that makes its point by repetition, each repetition being a little different and the phrasing of each difference exceptionally limpid . . . He appears either as a lonely youth or as a happy hooligan; you'd like to see him show a franker character, too, or see him in contact with different people."

In 1947, The Ballet Society (Balanchine-Kirstein) presented *The Seasons,* choreography by Cunningham, score by Cage, setting by Noguchi. The commissioning of a modern dance choreographer to make a work for a ballet troupe is exactly the sort of imaginative venture one might expect from Balanchine and Kirstein, but the latter found that the work

Carolyn Brown, for 20 years the greatest Cunningham dancer after Cunningham, in Variations V *(1965). She defines shape without succumbing to tension.*

was "interesting and pretty, but it had little virtuosic interest and was not particularly interesting for ballet-trained dancers to do . . . without acrobatic virtuosity based on four centuries of logical exercises, a dancer cannot hope to attract the mass public . . ." Kirstein is an acute observer of dance and art, and he was certainly correct in his assessment of Cunningham's ability to attract a mass public, but his patrician bias toward ballet led him to disregard one of the choreographer's remarkable qualities—his dance is highly virtuosic.

There has always been a special attention to technique in Cunningham dancing, despite the choreographer's interest in unschooled movements such as running and skipping. Cunningham says that he set out to find ways of making the body strong, resilient, and flexible, and decided that there must be more ways than were generally known. He did not want to exclude any kind of movement from his work—he finds that a negative way of approaching dance—but to deal with movement "in as many ways as my imagination could conceive . . . Any movement is possible in dancing—walking or virtuoso movements" because dancing is "the amplification of energy" and technique is "a kind of yoga."

Cunningham regards dancers as individuals who infuse movement with personal beauty and meaning as they perform. He finds that the trouble with virtuosity and technique is that the dancers come to rely on them, rather than on themselves, and everybody comes out looking the same. "Virtuosity narrows the scale," he says, and presents "less possibility for the diversity of human beings . . . so many dancers think that if they learn to do a step well, that's it, though great dancers go beyond. You have to get so far beyond it that you can make mistakes again, that something else can happen." He is not suggesting that dancers make mistakes on purpose, but rather that they perform like the great musicians who would rather miss a note now and then than fail to convey the music that lies within the notes. He does not demand something less than virtuosity, but something more.

With his usual logic, he points out that we all have legs, and that there are only two things we can do with them; we can bend them and we can straighten them. If you are a dancer and really straighten your leg, "Don't pretend it's straight, make it straight!—then they say you're a ballet dancer. If you bend them, you get way down in a deep *plié* and they say you've studied Chinese dancing." Really straightening the leg in the way Cunningham describes, and does, is a technical feat; the secret of his treatment of virtuosity is that every movement must be done fully and every stillness must be a moment of complete rest.

His dancers do not merely clarify the shapes of their bodies or change direction as sharply as a street turns a corner, they phrase steps without reference to music, and the choreography is always deeply involved with rhythm. *Canfield* once was performed at the Brooklyn Academy of Music in complete silence because the musicians' and stagehands' unions were quarreling over the right to handle the walkie-talkies. The performance was delightful. The rhythm of Cunningham's dances is intrinsic to the movement; it does not rely on a musical base.

When he first began making dances and working with Cage, the two men collaborated as choreographer and composer usually do; Cage wrote music, notated in the usual manner, often for choreography that had already been made. The two men worked within the framework of a length of time, specifying points at which the music and dance came together. As they prepared more works, the connections between dance and music became fewer. The first music was percussive and much of it was performed by Cage on a prepared piano, that is, a piano altered in tone by having pieces of various materials placed between the strings.

Cunningham and Cage then began to investigate the use of other kinds of sound and music. The choreographer points out that music changed after World War II when the tape recorder "brought the idea of space into music—it put it into inches." The first piece of tape Cunningham used was *Symphonie pour un homme seul* by Pierre Schaeffer and Pierre Henry, to which he was commissioned to make a dance in 1952. He could find no way to relate to that music in any conventional way, "because you'd always be late. It would be like a spook moving. There was no way to count it in any metered sense." So he tried another approach. He knew that the music lasted seven and one-half minutes, so he made a dance lasting seven and one-half minutes, put it together with the score, and went on from there. He is quite comfortable working this way, because time for him is not metered time "but a length of time you can divide any way you like." Human beings have agreed for thousands of years to chop time up into hunks of a particular size, but that does not mean there are no other ways of dividing it. Cunningham, using aperiodic time, is testing some of them.

By 1961, his repertory included dances with traditional music (Satie, Gottschalk), dances accompanied to some extent by untraditional music (a player piano was used in 1961 in *Crisis*), and dances that happen while diverse sounds also occur. His recent work includes very few dances that cannot be performed effectively in silence.

Cunningham's style entered its second major phase in 1951, when

Sixteen Dances for Soloist and Company of Three brought chance into his work. The following year he danced at the college at which Cage was teaching, and in 1953 he formed his company, consisting of six other dancers and two musicians, and began to concentrate on choreography for a group. The use of chance has nothing to do with anarchy or im- provisation. It began, Cunningham says, because he had made the sections of the dance and had more or less decided on their order, "but there were some things where I thought, 'It doesn't matter in this particular context, I could toss a coin,' so I tossed coins and accepted that particular choice." The coins determined nothing more than the sequence in which certain sections of the dance were to be presented. Cunningham had recently read an article about the Institute of Random Numbers, and learned that random numbers had been used for a certain scientific procedure and worked just as well as specific numbers would have done. Furthermore, both he and Cage knew of the *I Ching, the Book of Changes,* which, he explains, involves "Having a choice made not by yourself but by some- thing else out of a multiplicity of possibilities." The method worked.

Chance works, he says, "providing you accept what it is and not think it's something else or think it shouldn't be that." Students sometimes ask him what they should do if a chance operation commands them to do something they don't like, or something that will not work. Cunningham himself is willing to try whatever is suggested. "I never put any judgment on it. I'll try it out—whatever comes up, I'll try it out. Sometimes phys- ically it doesn't work, but by trying it out you find out something else because it's a constant way to open your mind out of what you know." He uses chance, as he uses everything else, as a tool of investigation.

Cunningham's friends tend to be artists and sculptors, and methods of using chance have been important in the formation of contemporary American art. The Surrealists, some of whom escaped to the United States from Europe during the late 1930s and early 1940s, transformed the Freudian technique of free association into psychic automatism. The artist would allow his hand to wander over the paper, creating spontane- ous patterns which could be used as the basis of conscious work. By doing this, he hoped to bypass the conscious mind and allow the images of the subconscious to reveal themselves.

The use of chance in art is suited to this century. "Accept," warned a Greek philosopher, "that anything which can happen can happen to you." The heritage of our time makes the caution terribly appropriate, when one remembers the "chance" that brought death or disruption to millions in the trenches of World War I, the purges and relocations of the Stalin era, the death camps of the Third Reich, and the destruction of Hiroshima and Nagasaki. The revolutions of more recent times and the violence in contemporary cities have continued the lesson. Perhaps the most relevant question of the age is, "Why me?"

There is a theoretical answer, of small comfort it is true, in the study of probability: There is an order that underlies chance. Toss a coin one hundred times and the odds are that it will come up heads fifty times and tails the other fifty. Furthermore, if it comes up heads twenty times in a row, the odds remain fifty-fifty that it will show another head on the twenty-first try. The bell-shaped distribution curve is the symbol of probability, the graphic demonstration of the philosopher's warning.

The operation of chance is a major concern of the time, and Cunningham is deeply aware of all things that mold his era. His use of chance, though, is quite different from that used by painters, and from that employed in music by John Cage. James Klosty points out that chance, for Cage, is "a way to disarm the power of the individual and elude the dictates of personal taste," while for the choreographer it is "less a philosophic choice than a pragmatic, potent tool."

Making *Suite by Chance* in 1953, Cunningham devoted months to constructing charts outlining the number of dancers to be used, spaces, sequences, movements of different parts of the body, and other components of choreography. Only then did he toss his coins to determine how the elements should be combined. He is a master of movement, space, and time, and any chart he compiles will be drawn with choreographic genius. He has worked out the possibilities on his body and in his mind, and has made, in effect, a series of dances. He can, therefore, trust to a controlled chance operation to determine how the parts should be assembled. Furthermore, he sees, as those who work in higher mathematics do, that a problem does not necessarily have one right answer. There are infinite possibilities, if we will only allow ourselves to become aware of them and open our minds to a wider angle of view than is customary.

After *Suite by Chance,* Cunningham made *Dime a Dance,* in which he used "open form," a method of composition developed by contemporary composers seeking to differentiate composition from performance. "Composing's one thing, performing's another, listening's a third. What can they have to do with one another?" asks Cage. In open form, the composition is written out, but the musicians decide at each performance which sections they will play, in what order, and with what combination of instruments. In *Dime a Dance,* Cunningham made the sections of the piece and rehearsed them with the company, but specified no sequence for their performance. Instead, members of the audience drew cards from a pack to determine the order of the evening. The method would not work very well with *Hamlet* or *Swan Lake,* since those works depend for part of their effect on dramatic structure. Cunningham, with his interest in infinity and in dance as its own statement, is not operating within that convention.

However, he does not ask, as Cage does, what composing, performing, and watching have to do with one another. He knows they affect one another, he also knows that this interrelationship does not require that each performance attempt to duplicate the last. It is axiomatic in dance that movement changes with the performer who executes it, and that no two dancers will create precisely the same effect with the same steps. It is an axiom Cunningham enjoys. He knows that "our elbows are different, our joints are different," and movement will look different on each of us. There is no reason to adhere to the convention that every performance must be the same, when one can rejoice in the differences.

In the winter of 1953–1954, Cunningham and his newly formed company offered a week of performances at the Theatre de Lys, off-Broadway. Neither *The New York Times* nor the *Herald Tribune* carried a review. Later in 1954, the choreographer was awarded a Guggenheim fellowship, prompting John Cage to make one of the most unambiguous remarks of his career. When the composer was asked what Cunningham intended to do with all that money, he said, "Eat." The company's special symbol, a Volkswagen bus, was purchased the following year. It was big enough to hold dancers, musicians, theatrical equipment, and a few personal belongings, and the troupe used it as Denishawn had used Pullmans, to travel the country. Cunningham dances in the years between 1955 and 1964 had their premières at, among other sites, the Brooklyn Academy of Music, Jacob's Pillow, Notre Dame University and U.C.L.A. In 1958, Cunningham was invited to participate in the dance program at Connecticut College, and the company worked there for several summers.

During the Volkswagen years, Cunningham continued to make group dances in a highly individualistic style. His pieces offered no narrative, no cause-and-effect development, no characterization, no directed emotion, no central focal point, and no central figure. His company was more an association of soloists than a hierarchy of corps and principals, despite the presence on stage of Cunningham and Carolyn Brown, who stood out even in a superb company because of their technique, and because they invariably went beyond it. His stage provided no frame for a central action, but was filled with dancers doing interesting things in various places. James Klosty notes, "There is no *best* spot on a Cunningham stage. In dances that permit the dancers to choose where they will move, there is no crush of bodies at stage center . . . the stage is not merely decentralized, it is demagnetized." If there is no best spot on stage, there is no best seat in the house, either. The principle of multiplicity, and of interaction between performer and spectator, require that the latter select the action to which he will attend.

Between 1961 and 1964, Robert Rauschenberg was the company's artistic adviser, designing costumes, lighting, and sometimes decor, making sure no nails were protruding from the floors of stages and involving himself completely in the life of the company. ". . . He created freshly, intuitively from theater to theater, even from night to night," writes Carolyn Brown. "He understood what was needed because more important to him than his own ideas was his absolute devotion to Merce's dances, his respect for the intrinsic worth of the choreography itself."

In 1966 Cage convinced another important young artist, Jasper Johns, to take on the job Rauschenberg had given up two years before. Johns was not attracted to the wandering life, as his predecessor had been, and he had different ideas about design. "I don't see the necessity for objects on stage during a dance," Johns writes. "That may be why I rarely have any ideas for sets . . . I have always felt that each dance should have its own distinctive costumes. A sort of visual novelty is provided which helps make it clear that one dance is not another dance. But I'm beginning to wonder if this is necessary." Since Johns does not like to work in the theater, he invited other artists to design for the company. Andy Warhol was one; Frank Stella was another. Johns himself conceived the idea of translating Marcel Duchamp's *The Large Glass* into a setting for *Walkaround Time* (1968).

Important contemporary artists have worked with Cunningham, and his treatment of space in some ways parallels developments in American painting. The movement that took leadership in art from France and bestowed it on the United States was Abstract Expressionism, also known as The New York School. The movement extracted and combined themes from two major styles of prewar Europe, Surrealism and Cubism. The Surrealists were interested in tapping the subconscious and in making paintings representative of the dreamstuff and other inner images. Many American artists, finding Freud's theories too intellectual, preferred to draw on the archetypes and collective unconscious of Jungian psychiatry as they searched for the matter of myth and for an art that would combine conscious and unconscious images. (Martha Graham's work with myth

Brown and Cunningham in Second Hand *(1970), sharing space, yet alone. Their different positions complement one another, their separation gives shape to the space between them.*

PHOTOGRAPH BY JAMES KLOSTY.

and dreams does not make her a Surrealist; her work is too thoroughly structured and too concrete in its imagery, although there are some elements of Surrealism in her dances.)

Cubism concerned itself with structure and point of view. A painting might examine a guitar as a whole, as an assemblage of parts, from above, from behind and from the front all at once. Cubist painters dealt with the use of geometric space and avoided the perspective of representational painting. They made a specific universe bounded by the dimensions of canvas and paint, accepted the choice and worked from there. The organization of painting also has been reconsidered throughout the century, as Cunningham has reconsidered the organization of dance.

The New York School involved painters with diverging techniques and theories, but much of the work it produced combined the intense personal expression of the Surrealists with the Cubists' concern with a painting as an object in its own right. Painters also began to experiment with art that was less an object than a process or an event. The canvas-filling labyrinths of Jackson Pollock's drip paintings have more than a little in common with the stage-filling calligraphy of Cunningham's dances. In both cases, separate events intertwine within a defined space, and the entire area is filled with energy that does not seem to begin or end, but simply to flow continuously through space.

Deborah Jowitt, reviewing a 1973 Cunningham performance for the *Village Voice,* quoted a little girl at whose school the concert had been given. The child told the choreographer that looking at his dancing "had been like looking at the inside of a watch," where everything was moving at the same time, but at different speeds, and "some things affected other things." That might just be the most perceptive review ever given to a Cunningham performance.

Cunningham's receptivity to the world around him did not diminish as his style evolved. In 1966 Jill Johnston noted that he seemed to be adapting devices from young choreographers who had, in fact, learned from him. (Among those who have worked or studied with him are

---

Merce Cunningham, today, still defines freedom with his body.
PHOTOGRAPH BY JACK MITCHELL.

Yvonne Rainer, Viola Farber, Dan Wagoner and Steve Paxton. Paul Taylor is an alumnus of both Cunningham and Graham.) Jill Johnston noted that at the end of *Place*, "Cunningham gets into a plastic bag and throws himself around in it," an act reminiscent of many works of the Saran Wrap Style favored by young choreographers at Judson Church. *Place* is one of the choreographer's darker pieces; Marcia B. Siegel sees it as ". . . an unquenchable ego absurdly struggling to effect some change."

Cunningham's interests are not limited to developments in dance; he is aware of engineering and the environmental changes it engenders. *Variations V* (1965) placed antennas on stage to be activated by the dancers who moved past them, sending signals to the orchestra pit. A series of photoelectric cells recorded changes in the intensity of light as dancers crossed them, and also signaled the pit. The signals activated electronic music-makers such as tape recorders, radios, and phonographs. Projected patterns played on the dancers, who moved through a stageful of contemporary debris, including a rubber plant carefully positioned by Cunningham during the course of his dancing.

Signals (1970) used laser projections in its lighting. In *TV Re-run* (1972), composer Gordon Mumma had the dancers wear belts containing sensors and transmitters. Their movements were translated into audible pitches, transmitted to the electronic gear in the pit, amplified, and fed to the audience through loudspeakers. Mumma thus completed a cycle; once, dance had been dependent on music; now, the score depended on the dance.

The company made a successful world tour in 1964, and four years later it finally had a successful season in America at the Brooklyn Academy of Music. The audience was finally ready to accept Cunningham. However, he has continued to dance primarily in small theaters and in spaces other than theaters. He still makes discrete dances, and the company performs repertory pieces on tour when requested to do so, but many of his performances, especially those at his studio or elsewhere in New York, are devoted to Events. The first Event was given in a museum in Vienna in 1964. There was insufficient room to allow the audience to wander to and from their seats during intermissions, so Cunningham designed a performance with no intermission. The dancers and musicians were in the playing-space, surrounded on three sides by the audience. The technique worked so well that Cunningham has been using it ever since.

An Event is generally rehearsed on the day of performance. The company's repertory is used as a bank of information, from which steps and sequences may be drawn and combined to form a completely new work. The organization of the work is written down and posted around the performance area "like choreographic shopping lists," as James Klosty remarks. the dancers maintain the order of the service by referring to the charts. Cunningham compares watching an Event to switching from channel to channel on a television set, watching a scene of this and a few moments of that. "One doesn't feel that's wrong—possibly the commercial people do—but you as a spectator don't feel it's wrong because that's the way it is, that's one of the possibilities." He also points out that ballet companies have been excerpting *pas de deux* from their repertory for quite some time, "but the ballet companies make nineteenth-century frames for them, so you can see this is a beginning and this is an end. Now, we don't think so much of ending, but of something continuing."

Events, he finds, are practical because they suit certain theatrical situations, and valuable because they mirror contemporary happenings. Cunningham understands that we look at objects and actions differently, and hear sounds differently, than our grandparents did, "because of the speed of life and technological advances." It is his intention to put the processes of the world, whether set in motion by humans or by nature, into his art. He remarks that he is more realistic than other choreographers because he does not impose an arbitrary order on events but shows things as they occur and people as they are. Whatever choice is offered, he abides by the rules he has made and tries it out. Whatever influences us—television, relativity, random numbers, our bodies—affects his dance-making. When a juxtaposition of events, or a surprising shape, or an odd encounter of rhythms creates a moment of humor, he enjoys it. His dances contain elements of wit that would never have gained admittance to the presentations of many earlier choreographers.

Still, the strongest force that moves his invention is movement. "Dancing is propelled by dancing," he says. I think dancing is its own necessity; I don't think it needs something else. It does have other things connected with it, but it wouldn't exist if it didn't have its own necessity . . . however one extends it in different directions, it would not be part of us if it did not have its own life."

* * *

Cunningham's penchant for cutting edge technology and unencumbered dance continued to fascinate Mazo. He documented the choreographer's deepening exploration of basic dance elements and his ground-breaking use of computers for composition.

Polarity (1990): *Stillness and Action:*

Choreographer Merce Cunningham . . . once remarked that there really were only two things a dancer could do with his leg: He could bend it or he could straighten it. Going a bit further, one could say that there are only two things a dancer can do with his body: he can move it or he can hold it still.

. . . [*Polarity*] is filled with suggestions of violence and of tenderness, or impassivity and energetic conviction, of tension and relaxation. It also makes the point that the difference between moving and not moving is very, very slight.

Is motion the absence of stillness, or is motionlessness the absence of movement? (Since molecular activity ceases only at an extremely low temperature—0 degrees Kelvin—it seems that movement is the *natural* state and stillness the unnatural one.) Once outside the physics lab, though, how do we measure motion? Only by contrasting it with its absence.

Some predators have eyes that react to movement, and some prey animals have evolved the defensive tactic of holding still. The rabbit that relies on its camouflage may escape; the one that runs could become a hawk's dinner. Interestingly, the backdrop for *Polarity*—the credit for the decor is shared by William Anastasi and Cunningham—displays a pair of bordered illustrations that might have come from a children's book. The stage-right panel shows an owl and another, larger bird of prey; the stage-left picture is a rough sketch of a rabbit.

At the opening of the dance, two men stand center stage, angled in to one another. One holds one arm up; the other seems rooted in the ground; neither moves. They look like kids playing *freeze.* One man flexes a foot; the other follows suit, and slowly, gently, they begin to slide those flexed feet a few inches through the air. After the initial motionless moments, a swaying becomes remarkably important and very nearly hypnotic.

Five dancers enter from stage right, as energetic as the flexed-footed pair is contained. They bend forward from the waist, sweeping their hands to the floor with elastic, relaxed backs. Now there are two groups of kids on the playground—a duo challenging each other in a game of physical control and a quintet enjoying a romp.

The rest of the dance repeatedly plays on the contrast between holding still and letting go. . . . Always, there is as much pleasure in looking at the still performers as there is in following the activities of the others, and always, the stage patterns prove that both groups are essential to the shape of the piece. (*The Record,* March 22, 1990)

Neighbors (1991): *Cunningham's humor:*

Merce Cunningham tends to be treated seriously, with a capital *S*. He is, after all, the godfather of postmodern dance, creator of a physically rigorous technique and an intellectually intense esthetic. He is even, by this time, a Grand Old Man of modernism.

However, the choreographer can be positively Puckish when he chooses, and he is at his most charmingly mischievous in *Neighbors* . . .

The new dance sends up the conventions and pretensions of ballet. It is also, of course, an elegant formal composition in the Cunningham style, measuring out time and space as if they were elements in a recipe. The basic ingredients—what the choreographer terms the gamut of movement—are extremely neat, controlled steps. Energy is held at a constant simmer, rather than being allowed to boil over and flood the premises. . . .

The jokes—which consist of body shapes, of alignments of dancers on stage, and of steps—are blended logically into the structure of the work, which is serenely beautiful. It's a joy to watch the way the choreographer transfers energy among the dancers, holding one motionless as a fixed point against which others can move or, a moment later, keeping the ensemble still while a single performer travels through space. (*The Record*, March 15, 1991)

Cunningham's use of computers: Trackers (1991), *an interview, and* Enter (1992)

With *Trackers*, his newest work, Merce Cunningham has become the first major choreographer to create a dance with the help of a computer. . . .

It is hardly surprising that Cunningham has become intrigued by computers; he has been fascinated by technology for decades, having been among the first to make dances specifically for television and to investigate the possibilities of the video camera. At a press conference before the season began, the choreographer remarked that LifeForms, a three-dimensional human animation software program, allowed him to explore new movement possibilities, and to look at dance from a different perspective.

The software, developed at Simon Fraser University in British Columbia, allows the user to shape the actions of a figure on the screen, and to move the figure—or a group of them—on a stage-like grid.

At the press conference, Cunningham noted that the program permits one to deal only with space, not with time. For a choreographer who treats music in a traditional way, this would be a serious drawback, but Cunningham does not make his dances to suit their scores; the music and the movement occupy the same theater at the same time, but are independent of each other.

Some sections of *Trackers* were composed using LifeForms, others were choreographed traditionally, and we can only guess which episodes were made in each way. The style and technique of the work are pure Cunningham; a viewer who did not read the program note would have no reason to think a new technology was involved.

The central motif of the dance is the counterpoint of clusters of dancers against individuals; the dominant image is one of mutual support. As it opens, Cunningham stands upstage right, still and strongly weighted, while two women face one another along a diagonal downstage. The women break into light, quick steps, tracing parallel lines as they travel across the stage; Cunningham remains in place, moving more slowly and more heavily while maintaining curved body shapes that contrast with his colleagues' erect postures. . . .

Late in the dance, Cunningham pulls a portable barre onto the stage and uses it, first conventionally to hold onto as his feet dart and stab the air, then as a walker as he crosses the stage. The barre—which dancers use in class—just might be a metaphor for the choreographer's computer, another device that can help us learn. We look to our friends for support and balance, but we also can progress with the aid of technology we invent for the purposes. (*The Record*, March 22, 1991)

. . . The world has altered radically [since the choreographer first made dances in 1942], and Cunningham, who has redefined the shape of dance, generally has perceived the changes long before they became topics of daily conversation.

Ecological concern was not yet common when he began inventing pieces that served as metaphors for the interaction of individuals and their environments. Cunningham was devising dances specifically for video before every tourist carried a minicam, and [in 1991] he became the first major choreographer to use a computer program in his work.

For him, scientific discovery, technological change, sociological change, and artistic creativity are interdependent. He is constantly reading, observing, and experimenting, and what he discovers finds its way into his dances. Most individuals can mouth truisms about the ways in which television and computers are affecting society; Cunningham suggests some precise physical reactions.

Seated on a bench in a small room of his company's Manhattan studio, Cunningham speaks in his habitually quiet voice; his big hands dart like fish through long-armed, open gestures. We see things more quickly than we did when he began making dances, he remarks.

"It came to me when I began working with video—that brought with it a whole different shape and speed of things. On a small screen, you don't have to see only one thing clearly; you can have a multiplicity of things in clear focus."

The computer and the television camera have revised not only the range but the rate of human perception. "The speed with which things change now is almost astonishing—look at the collapse of the Eastern European countries, falling like a pack of cards." People can see the immediacy of events, rather than having to wait for reverberations to reach them.

"As a result," he continues, "many more people in every way of life have realized that we no longer live in separate communities; we live in a single world. We know that problems are as complicated for others as they are for us—the holes in the ozone layer affect everyone, for example. That's why politics don't work; they stick to things domestic."

That . . . may have to change. The next generation will not see things —physically or metaphorically—the way this one does. [Cunningham's] been reading about massively parallel computers (many computers linked together to work on one problem simultaneously, thus solving it faster than one computer working alone). "You and I won't understand them, but 5-year-olds will be fine . . . they're growing up in the middle of it.

"Technological developments," he remarks several times, "aren't good and they aren't bad; they occur, and they must be accepted, considered, and used to the advantage of the species. . . ."

Art originates in perception, so it is logical that expanded vision results in innovative presentation. "Movement—not just dance—has been opened out," Cunningham says. "Space probes that send back photographs give us a different sense of the universe and new ideas about momentum. The computer can change the ways in which we see movement. I'm still learning to use my program, but it's opened up a lot of possibilities for me."

Technology affects audiences as well as artists. "I think we don't have a tradition of going to the theater anymore," Cunningham says. "Even in Centralia, Washington, where I grew up, we had a vaudeville house and everybody went. Then the movies came in, and everybody went there instead. Now, everybody watches the movies at home. Theater has disappeared, and it used to be part of your life."

That doesn't, however, necessarily mean disaster for performers. "If you think about it, the experience people had of Fred Astaire, who was a wonderful dancer, came through the movies. If that is so, it might be possible for the same thing to happen on a so-called serious level with television and with videos. I think both the stage and the visual media are valuable, and that they can exist at the same time. Videos might send people to the theater for a different perspective on something they liked."

The choreographer is an extraordinarily gentle revolutionary. The belief that his dances have no *meaning*—no manifest emotional content —results partly from his refusal to impose interpretations upon his audience. He has been trying to show, he explains, "that there are ways to do your work, and to do it seriously, without trying to tell people what to feel but by letting them find their own feelings. Anybody looking at the work should do it on his or her terms, not on mine."

But his dances do have political content, he says, "because of the individualism. There's an individual freedom about the way the dancers relate to each other and to the space."

A Cunningham dance is made of carefully and beautifully crafted steps, but the sequence in which they are performed and the arrangement of the dancers onstage was, when he began his mature work, unconventional. Instead of an ensemble dancing in unison, figures come together and move apart the way pedestrians maneuver along a crowded street. Each pursues his individual tasks while sharing space with the others. (*The Record*, March 15, 1992)

Merce Cunningham . . . celebrates the 40th anniversary of founding his company . . . with a dance named for the *Enter* key on a computer keyboard.

The choreographer worked out nearly one-third of the movement phrases for the hour-long dance using LifeForms, a computer program that allows the user to change the shape and position of human figures and to move them through space. . . .

Enter bears some resemblance to a computer game, not only because of the way figures dart through space but because of its interior logic. A computer operates through the rapid alternation of two switch positions: on and off. *Enter* operates by alternating stillness and motion. The dance also deals with the tension between crowded space and emptiness.

To these two concepts—one temporal, the other spatial—Cunningham added the use of chance operations to determine certain structural elements of the piece, including the duration of the various sections. The result is a strikingly beautiful dance.

Enter begins with the performers grouped tightly at the rear of the stage. One looks up; another has her arm raised; still others stand with arms outstretched. Marsha Skinner's backdrop, done in rich shades of red, brick, and brown, suggests the skyline of a city.

One of the dancers moves within the cluster, and then another shifts weight, but individual actions are masked by the closeness of the grouping. Then individuals escape from the crowd, spreading rapidly into space, like pool balls on the break.

Interestingly, as the pattern of movement expands, Cunningham deliberately leaves an open space center stage, precisely where a more conventional choreographer would concentrate the action. The dancers mark out an area by leaving it empty rather than by occupying it.

Emptiness occurs again and again during the dance, as does stillness. On Cunningham's own first entrance, he stands motionless, watching others dance. He walks upstage, raises one hand to the other, and stands statue-still again as first one woman and then another performs solos.

Since the stage has recently been full of motion, we're aware of the unoccupied space as well as of Cunningham's active inactivity. He is observing, nothing more, but observation is focused behavior, not passivity. The choreographer's still body becomes the focus of attention.

Cunningham always has avoided ensemble dancing, but *Enter* contains a few startling, energetic passages of synchronized motion, and even more striking ones of group stillness. . . .

The piece ends as it began, with a full complement of performers, but now the dancers are spread through the space, executing neat, energetic steps as the curtain falls. Emptiness is filled; activity is (temporarily) triumphant over stillness, and a great tension is resolved. (*The Record*, March 12, 1993)

On an Event (1994)—*new insights:*

An Event is an event is an event, as Gertrude Stein might have written had she lived long enough to see Merce Cunningham's choreography.

Stein's prose relied on the sound and rhythm of words rather than on their conventional meanings, and the writer reinvented grammar and syntax in an attempt to produce what she called *moments of consciousness.*

Cunningham has reinvented the structure of dance, and *moments of consciousness* is a pretty fair description of the impact his choreography produces. One of his more startling and effective reinventions is the Event: a seamless 90-minute dance made up of segments of works from his repertory, all linked together with such magnificent aesthetic logic that it's difficult to realize that the result actually is what Cunningham himself calls a *collage.*

    . . . One defining mark of this unusual form is that each Event is designed specifically for the space in which it will be danced, and the intimacy of the Joyce [Theater in New York City] allows us to experience aspects of Cunningham's choreography that don't show up nearly as well in larger venues.

The small theater, with its exposed, open stage, makes us intensely aware of individual steps; of the cool, chiseled shapes of those superlative dancers' bodies; of the astonishing articulation of their feet; of the interaction between the performers; and of the choreographer's decidedly teasing sense of humor.

When dancers advance across the stage with smooth, sweeping steps, we hear their feet brushing against the floor. In a larger theater, that whisper of feet would be lost; at the Joyce it becomes an integral part of the step, augmenting the sensation of carefully controlled strength. . . .

. . . [Some] aspects of the first Event . . . are invariably present in a Cunningham dance. There's the play of rhythm against rhythm; the intense concentration of the dancers, for whom nothing seems to exist but the moment in which they are moving, and the change of mood as one section of the work succeeds another.

Robert Rauschenberg, who appeared on stage in the very first Event . . . designed the decor for the current series and, with the assistance of Suzanne Gallo, also has furnished the costumes. . . .

It's a pretty safe bet that Rauschenberg also contributed the bright green garden hose that hung in a tight coil over a dancer's forearm during one segment of Tuesday's performance. The green looked ripely beautiful against the purple bodysuit, and if you've never thought of a garden hose as beautiful, maybe it's time to look again.

Cunningham and Rauschenberg are specialists in the art of surprise. Their business is to make us take a second look at things we've seen but never really noticed: Garden hose, bouncing feet, the way we shift our weight. Seeing afresh really is an Event. (*The Record*, September 15, 1994)

A Final Comment

. . . Cunningham continues to make steps and shapes, and phrases of movement that are positively astounding in their beauty. His combination of a balletic clarity in the feet and legs with a supple spine and a quick-turning neck allows him to develop movement of surpassing elegance.

Yet Cunningham long ago lost his power to shock (although the electronic sound-scores for many of his dances have not lost their power to irritate) and the cool formalism of his recent work doesn't startle the senses the way some of his early pieces did. (*The Record*, March 10, 1995)

VIII

NIKOLAIS, AILEY, TAYLOR

THREE SPECIALISTS

ALWIN NIKOLAIS IS the P. T. Barnum, the Tom Swift, *The Yellow Submarine* of dance. His company travels with thirty-five spotlights, eighteen light dimmers on three boards, twelve projectors, and a sound system.

His intentions are in some ways similar to those of Merce Cunningham, but his convention is utterly different. Cunningham separates dance, music, and decor and rarely discusses a work in progress with the composer or designer. Nikolais is a one-man band. Since 1958 he has not made a work for which he did not also compose the score and create the properties, costumes, and decor. When he makes a new dance he begins with elaborate preparations: He writes pages of notes, he plans scenic effects and prepares slides to be projected onto the stage, he chooses the materials to be used in the properties and costumes. When he finally begins to work with the dancers, he relates their movements to the decor and lighting, and makes certain they become aware of the environment in which they will perform. He designs his own light plots, of course, and has even been known to modify the lighting of the auditorium. The hangings and curtains, the boxes and levels of his stage define space, either by moving or by their position.

Nikolais presents a theater of color and shape, both of which change constantly. His dancers often are dressed in costumes that either alter or blur the lines of their bodies. Projected patterns, striking those costumes, further erase the outlines that separate people from the space they inhabit. A dancer may change color as he steps from one area of the stage to another, or he may execute a series of actions while a projector throws moving images on his stretching body. Movement plays upon movement, color alters color, shape defines and undefines shape. Nikolais' stage world is as changeable as a contemporary urban landscape; it reminds you of the famous joke about the New Yorker who advised a visitor, "Get a good look at that building you like so much—it may not be there to-morrow." Americans, particularly urban Americans, must constantly adjust to alterations in their environment, and the changes, although directed by people, frequently are effected by machinery, as are the mutations in a Nikolais dance.

The choreographer maintains that none of his dances is about machinery, but it is the mechanical aspect of his art that most spectators remember. After all, everyone has seen dancers moving; before Nikolais began his work, few people had seen them breaking out in a rash of purple polka dots. Nikolais is intent on creating an environment and observing its effects on people. The stretchable bags of *Masks, Props and Mobiles* are fascinating to watch as they change shape, but even more intriguing when you watch the bag as an extension of the dancer inside it, or consider the dancer as a creature being defined by the bag.

Nikolais, like Cunningham, is concerned with an Einsteinian, rather than a Freudian, universe. During his army service in World War II he decided that there was more to life than sex. "I thought the constant preparation on the part of both the male and the female—dressing, Madison Avenue, the whole thing—merely for sexual exploitation was too meager a value to place on living; that man wanted other things too; that to go around always looking in heat (one of my favorite expressions) was not necessarily the thing we should be devoted to."

If there is more to life than sex, there must also be more to dancing, and "since sexuality is an invitation to self, when you move away from that as your impetus for life, you have to go into environment—the relation of man to nature, the relation of man to things other than fellow man, the need to make peace with things other than fellow man." It was this premise that led Nikolais to abandon what he calls the "psycho-drama" that dominated modern dance from the demise of Denishawn until World War II, and to attempt to portray "man in a whole world, not man in a little personal world." This means that he must create a world, and he sees no reason to use the tools of the nineteenth-century theater when he has a toybox filled with contemporary apparatus at his command. "In the old days, it would take forty stagehands to change the environment; I can push a button and do it in one second." Some of his dances have two hundred cues within a half hour.

Martha Graham reflected, during the first twenty years of her career as choreographer, that the primary concerns of her time were Freudian psychology, the Depression, and the development of totalitarian governments hungry for conquest. Graham, therefore, worked in terms of psychological investigation, of a need for heroes and of national pride. Contemporary thought is more concerned with social psychology and with technology; Nikolais attempts to fuse the two.

Nikolais finds that the young dancers of his company do not concern themselves with the elaborate courtship rituals that were required when he was a young man in Connecticut, and that they are not ashamed of their bodies and their sexuality. As a result, they are freer to involve themselves with other matters than their immediate ancestors were and his choreography seeks to trace human development back to a "prepsychological state," a condition of atavism in which the relationships between people, and between people and the world, change constantly. "I had to represent that on stage by devices that would create what seems to be an environment, and simply create that as a metaphoric situation in which the dancers may then, through me, make a poetic statement and a piece of theater. The dancers move through light as one runs underneath a tree with spots of sunlight on it."

Interestingly, the choreographer's environments are created, owned, and operated by an omnipotent god. Nikolais has not danced since 1953, the year he first ventured into his new style of theater, but he is even more involved in a performance than many choreographers who dance in their own works. Nikolais, a large, genial-looking man with white hair, sits in the audience behind a control panel, and directs the joys and catastrophes taking place on stage. Even if the audience does not notice him, it cannot help realizing that the cohesive quality of the dance must have been created by one overseeing intelligence. Nikolais' environments often impose limiting circumstances on the dancers, and part of the interest lies in seeing how they will deal with the problem. The elastic costumes of *Masks, Props and Mobiles* are an obvious circumstance. In other works, the rules of the game are less immediately restricting; the dancers must simply flow in and out of a world that never stays still.

Somniloquy (1967) begins with a slide projection that resembles the opening of a cave thrown onto a scrim (a gauze curtain). Dancers appear behind the scrim, lighting their faces with flashlights they hold in their hands. Later, they turn the lights onto the gauze, spreading patterns on it. Colored slides change and change again making the dancers swim through red, silver, blue, green, purple, while the electronic score gains in intensity and pushes them to greater efforts. The projection for the final scene is a collection of white dots. The dancers move through the snowstorm, then stop abruptly as the projection goes out of focus. They move, and the scene focuses again. Several times the performers shift positions in a blur and snap back as the scene becomes clear. Finally, they disappear behind the scrim, leaving the stylized storm in possession of the stage.

Nikolais changes his dancers into flowers, into animals, into machines, and back again into people. His images can be threatening one moment and hilarious the next. There is no sense of stillness in his work; the dancers are either acting or being acted upon, and often both happen at once. Nikolais has been accused of making his dancers less than human, and frequently they do seem to be little more than moving screens on which slides may be projected. When he first began to develop his style, critics found it difficult to accept his pieces as dances, because they did not seem to be primarily concerned with dancing. Nikolais trains his dancers in what he calls a classical style of movement, derived from the methods of Hanya Holm, and insists that the performers must be strong enough to project themselves through the environment he makes for them. At times they fail, but we are all trying to survive in an environment that threatens to overpower us, one that changes shape and texture and will not wait for us to catch up with it.

The company has been blessed with several fine dancers, most notably Murray Louis and Phyllis Lamhut, who have left Nikolais for their own companies. However, while watching a Nikolais dance, one thinks less of individuals than of a performing organism. The effect of a Nikolais work is achieved through cohesion and change. Furthermore, no matter who is on stage, the audience is more aware of the choreographer than of any individual dancer. Although many of Nikolais' ideas have been adopted in dance and in drama, his work continues to be unique because his vision is so intense and personal.

"Tower" from Vaudeville of the Elements *(1965) by Alwin Nikolais. The dancers rely for support on their environment, which in turn would be useless without them.*

PHOTOGRAPH BY SUSAN SCHIFF-FALUDI.

He was born in 1910 in Southington, Connecticut. His mother believed that everyone should learn music, so Nikolais, like children the country over, received piano lessons. Unlike many other children the country over, he enjoyed them. His mother also managed to give him his first taste of theater; on her weekly shopping trips to New Haven she left her two sons off at the local vaudeville house. She stopped when she discovered that vaudeville had been succeeded by burlesque.

In New England, Nikolais recalls, dancing was sinful. "You didn't even think of studying that, but in a small town one never knew what kind of art one could get involved in." He took lessons from a painter who came to town, he worked with the local little theater, he took organ lessons at $4 each. He became interested in the technical aspects of each art; the Southington town hall, where the theater group performed, had a stage, but no effects, and Nikolais learned stagecraft by improvising.

When he was sixteen, he was enough of a musician to get a job accompanying silent films in the Westport Movie House, where he spent two years fitting sound to movement. He progressed to playing the piano for dance classes, and remembers coming to New York with a dancer who wanted to take class at Jack Cole's studio. At that time Ruth St. Denis was in her period of decline and Cole, who began his career as a dancer and choreographer by studying with Miss Ruth, had arranged for her to live and work in his studio. Cole asked Nikolais if he wanted to take class along with his friend, and the young man was on the studio floor, moving with the others, when he became aware of a figure in white gliding up behind him. "No, boy," said Ruth St. Denis to Alwin Nikolais, "the other foot."

In 1933, when he was twenty-three, Nikolais saw a performance given by Mary Wigman, who was on tour in this country. He was impressed with the dancing, but even more interested in the unusual percussion instruments on which the dancers accompanied themselves. He looked up Truda Kaschman, a teacher of the Wigman School in Hartford, and asked if she would teach him to play those instruments. She told him that he could only learn to play if he would learn to dance, which, he says, is what he'd always wanted to do anyway. While studying with Kaschman in 1936 he became the director of the Hartford Marionette Theater. He made his first appearance as a dancer ". . . together with two other boys, dressed in silver, representing Connecticut Industry, arising from fifty undulating girls, dressed in blue, as the Connecticut River."

He did his first choreographic work in 1936, making dances for plays produced by the Federal Theater Project in Hartford. He was committed to dance by then, and studied at Bennington during the summers of 1937, 1938 and 1939. Nikolais was thrilled by the activity and creativity of the Bennington years, and by the opportunity to watch and work with the major creators of a new art form. Among his teachers were Francesca Boaz, who taught percussion accompaniment for dance, and Hanya Holm, who advanced the Wigman style in America. (Holm's first major work, *Trend,* had received its première at Bennington in 1937.) In 1939, Nikolais made his first pure dance work, "Eight Column Line" for groups and soloist to the music of Ernst Krenek. The dance, which he co-choreographed with his teacher Truda Kaschman, was an evening-long piece which received a front-page review from the Hartford *Courant.*

His career as teacher, dancer, and choreographer was interrupted by the war, and his anti-Freudian revelation. After his discharge he returned to work, and in 1947 went to Colorado to continue his studies with Hanya Holm and to become her assistant. Her technique had become the foundation for his own way of teaching. Wigman's technique was metaphysical, while Graham's was psychological; the German dancer's method was less personal. "In the early days, if you danced with Martha, you couldn't dance, say, with Hanya. Humphrey-Weidman was freer, but Hanya's technique was specifically a dance technique for all dancers. With Hanya there was a science of esthetics and motion on which I could build. It was a technique which analyzed the psychical-physical interplay of the human being—the two constantly satisfied one another."

Most of his work had been done in Hartford, but in 1948 Nikolais came to New York to become the head of the dance department of the Henry Street Playhouse. (The Henry Street Playhouse was built in 1915, and Isadora Duncan, Sarah Bernhardt, and Eleonora Duse appeared there. It is not only a celebrated cultural landmark, but a celebrated cause of confusion, since the Henry Street Playhouse is not on Henry Street at all, but around the corner on Grand Street.) Nikolais inherited a theater in need of rebuilding, and a program in need of revitalization. He developed a children's theater, for which he made dance plays such as *Lobster Quadrille* (1948), *Sokar and the Crocodile* (1951), and *Merry-Go-Elsewhere* (1952). These pieces not only gave pleasure to children, but allowed a young dance company to gain experience in performance. And it is axiomatic in the theater that children are the world's toughest audience, because they always know when you're faking. As Nikolais built his company and his theater, he also was working toward a new form of dance. *Masks, Props and Mobiles* was produced at Henry Street in 1953, the same year that Merce Cunningham formed his company. During ensuing years, Henry Street and Nikolais became important. In the early days, the critics thought his work was pretty, but they were not at all sure it was dance. Nikolais responded by referring to his productions in other terms such as "theater pieces," being more interested in producing theater than in worrying about labels.

As he became more concerned with studies of environment, he banished role-playing from his dances, as Cunningham had done. "I eliminated St. Joan," he says, explaining the difference between his works and Graham's with a reference to *Seraphic Dialogue.* Dancers in a Nikolais work are not involved in traditional theatrical characterization. They are persons in an environment, and they are dancers, but they are not specific individuals with carefully defined histories or relationships. As a general rule, they are not even differentiated by variations in costume. Nikolais, like Cunningham, does not believe a dancer must assume a character in order to present the matter of dance, which is movement. Furthermore, the environment, the rules of the game, is what links the incidents in most Nikolais dances; there is no immediate cause-and-effect relationship between the action of one performer and the movement of another.

It was also in 1953 that Nikolais first put his name to a musical score. He developed from the use of percussion into making *musique concrete,* investigating sound as he did light and movement. He began to use tape recorders, on which he caught the sounds of parts of old automobiles and assorted bits and pieces he found in junkyards. He learned to do tricks with tape, to speed sounds and slow them, to edit tape and put sounds in the sequence he wanted. Then he saw the first Moog synthesizer, used one at Columbia University with the aid of a resident

Echo *(1969). Dancers change as they move through projections, which change as they fall on the dancers. A clear example of Nikolais' kaleidoscopic effects.*

PHOTOGRAPH BY SUSAN SCHIFF-FALUDI.

engineer and finally, with the funds from a Guggenheim fellowship, bought one.

Nikolais does not make a dance to music any more than Cunningham does, but the sounds he employs do more than share theater space with the movement. A Nikolais score accents that dance and adds a dimension to the environment; it is designed to suit the mood of the dance, to add another circumstance egging on the movers. His scores have been played, separately from their dances, in concerts of contemporary music. He has studied harmony and counterpoint, and his musical training is evident in the flow of movement he makes. He has written that hearing requires a more active process of interpretation than seeing. "Sound has the potential, therefore, of plunging the hearer into a much freer associative level than sight." Nikolais told a reporter for *Cue* magazine in 1909 that electronic music was proper for his kind of dancing because it comes "on its own terms," with recalling to the listener the romantic associations of, say, violin playing, and that traditional scores "make everyone think about the music rather than what the dance was about." Since "dance is the art of motion, not of emotion," a traditional, emotional score would detract from the presentation of the sculptural form of movement for which Nikolais is most celebrated.

He can, on occasion, be quite literal, as in *Tower,* first presented at the Tyrone Guthrie Theater in Minneapolis as one section of *Vaudeville of the Elements* in 1965. (Nikolais is fond of making evening-long works, then extracting sections of them for presentation in concert.) *Tower* begins as dancers walk jauntily onto the stage, each carrying a section of aluminum railing and each talking incessantly. As the choreographer himself says, "They never shut up." They begin piecing together their sections of fence into structures, but there is never quite enough room for all of them to fit and someone keeps getting pushed off the end. Still jabbering, they construct a tower (obviously, a Tower

At first, it seems as if the setting is defining the dancers, but the positions of hands and feet show that the dancers are defining the shape of the setting, too. Murray Louis is at left in this performance of Tensile Involvement.

PHOTOGRAPH BY DAVID BERLIN.

of Babel) which they decorate with warlike banners. Dancers run onto the stage with their emblems, competing with one another to place them in the most enviable position on the structure. The job of construction turns into a competition, almost a battle, exactly as in a children's game. In fact, you can see the entire episode on any playground in the country. The constant chatter grows louder, the tower grows more and more like a structure of war, and the entire edifice finally collapses under the impact of a most satisfactory explosion.

Tent (1968) is more closely related to the body of the choreographer's work, because it uses projections and less literal forms of movement, but again shows the use of a central property to define an idea. The dancers carry their huge tent on stage, hang it and begin to explore it. The structure first defines their world, then limits it. Once it has been erected, the dancers never venture far outside it; they spend their time shifting it into new shapes, crawling beneath it, looking out from inside it. They end up crushed under it, grovelling. In *Tent,* the dancers' movements are flowing; in *Tower,* they are quick, abrupt, and literal. The environment in a Nikolais piece determines the quality of movement.

In 1959, Nikolais was asked to make a piece for a television program, "The Steve Allen Variety Show," and since then he has devised a number of pieces specifically for television. He does not merely set movements to be recorded by the camera, but uses the special possibilities the medium offers. In *Limbo* (1968), made for CBS–TV, the dancers vanish into an invisible hole in the center of the screen.

Nikolais now operates his company as part of The Chimera Foundation for the Dance (the other important component of the compound beast is Murray Louis' company) and spends much of his time on tour. He performs throughout Europe (Paris adores him) and in South America and Asia. The central theme of his work continues to be the understanding of decentralization. Human beings have gradually learned that the earth is not the center of the solar system, that the solar system is not the center of the universe, and the human beings are not even the center of the earth, but only a component of its life. The protagonist of a Nikolais work is not an individual dancer, but a stage full of dancers limited and extended by their costumes and properties and moving along unexpected paths through a landscape that shifts as rapidly as the garden in *Through the Looking-Glass.*

Nikolais' brilliance is also his limitation. The totality of his work often is obscured by the components that make it up, and while he is concerned with environment, the audience cannot escape a continuing awareness of the tools that create the environment. He sometimes seems to be dominated by his materials, rather than to dominate them. He has, however, understood the major concerns of his time and found a way to portray them. His dancers move within a man-made world that is sometimes beautiful and sometimes terrifying. They frequently seem to be transmuted by that world, to be badly mauled and defeated by it, to be so fully dominated by it that normal emotion is banished from their lives. Yet Nikolais' wit somehow makes the universe endurable, and gives the audience an optimistic belief that they, too, will survive.

* * *

Kaleidoscope (1956): *Nikolais' work retains its interest:*

In a way, the most fascinating piece on the bill [of a joint program presented by Nikolais Dance Theatre and the Murray Louis Dance Company] was the oldest, a suite from *Kaleidoscope*, which Nikolais choreographed in 1956. There are three sections to the work, "Discs," "Pole," and "Clothes." Each title is a precise description of the dance it announces. In the first segment, each performer has a disc attached to one foot and uses it to announce his presence to the stage floor and to the audience. In the second episode, two dancers are linked by a long pole that they carry between them, and in the third, Nikolais muses on the adage that *clothes make the man*—both by the man's own standards and by those of his observers.

When *Kaleidoscope* first was shown—and for years thereafter—the theatrical techniques were so unusual that they drew attention to themselves. Now that Nikolais' ideas seem charming rather than shocking, the metaphors that the techniques were designed to serve are far more obvious.

Human beings function within an environment comprising nature, artifacts, and other human beings. We are not quite as independent as we would like to think, and because we cannot free ourselves from our surroundings, we had better learn to cooperate with them, and with one another. The thought seems mundane when presented in words, but it is striking when translated into theatrical movement. (*The Record*, December 19, 1987)

Blank on Blank (1987): *an exception to the rule:*

Every so often, a really imaginative artist can fool you: That's what makes him an imaginative artist.

Those familiar with the work of Alwin Nikolais expect each new piece to be a combination of dance and light show—a theatrical event that makes its point partly by camouflaging the dancers within their environment.

Blank on Blank, the Nikolais work given its world premiere last night [December 23, 1987] . . . is very different from the choreographer's mixed-media pieces. It makes most of its effects through movement alone.

The title, though, is a pun, and a bilingual one at that. Blank is almost the same as *Blanc*—the French word for *white*, which is the color of all the costumes in the piece. There is a painter's outfit, a nurse's uniform, a chic suit, and a batch of other variations on the theme.

Although some of the commentary on society is dark in the extreme, *Blank on Blank* might be called a white comedy.

To carry the pun a bit further, Nikolais has dressed his company in blank facial expressions, at least at the start. The chief movement theme of the dance also is involved in the title, because the performers often are leaning on one another or lying on the floor.

Support, or a lack of it, is a major motif. There is a striking moment early on when a performer swings like a pendulum, hanging from her partner's neck. Later, after a good deal of leaning, dancers knock their partners away, as if tired of getting and giving support.

Nikolais keeps his company on the floor during many striking moments—sometimes they curl up in small groups, sometimes they huddle together in large ones.

These compositions, which show people sprawling together as if for emotional comfort or for warmth, sometimes suggest the conditions of the homeless one sees on the streets of New York. This suggestion is amplified by the background projection: a pair of facing photographs of the famous statue of George Washington in the Wall Street area of the city.

The aggression, the loneliness, and the hardheartedness suggested by many of the images, however, are lighted by Nikolais' wit. The poses adopted by the dancers as they lean and press on one another are peculiar and uncomfortable-looking enough to be funny in the way that silent-screen comedy was funny.

One movement used several times toward the end of the dance— introduced by one performer, and taken up by others—is a loping, forward-leaning walk similar to the one made famous by Groucho Marx. This idea is reinforced by the start-and-stop action of the dance: At times, we seem to be looking at a series of still photographs extracted from a silent film.

In the final moment of *Blank on Blank*, the company lines up at the front of the stage, confronting the audience with expressions and actions of defiant aggression: One dancer picks at his nose, for example, while another cleans his nails. These actions are sufficiently incongruous—especially when performed in those neat white costumes—to get a laugh. (*The Record*, December 24, 1987)

Nikolais discusses some underlying assumptions:

Blank on Blank surprised first-night critics by its determined avoidance of special effects. . . . "It's difficult to put a whole multimedia program on," Nikolais explains, "and besides, there was something that I wanted to do. My multimedia works are colorful, but *Blank on Blank* is a portrait of do-nothing people. That's why I made it the way I did."

. . . The leading performer in a Nikolais dance is never a single dancer but a company, whose actions are amplified and altered by lights, slides, properties, and costumes. It is because he presented the stage as an environment, the choreographer says, that his company, "never created stars, as ballet does. Each dancer was supposed to be a star when he did a solo, and then to become part of the ensemble again. Think of it as a garden—all species live wonderfully together, but each has a strong identity. In dance, you don't get a contribution of quality from any individual unless he contributes to the whole."

There is a distinction, Nik says, between *movement* and *motion*, and dance consists of the latter. Movement, he says, is just that—an action. "Motion is the esthetics that rest within movement. Movement for most dancers is just a decoration of self, but motion is the medium of dance, and performers must have the intelligence to understand what they are doing and why and how they are moving. When you are a dancer, you work with such a delicate thing—your presence in space and in time, and the manipulation of space as part of an emotional context. That's far more than *movement*."

. . . "As a company director," he says, "you have a sense of responsibility to those kids who devote themselves to you. The kids in the school need a vision of where they are going." He displays tremendous concern and respect for the abilities of his students. "I don't see how anyone can teach," he remarks gently—Nik says everything gently and with conviction—"without believing that everyone in front of him is a genius. As a teacher, your job is to brush the crud away, and let the genius shine through. You can't teach without being concerned with the health and well-being of the people who are trying to learn."

He is also concerned with the well-being of his audiences. "I tell my dancers," he says, "to think this way: 'You're going on stage in front of these 1,000 people who have taken an hour to get here. You will all be here for two hours, and then it will take them another hour to get home. That's 4,000 lifehours—don't you dare waste them.'!" (*The Record*, September 30, 1988)

Alwin Nikolais and Murray Louis join ranks, but keep their individual identities.:
. . . Nikolais and Louis Dance is the new amalgamation of the Nikolais Dance Theater and the Murray Louis Dance company. Nobody will be astonished to discover that the individual styles of the choreographers have not been affected by the merger: Alwin Nikolais' environmental dance-theater pieces are still magical, and Murray Louis' neatly crafted dances continue to delight us with their joyous investigations of the range of human movement.

The two men have been associated artistically since 1949, when Louis joined Nikolais' company. Seeing the first of their four joint programs, you quickly realize what they have in common: Each is, at heart, a little boy let loose in a toy store. Neither Nikolais, who is 79, nor Louis, 63, has lost his ability to play or his capacity for wonder.

In Nikolais' *Video Game*, glowing stick-figure costumes sheathe performers whose movements, by resembling those of electronically generated cartoons, make deft comments on humanity. The serpentine arms that wriggle upward at the beginning of the same choreographer's *Crucible* require a second glance before we are quite certain that they are, indeed, arms. By submerging dancers in an environment of lights, properties, and sound, Nikolais manages to make us constantly question our senses. (*The Record*, October 19, 1989)

Alwin Nikolais (1910–93): The Nik of Time: an evaluation and conclusion:
It would be easier to recognize revolutionaries, in art or in politics, if they invariably looked the part. Alwin Nikolais, who died on May 8 at the age of eighty-two after a long battle with cancer, more closely resembled the popular ideal of a genial aristocrat—tall, strongly built, white-haired, erect of carriage, precise and gentle in his speech—than the traditional image of a firebrand.

Yet this autocratic, elegant, affable Connecticut Yankee was a visionary who reinvented the presentation, and with it the content of modern dance. The trouble with revolutions is that, if they are successful, people tend to forget who started them. . . .

In the 1978 *Gallery* the world is transformed into a garishly lighted shooting gallery, in which grotesque figures tumble over dead, hit by bullets fired by unseen, fun-seeking assailants. The technology—the gun-–produces disaster, but who produced the technology and found the most destructive way to use it? It is dangerous, Nikolais implies, to worship an artifact; we tend to invest it with our own worst qualities.

Nikolais himself was a genial, witty, utterly charming man, but his artistic vision was hardly optimistic. His carefully constructed societies self-destruct with remarkable regularity, sometimes because they cannot come to terms with the environment in which they exist. "The environment" was not a handy catch-phrase when Nikolais created his major pieces, and his message, like his medium, was somewhat in advance of its time.

The most prevalent criticism of Nikolais work during his most creative period—1953 through the mid-1970s—was that the choreographer was dehumanizing dance. He seemed far more interested in his miraculous magic-lantern shows and electronic sounds than in movement per se. His pieces do not display the virtuosity of individual dancers, and movement is merely one element, and not always the most commanding one, in his works. If one thinks about it, however, it becomes obvious that the moving human being is the defining element of the choreographer's environmental dance-theater. In dance, the body moves through space: Nikolais was among the first to suggest that the space determines the movement as much as the movement affects the space. That suggestion provides the central metaphor of his work.

As formalism came more and more into favor, Nikolais attracted less and less interest. Part of the problem was that he stopped being unique: Light shows had come and gone; computer games presented their players with worlds more detailed than any stage could accommodate; and every third teenager, it seemed, owned and operated a synthesizer. A second difficulty was that spareness was in and theatricality was out. The body itself had become the focus of attention, and Nikolais, as noted, had never separated the body from its environment. The dancer interacts with inhuman forces: Movement may be restricted by elastic ropes or it may be colored (literally) by projections.

Forty years after the revolution, it's hard to realize that here was a revolution. The Joyce [Theater] season [in July, 1993] may inform a new generation of dancegoers how much of what they take for granted was invented by Alwin Nikolais. (*Dance Magazine*, July, 1993)

An Alwin Nikolais Retrospective:

Retrospective showings, long a standard form in the graphic arts, seem to be catching on in dance. This spring [1993], we had the New

York City Ballet's Balanchine Celebration. Now, the Joyce [Theater] is offering a two-week Alwin Nikolais Retrospective. . . .

The twelve works are among those reconstructed during an 18-month-long residency by Nikolais and Murray Louis Dance at Rutgers' Mason Gross School of the Arts. Without that program, many of the older pieces probably would have been lost forever.

Nikolais' special gift was the ability to produce complex and fascinating multimedia presentations. The movement he devised, while often highly imaginative and witty, was less remarkable than the way he blended it with lighting, costumes, and stage decor.

In *Noumenon*, the choreographer transformed his dancers into pieces of moving sculpture by encasing them within stretch-fabric costumes. Instead of bodies, we see rectangles and triangles, planes and angles, bumps and bulges. At the same time, we can tell that the shapes are formed by moving arms, legs, and heads, and the charm and humor of the piece develops from the contrast between what we see on the surface and what we imagine going on beneath it.

Tensile Involvement sets the dancers within a stage-filling cat's cradle of fabric streamers. The movement seems shaped and restricted by the tension between the fabric and the dancers. In one fascinating moment, performers box themselves inside rectangles and move across the stage maintaining the shape of their *containers*.

The suite of dances from *Kaleidoscope* is equally inventive. In the first piece, the performers stand in profile, with one foot raised and the other flat on the ground. As the lights brighten, we realize that the dancers' stationary feet are strapped to discs.

It's great fun to see the inventiveness with which Nikolais used the discs: Dancers slam them down on the floor resoundingly; they set both feet on them and move by jumping along; they lie on their backs and set the discs spinning with their feet. What seems, at first, like a restriction instead becomes a challenge.

Wit—as opposed to broad humor—is difficult to achieve in dance, but Nikolais had a gift for it. Although two of these pieces were made 40 years ago—*Kaleidoscope* is three years younger—they seem surprising, as funny and as charming as they must have appeared to their first audiences. (*The Record*, July 23, 1993)

Alvin Ailey brings people into the dance theater who might not be there without him. He presents energetic, exciting, enticing dancing decked out in all the hoopla of show business: Settings, sexy costumes, music of many kinds, carefully plotted lighting. He is the only important entrepreneur of modern dance who will present programs made up of a work in the balletic idiom, another in a modern style, and a third made in jazz technique. Furthermore, he consistently programs as part of his regular repertory the works of other modern choreographers.

"I think that dance should primarily be entertainment," he told Marian Horosko during a taped interview in 1965. "The audience is more likely to get the message more easily if it hears something like 'Good Morning, Blues,' or 'The House of the Rising Sun' . . . It's a visual theater and an oral theater . . . beautiful people, beautifully dressed, doing beautiful and meaningful things."

Ailey is not to be reckoned a great choreographer in the company of Graham, Humphrey, and Cunningham, although one of his works, *Revelations* (1960), is indisputably a masterpiece, and one or two others come fairly close. He has manufactured a sizable assemblage of dances, of which some are quite good, some more than competent, and some better off forgotten. (It is too easy to forget that even the greatest artists produce their fair share of embarrassments. No artist's contribution can be measured by his single greatest effort or most remarkable failure. It is the canon of work, and the contribution to the progress of the art that counts.) As Ailey and his company have become solidly established as a group that gives regular performances for a middle-class, paying public, the choreographer has been accused, with some justification, of becoming too slick, too self-conscious, and too much a salesman of dance. Yet his salesmanship is never of the "A dollar down, a dollar when I catch you" variety. He stands behind his product, and his pitch is the same one employed by Ruth St. Denis in her vaudeville days—kinesthetic excitement, theatrical trappings, sensuality, and a touch of the exotic.

St. Denis' exotica was an evocation of the Orient; Ailey's is a tribute to black America. *Revelations* is choreographed to spirituals, and it contains visual references and jokes that are certainly more meaningful to black spectators than to white, but it is never parochial or exclusionist. The "Wading in the Water" section may recall memories to those who, like the choreographer, were raised in the traditions of a black Baptist church, but the beauty of the movement conveys the emotional content of that tradition to anyone who may be watching. The liquid arms and waists of the dancers speak of flowing water, a sense of cleansing and a complex of calming emotions, whether or not the spectator has ever witnessed a lakeside baptism. Ailey's work manages to convey at least some of the experiences of black people—such as the function of the church as an instrument of human and ethnic survival—to white people. His popularity was certainly enhanced by the Civil Rights movement of the 1960s, but he was making dances about blackness and beauty before the two were officially linked by a slogan, and he continued to make them after the great passion of the movement subsided.

Revelations and *Blues Suite*, with their theatricality, their rich music, their humor, their tenderness, and even their touches of bitterness are dances that can evoke pride in black spectators without either scaring white ones out of the theater or sending them home thinking "Now aren't they cute and ethnic?" Few works in the modern dance repertory can weld an audience together as solidly as can *Revelations*, and that is not merely a sociological achievement, but a theatrical one. One of Ailey's more important virtues is that he has built a company that provides the answer to one of a dance fan's most nagging questions: "I have a friend who has never seen a dance performance; what would make a good first time?" Ailey does not frighten anyone out of the theater. Novices do not leave a performance believing that dance is too refined, too intellectual, too complicated, too boring, too old-fashioned, or too new-fangled for them. Ailey is not babbling choreographic baby-talk either. He is a showman, he works hard to sell his audience on dance, but he does not condescend to the customers. His kinesthetic vocabulary is limited; his style is simple and in some ways, old-fashioned, but he has a genius for giving pleasure. His extended tours, in this country and in others, have helped create a market for modern dance; a six-week tour of the Soviet Union in 1970 ended with the company receiving a twenty-three-minute ovation in Leningrad—and that is a city that takes its dancing seriously!

Ailey intends his company to present new works, to revive and preserve dances made by modern choreographers, and to be a repository of the black tradition in American dance and music. To achieve the third goal, he presents dances made by black choreographers who are his predecessors or his contemporaries as well as his own creations. Donald McKayle's *Rainbow 'Round My Shoulder*, Talley Beatty's *Road of*

The corps massed for the first section of Alvin Ailey's Revelations. *The dancers' hands will open down and out in short, strong movements.* PHOTOGRAPH BY SUSAN COOK.

the Phoebe Snow, and sections of *Come and Get the Beauty of it Hot*, Katherine Dunham's *Choros*, Pearl Primus' *Fanga*, and other works by black dance-makers have been shown in the Ailey repertory, giving audiences some idea of the diverse sources and styles of black dance.

Both Dunham and Primus earned advanced degrees in anthropology, and their choreography traces the dancing of American blacks to beginnings in Africa and the West Indies. Dunham danced in and choreographed films, musicals, and revues; Primus devoted herself to a great extent to the study and preservation of original steps and sources, and both were instrumental in bringing to the American theater the driving, swaying, intensely honest dance that is as integral to the lives of its original performers as are the dances of American Indians.

Talley Beatty began his career with Dunham's dance troupe, and developed into a major choreographer in the jazz idiom, which requires different steps, different use of muscles, and a different sense of music than do modern dance styles. Jazz dancing is quick and sharp; it uses small, tense steps and long, pulling stretches; it conveys an almost unbearable sense of urgency at times and a feline sensuality at other moments. Beatty works with a company in Boston and makes dances for troupes outside the United States, but his works, which are as difficult to dance as they are charged with emotional current, are seldom produced in New York, except by Ailey. Donald McKayle studied with Graham, Cunningham, and Karel Shook. He has danced and choreographed for his own company and for Broadway shows and, like Ailey, brings together modern technique, theatrical presentation, and black American themes.

More black choreographers are working now, making dances of African, West Indian, and American subjects, using music from the vast territory of the black heritage and, equally important, doing so without catering to stereotype. It was not too long ago that black dancers were expected to restrict themselves to jazz, to tap, or to ethnic styles. Arthur Mitchell, a great alumnus of the New York City Ballet, formed a company to prove that black dancers could do ballet, and to give them a stage on which to do it. Alvin Ailey, in modern dance, has given black dancers the chance to do works in a variety of styles and, at the same time, has demonstrated that dance drawn from the experience of black Americans can mean a great deal to white audiences, and can be performed by white dancers.

His company contained only black dancers for the first six years of its existence, but the great gospel finale of *Revelations* is now performed by an ensemble of Orientals, African-Americans, and Caucasians. If black dancers have been freed, at least to some extent, from the cage of tap dancing, show dancing, all-black revue dancing and "Boy, you-guys-sure-got-a-natural-sense-of-rhythm" dancing, a good deal of the credit must go to Ailey. He has been called in to make dances by ballet companies, he has built and maintained a company of his own, and he has brought to the stage the works of other choreographers who might otherwise have been limited to a far smaller audience.

His presentation of Primus' *Fanga* at New York's City Center in 1973 may have been, for many members of the audience, their first exposure to African dance. The piece is a theatrical version of a traditional dance of welcome, and it is glorious in its virtuosity. African dance of this style requires a shimmering flow of waist and hips that makes the dancer seem almost boneless, a technique that is not part of the tradition of Western theatrical dancing. Undoubtedly, a fine West African dancer would be equally impressed at the sight of an American ballerina grasping an ankle with her hand, raising her foot to the level of her ear and hopping across the stage on the toes of her other foot. African dancers do not use that particular trick, any more than American dancers use the perpetually flowing waist and hips. However, the African dancer might decide to learn the trick and incorporate it into his style, while American dancers can enrich their techniques by observing the methods used elsewhere. Ailey's own dances do not employ a wide range of steps, but he brings to his stage a great number of styles and shows his audiences the immense possibilities of the human body.

He also regards his company as a museum of modern dance. In 1972, he asked Barton Mumaw to stage Shawn's *Kinetic Molpai,* and his repertory has included works by John Butler, José Limón, Anna Sokolow, Paul Sanasardo, and Lucas Hoving. Ailey's company is attempting to be to modern dance what American Ballet Theater and the City Center Joffrey Ballet are to their styles—a showplace for the choreographers, the styles, and the concepts of movement that have come together to augment an art. Ailey demonstrated his sense of history, and his appreciation of the theatrical element in modern dance, by dedicating a New York season to Charles Weidman in 1975. (It was the last tribute Weidman received; he died shortly afterward.) Ailey is not concerned with exploring new techniques or methods of presentation, as Cunningham and Nikolais are. Instead, he is obsessed with history and with theatrical presentation.

Ailey was born in Rogers, Texas, in 1931. When he was eleven, his family moved to Los Angeles where, seven years later, Ailey took his first dance classes with Lester Horton. He enrolled in UCLA, majoring in Romance Languages, intending to teach, but the offer of a scholarship from Horton pulled him back to dance. Horton, born in 1906, developed and taught a style of movement and choreography which uses a long, stretched-out body line, diagonal tensions, and long balances, which make the torso the center of everything that happens in the body. He had no qualms about taking his company to perform in a nightclub, if that was the way to make people look at dance, and some of Ailey's showmanship and desire to reach a wide audience seems to be a heritage from his teacher. Horton's teaching gave the country a number of fine dancers and established a definite style. The male solo "I Want to Be Ready" from *Revelations*, in which the dancer raises and lowers his torso and legs in slow, yearning reaches, resting only his hips on the floor, was developed by Ailey from a Horton floor exercise.

Ailey continued Horton's company for a short while after its founder's death in 1953, then came East in 1958 to dance on Broadway in *House of Flowers* with his partner from the Horton group, Carmen de Lavallade. (De Lavallade's career since then has included a season as first dancer with the Metropolitan Opera Ballet, the position of guest artist during American Ballet Theater's Twenty-fifth Anniversary season at the New York State Theater, and a distinguished assortment of roles in modern dance.) While in New York, Ailey studied at Martha Graham's school, took classes in modern dance with Hanya Holm and Charles Weidman, in ballet with Karel Shook, and in composition with Doris Humphrey. He appeared as dancer and actor, on Broadway and off, while forming his company and building it. He gave his first New York concert in 1957, and formed a company the following year. The American Dance Theater gave its first performance at the Ninety-second Street Y in March, 1958, presenting Ailey's *Blues Suite.*

The work is still in the company's repertory. It is made to the music of Southern black blues, which are sung as well as played. The movements

---

The floor technique of Ailey's teacher, Lester Horton, and the choreographer's own trademark, the arabesque, combine in the "Fix Me, Jesus" duet from Revelations.

PHOTOGRAPH BY SUSAN COOK.

are large, clear and unambiguous in their physical, emotional and musical meanings. The dance is bawdy, funny, and immensely appealing. "The House of the Rising Sun" sequence conveys a feeling of tired despair through the use of sharp contractions, short *jetés* that talk of imprisonment and the impossibility of escape, and clawing reaches at the air above the dancers' heads.

During the years following the company's debut, it made one or two appearances in or around New York each season and a few in other parts of the country. It enjoyed triumphant tours throughout the world, came home, and nearly disbanded for lack of funds. The State Department sent the troupe to the Far East in 1962, to Senegal in 1966, to nine African nations in 1967, and back to Africa and then to the Soviet Union, in 1970. (Ailey stopped dancing in 1965, believing that a dancing choreographer is overly tempted to compete with the other performers in his company. However, he continued to teach at Clark Center in New York, which was, for a time, the home of his eleven-member company.)

The tours continued, bookings in the United States began to come more easily, and in 1969 the company was invited to take up residence at the Brooklyn Academy of Music. A year later, Ailey again decided he might have to disband the company because there was not enough money to keep it going. Grants and funds became available, the company continued to grow, and in August 1972, the troupe joined New York's City Center of Music and Drama, of which the New York City Ballet and the City Center Joffrey Ballet also are components. In the same year Ailey choreographed Leonard Bernstein's *Mass*, and made the final segments of *The River*, a work to a score by Duke Ellington he had started the previous year, for American Ballet Theater.

Ailey was now part of the dance establishment. He founded a school, he gave regular seasons in New York, he took his company on tour; he was able to devote more effort to his goals of making his company a museum of modern dance and a center for black dance. His own choreographic style solidified into an energetic, muscular way of dancing that

---

Judith Jamison stands tall and proud in Cry, *Ailey's tribute to "All black women everywhere—especially our mothers."*

PHOTOGRAPH BY ABDUL-RAHMAN.

rejoiced in strength and exuberance, both of which are sometimes overemphasized. He is fond of arabesques and of a long, reaching line and fluttering movements of the hands and arms. He works well with masses of dancers, neatly spaced and moving in unison, and with diagonal lines. Two pieces choreographed in 1971, *Cry* and *Choral Dances*, show both the range and the limitations of his work.

Cry is a solo, made for the magnificent Judith Jamison and dedicated "for all black women everywhere—especially our mothers." Three recordings are used as the music: Alice Coltrane's "Something About John Coltrane," Laura Nyro's "Been on a Train," and The Voices of East Harlem's "Right on, Be Free"—jazz, contemporary blues, and soul music respectively. The dancer is driven from pride to degradation, and pulls herself back again. She unwinds the headcloth she wears as part of a proud costume and uses it as a rag with which to scrub floors. Her hands reach high and flutter down like birds; she contracts in anguish, swings her torso wildly from the waist, stretches in arabesque. She sinks to the ground, rises, writhes, bends double, pulls erect, and finally moves toward the wings in short, rhythmic, ecstatic steps as the curtain falls.

The dance is a virtuoso piece because it uses jazz movement, steps derived from African dance, Graham technique, Horton technique, and almost classical arabesques. It is exhausting to perform. Despite the number of sources, the actual vocabulary of steps used is not particularly large, and the phrasing not unusually conceived. The work succeeds because it is a showpiece for a brilliant dancer, because it suits its music, and because it is intensely, richly emotional.

Choral Dances is made to Benjamin Britten's "Choral Dances" from the opera *Gloriana*, and portrays a community celebrating a series of rituals and processions reminiscent in their solemnity of an Anglican church service. The movements often are long and stretchy; there is a lovely passage involving a long, diagonal line of dancers and a fine, clear series of groupings. Again, the vocabulary of movement is not large, but a mood is established clearly, and the music is well served.

Ailey's love for theatricality enlivens the poses, settings, and costumes of The Mooche, *a tribute to Duke Ellington and to four famous black entertainers.* PHOTOGRAPH BY SUSAN COOK.

Ailey is not a kinesthetically imaginative choreographer; he is a theatrically imaginative one. *Revelations*, *Choral Dances*, and *Cry* make their statements with steps and patterns closely related to the music and the mood it sets, and by heightening that mood through the use of costumes, lighting, and kinesthetic energy. Other Ailey works rely on narrative, on the emotional power of a specific situation or on costumes, setting, and special effects. As a rule, these works are less interesting and effective than those which are direct reflections of music by movement, which is then augmented by theatrical devices.

Ailey does not allow his enthusiasm to be diminished by the difficulty of a project he has set himself to accomplish. In 1975, he definitely determined to build a monument in movement to Duke Ellington, a plan he had considered for some time, and to present an Ellington Celebration during the summer of the nation's bicentennial year.

The choreographer began working with the composer in 1963, and got to know him better when they worked together on *The River*. Ailey was impressed by Ellington's elegance and vitality, as well as by his enormous talent. He recalls that they stayed in the same hotel in Canada while working on *The River*, and that Ellington would pound on his door at four in the morning, full of energy and calling, "Alvin, are you ready to work?"

In 1975, Ailey choreographed *The Mooche*, a celebration of four great black, female performers, to an Ellington score, and in May 1976, he offered the premiere of *Black, Brown and Beige*. *The Mooche*, which was first devised for television and then revised for the stage, makes more of its effect with theatrical devices—costumes and settings—than with choreography. The effects are fun to watch and the love which Ailey devoted to the piece is obvious, but the steps lack vitality. *Black, Brown and Beige* is somewhat more successful; it employs most of Ailey's favorite techniques—arabesques, diagonal lines and semicircles, short steps combined with large movements of the arms, backward arches of the torso, long, yearning reaches. Like much of Ailey's work, the dance lacks variety and focus, but it serves the music well.

Ailey is definitely not a member of the avant garde. In some ways, he has gone back to the simple, direct style of Denishawn. His dance celebrates athleticism, his presentations celebrate theatricality, his theater celebrates excitement. He has brought black audiences into the theater and shown white audiences something of the tradition of black dance. He has made his stage a place where various styles of dance can be presented in proximity to one another, and he has brought about a fusion of balletic, jazz, and modern techniques. His faults and his virtues are those of American show business. He can slip into banality, even into crassness on one evening, and rise to excitement, to a keen sense of theatrical presentation, and to emotional power the next. He has made life a little easier for black dancers and choreographers, and he has sent a lot of people away from the theater happy and willing to come back again.

* * *

Witness (1986): *Alvin Ailey continued to choreograph from life:*
 . . . *Witness*, a solo set to a traditional hymn, *My Soul is a Witness for My Lord*, deals with religious ecstasy. . . . [It]has for its setting three simple benches backed by flowing banks of candles. The dancer (Marilyn Banks) begins seated on the central bench: Her body contracts; her torso turns with wrenching power; her legs open and close again.
 As she rises and begins to cover space, employing such trademarks of Ailey's vocabulary as deeply stretched arabesques and hands that flutter like angry birds, Banks makes an emotional journey from despair to freedom and joy. . . .
 . . . *Witness* concerns itself with individual spirituality. It is, in effect, a distillation of themes that have occupied Ailey since *Revelations*. . . . (*The Record*, December 3, 1986)

Alvin Ailey: In retrospect:
 Alvin Ailey almost singlehandedly brought black dance traditions—and black dancers—into the mainstream of American art. Starting in 1958 with seven dancers, including himself, the choreographer built the Alvin Ailey American Dance Theater until it numbered more than 30 performers; by the time of his death on Friday at the age of 58, the company had played to an estimated 15 million spectators in 45 countries. . . .
 Ailey also founded the Alvin Ailey American Dance Center in Manhattan, a school that registers more than 2,500 students a year. The Alvin Ailey Repertory Ensemble, a junior company affiliated with the school, has become a well-known touring group. The senior company tours the world; the school draws students from around the globe. . . .
 . . . [Ailey's] output—approximately 80 dances as well as choreography for opera and theater pieces—included some outstanding and memorable creations. Equally important, he constantly tried to communicate his own delight in, and concern about, humanity to a wide public. He filled the stage with highly trained, magnetic dancers; with resplendent costumes; evocative settings; imaginative lighting, and with steps and gestures that commanded the eye. Energy.

Despite his deep commitment to creating a place for the work of black dancers and choreographers, Ailey's greatest devotion was to his art form, and to the emotions it could encompass.

Ailey wanted to put dance—all of it—on stage and let the audience revel in it, just as he did himself. He refused to limit his repertoire to the products of any one style or cultural heritage, even his own. He started his company as an all-black ensemble but kept it that way for only four years; eventually, rehearsals looked like a United Nations of dance.

In 1977, Ailey recalled the company's first State Department-sponsored tour in 1962: "I discovered as we traveled through Asia that there were blues in all cultures, that there were spirituals in all cultures, and that the people of any culture can express them. I got a lot of flak about it during the 1960s, but I think that an integrated company enlarges the statement I've been trying to make." An all-black company, he said, was a sign of "a kind of reverse chauvinism."

Ailey always strove to do more than was humanly possible. "You're always wanting to do more, wanting to be different, wanting to create," he told me the last time I interviewed him, almost exactly a year before his death; he was soon to be awarded the Kennedy Center Honor. (*The Record*, December 4, 1988).

During the same conversation, he spoke of the work he had done in "keeping the black tradition of dance alive. I took Talley Beatty's ballets and Donald McKayle's and George Faison's into the company repertory. I thought there needed to be a home for the works of black choreographers."

It was not only black choreographers, however, to whom Ailey felt a debt. He had strong ties to the entire tradition of American modern dance, and during his long tenure as a company director he provided stage space for works by Ted Shawn, Anna Sokolow, Joyce Trisler, John Butler, May O'Donnell, Elisa Monte, and other white dance-makers.

Although his most popular works were made to jazz or traditional music, from the outset of his career Ailey employed the scores of classical composers such as Ralph Vaughn Williams, Eric Satie, Benjamin Britten, and Samuel Barber. During last year's interview, he said: "It doesn't make any sense to label a work. . . . A choreographer can be black, and classical, and modern all within one ballet."

Ailey may ultimately be remembered more as a producer of dance than as a choreographer. Yet his finest creations—including *Blues Suite*, *Revelations*, and *Cry* . . . are undoubtedly masterpieces. His vocabulary was limited, but he could use it to stunning emotional and pictorial effect. High, driving kicks, stage-covering jetes, and repeated, almost manic spins filled his dances with excitement; deep arabesques and birdlike flutters of the hands lent them poignancy.

Some of his images—the archetypical working mother, all dressed in white, scrubbing the floor in *Cry*; the high lift framed by the ladder in *Blues Suite*, with its stretched bodies bespeaking sexual hunger; the woman riding high above her partner's back, posed as if for flight, in *The Lark Ascending*; the yearning, uplifted hands of the wedge of dancers at the start of *Revelations*—will be cherished forever.

Those images were drawn from the choreographer's own experiences as a small boy in Texas, as a student in Los Angeles, as an actor and dancer in New York. Of his early works, he once said: "The first desire" to make dances "came from the early soul experience, the fields and honky-tonks of the Brazos Valley. 'The Processional' and 'Wade in the Water' in *Revelations* came from images of my own baptism."

Ailey explored his feelings about the agonies and the triumphs of black Americans and put them on stage for the world to share. He took his admiration for such black choreographers as Katherine Dunham, who had preceded him, and his love for dance and theater of all varieties, and allowed them to guide him in making and producing dances-—despite illness, despite the financial straits his company constantly has navigated, despite his growing awareness that he never could accomplish as much as he hoped to achieve.

"Frustrations arise," he said last year "precisely because of our fantasies and desires, and fantasies and desires are what our art form is all about: making something where there was nothing."

For more than 30 years, Ailey made the dances his fantasies dictated, and gave a vast audience immeasurable quantities of joy. . . . (*The Record*, December 3, 1989)

Revelations (1960): *Always new:*

Revelations, seen for the thousandth time, or so it seems, still has power to thrill and delight us. (*The Record*, December 10, 1993)

In 1957, *Dance Observer* ran a review of a concert by Paul Taylor which consisted of an oblong of blank space: During one of the dances on the program, Taylor had stood without moving from the time the curtain rose until it fell. In 1962, the same choreographer produced *Aureole*, a dance to music by Handel that was taken, seven years later, into the repertory of the Royal Danish Ballet. Nine years after *Aureole*, Taylor presented *Big Bertha*, a devastating bit of social commentary in narrative form.

Paul Taylor is a choreographer who has learned something from everyone, yet has kept his own council. He has danced with Cunningham and with Graham, and had a solo made on him by George Balanchine. He has followed all three of those teachers without becoming the imitative disciple of any. The classicism of his wit, his phrasing, and his restraint are related to those of the ballet master; his respect for the individual dancers in his company and for the value of movement for its own sake are allied with the beliefs of Cunningham; his use of theatricality, although more sparing than Graham's, links him to her. Yet nobody would mistake a Taylor dance for the work of any other choreographer.

Taylor has made dances that respond with sensitivity to music, but he also has changed the score for a work after setting the choreography. He neither considers the music a separate experience from the dance, as Cunningham does, nor makes the music a servant to movement, as Graham does. Some of his dances have neither narrative nor characters; others use both. A sense of humor pervades his work, but his view of the world is not notably optimistic. He has been a brilliant dancer with an intensely personal way of moving, yet his choreography demonstrates the respect he holds for the individuality of other dancers; he did not need to stop making dances after he stopped performing.

During the early years of his work as a choreographer, Taylor managed to please and anger nearly everyone at one time or another. His early experiments with prosaic movement and untraditional sounds preceded by a few years the great interest in that way of dancing, delighting the avant garde and irritating the conservative wing of the party. When he began to work in more conventional forms, some of the experimenters felt betrayed, while the more formal dance-makers decided that he was a marvel. Taylor once considered leaving modern dance for ballet, but in 1972 he told Anna Kisselgoff of *The New York Times* that his movements were modern, not balletic, and "certainly not the third-stream meshing of modern and ballet that I don't like." Despite the disclaimer, many of his works express balletic conceptions in a modern dance idiom. Should the "third stream" continue to gain in importance, as seems likely, Taylor will undoubtedly be one of its heroes.

Paul Taylor.   PHOTOGRAPH BY JACK MITCHELL.

Edwin Denby, after seeing Taylor's company perform at the *Festival of Two Worlds* in Spoleto, Italy, in 1964, wrote ". . . such dance momentum had not existed before in the modern dance (i.e. in non-classic technique) . . . Taylor is one of the few choreographers who can sustain a large-scale dance with only from five to eight dancers. He is the first New York choreographer since Robbins who has taken the trouble to teach himself the continuous clarity of a well-made ballet. He has given the modern dance a new resource, one equivalent to (but not identical with) the classic dance-step phrase."

Taylor's work, like Cunningham's, is delineated in clear, rhythmic phrasing, one of the hallmarks of ballet. He generally sets his stage in a traditional manner, so that events of the greatest moment occupy the central area. One aspect of his style is the use of a limited number of steps which are repeated and rearranged to produce a defined visual and rhythmic effect, and this, too, is a technique of classical ballet. His is a flowing method of choreography in which movements are logically related to the ones that follow and precede them, although he is deeply concerned with sculptured figures and groupings. His dancers often seem to skim the surface of the stage like waterbugs skittering over a pond, and yet he has been known to tell the lightest and daintiest of them, Carolyn Adams, to dance with more weight. He is keenly aware of the floor and makes much use of the air. His dancers present the audience with a sense of the immediate, gently defining the space and time in which they happen. Taylor works in the idiom of modern dance with the conviction of an individualist and the sensibilities of a Classicist.

Taylor, like José Limón, set out to become a painter. He was born in Pittsburgh in 1930, spent his childhood in Washington, D.C., and enrolled in Syracuse University where he majored in painting and supported himself by winning an athletic scholarship as a member of the swimming team. During his junior year he saw some dance classes, then took some, then left school to study dance in New York. He won scholarships, as he had at college, and studied at Martha Graham's school, the

The intricacies of Taylor's choreography are evident in the many lines he can draw with only two bodies.

PHOTOGRAPH BY SUSAN COOK.

Juilliard School of Music (with the great ballet choreographer Antony Tudor), the Metropolitan Opera Ballet School and Connecticut College. He was an eclecticist from the beginning. During his student days in New York, he earned some money helping arrange window displays for the posh stores along Fifth Avenue together with two young artists of his acquaintance named Robert Rauschenberg and Jasper Johns. Those two had studied with John Cage at Black Mountain College, and when Merce Cunningham formed his company there in 1953, Taylor enlisted in it.

He danced with Cunningham's company during the unreviewed season at the Theatre de Lys and then, in 1954, left to form his own group and create his own choreography. The earliest work still in his repertory was made for that first company, and attracted a good deal of attention. *Four Epitaphs* (later revised to *Three Epitaphs*), was made to a recording by the Laneville-Johnson Union Brass Band and furnished with costumes by Rauschenberg. The music is an ancestor of jazz and was played at weddings and funerals in the deep South by local brass bands. It is slow, with a ponderous beat, and displays none of the virtuosic exuberance of later jazz. The dancers are not inclined to virtuosity either. They slump in on themselves and move from a forward-leaning crouch, as if it were beyond their power to stand erect. They resemble prototype models of human beings, discarded after more promising experiments had succeeded. The dancers are seen as if in two dimensions, which makes it more startling when one suddenly makes a movement that relates him directly to the audience. The dancers move as if they don't really have the strength to do this work, but will try anyway, and their muddy, shapeless appearance contributes to the image. *Three Epitaphs* manages to be funny and pathetic at the same time. Like much of Taylor's later work, it is highly theatrical and, at the same time, brilliantly understated. Taylor is the choreographic master of the throw-away line.

Few young choreographers can support themselves by devising dances. Between 1955 and 1961, Taylor danced with Martha Graham's company. He was the first Aegisthus in *Clytemnestra*, one of the original *Acrobats of God* and the creator and inheritor of several major roles. At the same time, he continued to investigate other ways of moving. He spent four years working with James Waring, a remarkably sensitive and eclectic choreographer who worked with humorous movement, balletic movement, simple movement, and nostalgic movement. (Waring died, too young, in 1975.) Taylor's work, first with Cunningham and then with Waring, contributed a good deal to the famous 1957 concert which resulted in the celebrated blank review. Certainly, the dances he offered were not in the tradition of Martha Graham. During one piece, he stood, dressed in street clothes, and shifted his posture slightly as a recorded voice intoned, "At the tone, the time will be . . . " In another work, dancers sat in chairs, got up, moved a bit, and had their dresses billowed by the wind, which also served as the soundtrack for the piece. A review in *Dance Magazine* called the concert ". . . a withdrawal—an excursion into nondancing—an effort to find the 'still point' in his approach to movement . . . *Duet* found Mr. Taylor standing still and Toby Glanternick sitting still. And that was all, except for an occasional piano plunk by David Tudor following a non-score by John Cage."

Although Taylor was working with Tudor, Cage, Rauschenberg, and other members of the Cunningham contingent, his work was quite different from Cunningham's. He was interested in movement for its own sake, and in the importance of the moment, but he was being more literal than Cunningham. The wind that blew dresses served as sound for the dance, something Cunningham would not have done. Also, Taylor worked in street clothes part of the time, and his dances were more prosaic and presentational than Cunningham's. Three years after the 1957 concert, he told Margaret Lloyd of the *Christian Science Monitor*, "I draw upon a catalogue of postures. My movements are scribbles of what people do—and people do sometimes stand or sit still, you know." Taylor continued to use postures and "scribbles"—his term for very quick movement—but he soon began to use them differently.

In 1960, Taylor and his company were invited to perform at the *Festival of Two Worlds* in Spoleto, and two works, *Meridian* and *Tablet*, were commissioned by the Festival. When the latter work was presented in the United States, Selma Jean Cohen commented in the *Christian Science Monitor*: "Mr. Taylor is excited about the curious movement possibilities of the human body. He likes to set a dancer in a clearly outlined pose and then suddenly have him run about with wildly flinging arms. He likes to have someone, serenely balanced in a classical position one moment, collapse into a shapeless heap the next. He likes to see a girl move with delicate fluidity while her male partner leaps with sharp, vigorous bounds around her."

The appearance in Spoleto started the company on a series of foreign tours, several sponsored by the State Department. It also helped establish Taylor as a choreographer of importance and, in 1961, he received a Guggenheim Fellowship in choreography to make *Insects and Heroes*, and left Graham to devote himself entirely to his own work. *Insects and Heroes* is a dance involving a monster and several dancers who are installed in cubicles furnished with overhead lightbulbs and pullchains with which to switch them on and off. The dance is neither narrative nor abstract; it is a sequence of events and encounters linked by the use of character, mood, and texture. In its consideration of an almost-human creature, it resembles *Three Epitaphs*. However, the movement and the presentation are more complex. Like *Three Epitaphs*, it is funny or sad, depending on your point of view. It is also a bit frightening, like a child's nightmare remembered some years later with a mature air of amusement. Taylor, like Graham, is a devisor of allegories and like Cunningham, a choreographer who allows the spectator a choice of interpretation. He can also be, as Humphrey was, concerned with the formal qualities of composition; some of his patterns are as deceptively offhand, and as beautifully shaped as a Japanese flower arrangement. His dances offer more precise emotional references than either Nikolais' or Cunningham's, but he, too, is dealing with interaction. His best works are composed of too many layers to allow the viewer to settle on a single, definitive reading.

Taylor tries to avoid restricting himself to any one convention or structure. "Any kind of movement is fair game," he says. "What matters is what you do with it and how it suits its environment." He is, however, perennially interested in particular ways of thinking, and he often deals with the concept of duality. "Things are very seldom one thing, and dance lends itself well to double, or triple, or quadruple meanings. Words can have double meanings, and gestural content can also have several layers of meaning—of course, all the meanings must be appropriate to the dance. I always try to make things clear and not to confuse an audience—you're going to confuse 'em anyway, let's face it––but I try to present a clear piece." His dealings with duality often result in what he calls "quirks," peculiar, surprising fragments of movement that show up like the bawdy puns in Shakespeare's sonnets. Taylor is, in fact, an irrepressible physical punster, and so good at it that the gestural jokes sometimes pop out spontaneously while he is working.

Taylor says his choreography is designed to show his dancers as individuals. The echoes of the arms of the three women give some idea of his sense of visual rhythm. Carolyn Adams is the woman in the lift. PHOTOGRAPH BY SUSAN COOK.

A year after *Insects and Heroes* came *Aureole,* a pure dance piece to music by Handel that is sometimes considered Taylor's best work. *Aureole* calls for the torso to be carried in a manner suitable to ballet, but breaks the line with wry accents of the feet. Bodies twist and curve into unexpected shapes while moving quickly and lightly across the stage. The delicacy of movement is spiced by unexpected shocks: A woman doing small, bouncy jumps disappears from the stage only to pop back followed by a second woman doing small, bouncy jumps; they exit, and finally return as a trio of small bouncers. *Aureole* combines lyricism with wit, a blending few choreographers have been able to accomplish. Humor in dance is moderately rare; wit is virtually nonexistent. The kinesthetic equivalent of the *mot juste* requires that both choreographer and audience know a language of movement sufficiently well to pun in it, and that they be sufficiently mature to laugh at something important to them, such as dance.

Taylor devised a magnificent solo for himself in *Aureole,* a highly difficult series of moves that rise, fall, and pause, but never seem to stop. Taylor is a big man, six feet one inch, about the same size and weight as Ted Shawn in his prime. The lightness of his movement combined with his size give a remarkable quality of ease to his performances. The size of his body and his lack of self-consciousness—he worked, not with a dancer's smile but with a bright grin—somehow led audiences to expect a slight clumsiness, a genial, bearish kind of movement when he came on stage. The contrast of this expectation with his sure control was part of his charm as a dancer, and his ability to use it part of his brilliance as a choreographer.

In 1974, Rudolph Nureyev appeared with the Taylor company and danced the choreographer's role in *Aureole.* Deborah Jowitt wrote in the *Village Voice,* "Taylor glides happily through his solo; when Nureyev does it, he makes you aware how *many* positions and tricky balances it contains." Nureyev, who was not yet comfortable in the style, showed the steps brilliantly, but as a ballet dancer shows them, making the audience aware of their difficulty and their separation from and links to one another. When Taylor danced the part, one never thought of him as a dancer performing a collection of difficult steps. There was only a large man flowing in a long, intricate procession of shapes. The sense of progression combines with clear phrasing, a sensation of effervescence and an almost tangible emotional warmth to make *Aureole* a masterpiece.

Scudorama, produced a year after *Aureole,* has a bitter flavor. Taylor had decided that "It seemed to be time to do an ugly dance" after having produced a superbly pretty one. He struggles to avoid falling into habits of choreography, and deliberately tries to prevent a pattern from forming. "One of my starting points is getting away from the piece I've just done." He also takes into consideration such practical matters as the need to balance a program for touring.

His choreography always makes use of sculptural postures and groupings and painterly scope and flow, of a contrast between horizontal and vertical movement and of a kinesthetic logic that serves as a frame for the work, but he does not always use these tools to produce the same sort of image. *Scudorama*, according to Marcia B. Siegel, "was beautiful as only violence can be beautiful—a thunderstorm, a four-alarm fire, or Times Square on a rainy night." The movement is percussive and twisting, the duets, trios, and solos have an air of decadence. The dancers begin the piece stretched out on the floor, they dance sometimes in street clothes and sometimes in dance clothes, and the whole thing resembles the kind of party you'd rather read about than attend. *Scudorama* is as harsh as *Aureole* is light; in both cases, encounters and emotion are presented without characterization, and the dramatic impact is created through mood and movement. The presentation is more theatrical than that of a Cunningham dance; the emotion is intensified.

In 1965, Taylor produced a biting satire on American life, *From Sea to Shining Sea*, except that he didn't set out to produce a satire. He began working with "an abstract collection of human activities, like brushing your teeth (if you can call that abstract) but it wasn't channeled into an American theme, it was to deal with the universal idiosyncrasies of human beings." As he continued his work, the choreographer decided that the dance needed more focus, and since many of the activities seemed typical of America, he dressed the dancers in red, white, and blue, continued to work in that vein, and came up with a classic bit of Americana.

Taylor is as much a choreographer of American values as Graham, but his comments are more social than psychological; his mythology is that of the comic strip, not of the epic; he is closer in style and tone to *Pogo* than to *Oedipus the King*. (Comic strips, of course, have a classical antecedent in the Old Comedy, in which Aristophanes and his colleagues made nasty remarks about the state of the city and the habits of the leading citizens. Neither Pogo nor Taylor is to be taken lightly.)

From Sea to Shining Sea is not the only dance which changed as Taylor worked on it. He believes that a choreographer has to let a piece grow, change and "Proceed on its own terms. It's scary to work that way because you don't have anything to hold on to; every day it's a new dance." The courage to work that way produces the quick, sketched-in quality that is one of the appeals of Taylor's dances. In the same way, he arrives at humor. He has said that he rarely sets out to be funny, but allows humor to develop out of movement, gesture, and timing. His quick eye, his delight in "quirks," and the particular quality of his creative mind, rather than a grim determination to be funny, are the originators of his wit.

Taylor's company made its first appearance on Broadway in 1963, the year of *Scudorama*. Since then, it has played Broadway fairly regularly, and has appeared at the City Center and the Brooklyn Academy of Music, established theaters for established companies, besides touring widely. The choreographer's methods became increasingly theatrical. In 1966, he attempted his most ambitious project since forming his company: *Orbs*. *Orbs* lasts an hour and is set to Beethoven's last string quartets. The work has six parts, an Introduction, a Conclusion, and movements called "Venusian Spring," "Martian Summer," "Terrestrial Autumn," and "Plutonian Winter." The dancers are cast as moons and planets; Taylor stands for the Sun.

In the first movement, the Sun introduces the planets to the pleasures of sex; the second brings violence and exhaustion; in the third, Taylor, as a minister, presides over the marriage of two planets; and the final movement is slow and cold. The wedding scene is performed in street clothes, the rest in dance clothing. A line of thematic and kinesthetic logic links the sections of the dance, which portrays changes over which humans have no control. The humor and lyricism of the dance are dictated by the scheme of its conception. Perhaps more important than the attempt to control a dance in this way was Taylor's courage in choosing music as great, and as difficult, as the Beethoven quartets.

Taylor is a remarkably musical choreographer. He has used scores of the baroque masters and of John Cage. He has commissioned music, he has worked with pastiche. In his use of music, as in everything else, he goes his own way. He began making *Scudorama* to Stravinsky's *Sacre du Printemps*, but switched to a score by Clarence Jackson. He worked out the movements before setting *Post-Meridian* (1965) to an electronic score. *Public Domain* (1968) uses music commissioned from John Herbert

---

Rudolph Nureyev and Eileen Cropley in Aureole. *Although the work is in the repertory of the Royal Swedish Ballet, Taylor says it is a difficult dance for ballet dancers to learn.*

PHOTOGRAPH BY SUSAN COOK.

McDowell. It begins with Tschaikovsky and works its way forward and back through Brahms, Puccini, Gregorian chant, and everything else that can be performed without the payment of royalties. The dance also offers a taste of nearly every kind of movement, and changes mood and pace as abruptly as the score. At times, the juxtaposition of music and movement are incongruous, and therefore funny. The dance is a comment on, among other things, the dance's need of music, and its need not to rely too much on it.

Public Domain was followed a year later by *Private Domain*, with a score by Xenakis. The setting by Alex Katz created a series of private domains by using large panels which divide the stage into three segments, and sometimes obscure the movement more thoroughly than do the fans in Cunningham's *Tread*. The dancers wear swimsuits, and the movement is rich in erotic imagery. It is typical of Taylor that he followed a work almost in the tradition of Dada with one that combines the eroticism of Graham with some of the presentational methods of Cunningham, and yet made two dances that were distinctly his own.

Two years before *Private Domain*, in 1967, he produced *Agathe's Tale*, a delightful bit of narrative bawdry that might have come from Chaucer, about a virgin who is seduced by the Devil and enjoys it immensely. The plot is obvious, the work is beautifully costumed, and Taylor does not ask the audience to supply its own meaning. The subtleties in *Agathe's Tale* reside in the movement; the piece can be enjoyed by anyone, and generally is. However, the choreographer's intelligence and erudition are evident, as they always are: Some knowledge of medieval stories and miniatures aids enjoyment. The ability to realize that the title is not merely a pun, but a literary reference, also helps. There are references in many of Taylor's works—to music and dance in *Public Domain*, to myth and astronomy in *Orbs*, to American history, to contemporary mores, to literature in many of his other pieces. The apparent simplicity and self-imposed limitations of his choreographic vocabulary are deceptive; Taylor is a highly literate choreographer, and although the wit, the power, and the beauty of his work are self-evident, the dances benefit from a literate public.

Big Bertha (1971), apparently a simple story dance, demonstrates Taylor's complexity. A family of three—father, mother, daughter—comes on a music machine, presumably in an amusement park. The life-sized doll attached to the machine accepts a coin, swallows it, and the music begins. The family dances together; the music stops; the machine eats another coin. The family, a middle-class, Midwestern American family enjoying a Sunday outing, is perfectly content. Then things begin to go wrong; instead of conducting the music, the mannikin begins to direct the family. Father slaps Mother; Father rapes daughter; Mother stands on a chair, strips to her red skivvies and does a kootch dance. The music machine gains all the amusement possible from the family, then lets them go.

One can read *Big Bertha* as a parable of the rape of America by the Machine, of the worship of the Machine by America, of the subconscious desires of a Dick-and-Jane family, or of a number of other things. The dance is short, but it is intense and layered. Graham's Puritan–Pagan conflict is here, as is the social comment of Humphrey and the satire of Weidman. The dance is beautifully constructed, but the movement is used, not for itself, but to make a statement in theatrical terms. However, Taylor is not content to make a single statement; like any good social satirist, he uses a single situation as a metaphor to sum up the actions and beliefs of a society. *Big Bertha* is a major work, terse though it is.

Another American satire, *American Genesis*, received its New York premiere at the Brooklyn Academy of Music in 1974. As the curtain fell on the first act of the three-act work, Taylor fell, too. Nobody in the audience realized that anything was wrong, but Taylor did not get up and the performance was postponed. He had been ill, and the strain of performance was too much for him. It had been noticed the previous year that Taylor had been gaining weight and was not dancing with his accustomed strength, but in keeping with his practice of privacy he said nothing about his physical condition. He continued to perform after the incident in Brooklyn and danced his roles in *American Genesis* later in the year. Shortly after that, he quit the stage, at least temporarily. He has not announced his retirement, nor has he said he will not dance in the future.

There had been some speculation that Taylor might also stop choreographing, since most modern choreographers are the central dancers in their own companies. However, Taylor, like Ailey and Nikolais, has no intention of ending his work. He is interested in displaying the personalities of his dancers, and he does not believe that choreography should be a vehicle to parade the dancing of its inventor. Furthermore, he says, he has always tried to separate Taylor-the-choreographer and Taylor-the-dancer, so he found no change in his choreography when he decided to stop appearing on stage. Certainly, *Esplanade* and *Sports and Pleasures*, the first works he produced after putting himself on the bench, are among his successes. They are witty, neatly crafted, deft in their definition of relationships and their handling of time and space.

Taylor is not an explosive innovator like Graham or Cunningham, or a showman on the order of Nikolais or Ailey. He is an artist and craftsman with a keen appreciation of the possibilities presented by time, space, shape, and the paradoxes that make existence interesting. Modern dance has been, since its inception, an art made by anarchists—by individuals who have something to say and intend to say it in their own way and in no one else's. Taylor has funneled the many methods of modern dance through his sensitivities, and has created a personal and important body of work. He is more closely allied with the Classicism of Humphrey than with the Romanticism of Graham: He often limits his pallet of steps, he is concerned with form, he deals more with relationships between people than with the motivation of individuals, he is often elegantly witty, a quality thorough-going Romantics often take themselves too seriously to afford. His work is cool, rather than hot; he produces satires rather than tirades. However, his dances are not cold or contrived, and he is devoted to exhibiting his dancers as individual human beings. He is an individualist without being aggressive about it, a Classicist without compulsive symptoms. In many ways, he provides a bridge between what has happened and what may be getting ready to occur.

* * *

Last Look (1985): *Art imitates life:*

Last Look is a short, brilliantly orchestrated exercise in concentrated violence. . . . It portrays the world as a psycho ward, as an amusement park hall of mirrors, as a living rubbish heap.

On the way home from City Center, where the Paul Taylor Dance Company offered the world premiere of *Last Look* last night, I passed a newsstand that displayed a photograph of Thomas Hearns after Marvelous Marvin Hagler had finished with him. Hearns and Hagler are professional boxers, and what they do to each other is their business, but the idea of an audience cheering vociferously as one human being pounds another into hamburger is more than a little frightening. It is this very violence that Taylor reflects in his dance.

Taylor daringly has chosen a movement vocabulary composed of tense, staccato actions, many of them almost spastic. The stage is set with a series of mirrored oblongs, and, as the lights come up, a heap of some sort is revealed in front of the mirrors.

The heap, we realize as the lights grow stronger, consists of bodies piled together. First one dancer and then another separates himself from the pile, jerking and curling back in obvious horror.

The dancers come awake, moving jerkily with tiny steps, sharp jumps, and tremors that run through their entire bodies. We might be observing the violent inmates of a psychiatric hospital, or a group of alcoholics or addicts enduring detoxification. . . .

The steps are brilliantly devised. The seemingly random violence of the action is not random at all; each step is a precisely designed visual metaphor. *Last Look* is an ensemble dance, but it is filled with individual details that stand out in the memory: Kenneth Tosti scratching at his chest like a monkey; four dancers holding the feet of a fifth, who is trying to jump; a group of men moving sideways like crabs.

Performers emerge from the mass of dancers to enact, by ones and twos, their particular vision of hell, and each sequence is more violent than the one before. . . .

In the culminating section of the dance, Raegan Wood is tossed back and forth among the four male dancers in the piece, and finally held upside down, dangling helplessly in their midst.

Finally, David Parsons gets a look at himself in the mirror, shrinks back from the image, and looks again. The other dancers run, jump, clutch, and finally huddle together in a heap, just as they did at the beginning. Even here, there is no peace—Linda Kent is thrust back again and again before she can find a place in this leaf-pile of humanity.

Taylor has used the image of humanity as a pile of used-up bodies before, in his *Big Bertha*, made in 1970, but *Bertha* is a black comedy. *Last Look* does not permit the soothing defense reaction of laughter. The choreographer has shown a society shaking itself to pieces, a culture attacking itself, beating itself, brutalizing itself into oblivion. . . .

Last Look is not a pleasant dance, but it is a remarkable achievement. (*The Record*, April 17, 1985)

Paul Taylor on music and choreography:

All you need to know about Paul Taylor is this: There is no better choreographer alive.

In art, unlike in athletics or in spelling bees, there never is an undisputed "best"; art defies absolute, objective measurement. In each era, though, a small group of creative individuals become the acknowledged peers of their artistic realms. Since 1974, when he retired from performing at the age of 44, Taylor has gone from being a very good choreographer to being a great one, one of the peers of contemporary dance.

His works are intensely virtuosic, superbly organized, high responsive to music, and intellectually intriguing. Every Taylor dance has an ideational and an emotional center, and it also has several layers of meaning, including the immediate content of its beautiful, daring movement. In an interview [in 1974], Taylor pointed out, "Things are very seldom one thing, and dance lends itself well to double, or triple, or quadruple meanings. Words can have double meanings and gestural content can also have several levels of meaning—of course, all the meanings must be appropriate to the dance."

In an interview a few weeks ago, seated at his desk in his 19th-century sea captain's house on Van Dam Street, the choreographer remarked, "Sometimes I know what a piece will be about when I start to make it; sometimes I don't ever want to know. . . . "

Several of Taylor's finest dances have been made to baroque scores. "I really prefer to use new music," he explains, "but sometimes baroque is practical—you don't have to pay for it or wait around while somebody writes it for you."

Aureole (1962), one of Taylor's first great dances, was made to music by Handel. "The use of a baroque score was perverse," Taylor explains, baring his wonderfully wicked grin, "because the piece was to be done at that bastion of modernism, the American Dance Festival at New London. It was quite delightful to be taking a piece of music they wouldn't like up there. Then everybody liked it and that sort of took the wind out of my sails."

Taylor is far too tall to be a leprechaun, but his wit and his slightly off-center view of the world make one wonder, sometimes. He is as comfortable with joke baroque as with the real thing because, he remarks, "All musical instruments seem completely zany to me. When you think of all the time and effort that has gone into these peculiar contraptions that make such odd noises—they're really like Rube Goldberg inventions—it makes me laugh with delight." . . .

"Traditional instruments—the violin, the harp, and so on, seem as ridiculous as anything Peter Schickele [a.k.a. P. D. Q. Bach] plays," he continues. "Trying to define musicality for myself has been a very interesting part of my life. Matching—you know, when the music goes 'Clonk', the dance goes 'Clonk'—is Mickey-Mouse. Musicality in dance is the dialogue between music and movement. You can communicate subliminally by the way dance uses the music or the way music uses the dance.

"It's always been very easy for me to make movement match the sounds; I've had to fight that in order to be more adventurous. There was a time when I decided to learn to read music, but then I thought better of it. Perhaps if I could read music I might not listen so hard."

Objects, including musical instruments, are not innately beautiful to Taylor, but living bodies are, "even if they're a little weird at times. People—being one, I look at it quite differently—are beautiful," he says. "I do think there could be quite a few improvements in function—our bodies are not made to stand upright on two feet, for one thing—but I like looking at bodies. Also animals and bugs and anything that moves." . . .

Some choreographers have found that giving up performing limits their desire or ability to make dances, and nearly all choreographers—especially in the highly personal environment of modern dance—fear that will happen. Taylor, however, became a greater master than ever.

"I was able to channel my focus," he explains. "By not dancing, I was able to channel more energy into choreography. I was able to gain distance, too—when I was dancing I couldn't go out front and see the dancers—and that gave me a more objective perspective. In effect, I was freed." (*The Record*, March 28, 1986)

Ab Ovo Usque Ad Mala (From Soup to Nuts) (1986): *Taylor's humor:*
Paul Taylor's *Ab Ovo Usque Ad Mala* is the funniest thing to happen to Rome since Caligula made his horse a senator. Well, maybe only since Zero Mostel started on his way to the forum, but you get the idea. Some passages look like the Rape of the Sabine Women as choreographed by the Marx Brothers; others suggest *Julius Caesar* performed by the original cast of *Marat/Sade*.

Ab Ovo Usque Ad Mala is subtitled *From Soup to Nuts*, which is not a free, but a relatively inexpensive translation. The new dance . . . is set to the *Royal Firewater Musick* and the *Howdy Symphony*, both by P. D. Q. Bach as edited by Professor Peter Schickele. . . .

Ab Ovo is Taylor making fun of himself, which is a lot more difficult, and a lot braver, than making fun of someone else. The piece is filled with parodies of Taylor's most admired dances, including *Esplanade* and *Arden Court*. . . .

Taylor is too fine an artist, you see, to simply parody style: He takes on substance as well. The men of the company are fitted out with cut-off togas, false beards, and false hair sprouting from their legs and forearms. They are indeed a race of hairy-chested men, and their very appearance parodies the muscular virility Taylor cultivates in his male dancers.

The women, equally Roman in dress, get to perform many of the pretty little steps and goddess-on-a-pedestal poses the choreographer sometimes assigns to the female ensemble. They also, however, flex their biceps and order the men around with imperious gestures.

Taylor is not only mocking his own style, he is making some sharply pointed comments about the roles to which men and women are assigned in dance, and in society. . . .

Taylor uses some visual jokes that were old when burlesque was young, and some that obviously are the products of his own inspired madness. When a woman does a delicate, whirling step, a man seated on the floor—Taylor is fond of seating dancers on the floor—takes the opportunity to look up her billowing skirt. When a pair of dancers find themselves in a typical Taylor pose—the woman's leg resting over the man's arm—the man taps his partner's knee with the side of his hand, producing the familiar knee-jerk reflex. When a woman flings herself into a man's arms, she very nearly knocks him into the wings.

. . . The brilliance of *Ab Ovo* lies in its functioning on three levels at once: as direct physical humor, as self-parody, and as social commentary. (*The Record*, April 13, 1986)

Brandenburgs (1988). *pure dance:*

Good grief, Paul! Here I was, prepared to knead my brain for hours to figure out the underlying meaning of your new dance, and all it's about is dancing?

Part of Paul Taylor's special genius is his ability to make dances in which movement acts a metaphor; works that stir viewers' thoughts as well as their emotions and kinetic responses. However, the choreographer's newest piece, *Brandenburgs*, is simply about dancing. And about joy. And about the music of J. S. Bach. And, possibly, about classical form. And maybe—this is just a guess—about the American style of classical dancing and George Balanchine's contribution to it.

Brandenburgs . . . is made to the music of Bach: the first two movements of the *Brandenburg Concerto No. 6* and the complete score of *Brandenburg No. 3*. It is a beautiful, elegant, energetic dance.

Baroque music has long been a favorite of Taylor's. Only last year, he choreographed *A Musical Offering* to the Bach score, and many of his finest works use music of the period. The dance that *Brandenburgs* recalls most strongly is *Aureole*, which Taylor made to music by Handel in 1962. *Aureole* was a "white" modern dance—after the classical 19th-century white ballet, a la *Swan Lake*, in which all the dancers wear white. And while *Aureole* seemed strange to many at the time, its beauty won everyone over.

Like *Aureole*, *Brandenburgs* clothes its principal dancers in white and employs quick, joyful movement. It also uses some Taylor trademarks —including rapid little sideways steps (the equivalent of ballet's *bourrées*), and arms that scoop the air as a dancer runs or skips. Yet *Brandenburgs* is in some ways more restrained, more sophisticated in construction than *Aureole*—not surprising, since Taylor now has a larger company.

The new dance uses an ensemble: five men who wear dark blue tights belted with gold. At the opening, these five form a kneeling diagonal broken by the placement of the dance's four principal performers, who are dressed in white trimmed with gold. Christopher Gillis, who also kneels, is surrounded by three standing women. . . .

This is where the Balanchine reference, intended or not, comes to mind. Seeing a man and three women, all in white, in a classical pose recalls *Apollo*. The thought is reinforced a few minutes later, as Gillis takes each woman in turn by the hand and dances with her. For a moment, it seems as if he will take the hands of all three women in his palm at once, as Balanchine's Apollo leads the Muses, but the action is not completed.

The important point, however, is not immediate reference, but the fact that Taylor employs classical forms and clarity of action within a musical context, which is just what Balanchine did in his ballets. The structure of *Brandenburgs* and many of its steps might be said to be balletic, but it would be far more accurate to say they are classical.

It is possible to see a whirling series of spins as the modern-dance version of *chaîné* turns, but they are, in fact, executed differently. What is important is that they are simple, clear, exceedingly rapid turns, performed without extraneous decoration. That dedication to essentials, and the concurrent concern with logical structure development, are what make *Brandenburgs* a dance in the classical style. . . .

Taylor plays lovingly with rhythms, setting a principal to dancing on the underlying beat of a musical passage while the ensemble, behind her, is guided by the more rapid, ornamented notes that skitter along above it. The music is the foundation on which Taylor's choreography rests, from beginning to end. . . . (*The Record*, April 7, 1988)

Minikin Fair (1989): *Imaginative and funny multipeds:*
One of the consistently astounding aspects of Paul Taylor's genius is his ability to see at least two sides to every question. It has become almost traditional for Taylor to present his new works for each year in pairs: one light and one dark.

This season's light-hearted dance [is] *Minikin Fair.* . . . [It] is a toy circus brought to life—at least, it's that when it is not an old-fashioned village revel. . . .

The thematic joke of the dance involves feet. First we see Joseph Bowie encased in a green cocoon that permits him to roll, to slither, and to travel on his hands, but never to walk. A bit later we are introduced to a trio of Monopedlets—women who each have one foot bare and the other covered with a large, red shoe. Then comes a group with two feet (two red shoes), and then a quartet of men with three feet each. Yes, three feet: The third is a red shoe at the end of a stick, at times used like a cane. Finally, of course, come the people with four feet. Right; women with two red shoes on sticks.

The rhythms and patterns of movement Taylor sets up for his groups of multipeds are gloriously imaginative and funny, and when the dancers finally shed their extra feet, Bowie, still imprisoned in his green folding sheath, roams the stage gathering up the discards with a hopeful grin on his face. . . .

There is a theme, too: for all its zany humor, *Minikin Fair*, like every Taylor dance, is a metaphor, or, more precisely a series of metaphors. It is about performing—specifically, about dancing ("finding one's feet"); it is about imagination (specifically, the wonderful childlike imagination that an artist must preserve as he matures), and it is about spring (the season of rebirth and of creation). (*The Record*, April 17, 1989)

Company B (1991): *as good as it gets:*

This is as good as it gets. Also as good as it's ever been or is likely to be. Paul Taylor's *Company B* . . . is that rarest of artworks, an unquestionable masterpiece with intense and immediate popular appeal.

The dance, made to songs of the 1940s recorded by The Andrews Sisters, evokes the fragrant boy-meets-girl America of the years preceding World War II, and (very gently) mourns its destruction by battle, fear, and death. There's nothing wrenching about that mourning: the dance is choreographed in a major key, not a minor. Taylor simply knows that our national youth ended with Hiroshima, and that youth, once gone, can never come again. Memories can, though.

Company B recaptures the springtime of swingtime with Lindy steps, snapping fingers, flirtatious sashaying and biceps-flexing, a Hora circle (to *Bei Mir Bist du Shon*), and dance-all-night energy.

Yet those bright, neat, on-the-beat steps are only a foundation on which the choreographer has built movement of astonishing inventiveness and remarkable musicality. The sharp, almost mechanical upper body movements in Andrew Asnes's solo to *Tico-Tico* (it's a cuckoo clock, remember?) are filled with masculine braggadocio; the smooth, brief shift to double-time in *There Will Never Be Another You* not only surprises the eye but reminds us that the dancing couple doesn't have much time together. Sandra Stone's solo to *I Can Dream, Can't I?* changes suddenly from sweet, gliding steps to urgent staggering ones, and Jeff Wadlington's to *Boogie Woogie Bugle Boy* is so inventively virtuosic that the air seems to sparkle around the dancer's legs.

However, dance is concerned with more than steps, and a great dance encompasses a great deal more. Taylor's theme here is innocence —not of individuals, but of an entire culture—and its passing. A bright-eyed naivete is evident in the music, and the choreographer heard it. for example, despite the pronunciation of "Yankee" as "Yahnkee," The Andrews Sisters' recording of *Rum and Coca-Cola* is as authentically West Indian as pasta: It's swing, not calypso, and it's not really bawdy, it just pretends. Dancing to it, tiny Mary Cochran raises her skirt thigh-high, to the delight of the company's men, who lunge after her like hungry puppies, but Cochran dances as if she didn't know what "working for the Yankee dollar" really means, and neither do the boys.

In the same way, Wadlington's pelvic thrusts in *Bugle Boy* are tossed into a dance filled with all-American-boy athleticism, and the women who mob Patrick Corbin in *Oh Johnny* look like bobby-soxers chasing a crooner but unsure of what they'd do if they caught him.

The death of innocence is just as delicately evoked. During the second dance of the 10 that constitute the work, *Pennsylvania Polka*, as Francie Huber and Hernando Cortez romp across the dancing space, four men appear in silhouette upstage; two extend straight arms to the side, two raise bent arms over their heads, and they are fully in position before we all realize that the first pair is aiming guns and that the second duo has been shot. . . .

Constance Dinapoli is left kneeling as David Grenke joins the marchers after *There Will Never Be Another You*, but Taylor is too fine an artist to leave her there, or to bring all the boys back but one. They return to dance again to the opening song, *Bei Mir Bist du Shon* with all their original vitality, but we know that they—and their girls—have changed too much ever to be as innocently playful again. Whoever you were at a given moment, there will never be another you quite like that. But you can still find reasons to dance.

Paul—Bei Mir Bist du Genius. The dancers are great, too. (*The Record*, October 24, 1991)

Musical Offering (1987, reviewed in 1992): *Finding peace:*

Musical Offering . . . shows Taylor's genius in top form. In this work, subtitled "A requiem," the choreographer plays on his favorite theme —the duality of human nature—in beautifully subtle ways. Movement motifs that might be described as "primitive"—two-dimensional shapes;

weight shifting metronomically between widespread feet—are contrasted with light, fast jumps and curving paths of travel.

However, even the curvilinear movements are given archaic contours, and the dancers are dressed in loincloths, accenting their primitive status.

Most important, the stark, undecorated movement is performed to the lyrical, ornamented, elegant music of Bach, and fits it beautifully.

Taylor does not descend to such simplistic concepts as "Good" and "Evil", but instead makes us aware of the contrasting qualities of the human animal, and of the world we create from them. Karla Wolfangle is raised high by four men, like a pagan idol; later [Caryn] Heilman is brought on stage in an image suggesting the descent from the cross.

All of us, crudely or with finesse, seek peace, and at the end of the dance, as opposites are reconciled, we find it. (*The Record*, October 29, 1992)

Funny Papers (1994): *Superdance!*

Funny Papers . . . is choreographed to novelty tunes that span decades of American popular music: delightful oddities such as *Does Your Chewing Gum Lose Its Flavor (On the Bedpost Overnight)* *Itsy Bitsy Teenie Weenie Yellow Polka Dot Bikini*.

To make the work, Taylor took dances choreographed by six members of his company [Sandra Stone, David Grenke, Patrick Corbin, Andrew Asnes, Mary Cochran, and Hernando Cortez] and "amended and edited them. . . . "—but the final product, dazzling in its conception, its humor, and its technical brilliance, is pure Taylor.

. . . Taylor . . . [is concerned with] the American way of laughter.

Funny Papers takes clichés of movement and of self-definition (gender roles come in for a good deal of teasing), exaggerates them, and plays them back to us. Yet there's nothing vicious about the mockery; it's generally good-natured and always gloriously funny. . . . Furthermore, the phrasing is truly mind-boggling. Taylor plays delicious games with tempo, now doubling it, now slowing it, now holding to the beat.

It's a lark; it's a takeoff; it's Superdance! (*The Record*, October 14, 1994)

TWYLA THARP

ADVANCE FROM THE 1960s

THE 1960s WILL be transformed, with the passing of time, into a mythical age like the Revolution, the Civil War, the great era of radicalism that preceded World War I, the Jazz Years, and the Depression. The nation emerged from the bland self-satisfaction of the Eisenhower Presidency and the parochial hatreds of the McCarthy purges into tumult, torment and, temporarily, triumph. The decade witnessed the greatest extension of sexual freedom since the 1920s, the most dedicated challenge to established authority since the strivings of the Wobblies, and one of the most rampant epidemics of self-delusion in American history.

When Lyndon B. Johnson announced that he would not attempt to retain his office in the presidential election of 1968, the young people who had mobilized themselves into the Civil Rights movement and the war against the Vietnam war thought, for a luminous moment, that they had won. Laws had been changed; wrongs had been righted; progress would continue. But Johnson was succeeded by Richard Nixon; the war went on; the black, the poor, and the unconsidered, who had earned some legal redress and some measure of dignity, still lacked a full share of power. The realization came that winning the campaign for human freedom was too massive and prolonged an undertaking for the army of any single generation, and the battalions of youth could not content themselves with a series of small victories. The retreat of the 1970s began.

The mythmakers will concentrate on the excitement and courage of the 1960s, and forget that it was a time as well stocked with folly as with greatness, as defined by a retreat into neo-Romanticism and mysticism as by an advance into responsibility. It was, though, a time of dedication, of needed rebellion, and of vital questions asked in anger. The passivity of the following decade has served to show how important and disturbing the questions were.

The most perplexing question posed by modern dancers was, "What is dance?" Some young choreographers decreed that theatrically intensified emotion detracted from the observation of movement. Others decided that technique was limiting, and chose to explore prosaic movement, abandoning the trained bodies of dancers for the less beautiful and less flexible, but less elite and, to them, more interesting, bodies of average human beings. Games, skits, and tasks were integrated into dance; mundane objects such as plastic bags, motorcycles, and mattresses were hauled onto the stage. Anti-dances were made on nondancers.

Other choreographers investigated pastiche, images from films and other media of popular culture, and the limits of human endurance. Some accepted as a credo the dicta of one of their number, Yvonne Rainer: "No to spectacle, no to virtuosity . . . no to the involvement of the performer or the spectator . . . no to moving or being moved." Many also said "No" to sexual overtones in dance. Some dancers performed naked, in an apostrophe to the new sexual revolution, to attract attention, to shock their surrogate parents in the audience, or to proclaim that neither nudity nor gender was important. The conventional roles for male and female dancers established by ballet were altered even more drastically than they had been by Merce Cunningham; in many instances they were obliterated, as the dance-maker dealt only with bodies, not with bodies which, because of their genders, had psychological or sociological connotations. In short, the answer to nearly every historical concept of Western dance was "No."

During a performance given by Yvonne Rainer's group, The Grand Union, a group of people walked part-way across a room to a wall, touched it, turned, and walked back to the starting line. Then they did it again, and again, and again. A spectator interested in observing the way different walkers moved, or the changes in the mass of the group, could be fascinated, but most works of the period seemed far more interesting to perform, or to conceive, than to watch.

American painters were making use of pedestrian objects such as soup cans, flags, and comic strips; theatrical works were being reconsidered. Young people, rejecting the political and social values of their elders, also found it requisite to reject their artistic criteria and seek new ones. Their hunting ground was the contemporary world—its objects, its beliefs, its people. Many dances of the period were related in structure and concept to the theatrical occurrences known as happenings, environments, and events. The first happening was produced at Black Mountain College during the Cage regime, and the genre relied on many of the precepts that were developed by Merce Cunningham.

Happenings and the dances related to them denied the value of dramatic structure and defined, motivated characters. Their inventors avoided presenting works which could be interpreted logically, which could be sounded for the meaning or purpose, or which could emotionally affect the audience. Yvonne Rainer worked at constructing a dance which would be "completely visible at all times, but also very difficult to follow and get involved with."

This form of presentation was a political statement. The producers hoped to demonstrate that there was a relationship between a message, the person who sent it, and the people who received it, and to force the receiver to decide what, if anything, the message meant without any help from the sender. Their work was a protest against the notion of packaging products and ideas in such a manner as to convince the public to buy them. It suggested that the electorate should avoid taking at "packaged" value the statements issued by the government as shoppers should distrust the advertised qualities of manufactured goods. The dances and theatrical events were designed to force the members of the audience to think for themselves. Many thought the whole business was nonsense and went home.

Happenings used chance techniques, as Cunningham did. Performers might be given a list of words to say or actions to perform, but no directions as to when each item on the list should be accomplished. Objects were not used as properties, subject to the action of a performer, but became integral parts of a dance or production, performers in themselves. The choreographers and producers sought to bring together the sensory stimuli that might be experienced on a busy city street, an image similar to some of those used by Cunningham to describe his work.

Surrealism had expressed itself in symbols; Abstract Expressionism represented the feelings of the artist. Pop Art, happenings, and the new dance dealt neither with symbols nor with emotions, but only with objects and people. Any comment was contained in the event. There was an element of Dada humor in many pieces, and a good deal of selfconsciousness in many others.

Allan Kaprow's *Calling*, performed in August 1965, began with the performers standing on street corners. They were taken into an automobile, wrapped in aluminum foil, and left unattended in the parked car until called for by performers in a second vehicle. During ride number two, the person was stripped of his foil, wrapped as a parcel and deposited at Grand Central Terminal. After working loose from his wrappings, he called to other human parcels—and they to him—then left the station. In the final episode the performers dialed phone numbers and waited a long time for an answer. When it came, the caller asked to speak with a particular person, and the recipient of the message hung up.

One can find pungent social comment in *Calling,* but the discovery comes from reading a description of the work, rather than from watching the presentation of any episode, or even of the entire sequence. The pieces make much of its comment when experienced intellectually in private, rather than emotionally in public, although a passerby watching someone unwrap himself from a burlap sack in Grand Central Terminal probably would undergo some kind of emotional experience.

Conveying such an experience, though, is clearly not the aim of a piece which carries the subtitle, "A Happening for Performers Only." The sensations of the performers, not those of the spectators, were considered important. In that respect, many theater and dance pieces of the time were amplified children's games. Games, tasks—such as drawing a line on the floor—and other problem-solving activities formed the material of many dances. Others dealt with problems related specifically to movement. Many of the solutions (and the problems) were banal, boring, and limited, but others supplied useful material for future work.

A major subject of investigation was the relationships of performers to their audience. Some choreographers danced in public spaces and in the streets. Others made the audience part of the work, rubbing out the line between performer and spectator, and this, too, was sometimes construed as a political comment, a statement about the position of government and governed. A third group worked only for a coterie audience, or did not much concern themselves with whether an audience arrived or not. Theater exists only in the presence of an audience, and a new form of art succeeds only when an audience accepts it. Artists who, like living-room politicians, prefer to preach only to those who agree with them, are unlikely to change art, as the spouters have little chance of altering social conditions. No major artist allows the audience to dictate the content or manner of his work, but neither does he present that work without the hope of eliciting a response.

Another aspect of the new dance was that much of it was, and is, excessively intellectual. It has a kinship with the Conceptual Art of the

1970s, in which a work need only be planned and described, not executed. One question posed by the investigators was whether or not dance need be an emotional art. The answer, apparently, is that it must. Motion evokes emotion, and it has been the business of theater to heighten emotion since before Aristotle wrote that the task of tragedy is to evoke in the audience sensations of pity and terror. A performance that evokes emotion in the performers, but does not amplify it for the spectators, may have therapeutic value but serves little theatrical purpose. Many of the choreographers of the 1960s limited themselves to one aspect of movement, one set of ideas, one fixed set of propositions, and have found no way to go further.

One reason for limiting movement was a desire to experiment with the use of nondancers, thus posing the question, "What is a dancer?" The answer, despite all attempts to prove otherwise, is that a dancer is a human being with a highly trained body, capable of virtuosic movement and a developed sensitivity to rhythm. Examining the movements of an ordinary, untuned body was part of an attempt to make dance a more democratic art. One of the rallying cries of the 1960s was "Participatory Democracy," and every young orator declaimed his concern for "The People." Young citizens had finally figured out that the American government and the American populace are separate entities, and assumed the laudable goal of changing that situation. Their aim was reflected in their art, where the results were less gratifying than they would be in politics. Furthermore, choreographers regarded the untrained body as a valuable tool, as they saw everyday objects as important components of art. The experiment had value, in pointing out that art is integral to, not separate from, human experience, but it also proved that the artist is the member of an elite, whether he, or others not as gifted, likes it or not. Dance which limits its means of expression to the movements of which an untrained body is capable trims its vocabulary to the choreographic equivalent of baby talk.

Many of the questions raised by the dances of the 1960s were posed at the Judson Dance Theater, housed in New York's Judson Memorial Church. The theater began in 1962 with classes in dance composition offered by composer Robert Dunn, and it grew to be to a new generation what Bennington College had been to those whose values were being challenged. Judson was not the only space in which the new choreographers could dance, but it served as a focal point for the movement. Some dance-makers performed in streets, on rooftops and in public and private buildings. Several choreographers, including Meredith Monk and

THE HOUSE
PRESENTS

"NEEDLE-BRAIN LLOYD
& THE SYSTEMS KID"

A 2 PART - 4 SCENE THEATER PIECE / SATURDAY, JULY 18, 1970
CONNECTICUT COLLEGE AMERICAN DANCE FESTIVAL

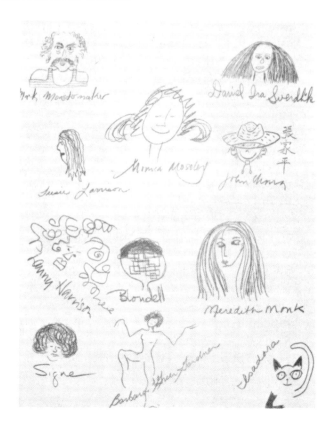

PROGRAM

Scene I
4:00 p.m. in the Arboretum
followed by

Scene II
at the College Green

— dinner break —

Scene III
9:15 p.m. at the College Green
followed by
Scene IV
in the Arboretum

Directed by Meredith Monk

Performed by The House and the Augmented House
from Connecticut

Music © Meredith Monk, 1970.

A program for Meredith Monk's Needle-Brain Lloyd and the
Systems Kid, *performed at Connecticut College, New London.
The division of scenes and diversity of credits give some idea of
the scope of the piece.*

Rudy Perez, made pieces which employed more than one site. Monk's *Needle-Brain Lloyd and the Systems Kid,* presented at Connecticut College during the summer of 1970, required its audience to move from place to place. To view the final sequence, which was presented after dark, the spectators were directed to follow a path down to the lake (performers holding flashlights were stationed along the way) where they could watch dancers rowboating away into the dark. Two years later Perez offered a work at Connecticut which required the audience to follow it from a conventional theater to various outdoor sites; one sequence consisted of a series of patterns made by moving motorcycles, and took place on the parking lot.

Monk's *Juice* (1969) had three episodes, the first staged at the Guggenheim Museum, the second, three weeks later, on a conventional stage at Barnard College and the third, the following week, in the choreographer's loft. If nothing else, *Juice* set some sort of record for length of intermissions. Anna Kisselgoff, reviewing for *The New York Times,* found that, "Seen as a whole, 'Juice' was a true abstract drama. It was nonlinear in content, but its characterization of the protagonists unfolded steadily and progressively . . . Miss Monk's formal concerns frequently deal with layers of reality." Costumes, songs, and recitatives contributed to the development of the characters. As the work moved from locale to locale, it diminished appropriately in scale. The first episode filled the winding ramp of the museum with performers. The final one used no dancers at all, but consisted of a showing of the costumes and properties used in the first two sections and a videotaped performance by each of the work's principals.

Monk is not strictly a choreographer. Her works use vocal music and are best considered theater pieces rather than dance. Many of her important works have been divided into short segments, each of which, through the use of decor, speech, music, and movement, presents several layers of information. Deborah Jowitt calls her works ". . . journeys through a dense landscape of meticulously shaped events . . . Certain everyday signs and sounds acquire a surreal edge because they're isolated from their usual context or performed with neat deliberation and intensity."

One of Monk's more celebrated pieces, *Title: Title,* was offered during a festival of avant-garde dance at the Bill Rose Theater in February 1969. The performance began with a recording of Ethel Merman singing "There's No Business Like Show Business" to an empty stage. In the lobby and in the balcony, Monk had placed sealed cartons, each furnished with a peephole, and each containing a performer who was eating or reading. Monk did not merely move theater into a museum, she moved a museum into a theater.

Her longer works, such as *Vessel* (1971) and *Education of a Girlchild* (1972–1973), contain some of the same surprising juxtapositions of elements, and offer more emotional information. She does not call her creations dances: *Vessel* was an "operatic epic," *Juice* a "theater cantata," *Education . . .* an "opera" and *Needle-Brain Lloyd* a "live movie." The subtitles give some idea of the number of media from which Monk draws concepts. She places objects and events in circumstances in which one would not expect to find them, and thus enhances the importance of the bits of information offered by each moment. She also carries the idea of happenings and their dance cousins to their farthest extreme, treating people as if they were objects. She encased performers in cartons, as if they were packaged goods. By referring to a work as a "live movie," she called to mind Hollywood's practice of dehumanizing its stars with its use of makeup, costumes, precise positioning, and the technical paraphernalia of sound-stage shooting. An actor becomes an animated prop to be defined by camera-work and editing. Monk uses performers in a similar manner, with a similar purpose.

She believes that each piece should develop, in part, from the locale in which it is performed, and prefers not to do a work on a site other than the one for which it was made. Her fascination with theater and stylization add to the character of her work. She can present mundane events in glamorous style, as the movies do, and translate emotion into a specially created reality, as classical opera does. Monk's work, like that of Alwin Nikolais, is too personal to be imitated exactly, and the requirements she sets for her work make it unlikely that she will attract more than a limited audience. However, her ideas have influenced other artists, and will probably continue to do so.

A different approach was adopted by another of the revolutionaries, Twyla Tharp, the most important American choreographer to appear since Jerome Robbins. Tharp worked at Judson, in museums (the Metropolitan Museum of Art), in open spaces (Central Park), and at the Alaska Pavilion of the New York World's Fair. She made dances far removed in concept and content from those of traditional choreographers. For the first five years of her career, she worked at being the most iconoclastic of the iconoclasts, the farthest forward of the avant-garde, as Martha Graham had done during her long woolens period. She performed as if performing did not interest her at all, as if dancing were a necessary but unfortunate by-product of making dances. However, she has been, from the very beginning, concerned with two of the three interests of classical dance-makers—space and time. The third classical interest, sex, is not a theme of her work. Her first company, like Martha Graham's group, was a procession of vestal virgins; she used them as dancers, not as female dancers, and when she enlisted a man in the troupe in 1972, she used him as an individual, not as a male individual.

Tharp is a slight, intense, brilliant woman whose speech needs to maintain a rapid clip in order to keep pace with her mind. She stands five feet, three inches tall, has a dancing weight of 105 pounds, and wears her dark hair in a short, squared-off bob which she flicks away from her eyes while dancing with a toss of the neck that has become a patented trademark. Her dark eyes and thin mouth specialize in the expression of a housewife who is also a mechanical engineer listening to the pitch of a door-to-door salesman pushing jerry-built vacuum cleaners. Her candor is so intense it is almost frightening.

Tharp was born in Portland, Indiana. When she was two, her mother, who had studied to be a concert pianist, started her on ear training. Two years later, Mother enrolled her in tap-dancing lessons. The family moved to California, where Tharp spent the 1950s studying everything her mother thought might come in handy: ballet, baton twirling, piano, viola, drums, harmony, counterpoint, typing, and shorthand. As a friend remarks, "If they teach it, Twyla studied it—for at least a year." As a result, she has a notable theoretical and practical knowledge of music. She can play; she can read a score and work from one.

In 1961, she transferred from Pomona College in California to Barnard College, partly so that she could study dance in New York. She still did not plan to be a dancer; her degree from Barnard is in Fine Arts. Tharp studied dance as she had studied music: if they teach it, she learned it. She worked with Martha Graham, Alwin Nikolais, and Merce Cunningham; she studied ballet with Margaret Craske, Richard Thomas,

Twyla Tharp's first dance, Tank Dive *(1965), used stylized, over-sized shoes as props and Petula Clark's recording of* Downtown *as a score. It was four minutes long.*

PHOTOGRAPH COURTESY OF THE TWYLA THARP
DANCE FOUNDATION, INC.

Barbara Farris, Erick Hawkins, and Igor Schwezoff; she took classes in jazz technique. She began her career as a dancer in Paul Taylor's company, where she worked for two years before setting out on her own. In 1965, her first year of independent work, she made five dances and began what, in retrospect, has been a logical progression of choreographic essays.

Tank Dive (1965) started when Tharp entered the auditorium of a theater at Hunter College. She moved forward and stepped into a large pair of shoes which had been placed on the floor, then leaned forward as if she were skiing. From there, she advanced to the stage and stood for a moment in *relevé*, holding the floor with her toes while keeping the rest of her foot a vertical extension of her leg. A blackout ended the sequence. The second section of the dance brought two men into the auditorium to accept small flags proffered by two women. Blackout. The lights came up showing Tharp on stage, in *relevé*. She ran to the back of the theater, swung around a pole, slid out toward the center of the floor and stood, briefly, in *relevé*. Final blackout. Elapsed time: four minutes.

It seems a bit odd that this series of three disconnected episodes should have been the beginning of a cycle of works that involves constant, flowing movement weaving itself over a stage, or that *Tank Dive*, performed by nondancers, should develop into choreography that can be executed only by highly skilled and disciplined dancers. But the basic elements that make Tharp a remarkable choreographer were there. The blackouts provided an element of surprise; the dance made use of a large expanse of space; the work had a clear sense of time. The same elements are apparent in a masterpiece Tharp crafted in 1972 for her own company and the City Center Joffrey Ballet. *Deuce Coupe* surprises by employing carefully planned near-collisions of dancers, it uses several styles of movement, it fills the three dimensions of the stage, and it plays rhythms off against one another.

Tharp's work with ballet companies, which would have seemed an unlikely development at the beginning of her career, also is logical. "Ballet technique," she has said, "is the technique most worth investing your time in. It is the most thorough, the most versatile, the most logical, rigorous and elegant . . . I think jazz technique is important, too, very important. Rhythm is a tool I've become more interested in rather than less interested in as I work with it." Her reasons for valuing ballet technique are a key to understanding her work; she wants a method of dancing at her disposal that will allow her to use bodies in interesting ways. She says ballet technique is "rigorous," not restricting; in her dances, technique is to be used, not worshipped.

The year after *Tank Dive* the choreographer made a dance for three women in which, during the first section, each performer carried a stop watch and moved in straight lines. The second episode employed tap dancing, which shows up in other Tharp pieces, the third brought a large box into the dancing space which made it impossible for the audience to see all of the dance, and the fourth relaxed into flowing movement. The first sequence is reminiscent of theater games and tasks; the tap dancing suited the delight of the period in camp, and is part of Tharp's childhood; blocking part of the movement from the audience had been tried by Cunningham. The young woman was investigating, experimenting, playing, and learning. She made works for different spaces, for differing numbers of dancers, with different sorts of sound.

During the late 1960s, Tharp contrived dances that used no lighting effects and few, if any, properties. Although she choreographed to music, the audience was not permitted to hear the score; her dancers worked in silence, to the amplified beat of a metronome, or with the aid of a timekeeper who called out the most important beats. She used stylish costumes, but they were the only concession she made to theatricality. Her dances were concerned only with space and time, and she dealt with these qualities coldly and precisely, as if she were drafting a set of plans for a warehouse. Tharp, like the constructors of happenings and theater games, was concerned with solving problems, but the tasks she set for herself were far more complex than the baby-games employed by her contemporaries, and her resolutions resoundingly more brilliant. Contemporary reviews demonstrate the effect her asexual, intellectual, determined dances had on trained observers. Marcia B. Siegel wrote, "Miss Tharp has a mind IBM would be proud to have manufactured . . .," and Arlene Croce regretted that there was no more to her style than intellectual brilliance and technique: "The Tharp company is spectacular, but its virtuosity is mostly mental. It works like a feat of visual ventriloquism. It isn't, however, very attractive . . ."

Dancing in the Streets of London and Paris, Continued in Stockholm and Sometimes Madrid (1969)—hereafter known as *Dancing*—was, oddly enough, performed in Hartford and New York, and in museums, not in theaters. The work was made in individual phrases which could be moved into different spaces, giving it some relationship to a Cunningham Event. It used no score. Dancers called out time checks and watched one

The Bix Pieces *as performed in the Delacorte Theater in New York's Central Park, September 1972. Twyla Tharp and Sara Rudner each appear twice in this photograph, which illustrates the easy, twisting waist that is a special attribute of Tharp's style. (Above)* **PHOTOGRAPH BY WILLIAM PIERCE.**

Deuce Coupe *(1973), which Tharp made on her own company and the City Center Joffrey Ballet. Ericka Goodman (in white) performs one of the classical ballet steps which formed a point of reference from which the dance developed. The graffiti on the backdrop were executed during each performance. (Below)*

PHOTOGRAPH BY HERBERT MIGDOLL.

another on closed-circuit television. Performers in different areas of the building did different things, sometimes flowing into the audience, sometimes requiring the audience to follow them. They performed workaday tasks such as switching clothing, or reading while dancing; they were allowed, at times, to imitate gestures made by members of the audience; they performed intricate feats of virtuosity. *Dancing* incorporated virtually every technique that was tried during the 1960s; it was a compendium of radical dance. It signaled the end of its choreographer's experiments with that particular style.

By the time she devised *Dancing*, Tharp had evolved a characteristic way of moving. Her dancers had to be ready to change direction suddenly, to hold a sustained pose and then quickly shift their weight off center and back again, to allow their bodies to take on unexpected shapes, to let their arms dangle freely while their legs held a rigorous position. Deborah Jowitt stated it precisely in a review of Tharp's company's appearance at the Billy Rose Theater: "This style . . . involves acquiring a strong classical technique and then learning to fling it around without ever losing control." Tharp says her dancers must "ease the tension in the tops of their bodies while using all the technique of their legs."

Tharp's dancers move over the stage with expressionless faces that would make them fine poker players. They often seem on the verge of smashing into one another, and never do. They move in all-over patterns on stage, making lines that intersect, parallel, go over and under one another like the forces in a Pollock drip painting. Dancers on different parts of the stage do different things at the same time, or the same things at different times. The dancers sometimes are dotted on the stage as randomly as sprinkles on an ice-cream cone, but their relationships to one another seem to have been calculated with a pair of calipers, if you look closely. Tharp's choreography always seems spontaneous, and is invariably meticulously crafted. Her dancers can make movements that seem offhand and casual because her dances are founded on a strong, carefully developed structure.

The rhythms of her dances are exceptionally complex. Tharp admits that they are difficult for dancers to grasp and are as much a part of the pattern as the movement. Sometimes Tharp will pass a phrase, count by count, from dancer to dancer, as if playing a parlor game. She opposes dancers to one another in time as she does in space, and makes the opposition appear uncalculated. That apparent lack of calculation results from five hundred hours or more of rehearsal.

Tharp experimented with all the techniques of the dance rebels: austerity, disinterest in performance, lack of a score. Then she returned to music, and swam into the mainstream of choreography. No other dance-maker of her generation accomplished the transition from the avant-garde with such success; in fact, none of the others really made it. Tharp spent five years in her iconoclastic phase, then began her transition in 1970, when she made *The Fugue*. The following year, she performed with her company at the Delacorte Theater in Central Park, offering *The Fugue* and *Eight Jelly Rolls*. *The Fugue*, a percussive trio, is really a fugue, although it is danced without a musical score. The stamps of the dancers' feet provide a rhythmic base. The three performers execute their steps in fugal form, and the changing positions of their bodies and of their placement on the stage allow the audience to see each motion and pose from several angles. It is interesting to learn how the impact of a movement changes when the step is presented in profile, instead of head-on, or when the dancer doing it changes his spatial relationship to the other dancers on stage. *Eight Jelly Rolls* let the audience hear the score (it is made to the music of Jelly Roll Morton and His Red Hot Peppers), inaugurated a series of dances in the tradition of jazz, and established Tharp as a major choreographer. The dance was a tribute to the jazz of the 1920s and to the show-business style of dancing that went with it. It showed, in classically based movement, its choreographer's understanding of the kinesthetic principles that support all forms of theatrical dancing—and it was highly theatrical. Tharp was playing to her audience, forcing them to notice movement and react to it.

Eight Jelly Rolls had the odd balances, the dead pan humor that mocks Art with a capital A; the flow of movement, the kinesthetic paradoxes, the sudden interruptions—but it also had pizzazz. There was a magnificent sense of showmanship in the way she used dancers and in her choice of dancers. For openers, they did not look like one another, as members of a dance troupe often seem to do. There was a six-foot-tall woman who seemed gangly until she began to move, and a small, remarkably sexy woman. There was Tharp herself; slim, nonchalant, poker-faced. There was no attempt to make the performers resemble one another in physique or personality; all they had in common was a sense of humor and virtuosic technique.

Tharp does not use jazz movement as Talley Beatty does, nor does she employ ballet steps as George Balanchine does. Instead, she blends the two into a unique way of moving that suits the mood of the music without becoming subservient to it. In *Eight Jelly Rolls,* Tharp had, in effect, taken Morton's music as a text on which to preach or a theme on which to write a commentary. The music was honored, yet seen in clear retrospect; the 1920's were recalled, not with sentimentality, but with honest charm and humor. One of the dancers did a gentle parody of burlesque, performing bored bumps while languidly hanging one arm in the air. In another episode, Tharp plays with the problem of balance, and dancers gently stagger, weave, and lurch in a kinesthetic evocation of smoke-filled speakeasies.

In 1971, Tharp turned her attention from jazz to ragtime with *The Raggedy Dances*. Again, she commented on the movement and musical styles of a period while maintaining the energy and style of her own idiom. The stage was aswirl with dancers, each showing an individual body, personality and way of moving, yet each integrated into a design. They shifted easily from big motions to little ones, from stillness to movement, from one direction to another, keeping the expressionless faces and relaxed shoulders that were by now a Tharp trademark.

The choreographer moved on to *The Bix Pieces* (1972) and *Deuce Coupe* (1973). *The Bix Pieces* was danced to the music of the great cornetist of the 1920s, Bix Beiderbeck, and choreographed to the six quartets, Opus 75, of Franz Joseph Haydn, whose music Tharp loves. One of the quartets was used in performance. Tharp did not use the Beiderbeck music for choreographic purposes because she was afraid "of becoming too specific, of parodying, of getting what comes to mind when the music is first heard, rather than having to think of it more basically." Changing music is not unusual for Tharp. She began to make *Push Comes to Shove* (1976) to Bach, found the selection too somber, thought seriously about Mozart and returned "to my first love," Haydn. She notes dances on the musical score, and says that if she changes her selection, "You

---

Eight Jelly Rolls *was one of the dances based on jazz that helped Tharp to develop a reputation as a choreographer in the mainstream of dance. The different shapes and sizes of the dancers make the troupe look less like a traditional company than a party of individuals. (Left to right) Rose Marie Wright, Nina Weiner, Isabel Garcia Lorca, Tome Rawe, Sara Rudner, Twyla Tharp.* PHOTOGRAPH BY TONY RUSSELL.

just count it in threes instead of fours; changing music does change the dance. Of course it does—but it can be done."

The Bix Pieces is quintessential Tharp: the strangely assorted company moving with the eased shoulders of jazz on top of the firm legs of ballet, the sequences of movement apparently dashed off as a painter might scribble first sketches, the amalgamation of many kinds of movement including some deftly inept baton-twirling by the choreographer. In addition, the piece used a new technique, a script, which was performed by an actress during one sequence of the dance. As the lines were recited, Tharp pointed with her baton at dancers who illustrated the words in movement, using them as a teacher might use an animated cartoon.

Both the script and the dance demonstrated the choreographer's concern with time, both in an immediate sense and in a poetic one. "I hated to tap dance when I was a kid," the script begins, "but *The Bix Pieces* is about remembering. It is an attempt to remember and acknowledge my beginnings: My tap-dancing lessons, my ballet lessons, my baton-twirling lessons, my piano and viola lessons, my father. My father died this spring, and this dance was to commemorate the time when he was young." Tharp's son was born that spring, too, and the dance does not forget that either.

In the next section of the script, the actress reeled off a series of numbers as quickly as a calculator could flash them, and at each number, a dancer illustrated a move. Then, the individual steps were incorporated into a sentence: "To make movement [move] which is nonlinear [move] non-positional [move] and non-[move] stop, one makes movement [moves] so full [move] of these things [move] that one soon stops [stop] seeing them."

The effect was a *tour de force,* the same sort of achievement that makes audiences applaud the acrobatics of a classical *pas de deux.* A few seconds later, the trick was repeated as the actress listed the nine categories into which balletic movement may be divided while one dancer demonstrated the ballet steps and another showed their equivalents in jazz movement. The short course in the history of theatrical dancing was paralleled by the remark that one theme in the Haydn score did not originate with that composer. "Can anything be new, original, private?" asks the actress who speaks for the choreographer. "October 9: 'Today I thought of writing a dance to the *Goldberg Variations,* just because it's already been done.' It seems to me that art is a question of emphasis. That aesthetics and ethics are the same. That inventiveness resides first in choice and then in synthesis—in bringing it all together. That this action is repeated over and over again, the resolutions being somehow marvelously altered each time."

The script combines technical, biographical, and emotional information, as the dance does. The work uses two kinds of music, many kinds of movement, words, and theatrical properties, and unifies them in a logical work of art. The style is cool; the emotion is transmitted as an undercurrent. Tharp drew on her memories as she drew on Beiderbeck, to create the dance. She filtered her memories through theatricality and her choreography through another score, perhaps for the same reason—fear of "becoming too specific."

Deuce Coupe (1973) was commissioned by the City Center Joffrey Ballet, a company that sells tickets by selling youth, excitement and whatever is chic at the moment, and was performed by Tharp's own company and the Joffrey dancers. This time the choreographer did not have to create the illusion of a filled stage with a group of six dancers; she had a large company at her disposal and used it to paint a continuing flow of movement across the space framed by the proscenium. Behind the dancers, a group of New York hoodlets (the street kids, the graffiti group) used their spray cans to paint their names on the backdrop in vibrant colors, just as they paint them on subway cars.The dance used music recorded by The Beach Boys, a popular singing group who were not in the avant-garde of rock but worked in a style popular with the kids who feed juke boxes. The choreographer again related contemporary movement to its classical equivalents. One dancer performed a series of ballet steps in alphabetical order, appearing at intervals throughout the dance to present a new entry from the dictionary, while the other performers used a large pallet of movement, including steps derived from the discotheque dancers of the 1960s.

The styles of movement complemented one another. Steps were used to parody themselves and to make a point about others. In *Deuce Coupe*, Tharp did for the popular dances of the 1960s what Jerome Robbins had done for the vogues of the two previous decades—she incorporated them into theatrical dancing and, in doing so, commented on the era that produced them. Deborah Jowitt writes that the dance ". . . shows us the Joffrey dancers looking like the real young people they are, instead of the effervescent Youth they are often called upon to play." *Deuce Coupe* mocked the frenzies and follies of the 1960s, demolishing the pretensions of an area while saluting its accomplishments.

Formations of dancers sprawled across the stage in true, youthful,

1960s' untidiness. Movement was constant, quick and unrelenting. So much was happening at once that it was impossible to see and remember it all. The dance was purely urban; it dealt with the movements of big cities and university towns, not with those of rural or suburban cultures. The dancers sagged and pranced, stopped short and changed direction, drew attention to first one part of the stage and then another, filled vertical space by crouching, reaching, or leaping. Under the incessant activity was a beautifully drawn pattern, but as the pattern of an era is seldom understood by those who live in it, the full pattern of the dance was too complex to be comprehended at one viewing. Near the end of the ballet, a group of performers far to stage left lifted another high and held her, like the soldiers elevating Hamlet's corpse. *Deuce Coupe* was not merely a statement about the 1960s, it was an epitaph for the decade.

The success of *Deuce Coupe* led the Joffrey Ballet to commission another work from Tharp that same year. *As Time Goes By* does not augment the Joffrey with Tharp's company, and it is a classical ballet. It is made to the last two movements of Haydn's *Farewell Symphony* and is prefaced by an opening solo performed *en pointe* and in silence. *As Time Goes By* uses classical technique but it, too, is a tribal rite concerned with repetition and change. It is carefully structured, and it employs the Tharp hallmarks of constant movement, formations appearing and vanishing, unexpected changes, and complex phrasing. Whatever you expect to happen next, doesn't.

Working with her own company, Tharp continued her investigations of jazz with *Ocean's Motion* (1975), to Chuck Berry's music, and *Sue's Leg* (1975) to Fats Waller's. She also was commissioned to make a dance for American Ballet Theater, *Push Comes to Shove,* which was first performed in January 1976. *Push Comes to Shove* is choreographed to Haydn's *82nd Symphony,* with a brief prologue in ragtime. One of the central roles was made on the great classical dancer Mikhail Baryshnikov,

Twyla Tharp's Push Comes to Shove, *choreographed for American Ballet Theater (1976). Mikhail Baryshnikov is at far left, Martine van Hammel is the woman with crossed arms. The corps demonstrates the shifting patterns of Tharp's stage and its changing points of focus.* PHOTOGRAPH © MARTHA SWOPE.

who moved through his solo exactly as if he were dancing the role of Twyla Tharp, deadpan expression and all. The second movement of the symphony is devoted to a magnificent piece of choreography for the *corps de ballet,* a classical passage that Tharp has restated with changes of viewpoint and lines suddenly slightly askew. Again, formations change quickly; nothing holds still long enough to be analyzed, but the constant play of motion is brilliant. This seems to be part of Tharp's heritage from the Judson contingent; her dance is meant to be experienced while it happens, not chewed over afterward. *Push Comes to Shove* contains parodies of balletic curtain calls and other conventions of classical dance, but it is not a parody or a derogatory statement. It makes statements about performance and presentation, and about methods of movement; it praises the Classical convention while mocking some of its accoutrements. Its physical beauty makes the statement common to Tharp's work, a statement that had been made earlier by Merce Cunningham, that the business of dance is dancing.

In March 1976, shortly after the premiere of *Push Comes to Shove,* Tharp and her own company presented a season at the Brooklyn Academy of Music and played to full houses. Tharp had been developing a following among dance fans, but the one work for ABT did more to ensure her success than all the work that had preceded it. She was the subject of interviews, articles, and profiles, not only on the art pages of newspapers but on the glossy pages of magazines. Her bobbed hairstyle suddenly appeared on women all over New York, just as Loie Fuller skirts had been adopted by the women of Paris eighty years before. Contemporary civilization makes a fad of genius, as it does of everything else.

The Brooklyn season was the occasion for a new work, *Give and Take.* The first section was made to Gregor Werner's *Prelude and Fugue in C Minor,* the others to pieces of American music. Two of those, John Philip Sousa's *The Liberty Bell* and *The Stars and Stripes Forever,* had already been used by George Balanchine for his ballet, *Stars and Stripes,* and Tharp's dance acknowledges her admiration for Mr. B. There are hints of *Stars* and of *Agon* in the choreography. *Give and Take* deals with American ways of dancing, and with Americans' ways of looking at themselves.

Twyla Tharp.   PHOTOGRAPH BY GJON MILI.

It recalls those who faint on the sidelines of parades and those who drink their way through football rallies. It contrasts what we do with what we say we do; it presents bouts of determination and moments of indecision. At times, Tharp packs her dancers into a crowd; at others, she leaves one lonely on the stage. At the very end, a dancer stands perfectly still, holding a long, high *relevé*. As the stage lights dim, she drops back into a normal stance and walks quickly from the stage, as if demonstrating to us that nothing ends neatly and perfectly, and that even the most impressive pose must, in time, be given up.

Tharp, like many choreographers of her generation, is not interested in maintaining a repertory; she believes that rehearsing old dances demands time that can better be spent in making new ones. Some of her works, such as *The Bix Pieces,* now can be seen only on tape. Others have been rearranged into new forms—*The Fugue* has been transferred from three women to a woman and two men, and *The Raggedy Dances* has been redone in abbreviated form, as a duet. *Deuce Coupe* has been succeeded in the Joffrey repertory by *Deuce Coupe II*, a more tightly constructed work that does not require the participation of Tharp's own company. It lacks the energy and vitality of the original, but Tharp says, "It's like comparing a bunch of wild flowers with straw flowers. The wild flowers are much more beautiful, but they only last for an hour, then they're gone. The straw flowers are not quite so wonderful, but they can be preserved."

Tharp and her contemporaries developed in an era in which products were designed to become obsolete quickly, to be disposed of and turned in for new versions. The rebels of the 1960s disliked the thought of permanence; possessions were limitations on freedom. Tharp has advanced beyond the 1960s—beyond the disdain for an audience, the fear of involvement, the need to rebel for the sake of rebellion. She celebrates the lack of discipline of the 1960s within a crafted form. She has freed herself of the tyranny of intellectual form to allow passion to show through it; her work is cool, but not frigid. She works with her own company and on commission; she presents a synthesis of ideas of dance, interpreted by an individual mind.

Tharp is too interested in devising new dances to revive old ones, and too busy creating to become mired in reverence or self-adulation. "Why do we have to crawl to art on our knees, and put brambles in the path? It's something you do. You eat, you sleep, you do other things, and in between you make a little art."

* * *

The Upper Room (1987): *Tharp presents classicism:*

Stop, Twyla! I can't count that high. I can't calculate that quickly. I can't see that much in 40 minutes and survive to write about it.

Twyla Tharp's *The Upper Room* . . . is an essay in unbounded energy, higher mathematics, and structural choreography. It is an astonishing piece of work.

Twyla Tharp Dance . . . is an assemblage of highly talented, intensely disciplined dancers whose bodies are totally at the service of one of the keenest minds in the performing arts.

The Upper Room stretches those bodies and that mind as far as anything Tharp has produced. The dance is constructed to a score by Philip Glass and has been costumed by fashion designer Norma Kamali, who has dressed the dancers in striped, raglan-sleeved pajamas that, as layers are removed, become warm-up suits.

Jennifer Tipton has devised a curtain of light at the rear of the stage, as she did in 1983 for Tharp's *Fait Accompli.* . . . In *The Upper Room* [dancers] often cut through the mist like headlights piercing a fog.

There is too much dance here to comprehend in a single viewing. One must be content to sense the structure of the piece rather than to analyze it, and to be thrilled by the energy and virtuosity of the performances rather than to expect a moment-by-moment comprehension of all that is happening on stage.

Tharp's technique frequently dispenses with the preparations common to classical ballet and to much modern dance.

There are no pauses between one step and the next to prepare us for what is about to happen, or to allow our minds to reflect, even for an instant, on what has happened. Instead, the stage is filled with movement that progresses with implacable logic but does not stop, like a professor, to explain how proposition A produces solution B.

Tharp begins with two dancers . . . upstage center. Their steps, including a simple, back-pedaling run that appears again and again in the course of the dance, provide the basic thematic material that is to be developed.

Three more dancers appear and play with the material, restating it in a number of ways. Tharp increases the number of performers on stage and develops a series of spatial patterns (often diagonals) and clearly defined body shapes (often taut, shortened arabesques).

The first performers wear soft shoes, but Tharp soon introduces a group of women in pointe shoes (Kamali has colored them red), and develops a dialogue between weighted dancing and upward-reaching dancing.

This reaches its climax in the most melodic section of the score, during which Tharp employs a clear classical vocabulary, including, it should be noted, preparations.

One key element of this exercise is to point out that classical vision structure (canon form, inversion of steps, balance of pattern, etc.) does not depend on footwear, on preparation, or even on academic definition of line. Classicism, Tharp seems to be saying, depends upon structure.

The Upper Room is basically contrapuntal. It begins with a simple theme for two dancers, brings in a second theme and a third, and interweaves all the individual lines into a continuously moving, changing, fully integrated structure. It is brilliant choreography, and it is magnificently danced. (*The Record*, February 1, 1987)

Tharp joins American Ballet Theater as Artistic Associate:

What on earth is Twyla Tharp, one of the most innovative, outspoken, radical creative forces in dancing doing as an Artistic Associate at American Ballet Theater? ABT is an institution; Tharp is an individualist. ABT specializes in classical ballet; Tharp has earned a reputation as a revolutionary.

Some years ago during an interview, Tharp asserted, "I will never again tie my fortunes to those of one of the big ballet companies." Yet ten months back, after dissolving her own troupe, Twyla Tharp Dance, the choreographer signed on with ABT and is busy rehearsing a series of new works for the company. She has made dances for ABT in the past, the first and probably the most famous being *Push Comes to Shove* (1976). She has also produced two works for the Joffrey Ballet and one, in collaboration with Jerome Robbins, for the New York City Ballet.

During the last years of her own company she made increasing use of the classical vocabulary (in truth, she has always been a classicist) and of dancers trained in ballet. But what happened to the artist who taught us that popular music was suitable for serious dance, who devised a style of movement unlike any seen before, and who constantly astonished audiences with her imagination and inventiveness? She ran out of money, that's what. . . .

Tharp's move to ABT has implications that link financial considerations with artistic ones. She has, as noted, been relying more on the classical vocabulary in recent years, whereas during the mid-Sixties and early-Seventies, she devised her own.

"In the beginning," she explains, "I was making most of the movement on myself, and the few dancers who worked very closely with me. I could invent the vocabulary of each dance. You can't do that when you figure the cost per hour of rehearsing and maintaining a major company. Forty hours of rehearsal cost a lot of money. So you use the vocabulary that everyone knows. If there were another technique that was so readily available to dancers, and so expressive, I'd be glad to use it."

There were, to be sure, other factors that influenced Tharp's choice. She has always had a keen sense of the prevailing climate of art, and classical formalism is a highly praised quality of dance these days. Perhaps more important, she has retired from performing.

"Figure it out for yourself," she says. "There has to be a reason to go through the grind of running a company in this irrational, capricious, insane type of business. The reason for me was dancing."

Tharp, who was thoroughly trained in ballet, has chosen, for several reasons, to change idioms. As ballet and modern dance continue to borrow from one another, other artists decide, at a certain point in their careers, to follow her example. It would not be the first time that Twyla Tharp started a trend. (*The Record*, May 7, 1989)

At 50, Tharp Returns to the Stage . . . with a New Troupe:
"Why am I dancing again?" repeats Twyla Tharp, in her customary machine-gun rhythms. "Because I'm belligerent, that's why."

Tharp? Never.

Tharp has indeed been called belligerent, abrasive, aggressive, and defensive. She's also almost frighteningly brilliant, daringly innovative, gloriously deadpan funny, and one of the outstanding choreographers of her time. And she's back . . .

Ten years ago, when she was turning 40, the choreographer made a dance with a prize-ring metaphor called *Fait Accompli*; the "accomplished fact" was her performing career. Now, six months past her 50th birthday, with quite a lot of gray in the famous short hair, she has choreographed a new work called *Men's Piece*, and she's dancing in it.

. . . Tharp cools the machine-gun fire and says, quite logically, that she's dancing again because she wants to. "You have a sense that there are certain things you want to do," she explains, "and you find ways to do them.

"Also, at a certain point, you're not asking permission anymore." . . .

. . . [Tharp's] working life has held plenty of segments and division—films (*Amadeus*); Broadway (*Singin' in the Rain*); television; her own company (1963–87); and American Ballet Theater (artistic associate, 1987–89).

Tharp, who had a strong working relationship with Mikhail Baryshnikov, dissolved her own company to join him at Ballet Theater when he was artistic director there. Her tenure came to an end with his departure, although the company has continued to produce and dance her works with great success. Finding herself in the uncomfortable position of a concert choreographer without a company, she used her determination and her varied experience to develop work for herself. . . .

Having one's own company, she says, is rewarding, "but it presents artistic problems. The choreographers in that situation have to push their own visions as hard and as fast as they can, but they may not feel the revitalization that comes from working with other dancers and other media." . . .

. . . She has insisted for years that art can be serious and commercially successful at the same time. Film, television, theater, and videos, she asserts, can help support concert performance. . . .

She makes pieces in her own style and in the classical manner, depending on the dancers and the performing circumstances. "I think range in art is important," she explains. Furthermore, she has always insisted that fine art and commercial art should not be separated by some form of cultural chaperone. "I'm not going to sit up on some ivory tower and say, 'Hey, guys, come support me,'" she says. (*The Record*, January 26, 1992) and

Tharp Explains it to You:

The best talk show around is not on late-night television: It's at City Center, where the host is Twyla Tharp.

Of course, Twyla doesn't just talk, she dances. . . . An exceptionally fine 16-member company also dances, performing works from the choreographer's repertory as well as a "sneak preview" of her newest piece, made for the Martha Graham Dance Company.

The center of the program, though, is Tharp's commentary. Standing at a podium stage right; panting when she's trying, by turns, to dance and talk; tossing off choice phrases in her best deadpan style, the choreographer tries to make us aware of the process involved in creating and performing dances.

One of her parlor tricks is to demonstrate a phrase of choreography her dancers never have seen, have them follow her through the steps, and then rehearse them in the movement . . .

. . . [A]s Tharp gives corrections ("These are circles of the knee, not circles of the pelvis, circles of the tummy, or circles of the right shoulder"), we gain some understanding of the choreographer's craft.

We see that a movement phrase has a theme; that its steps are somehow related to one another; that imprecise execution can alter its effect.

We get some idea of the logic—rhythmic, kinetic, or dramatic—that goes into shaping a dance.

This season is Twyla-on-a-budget. There are no costumes, no sets, no fancy lighting, no smoke machines.

"Theater," Tharp says, "is magic; it's an illusion created by extremely skilled people." As she intends, the bare stage and the lack of theatrical illusion focuses our attention on the steps themselves and on the dancers who perform them. We are not seduced by "magic" into forgetting how difficult it is to dance, nor are we distracted from the interplay of movement and music. Instead, we are reminded of the impact that dance can make all on its own. (*The Record*, September 17, 1993)

On *Demeter and Persephone*—Tharp's work for the Martha Graham Company:

. . . [T]he Martha Graham Dance Company['s] . . . season-opening gala . . . culminat[es] in the premiere of the first work the troupe has commissioned from an outside choreographer, Twyla Tharp's *Demeter and Persephone*. . . .

Indulging in one of those bits of quirky logic she loves so well, the choreographer has set the Greek legend of the abduction of spring by the god of the underworld to klezmer music—the folk songs traditionally performed at Jewish weddings in Eastern Europe.

Perhaps it shouldn't work, but it does. The rhythms suit those of the Greek circle dances at which the choreographer hints with crisp, high-kneed steps and arms a la Zorba, and the music's evocation of rejoicing despite oppressive circumstances is appropriate to the wailing of Demeter, mother of the abducted goddess.

Tharp begins with a choral episode, at once brisk and formal. As the story progresses and Demeter . . . mourns the loss of her daughter, the choreography introduces elements of the Graham vocabulary with its anguished contractions and yearning reaches. Indeed, a few episodes refer directly to Graham's own works, but they are so neatly and appropriately integrated into the dance that only those who know the Graham repertory will notice. . . .

. . . [T]he choreography is witty and filled with little rhythmic surprises and an adept mixture of styles.

. . . Tharp [has] explained that *Demeter and Persephone* is a passion play performed by pilgrims on their way to be initiated into the Eleusinian mysteries. The work, with its constant flow of disciplined but ecstatic movement, does suggest a strong sense of community and has the fervor of impromptu story-telling.

The myth is played out in dramatic images that flash out of the energetic, neatly patterned communal dancing. The ensemble suddenly dissolves into a set of individuals, each taking a specific role, then comes together again. Persephone . . . is lifted high by her captor; [Demeter] reaches out desperately; two goddesses come on in a funny, bent-over soft shoe to tease Demeter into smiling once more.

At the height of the story, the principal performers come into sharp focus; at the end, they blend back into the group, dancing their way offstage. *Demeter* is a fine example of formal choreographic structure; equally important, it's great fun to watch. (*The Record*, October 8, 1993)

Americans We (1995): premiere by American Ballet Theater:

Americans We . . . [is] as masterpiece. . . .

. . . [Made] to a selection of 19th-century American musical pieces, . . . [it is] lyrical but is physically daring and dazzling as well. Tharp sends the dancers rollicking across the stage, prancing like circus ponies and spinning in air like acrobats. . . .

The leading dancers exemplify American types, familiar from stories and folklore. Tharp brilliantly takes the theme still further, hinting at the styles of important American choreographers: Agnes de Mille, Jerome Robbins, and, especially in the glittering finale, George Balanchine. It's not just "Americans We" that she's talking about but "American Dancers We."

Square dancing, march formations, and yes, pure ballet, make it clear that Tharp has taken her text from Isadora Duncan: "I see American dancing." . . . (*The Record*, May 4, 1995)

EPILOGUE

WHEN ISADORA DUNCAN and Ruth St. Denis watched Loie Fuller perform in Paris, American ballet was a candidate for obsequies and the nation's dance in general was an unconsidered—almost a nonexistent—art. Now, dance is more popular than at any time in American history and ballet is so voraciously alive that it is swallowing some of the audience of modern dance. It has also chewed thoroughly on some of modern dance's assumptions and conventions. The modern camp, in turn, has digested some of the precepts of ballet. The two forms of dance are not in open conflict as they were when Martha Graham and Doris Humphrey were seeking to develop contemporary ways of dancing; it is generally accepted now that modern dancers will study ballet technique, and that ballet companies will commission works from modern dance choreographers.

Traditional ballet is a Romantic art, replete with grand gestures, rich costumes, beautiful bodies, and bouts of passion. The eternal feminine leads us ever upward intensifying the metaphor by balancing on *pointe,* and the leading artists of both sexes are presented as objects of desire. In an epoch notably short of heroes, ballet provides us with superhuman surrogates who defy the laws of gravity; in a period of economic and political turmoil, it offers glamor and stability; in a time of mechanized mediocrity, it presents a vision of aristocracy and individual excellence. But ballet is also an intensely formal art that depends on a strict vocabulary, precision, logically evolved structure, and the careful arrangement of groups. Some of the greatest modern ballets—Balanchine's *Agon,* for example—deal more with form than with emotional content, and are made to music suitable to the Classical cast. These ballets attempt to interpret the conditions of the age, rather than to negate them. However, the average ballet fan seeks the Romantic face of the art, and asks to be swept away by music and gesture that bring some power of emotion into a rushing, untouchable world.

Martha Graham and Doris Humphrey defined the Romantic and Classical aspects of American modern dance; Graham's passion exemplified America's Romanticism while Humphrey's strict form defined its Classicism. Since the end of World War II, the Classicists have been dominant. Few important modern choreographers in recent years have made dances on the subjects of individual revolt or passion; most have been more interested in sociology than in psychology, more concerned with movement than with metaphor. Graham's greatness still pervades the art; few major choreographers have not learned something—technique or philosophy—from her. But what they learned caused many of them to seek a new direction. Graham's greatest work brought Romanticism in modern dance to a peak; she was an impossible art to follow. Furthermore, the time in which she made these monumental dances demanded an art of personal statement; succeeding decades produced an environment requesting a more restrained, detached, form of comment. When, in the late 1960s and early 1970s, proclamations were needed again, modern dance was following a longer road into Classicism; the statements were made by ballet and by rock.

Since the advent of Merce Cunningham, modern choreographers have generally concerned themselves with formal and societal matters rather than with personal ones. Cunningham and Paul Taylor are not ballet choreographers, but they are speaking, in a different vocabulary, of the same subjects treated by the formal aspects of ballet: shape, groupings, relationships in space, rhythmic phrasing, the physical possibilities of the body. Nikolais deals with environment; so, in another way, does Meredith Monk. All have more in common with Humphrey than with Graham. All are more closely allied to the art of Piet Mondrian or Frank Stella than to that of Vasily Kandinsky or Joan Miró, to the novels of John Barth and Thomas Pynchon than to those of Hemingway or Faulkner.

The dance revolt of the 1960s resulted in the establishment of an off-off-Broadway of dance where performers and choreographers can experiment. College dance departments and home-grown troupes throughout the country provide other opportunities to work. The percentage of

Moving ahead, but glancing back. Baryshnikov in Push Comes to Shove.   PHOTOGRAPH © MARTHA SWOPE.

choreographers in the national population has never been as great as it is now. However, many younger artists perform for a coterie audience, or are more concerned with being avant-garde than with being dance-makers. Others have severely restricted themselves in their choices of movement. Some of the talented ones will grow out of their limitations.

Interesting work is being accomplished; modern dance has not lost its ability to attract experimenters. Trisha Brown makes simple movements, but she makes them in unexpected places—she walks on walls with the aid of a harness. The Multigravitational Aerodance Group works on a structure resembling a circus apparatus. Pilobolus chooses the names of its works from botany, blends its bodies into groups that form the shapes of strange but friendly beasts, and has created a new technique based on yoga and gymnastics. Most of the experiments seem to be concerned with form and technique, with intellectual concepts rather than emotional content, with method rather than message. The avant-garde has, to a great extent, accepted the Classical aspect of the tradition, and, in some cases, has taken it to its extreme. For a time, at least, that side of the art is likely to continue in ascendance, although the continued interinfluence of ballet and modern dance may soften it.

Twyla Tharp stands as a synecdoche for contemporary dance. Tharp works with her own troupe (generally considered a "modern dance" group) trained to perform in her style, but she also receives commissions for companies committed to Classical ballet. She composes her dances with traditional ballet steps, but she uses them to remark on contemporary concepts and rhythms. Tharp realizes that a Classical technique may be used to express ideas unconsidered by the age that devised it, and that tradition may provide a foundation for new methods of construction.

Isadora Duncan trapped herself by concentrating on personal emotion without developing a systematic method of passing on her passions to her students. Many members of the newest generation of dancers are confined in form, apparently without a personal passion to convey. Of course, Isadora Duncan was a genius; so is Martha Graham; so is Merce Cunningham; so is Twyla Tharp. Genius can express itself through Classicism, through Romanticism, or through any amalgam that the time demands. A passion will be found, suited to its time, since the recurring production of genius seems to be the most important work of the human race, and genius is a passionate measure of its era.

May 1976
New York City

* * *

Joseph Mazo's writings since the publication of the original Prime Movers convey his observations of the continued close relationship between modern dance and ballet, the development of intriguing choreographers, and the re-establishment of emotion and personal experience as vital impeti for making dances.

Excerpts from articles are grouped only by choreographer in this section, although relationships clearly exist among these dancemakers.

Erick Hawkins

Ahab (1986): *An innovative, ritualized dance-drama:*

Erick Hawkins's *Ahab* is not a dance but a dance-drama. It is the contemporary American equivalent of a Japanese Noh play.

The piece, which of course is based on *Moby-Dick*, . . . like a Noh play, is performed in a highly ritualized manner, combining music (by Ross Lee Finney), a spoken text (drawn from Melville's novel), dance, and dramatic presentation. The dancers who perform the smaller roles are masked, suggesting that the characters they portray are to be regarded less as individuals than as figures necessary to the action. . . .

Ahab's wooden leg is suggested by a white shoe and stocking; the exotic nationalities of the harpooners are defined by their masks. Nothing is *realistic*, because nothing is permitted to detract from the poetic reality of Ahab's search for the white whale and from the tragic culmination of that quest.

The movement, too, is deliberately limited in its vocabulary. Hawkins [as Ahab] paces the deck with the unbending bearing of an Old Testament prophet. The harpooners, grasping their weapons, lunge forward with awkward, almost primitive, leaps. . . .

Even *realistic* actions—Ahab nailing a gold coin to the mast or ripping up a chart—are performed harshly, with a maximum of economy.

These techniques allow us to understand Ahab's emotions without becoming empathetic to them. We behold the story from a respectful, ritualized distance. It is the whole of the tragedy, not its specific incidents, that the choreographer wishes us to understand. As a result, a dramatic tension is created that is released only when a clap, like that used in Japanese theater, signals that the event has been completed. . . .

. . . Hawkins has discarded traditional Western dance techniques and theater practices, and in doing so has created a powerful, stimulating, imaginative piece of dance theater. (*The Record*, September 24, 1986)

Erick Hawkins: Unique among the unique

Modern-dance choreographers are individualists by definition, but Erick Hawkins is unique even among their diverse company.

First off, he has a degree in Greek from Harvard. (He had gone there intending to study piano, only to be told that he was too advanced to join the beginning music theory class.) "I enrolled in classics by sheer accident," Hawkins says, "but once I got into the Greek idea I was fascinated. The Greeks created the one civilization that accepted the body and did not think it was dirty. The Greeks thought a fully developed body was important."

Second, he worked with the two greatest innovators of American dance, George Balanchine and Martha Graham, before setting out on his own. "I was very bright," he explains, "I went to the best."

Hawkins began his performing career in ballet at a time when ballet and modern dance were in the midst of a blood feud. He was, he recalls, the first male student at the School of American Ballet, which was founded in 1934, and he danced with the American Ballet and with Ballet Caravan, both precursors of the New York City Ballet.

In 1938, filled with admiration for Balanchine but seeking a technique that might further aid his own work, Hawkins showed up at Graham's studio to take class. Shortly thereafter, he became the first male to dance with her company, and "possibly the first man to dance without a shirt on," he remarks jokingly.

Hawkins began to choreograph in 1937, but it was not until the 1950s, after a successful dancing career with Graham—and a less successful marriage to her—that he devised a unique style of movement, different from that of Balanchine, Graham, or anyone else. . . .

His idiom has long been favored by a limited group of connoisseurs, but now, nearly 30 years after he developed it, the style is becoming popular. "I feel a little bit like John the Baptist," Hawkins remarks. "I am trying to say things I know are true and nobody has wanted to listen. Lately, though, things are getting better—people are starting to pay attention." . . .

The first thing one notices about Hawkins's movement is that it is soft, employing neither the percussive attack of Graham's technique nor the intense, self-conscious stretch of ballet. It is, the choreographer explains, based on the needs of the human body and on the concepts of Buddhism. (Remember, we are dealing with a man who cites Plato, Nietzsche, and Alfred North Whitehead in the course of casual conversation.) "Having had a grounding in Western civilization at college

—I was fairly far along in the dancing by this time—I found I wasn't happy," Hawkins relates. . . .

"I began to read Suzuki's 'Essays on Zen Buddhism.' The book was like a blank wall—I couldn't get an understanding of it—but because of the aesthetic appeal of the drawings, I began to read further. I found the Blythe translation of haiku—I still think haiku are the greatest poetry that has ever been—and slowly I came to the essence of Buddhism.

"The Eastern way of knowing is through immediate apprehension —direct knowing. The Buddha knew the divine not through doctrine but through his body. That is the basis of my technique—you just do the movement, you don't get in your own way. Free-flowing movement is kinaesthetic truth."

Certainly, Hawkins is a supreme advertisement for his own theories. Until six months ago, when he slipped on an oil slick in a parking lot and temporarily interrupted his regimen of swimming and dancing, he weighed precisely one pound more than he did at 21. . . . Informed guesstimates put his age at 78.

Although Eastern thought has influenced his movement and the content of many of his dances, his philosophy of theater follows that of Plato, who wished to ban violent passions and ugliness from the stage. "Any psychological negativity in a work of art is as useless as effort is in movement," Hawkins asserts. "Everybody is faced with the challenge of going ahead until the day he dies: Works of art should give everyone in the audience the courage to be the hero and to face the monster.

"I don't show ugliness in my work and a lot of people say that I'm simply escaping. But the traditional role of art all over the world is to bring the audience to enlightenment. You can't just show ugliness and violence without also showing ways of transcending them."

The choreographer's newest work, . . . is called *God the Reveler* and is based on the attributes of Dionysus, the Greek god of wine and of the theater. "At Delphi," Hawkins says, "Dionysus was the equal of Apollo. Greek vases show the two gods shaking hands. To be only Apollonian in a work of art is academic; carrying the dionysian idea to its extremes is to be absurd.

"I'm very Apollonian, actually, but in the new piece I'm trying *unleashedness.* A work of art needs both Apollonian and Dionysian qualities. Artists who give us the most satisfaction blend the two."

There is a third strain in Hawkins's work, one as important as Buddhist thought and Greek philosophy, and that is old-fashioned American pride.

"All over the country," Hawkins, who was born in Trinidad, Colorado, points out indignantly, "people perform *The Nutcracker* at Christmas time. That's silly. It's what they performed in Russia 100 years ago. An American child doesn't even know what a sugarplum is. When I was in Washington [DC] recently we drove past the Lincoln Memorial, and I found myself thinking, 'Look at that! Make a Greek temple as a memorial to an American man who was born in a log cabin—how dumb can you get?'" . . .

Hawkins and his company performed *Plains Daybreak*—a stunningly beautiful dance based on the mythology of the Plains Indians—for 12,000 schoolchildren in two days at the Seattle Opera House. "We played music by an American composer, showed them the work of an American mask-maker, and presented American animals—the coyote, for example—in an American legend. They loved it," Hawkins says. (*The Record*, November 29, 1987)

Many Thanks (1994): *Simply beautiful*

Critics usually try to avoid using the word *beautiful*. It's hackneyed, it's imprecise, and it sounds naive and vaguely unprofessional. Yet once in a while, like it or not, we're stuck with it. The dances Erick Hawkins and his company are presenting at the Joyce Theater [in January, 1994] are beautiful—elegantly shaped, delicately nuanced, and utterly free of excess.

The body shapes are clear and sweetly curved; the movement is flowing and soft, and each passage of the choreography seems to develop from the last as naturally as a branch grows from the trunk of a tree. . . .

[*Many Thanks*] begins with absolute simplicity, as three dancers standing center stage execute a step so clear and uncomplicated it might have come from a children's game. They cross one foot behind the other, then return to starting position, gently but emphatically swinging their arms.

This simple shift of the body from side to side is so filled with innocence that only a highly sophisticated choreographer would dare to use it. It also creates a base from which Hawkins can build an inexorably developing pattern of movement.

More dancers enter, at first repeating the theme and then breaking out of it, into a deliberately increasing range of movement that expands not only horizontally across the stage but vertically as well. . . .

The end of the piece is quietly spectacular. All eight dancers are tightly grouped upstage right, and the men, one by one, hurl themselves into leaps that bring the dancers down into deeply stretched, floor-hugging lunges. The leaps are repeated as the men force themselves forward toward some vastly desired goal while behind them the four women tilt their heads back to look at the sky.

The movement is filled with intense physical energy, yet the dancers execute it with an apparent lack of effort. We're never permitted to realize how difficult these steps really are, or how much strength is required to perform them. We simply bask in the comfortable warmth of those clearly yet softly defined shapes and the flow of unfolding patterns.

The program also included *Intensities of Space, and Wind* and *New Moon*, both masterpieces of contemporary choreography. *Intensities* deals with the complementary qualities of empty and filled space, and movement and stillness.

New Moon is an utterly joyful dance in which curving shapes and paths of movement hint at constant renewals of life and its promise.

What is remarkable—although in a more sensible society it wouldn't be—about these dances, which affirm the human capacity for fresh starts and poetic self-expression, is that they have been made by a man who, according to the accepted dictates of our culture, should be living in a retirement community. In April, Hawkins will celebrate his 85th birthday.

Many Thanks, his most recent masterpiece, reminds us that there is no mandatory retirement age for genius. (*The Record*, January 28, 1994)

Erick Hawkins died November 23, 1994.

Judith Jamison

Divining (New York premiere, 1984): *presenting a new talent*

There's an exciting, original, energetic new choreographic talent in town: Her name is Judith Jamison. . . . [T]he first major work by the woman who used to be everyone's favorite Alvin Ailey dancer is very impressive indeed.

[In t]he dance, called *Divining*, . . . [t]he curtain rises—very, very slowly—to reveal four dancers dressed in white and set in a diamond pattern center stage. They sway from the waist, first forward and then to the back, like trees bending in the wind. This sensuous, measured manner of movement, which seems part of a ritual invocation, becomes a major motif of the dance. . . .

The verb "divine" means "to make out by supernatural or magical insight," and Jamison's dance suggests the discipline, the concentration and the controlled ecstasy the procedure traditionally requires. The choreographer has created onstage an entire culture—one that is at once "primitive" (close to nature) and sophisticated in its movements and self-awareness. (*The Record*, November 30, 1984)

Judith Jamison, Artistic Director:

Judith Jamison has been named artistic director of the Alvin Ailey American Dance Theater, succeeding the company's founder, who died December 1, [1989].

"This is like coming home to a place where I've been in my heart for years, even if I haven't been here physically," Jamison said at a press conference. . . . Jamison joined the company as a dancer in 1965, and soon became an internationally recognized star. . . .

"Mr. Ailey asked me to do this a long time ago," she said. "And he kept asking. It was one of those have-tos of life." She is not going to attempt to "fill Ailey's shoes" because, she explained, "We all have our own shoes to wear. . . . Mr. Ailey believed in the individuality of the artist; I am still Judith Jamison and I will be working to reflect both his vision and mine." (*The Record*, December 21, 1989)

Hymn: *A tribute to Ailey:*

. . . Artistic Director Judith Jamison's *Hymn* . . . is an inventive, exciting, and moving piece of dance theater.

Hymn might almost have been spelled "Him", since the piece is a tribute to the company's founder Alvin Ailey. . . . Yet the work goes deeper, saluting the spirit of dance as well as the spirit of a dancer.

The text, written and performed by Anna Deavere Smith, is derived from taped interviews with Ailey dancers. The first is a recording of Ailey himself; . . .

Although choreographers who use a spoken text often err by dividing our attention—its not easy to look and listen at the same time—Jamison avoids the trap.

One reason for her success is that she has avoided literal gesture, inventing instead movement that abstracts the emotional and rhythmic content of each interview. Words and music complement each other, rather than compete. . . .

Carefully calculated shifts of rhythms, texture, and density—the number of dancers on stage—keep us constantly alert and interested as one episode succeeds another. Deavere becomes an alter ego for each of the solo dancers—speaking in her own many voices, thus linking the sections and maintaining the overall theme. (*The Record*, December 10, 1993)

Garth Fagan

[Garth] Fagan, who began his career touring with the Jamaican National Dance Company, founded the [Bucket Dance Theatre] in 1970, when he arrived in Rochester, N.Y., to join the faculty of the nearby State University of New York at Brockport. Working with students who had little or no previous dance training, he created a company that has been widely applauded throughout the country. . . . (*The Record*, March 28, 1985)

It has taken some of us—including me—several years to become comfortable with the spare, strenuous, deliberately disjointed choreographic style of Garth Fagan. There is nothing familiar about it, nothing that suggests well-known reference points of permits easy comparisons. Fagan's work demands that we come to it without preconceptions; that we watch with the same intensity the dancers bring to their performances. (*The Record*, November 16, 1989)

Until, By & If (1990): *A fine example of Fagan's dances and dancers*
Fagan's style and vision are unique. Nobody invents body shapes like his or devises such intricate interplays of rhythms. No other choreographer displays the body at such unexpected angles, and no one produces such unusual images so naturally and unself-consciously.

The performers, too, are remarkable, as energetic as tadpoles, disciplined as drill sergeants, physically impressive as dancers, yet the demands they make on their bodies never hinder the free, proud presentation of individual personalities.

Fagan's dances are most easily appreciated for their physical intensity, but they are constructed with steel-beamed logic and challenge the mind as well as the eye. . . . [In] *Until, By & If,* . . . [t]he choreographer has incorporated an epigraph from the Caribbean poet Derek Walcott: "until your winters grow more kind/by the dancing firelight of the mind." The first line prefaces the opening section; the next, the second; . . . "If" is the unannounced third segment. . . .

. . . "Until" seems to be a battle with gravity; the dancers move heavily, pressing down on one another's bodies and curving into awkward, uncomfortable-looking postures. "By" is romantic, filled with couples, their soft, yielding shapes nestling tenderly as they recline on the floor. "If" is freedom; the dancers still are paired, but we're aware of individual bodies moving vertically, and of flowing, thrusting chests and pelvises as partners incite each other to share joy and pleasure.

It's no accident that the piece begins with a wedge-shaped mass of dancers advancing stiffly with small, earth-hugging steps and ends with a couple face to face, rejoicing in the flexibility of their bodies and effortlessly lifting their feet. Fagan has choreographed a journey from the winter chill that binds both minds and bodies to the love and freedom of emotional summer.

Until, By & If is set to three jazz pieces by Don Pullen. . . . The music, like the dance, is at once intellectual and passionate. (*The Record,* November 15, 1990)

Moth Dreams (1992): *A dance autobiography*

Griot New York, the astonishingly beautiful dance Garth Fagan made last year, is a condensed emotional history of black people in America. *Moth Dreams* . . . is a condensed emotional history of Garth Fagan. . . .

The [Garth Fagan Dance] performers' control of balance and shape, their almost unnoticeable transitions between steps, their muscularity—never disturbed by tension—and their musicality make the company one of the country's finest.

No other troupe dances quite this way, because no other company dances for Fagan. The choreographer not only has developed his own technique, he has—especially during the last few years—gone far beyond technique into style and substance.

Moth Dreams is an abstract dance, in the sense that Picasso's *Guernica* is an abstract painting; we see a succession of images, each clearly depicted yet unrealistic enough to carry an abundance of meanings. . . .

The first section, "His Dream," is made to music by Andre Julivet. Its edged images are intended to suggest the strict academic mind of the choreographer's father, an Oxford-educated scholar who was chief education officer of Jamaica, where Fagan was raised.

The third segment, "Her Dream," has a commissioned score by Wynton Marsalis. . . . It's an homage to Fagan's mother, who loved beautiful clothes and the life of the emotions. . . .

The central episode, to music by Thelonious Monk, is "Their Dream" —Fagan himself—portrayed by the brilliant Norwood Pennewell in a beautifully made solo. Here, the long-held poses that stretch across the music, little skittering side steps that catch its accents, and light, easy movement that suggests the essence of jazz without being technically *jazzy,* Fagan displays his unique style of choreography to its best advantage.

Pennewell, in gray overalls and a baseball cap, becomes the eternal adolescent, caught between action and dreaming, between aspiration and anxiety. The choreographer creates the mood partly with steps— which here are unusually simple for him—and even more with rhythms.

The dance phrases sometimes match the musical ones, but at least as often they play with internal rhythms, prolonging a step so that the dancer seems to be hearing a deeper music than we do.

What he hears, its becomes clear, is the mixed music of Fagan's childhood, finally brought into harmony by the mature artist the once-divided boy has become. (*The Record*, September 24, 1992)

Jukebox for Alvin (1993) *performed by the Alvin Ailey American Dance Theater: A tribute to a friend and mentor*

Ailey long had wanted Fagan to create a piece for his company, but schedules never seemed to mesh. Now, four years after the choreographer's death, Fagan has produced a tribute to his late friend and mentor that is astonishing in its beauty and in its complexity.

Jukebox [for Alvin] . . . is a pure-dance work rich in imagery and emotion. . . .

Fagan and Ailey shared a wide-ranging taste in music. Acknowledging this, the first section of *Jukebox* is set to music by Antonin Dvorak, the second to Taj Mahal, the third to Keith Jarrett, and the last to Sly Dunbar and Robbie Shakespear. . . .

[At the very end], Fagan clears the stage, and the last three performers continue to dance—serenely, securely, and comfortably to the beat—as the curtain falls. They look as if they could continue forever, which, it seems, is the impression Fagan wants to create. Ailey is no longer alive, but the dance—his dance—goes on. (*The Record*, December 13, 1993)

Trisha Brown

Ms. Brown is one of the most celebrated and important choreographers of postmodern dance. In her earlier days, she became known for works in which dancers walked on walls and danced on rooftops. More recently, she has collaborated with contemporary artists and musicians on dances for the proscenium stage, but her fascination with structure has not diminished. (*The Record*, September 19, 1985)

Trisha Brown's style:

Ms. Brown's works suggest a constant flow of energy that travels through the body of each performer and through the company as a whole. The dance vocabulary Ms. Brown employs relies on fluid motions; the body almost never comes to full stretch but seems soft and relaxed, ready to respond to any kinetic impulse. Her group dances suggest clumps of giant, feathery seaweed moving freely in ocean currents.

Ms. Brown's dances are intensely intellectual. Nobody is likely to be deeply moved by any of the pieces, and yet the sweet shapes of the steps themselves and the repeated rigor of the rhythms provoke a definite sense of well-being.

Ms. Brown has wit, too. The sight of two dancers bumping chests like a pair of playful Great Dane puppies (in *Set and Reset*) is certain to elicit a gentle smile from any spectator. . . . (*The Record*, September 19, 1985)

Astral Convertible (1989): *A striking set, remarkable choreography*

The most immediately striking feature of *Astral Convertible* is not the fluid and beautiful choreography of Trisha Brown but the technologically impressive decor designed by Robert Rauschenberg.

The artist has placed the dance . . . within an urban landscape defined by a group of metal scaffolds that range in height from 2 to 8 feet. Each of these towers is fitted with sensors that detect the bodies of the dancers and the reflective fabric in their costumes. As the performers move, they activate the sensors and stimulate changes in the lighting . . . and the music. . . . The entire enterprise—except the dancing, of course—is powered by automobile batteries; hence the name of the work.

It seems only fair to point out that the idea is not completely novel; Merce Cunningham has employed similar techniques at least twice. In *Variations V* (1965), Cunningham's dancers moved among five antennas, breaking electromagnetic fields and thus producing changes in John Cage's electronic score and in the slide projections and films that formed the background of the piece. In *TV Re-run* (1972), composer Gordon Mumma had the dancers wearing sensors in their belts; movements were translated into audible pitches that were amplified and broadcast to the audience.

In Brown's new work, as in Cunningham's older ones, the decor can alter our view of the movement. A line of Brown's dancers may be hidden like gentle snipers behind a tower only to suddenly delight us by their unexpected appearance. The changes in sound, as performers cross invisible lines, make us aware that we constantly affect not only people but objects, and that they, in turn, unknowingly react to us.

However, the most remarkable element of *Astral Convertible* is the choreography. As in so much of Brown's work, the dancers seem to be negotiating a treaty involving the law of gravity. At the very beginning, performers dressed in bodysuits of metallic gray are stretched on the floor. They rise by stages, and, just as we think they are going to come to their feet, stop and slip back to the floor. The curled shapes of their bodies as they reach the apex of their efforts to stand are lovely, and the surprise we feel at their collapse is arresting.

There is no sense that the dancers have failed to rise; they simply accept the fact of gravitational force, relax, and try again. It is a pattern that reappears frequently in *Astral Convertible*; in one repeated motif, dancers reach behind them, grab their lifted heels with one hand, then fall forward, giving in to the pull of the earth.

Dancers are constantly tilting a bit too far in one direction or another, comfortably accepting the consequences, and rebounding immediately. . . . In *Astral Convertible*, whatever goes up must come down, but whatever falls down will just as certainly come back up.

Brown's style of movement is sweetly soft. Impulses from the pelvis and shoulder turn and twist the dancers' bodies as if they were so many sea plants, reacting naturally to the current. Sudden, energetic bounds punctuate this easy action and contrast with the elegant, curling body shapes that dominate the choreography. Gentleness does not imply limpness or a lack of vitality, however; the movement is filled with energy, and the dancers clearly are strong as well as supple and centered. The inventive, fluid shapes of the steps, set against the rigorous mathematical complexity of the developing patterns, makes the dance fascinating and intensely enjoyable to watch. (*The Record*, March 16, 1989)

If You Could See Me (1994): *Would you know me?*

When we talk about *seeing* a person, we usually mean seeing his or her face. We remember reading that "the eyes are the windows of the soul" and that we judge someone's mood from the expression of his mouth.

We talk about meeting "face-to-face"; performers prefer to present themselves face-front, and TV and film directors make emotional and dramatic capital of close-ups—which emphasize a performer's features.

Yet dancers are more concerned with bodies than with faces, and Trisha Brown's acute mind has come up with a question that, being a choreographer, she poses and answers physically. The title of her new dance, the first solo she's made for herself in 15 years, is really the first phrase of the question. "If you couldn't see me" (meaning: If you couldn't see my face), Brown asks, "would you know me?" . . .

Having set herself the question and decided upon the answer, the choreographer proceeds to prove her point. Throughout the 10-minute solo, Brown is always turned at least partly away from us; a great deal of time she shows only her back, and the rest of the time her features are concealed by her hair.

That being the case, do we know her? Of course we do. Nobody else moves quite that smoothly, drifting so gently and yet so precisely from one position to the next. Nobody else travels over the stage so easily that we hardly notice how quickly she's gone from one side to the other. Nobody else would have a leg-swing gently echo an arm-swing as energy flows almost visibly from one part of her body to another.

Brown's way of moving is fluid, and effort is always camouflaged, yet it's also amazingly clear. We see every action distinctly as the choreographer focuses our attention without seeming to. We're caught, as she intends us to be, by the moment when she rolls her head back on her neck, letting us think that she's finally going to give in and let us "see her." Of course, she never does. . . .

Chess masters and mathematicians describe particularly elegant games and solutions as beautiful. Brown's dances, investigations of physical and intellectual premises, are beautiful in the same way, as well as in their physicality. (*The Record*, May 6, 1994)

Laura Dean

Ecstasy (New York premiere, 1994) *and* Infinity (New York premiere, 1994): *Rapturous dance*

Ecstasy is the appropriate word. It's the title of one of [Laura Dean's] dances . . . , but it also sums up the nature of her work. Her dances are outbursts of rapture.

Dean goes straight to the heart of choreography—to the pulsing, insistent rhythms that impel us to move: we breathe, our hearts beat, and we go on from there. The patterns of her dances are dazzling in complexity—people flash through space like comets, tracing burning paths in the air—yet the steps are often as direct and chaste as those of folk dances.

When she first began to choreographs more than 25 years ago, Dean relied largely on deliberately naive, geometric patterns and on unadorned movement—most notably dervish-style spinning—to produce works that were deeply meditative and nearly hypnotic.

Slowly, she expanded her vocabulary, and her dances now are as thoroughly theatrical as they once were inner-directed. *Ecstasy* and *Infinity* . . . even hint at tap-dancing. The floor is miked and the snaps and clicks of feet striking the stage are part of the rhythmic pattern. Gently swinging arms—a stylized suggestion of old-fashioned hoofing—complete the image. . . .

Steps, however, are not the focus of Dean's choreography; patterns are. They, too, look deceptively simple until you realize that you can't figure out how the flow of dancers is being accomplished; how the space seems to be constantly expanding and contracting; how the lines of energy keep streaming and swirling over the stage without a pause. . . .

In both works, though, the flow of movement never stops—the force of the drummed rhythms won't allow it—and it carries us along the way a current tows a swimmer. Dean's choreographic waters are clear, warm, and filled with the energy of life.(*The Record*, April 29, 1994)

Ulysses Dove

Ulysses Dove: Going "beyond the [Ailey] company"

[Ulysses] Dove became interested in dance while he was a premed student at Howard University. He saw a performance given by American Ballet Theater and was moderately impressed; then he saw one by Martha Graham's company and went away determined to study dance. He changed schools, changed majors, came to New York to continue studying, and in 1970, only a few months after being graduated from Bennington, he was invited to join the Cunningham company. Three years later, he began dancing with Ailey.

Ailey himself is exceptionally proud of dancers who "go on beyond the company" as he puts it, and he is delighted by Dove, who has gone far indeed. Between 1980 and 1983, the young dance-maker was the assistant director of the newly formed modern dance wing of the Paris Opera Ballet . . .

Dove has studied or performed with many of the major artists of modern dance, and in teaching and in choreographing, he says, he took from each "the essence of dance; not so much technique as the meaning of dance itself."

Among the skills he demands from his dancers, be they European or American, is an awareness of a continuous line of action.

"A phrase starts when you come onto the stage," he explains, "and it continues until you leave. The pauses you take are part of the phrase, as they are when an actor says, 'To be—or not to be.' You can run it all together, but then it does not make sense."

Dove is extremely concerned with the structure of each piece of choreography. He tests steps on himself before demonstrating for the dancers partly to see how the work feels as well as how it looks, and partly because a really wonderful dancer can distract a choreographer. . . .

. . . The first dance he ever choreographed was made for Ailey's second company in 1980.

"I had hurt my back and couldn't go on tour, and Alvin said, 'Why don't you do a piece while you're in New York?' I'd been thinking about it for some time, so I tried it, and it worked." (*The Record*, July 6, 1984)

Episodes (U.S. premiere: 1989): *Human encounters along life's crossroad*

Ulysses Dove's dances don't take place, they explode. Dove, a soft-spoken, gentle, reasoning man, creates choreography of astonishingly violent intensity. His most recent work, *Episodes*, with its sudden leaps, clutching catches, and taut, body-lengthening stretches, might be a visual translation of the Latin adage, *carpe diem* ("seize the day"). . . ,

The dance consists of a series of human encounters that take place on two long, intersecting diagonal paths: a crossroads defined by light. As the first note of Robert Ruggieri's electronic score erupts in our ears, two men burst onto the stage, the second crowding the first as they run with long, urgent strides. They do not move like two per-formers who have been instructed to run; they cover space as if their lives depended on reaching the end of the runway, and the second man crashes after the first as if catching him were all that mattered.

That driving race, ending in pouncing jumps, states the metaphor of the dance. There is no time to waste in this life, no second that is not precious; each moment, and each encounter with another human being, must be snapped up as quickly as a frog's tongue catches flies.

It is typical of Dove's choreography that the violent actions of the dancers are channeled and made more intense by the formal structure of the dance. The performers may not venture outside the two strips of light; when two men finally break the pattern, to circle one another where the roads meet, the effect is almost shocking. In creating so strict a pattern, Dove set himself a fascinating structural problem, which he then brilliantly solved.

The first series of entrances come from the same place—upstage right—so that when Dove eventually brings a dancer on from down left, we are strongly aware of the change. Just as we get accustomed to watch-ing dancers pursue one another, we see two of them passing in oppo-site directions. When we become comfortable with entrances at break-neck pace, a man saunters across the stage. As soon as the choreographer has established to our satisfaction that the dance is a series of duets, he introduces a trio.

However, Dove is not concerned with form for its own sake, and *Episodes* is a drama, not a study. Men and women pursue one another along the paths of life, sometimes being welcomed, sometimes receiving a rebuff, sometimes getting themselves knocked down and walked over.

The character of the movement is aggressive and even predatory. The men stalk the women and are, in turn, hunted by them. . . .

Women spin through the air until men catch their thighs and haul them in, chest-high. Men stretch into deep lunges and extend themselves just as completely while in air. Everything happens quickly; there seem to be no transitions, just percussive attacks that lead from one step to another. Furthermore, the dancers' actions are never gentle; even when two of them support one another, they do so in a way that suggests shock, anger, or need, but hardly ever tenderness. (*The Record*, December 14, 1989)

Ulysses Dove died in 1996.

Jawole Willa Jo Zollar

Nyabinghi Dreamtime: *Urban Bush Women on a journey to freedom:*

Other people's religions, like their social conventions, generally seem more like artifacts to be studied than traditions to be experienced. Part of the astonishing brilliance of Jawole Willa Jo Zollar's *Nyabinghi Dreamtime* is that the work draws us into the ecstatic communion of a Rastifarian ritual, not as detached observers but as participants in anguish and in rapture.

Urban Bush Women, the remarkable troupe of dancers and musicians Zollar formed 10 years ago, . . . draws its material from the traditions and cultures of the African Diaspora.

The dance depicts a journey from slavery to freedom, from despair to hope, from anger to security, from anguish to redemption. It is the same passage Jews recall at the Passover Seder, beginning with the words, "Because we were slaves in Egypt."

Zollar describes the voyage using movement as her metaphor, beginning with downcast stillness, then advancing to tense-bodies, uncontrolled actions through passages of rapturous freedom to a trusting, fulfilled quietude. Nyabinghi is a Rastifarian rite that lasts from three to 21 days. Two years ago, percussionist Junior "Gabu" Wedderburn, who composed the score for the dance, took the company into the hills of his native Jamaica to witness a Nyabinghi ceremony.

Zollar has transferred the observance into choreography so meticulously organized and strikingly performed that it doesn't look like choreography, but like spontaneous action.

The women on stage seem impelled to dance by the persistent, passionate drumming and by their own inner needs. Until the very end, they never move in complete synchronization, yet each performer is rhythmically and physically a part of the celebrating community.

At first, we see women kneeling as they chant about a sister who is lost and whom they must "bring back to Zion." The spiritual rescue of that woman—who kneels far from the others, before a candle—provides the dramatic material of the dance. She is roused, whipped with palm fronds, and gradually brought into the community, first dancing alone and finally as a member of an ecstatic group.

The dancing is drawn from African tradition: backs are bent, feet are flat when they strike the floor, even in landings from jumps; chests, arms and hips move in isolation from the rest of the body. The bodies are tense; elbows pump with frantic anger; individual actions seem almost spastic and random, as if generated by forces beyond the dancers' conscious control.

Dancing is only one means of expression in this community. The drums—of various timbres—enthrall our ears with complex, demanding music, and human voices add another, yearning note. When a drummer begins to sing about "400 years in Babylon"—any conquering, enslaving culture is Babylon—the women join in responsively. Their songs have a familiar quality; while in Jamaica, Zollar realized that she had heard the same kind of singing in the church she attended as a child in Kansas City.

As the dance progresses, the spasmodic movements become less prevalent and are replaced by joyously open steps until the dancers finally travel around the stage as a contiguous, united group. At the end, however, solemnity replaces ecstasy: the performers—dancers and musicians alike—raise candles high above their heads and hold them there, flickering with promise, as the lights fade.

The reds and greens of the dancers' costumes, the small, hopeful lights of the candles, and the heartbeat throb that underlies the drumming, all compel us to share the experience. Salvation is possible, and we have been allowed to partake of it. . . .

The dancers are gifted and daring, the music is compelling, and the choreography is both inventive and inspired. Quite simply, Zollar and her company are artists of major importance. (*The Record*, May 13, 1994)

Ralph Lemon

Ralph Lemon: Taking choreography seriously:

At 35, Ralph Lemon is one of a generation of so-called "emerging choreographers"—a description that makes it sound as if they were climbing out of a swimming pool. . . .

In 1979, Lemon left Minneapolis, where he was a member of a dance company, for New York; he worked with respected choreographers—including Blondell Cummings and Meredith Monk—and began producing his own dances. In 1985, he incorporated his own company. Two years later, he won a Bessie Award and an American Choreographers Award; the following year, he took the gold medal in the Boston International Choreography Competition.

Last fall, Lemon was commissioned by the Lyon Opera Ballet to make a work to music by Frank Zappa; the dance had its premiere during the Lyon Biennale de la Danse, a prestigious international event. Next month, he will be traveling to Braz, Austria, to execute a commission.

In short, he has established himself on the international stage . . . .

"It's [a choreographer's] job," he [explains], "to keep pushing. I don't want to pin anything down yet because I don't know what I'm doing yet. The job is to destroy myself, and to go on finding out what I'm doing and what I know. With each new dance, I have to destroy what I did with the last one. If I try holding on, I won't learn what else I can do or where dance can go."

As a black man, Lemon is a spokesman for an artistic generation on another level as well. It is less than 35 years since Alvin Ailey began bringing black dance and dancers into the mainstream of concert performance.

Modern and post-modern dance are producing a strong contingent of African-American choreographers whose work may, or may not, incorporate ethnic themes and traditional music. Garth Fagan, Bill T. Jones, Ulysses Dove, and Bebe Miller (with whom Lemon danced in 1986–87) work in different styles and cannot easily be type-cast. (*The Record,* May 7, 1991)

Lemon: A Mover and Shaker in Choreography:

Ralph Lemon's dances turn the stage into a pulsing, restless ocean of movement. Although the choreographer sometimes will focus the eye on an individual image or a moment of stillness, he concentrates on flowing patterns made of interlocking phrases. . . .

Movement itself—sheer, satisfying, inventive physicality—is of intense importance to Lemon. However, movement does not exist merely for its own sake; it supports a powerful emotional intent.

The very title of [his] new pieces—*Phrases Almost Biblical* and *Their Eyes Rolled Back in Ecstasy*—suggest mysticism and a search for salvation. *Phrases*, especially, is filled with references to flight. Dancers soar, only to be drawn back to earth by gravity, and take off again; they fall loosely to the stage floor and rebound effortlessly; they turn in air, swinging their legs out horizontally.

The piece is danced in silence, except for occasional dance-rehearsal words—"And!" "Again!" "Stop!"—spoken by a recorded voice, the amplified sound of breathing, and a burst of church bells.

The bells sound again, surprising us, in *Their Eyes Rolled Back in Ecstasy*, and Lemon has introduced into that dance a few easily remembered moments from *Phrases*, such as the striking image of a tiny woman hanging from a larger one's arms, half child, half symbiont.

Ecstasy thus is a continuation of the earlier *Phrases*, but it is a more thoroughly controlled piece of choreography.

For one thing, it's more horizontal: We're aware of entrances and exits and of repeated patterns. We see very clearly the way dancers propel one another through space or rebound from each other's bodies like billiard balls coming off the cushions. The choreography makes us aware of the changes in groupings, rather than letting the dance move almost seamlessly past our eyes. . . .

Their Eyes Rolled Back in Ecstasy/Solo, danced by Lemon himself, seems to be almost a meditation on the pose—lying prone, with one arm hooked sharply near the head—with which the group work ends.

While *Phrases* and the group *Ecstasy* are dances about flowing motion, the solo is concerned with deliberate, uncertain movement and with stillness. At the beginning, Lemon moves tentatively, rising from the floor as if unsure of how to move on two legs. He sustains poses for a long time as if testing the feel of them before gaining confidence and the freedom to continue his journey.

Taken together, the works are physically fascinating and emotionally intense. (*The Record*, January 29, 1993)

Mark Morris

Three Preludes (1992), *performed by the New York City Ballet: Baryshnikov dances Morris:*

. . . *Three Preludes* [is] a solo made for [Mikhail Baryshnikov] by Mark Morris. . . .

The ballet, choreographed to piano music by George Gershwin, playfully suggests the sophisticated style of dancing epitomized by Fred Astaire. Baryshnikov comes on stage with a small, feet-together jump, his back to us, and the gentle surprise of that entrance prepares us for the theatricality to come.

He advances in profile, rising onto half-toe and descending again as his white-gloved hands flex and relax. In the second, adagio, movement, he bends smoothly at the waist, giving his steps a jazzy, off-center quality. His hands sweep high; they bend, they play with the rhythms of the music. The dancer slips into a sitting position on stage, facing away from the audience, and rests easily for a moment.

Three Preludes is notable for the variety of steps Morris has devised, and for the logic with which he has linked them.

The central point is that everything looks effortless: leaps, lunges, sweeping arms, bends of the torso, all are executed with seamless ease. Yet it's all achieved only by carefully monitored effort: Baryshnikov's arms open upward to the full extent of their reach; his small, noiseless steps cover a carefully calculated amount of space in an equally precise segment of time.

Timing, in fact, is key. Morris gets smoothness and surprise by the way he phrases the steps—that first entrance and Baryshnikov's abrupt exits at the end of each segment—and the dancer's intense physical control accents those phrases. Baryshnikov, for his part, lets a bending of his knees or fingers bring out the gentle humor of Morris' choreography.

Everything about the short ballet—even the single spotlight focused on the dancer—recalls the charm and charisma of an old-fashioned nightclub act or vaudeville turn. Gershwin's music, of course, suggests Broadway and American classicism, and Morris pays tribute to those styles.

The choreography is based on the vocabulary of academic ballet, but its presentation and structure create images of popular theater. The piece might be read as a catalog of the virtues Americans have come to value in dancing—and, by extension, in ourselves: daring, virtuosity, confidence, humor, and an almost casual style of execution.

Baryshnikov's charm and magnetism allow Morris to display another admired aspect of American performance—the star in the spotlight, alone, unchallenged, and compelling . . .

Such humility comes from the knowledge of tested skill, and of talent, and of a job well done. Baryshnikov and Morris can claim all three.

(*The Record,* June 18, 1992)

L'Allegro, il Penseroso ed il Moderato: *Highly acclaimed . . . with reservations:*

Mark Morris' *L'Allegro, il Penseroso ed il Moderato* is as joyfully and charmingly naive as only a highly sophisticated intelligence could make it.

The evening-length, highly acclaimed dance . . . [is set] to an oratorio by Handel, composed in 1740, with a libretto arranged from two poems by John Milton that were written about 100 years earlier. The first poem celebrates joy, the second, melancholy.

Knowing his history as well as he does his music, the choreographer suggests the lavish entertainments of the baroque era with their nymphs and shepherds, yet he is too smart to imitate them. Adrienne Lobel's set consists of a simple frame and colored screens that rise and fall; the costumes by Christine Van Loon are tights and loose shirts for the men and soft, simple dresses for the women.

Furthermore, the work is anything but aristocratic in conception. There is no central figure, no central couple, no protagonist, antagonist, or indeed, any agonist at all. Dancers, usually in clusters, emerge from the shifting shapes of the ensemble and then return to it, performing as members of a community rather than as self-defined individuals.

The movement reminds us that Morris had youthful experience performing with a folk-dance troupe: There's a great deal of precisely crafted ensemble work in the piece, and its most striking and beautiful passages result from the development of patterns, not of steps.

The weaknesses of *L'Allegro* stem from the same source as its virtues. The lack of individuality and the choreographer's preference for symmetrical groupings eventually place limitations on the work's visual interest, and deliberate naiveté has its limitations. (*The Record*, July 16, 1995)

Bill T. Jones

Still/Here (1994): *Choreographing from life:*

Bill T. Jones—42 years old, tall, sleekly muscular, astonishingly handsome, recipient of a MacArthur "genius" grant, and in constant demand as a dancer and choreographer—was diagnosed HIV-positive 10 years ago. He's still here, and *Still/Here* is the name of his new dance-theater work . . . .

During the past two years, Jones has visited 11 American cities, conducting and videotaping "survival workshops" with people who are dealing with life-threatening illnesses. However, *Still/Here* is not about illness, or dying, or even survival: It's about living.

Sipping tea at a Manhattan hotel and speaking with silken-voiced intensity, Jones recalls receiving his diagnosis: "I thought initially I was going to keel over. I was hoping I would make it to my Joyce Theater season that year, and then to my BAM season in 1985. Now, I don't think that way. I've decided to use the conditions of my life and not be used by them."

He quotes a woman who took part in one of the workshops as saying: "The thing about a life-threatening illness is that it raises questions any reasonable adult should be thinking about."

Common themes emerged in the workshops: "People found introspection was a survival technique," Jones remembers. "People have to have a spiritual component in their lives to go the distance—and an atheist can have a spiritual experience, too."

Living is a complex process, and *Still/Here* is a complex work. It incorporates Jones' choreography, performed by his own company, with Gretchen Bender's videos, some of which Bender abstracted from tapes made during the workshops. . . .

Jones is identified as a choreographer, but like his massive *Last Supper at Uncle Tom's Cabin* of 1990, *Still/Here* is more a piece of theater than conventional dance. "You have to remember," he explains, "that I started from theater and that I started late as a dancer. My early influences were literary and cinematic.

"I'm a storyteller; storytelling is something I inherited from my mother and father. Besides that, many of my friends were visual artists, and we'd sit around and talk about technique."

The central factor in *Still/Here*, as in all his work, is movement, but other art forms augment and heighten it, sometimes by contrast. Five screens provide a "media environment" for the presentation of Bender's videos.

"I like the cultural reference video brings," Jones explains. "Video is intrusive in our culture. Dance is flesh-based work; video is distancing. discontinuity—a certain kind of counterpoint—creates a level of abstraction." Video—or decor, or costuming—is intended to function in concert with the dance, not to distract from it. "I always want to make a piece of dance my company can do beautifully," the choreographer says. "I'm not going to hand my dancers impersonal material. The movement is informed by this experience, by emotional content."

Since Jones' work is so strongly evocative of emotion and so intensely related to social issues, it comes as a bit of a surprise when he remarks that his favorite choreographer is the great formalist Merce

Cunningham. (At a Cunningham concert a few years ago, Jones remarked with obvious sincerity: "I'm here to learn something.")

Yet, he goes on, "I don't live in the same world as he does. What are the questions he faces, and what are mine?"

Asking questions is the key to Jones' technique in approaching a project: "What questions do I ask to do this work?" It's a method, he says, that arose logically from the circumstances of his upbringing.

He was raised in upstate New York (he lives in Rockland), one of 12 children. His childhood was informed by his mother's religious certainty, he says, but also "by our being migrant workers at the bottom of the pecking order.

"That made me think: How can I be a second-class citizen when I'm told I can be president if I work hard enough? The world is full of hypocrisy: What do you do with the rage and consternation you might feel?

"Young people sometimes go off the deep end when they find out how the world really works—I refused to become cynical and give up. I learned to wake up and to say what is going right and what's not."

His own rage and consternation became material for dances. Unlike many choreographers of earlier generations who made works questioning the integrity of American society, Jones didn't start from a protected status. He's black; he's gay' he's an artist—that's three strikes right there.

Yet Jones didn't creep back to the dugout. In a way, he is proof that the system can live up to its claims: He did work hard, and he is a successful and respected artist. At the same time, he's an artist with honest reasons to challenge the smug self-satisfaction with which society often regards itself: the attitude he calls, when discussing *Still/Here*, "the arrogance of the well."

"The arrogance of the well—the arrogance of youth," the choreographer explains, "lies in saying, 'This doesn't involve me.' Think about someone you love and how life is for them; that puts it into perspective." (*The Record*, November 29, 1994)

Still/Here (1994): *Death in the abstract:*

It is impossible, I think, to watch Bill T. Jones' *Still/Here* without feeling the certain and uncomfortable realization that one day you're going to die, and wondering how you'll deal with the death sentence when some doctor or other pronounces it. Those you love are going to die, too, and you'll have to go on without them. How will you deal with that?

Oddly enough, although the dance-theater work is sometimes disturbing, it is not in the least depressing. In Elizabethan-Jacobean tragedy, the hero almost always speaks a line affirming his sense of self and choosing, rather than blindly awaiting his fate: "This is I, Hamlet the Dane;" "I am Duchess of Malfi still." It is that spirit, at once accepting and defiant, that animates *Still/Here*.

To prepare the evening-long piece, . . . [Jones] conducted "survival workshops" with people afflicted by life-threatening illnesses. Tapes voices and visual images from those sessions provide some of the material for the work; Jones' choreography, abstract where the tapes are precise, creates a counterpoint.

Gretchen Bender's videos, projected on five screens that move in and out during the course of the work, show us the faces and bodies of workshop participants. the lyrics used by composers Kenneth Frazelle (*Still*) and Vernon Reid [founder of the rock band Living Colour] (*Here*) are largely selected from workshop dialogues. (Odetta's performances of Frazelle's songs ranged from the delicate to the ferocious and contributed greatly to their power.)

Yet the images, moving though they are, seem somehow less real, less dramatically intense, than the figures of Jones's dancers: broad-shouldered, big-bellied Lawrence Goldhubber; tall, lean, shaven-headed Odile Reine-Adelaide; muscular Torrin Cummings; short, powerful Arthur Aviles—one of the finest dancers we have—and all the rest.

Executing the choreography, which sometimes is gestural and sometimes abstract, they become personifications, not only of the specific human beings whose words they amplify but of humanity itself. Nobody is simply performing steps: The dancers invest every action, no matter how simple or how athletic, with emotional intensity.

No matter how vivid the performances, though, the dominant force in the piece is the power and perception of Jones's vision. one reason *Still/Here* is not depressing is that, from the simple, dignified patterns of the opening until the end, nobody onstage is ever alone for long.

Dancers constantly support each other, often in paired partnerships but frequently in larger groupings. The full company surrounds a dancer, holding him up and lifting him high. . . .

Toward the end of the second section ("Here"), a taped voice asks, "How could you conceptualize your life if you could draw it as a line?" The piece itself seems an answer to that question. The first half is generally studied and formal, the second begins with similar disciplined movement but erupts into an episode of wild, physically violent individualism before resolving again into calm.

Movement motifs from the first act are repeated in the second, gaining in meaning. In "Still," Aviles appears in profile performing a squared-off arabesque that keeps his back absolutely parallel to the floor. It's a striking posture and an amazing display of skill, but its full meaning doesn't come clear until, near the end of "Here," Aviles executes a variation of the pose, this time facing upstage, and his body becomes an arrow pointing toward the future.

Before the performance began, Jones, who does not dance in the piece, appeared on stage with his mother, Estella, dancing with sharp, powerful gestures as she sang a bit of a gospel hymn and then prayed movingly in rhythmic gospel-preacher style, for the sick, the well, and the mothers of suffering children. Amen. (*The Record*, December 2, 1994)

Bill T. Jones teams with poet Toni Morrison and musician Max Roach.

Degga [premiering the next week as part of New York's Lincoln Center's summer Serious Fun! Series] . . . offers as impressive a lineup of collaborators as we're likely to see: Bill T. Jones, Toni Morrison, and Max Roach.

. . . ["Degga"] means "hear" or "understand" in Wolof, a Niger-Congo language. . . . The piece is about somebody learning; about acquiring knowledge. . . .

The morning of the rehearsal, a newspaper story reports that the House of Representatives is moving toward a vote that would end all financing for the National Endowment for the Arts in two years. The article notes that the NEA was being attacked for supporting works that dealt with "homosexuality, nudity, and religion."

Jones . . . looked over the story and suddenly said, in a quiet, surprised voice, "Homosexuality, nudity, and religion—they're talking about me." His name was not mentioned, of course, but Jones is openly gay and HIV-positive, and his mother's deep religious faith was an important influence on his childhood. He makes works that often deal with homosexuality and religion and sometimes employ nudity.

The end of the NEA would not mean the end of Jones's work. . . . Yet his is deeply concerned, because, he says, "NEA funding says that America wants art. the question being asked is, 'Is art as important to us as highways?'"

Jones is resident choreographer of the Lyons Opera Ballet in France, where he just signed a three-year contract. "I don't want—I can't —look to Europe for a place to create," he says quietly. "I'm an American. France could not have invented Bill T. Jones." (*The Record*, July 21, 1995)

This was one of Joseph H. Mazo's last articles. He died July 26, 1995.

BIBLIOGRAPHY

IT WOULD HAVE BEEN possible to document every quotation, performance, and event with a footnote in proper scholarly fashion. However, I have an aversion to footnotes in popular writing. The little numerals, asterisks, and daggers that call one's attention to the documentation are as demanding as a telephone. We feel obliged to obey their commands to look at the bottom of the page, interrupting the far more important and interesting business of learning what happens next. I wanted readers to be free to concentrate on the development of an art without distractions.

Dispensing with footnotes does not mean one can do away with documentation altogether. It is dishonest to present a book based on research without giving credit to the writers and scholars who produced the original material. That is as reprehensible as inventing facts, and furthermore, it is unsporting to leave readers without some way to check data. It is also my hope that some readers will want to learn more about the subject, and the following list of books and articles can serve to guide them.

Another difference between popular and scholarly writing is that a scholar is obliged to rely primarily on original sources while a popular writer may cheat now and then, and trust the work of his predecessors. As a matter of fact, I have nearly always investigated primary sources, but in a few instances I have relied on secondary materials and it seems only fair to say so.

My primary sources have nearly always come from the Dance Collection of the New York Public Library. The collection includes books, magazine articles, newspaper clippings, photographs, drawings, tape recordings, and motion pictures. All films and tape-recorded interviews (other than those I conducted) as well as many of the newspaper and magazine reviews to which I refer can be found there. I have not listed in this bibliography the date and source of every review used in preparing the text, although I have listed critical pieces that are essentially essays. Those interested in specific reviews will find them on file at the Dance Collection.

This bibliography mentions only materials I used directly during the preparation of *Prime Movers;* it does not include all the works bearing on the subject I read or examined during the eighteen months it took to prepare and write the manuscript. Some of the works I have listed may seem, at first glance, to have little bearing on the subject. In such cases, I have made a short note explaining the relevance of each work. I have also noted some books that are outstanding in their fields to make it easy for anyone who wants information about a specific choreographer to find a particular good source.

Four books need to be mentioned separately from the rest because they served as starting places and standard guides. My basic reference to American history has been Samuel Eliot Morison's *The Oxford History of the American People.* My desk reference to dance has been *The Dance Encyclopedia.* For quick reference and reminders in the field of general information, I have trusted *The Columbia Encyclopedia.* My desk dictionary is *The Shorter Oxford.*

BOOKS AND ARTICLES

Allen, Frederick Lewis, *Only Yesterday: An Informal History of the 1920s.* New York: Harper & Row, 1931.

Anderson, Jack, "Louis and Nikolais: Sharing the Stage," in the program of the Brooklyn Academy of Music, January 1972.

———, "Some Personal Grumbles About Martha Graham," in *Ballet Review,* Vol. II, No. 1, 1967.

Andrews, E. D., "The Dance in Shaker Ritual," in *Dance Index,* April 1942.

Armitage, Merle (Ed.), *Martha Graham.* New York: Dance Horizons, 1966. (First published in a limited edition in 1937; contains important essays about Graham's early work.)

Barnes, Clive, "The Cold War in Modern Dance," in *The New York Times Magazine,* July 28, 1968. (Deals with Cunningham and Taylor.)

——————, "Graham's New Myths and Diversions," in *The New York Times,* November 14, 1965.

——————, "Looks at Lightning," in *Dance and Dancers,* October 1963. (About Graham.)

——————, "Martha in Europe," in *Dance and Dancers,* January 1963.

Battcock, Gregory (Ed.), *The New Art: A Critical Anthology.* New York: E. P. Dutton & Co., 1966.

Becker, Ernest, *The Denial of Death.* New York: The Free Press, 1973. (A major work of contemporary psychology and anthropology.)

Beiswanger, George, "Dance Over the U.S.A." (Part I), in *Dance Observer,* January 1943.

——————, "New Images in Dance," in *Theatre Arts,* October 1944. (About Graham.)

——————, "New London Residues and Reflections" (Part V), in *Dance Observer,* March 1957, (About Limon.)

Bergman, Maurice A., "A Young Creative Dancer Urges More Americanism in the Dance," in *The Jewish Tribune,* January 27, 1928. (Interview with Tamiris.)

Bernstein, Irving, *The Lean Years: A History of the American Worker, 1920–1933.* New York: Houghton Mifflin Co., 1960.

Bossaglia, Rosina, *Art Nouveau: Revolution in Interior Design.* New York: Crescent Books, 1971.

Briggs, John, *Requiem for a Yellow Brick Brewery: A History of the Metropolitan Opera.* Boston: Little, Brown & Co., 1969. (As delightful as its title.)

Buckle, Richard, *Nijinsky.* New York: Simon & Schuster, 1971. (Contains a thorough description of the Diaghilev season of 1909 which brought about the rebirth of ballet in Western Europe.)

Bugbee, Emma, "Martha Graham Warns Girls of Hardships of a Dance Career," in *The New York Herald Tribune,* January 21, 1941.

Cage, John, *Silence.* Middletown, Conn.: Wesleyan University Press, 1973.

Campbell, Joseph, *The Masks of God; Creative Mythology.* New York: The Viking Press, 1968. (The fourth volume in a series which should be studied by anyone interested in the concepts of Jungian theory in modern interpretation of myth or in the creative process.)

"Choreographic Success Story: Triple-Threat Tamiris," in *Cue,* June 8, 1946.

Chujoy, Anatole and Manchester, P. W. (Eds.), *The Dance Encyclopedia,* revised and enlarged edition. New York: Simon & Schuster, 1967. (The standard reference in the field.)

Cohen, Ellen, "Alvin Ailey, Arsonist," in *The New York Times Magazine,* April 29, 1973.

Cohen, Selma Jean, *Doris Humphrey; An Artist First.* Middletown, Conn.: Wesleyan University Press, 1972. (An autobiography, edited and completed by Cohen.

The volume includes essays by Humphrey and a chronology of her dances by Christina L. Schlundt. A thorough, scholarly and intensely valuable book.)

Cohen, Selma Jean (Ed.), *The Modern Dance: Seven Statements of Belief.* Middletown, Conn.: Wesleyan University Press, 1965. (Among the statements are essays by José Limón, Paul Taylor, and Alwin Nikolais.)

Cohen. Selma Jean, "Merce Cunningham: A Profile," in *The Dancing Times,* August 1964.

Coleman, Emily, "Martha Graham Still Leaps Forward," in *The New York Times Magazine,* April 19, 1961.

Coleman, Martha, "On the Teaching of Choreography," in *Dance Observer,* December 1950. (Quotes Nikolais.)

Cooper, H. E., "Loie Fuller," in *The Dance Magazine,* February 1927.

Croce, Arlene, *"Avant-Garde on Broadway,"* in *Ballet Review,* Vol. II, No. 5, 1969. (The celebrated season at the Billy Rose Theater.)

——————, "Twyla Tharp's Red Hot Peppers," in *Ballet Review,* Vol. IV, No. 1, 1971.

——————, "New York Newsletter: Merce Cunningham and Jerome Robbins," in *The Dancing Times,* March 1970.

——————, "New York Newsletter: Some Thoughts on Alwin Nikolais," in *The Dancing Times,* February 1970.

Cunningham, Merce, "Summerspace Story," in *Dance Magazine,* June 1966.

Darling, Harriett Tarbox, "And the First Was Loie Fuller," in *The Dance Magazine,* March 1926.

de Mille, Agnes, "Dialogue on Dance," in *Channel 13/WNET Program Guide,* January 1966. (About Graham.)

——————, "Martha Graham," in *The Atlantic Monthly,* November 1950.

Denby, Edwin, *Looking at the Dance.* New York: Curtis Books, 1973. (Originally published by Horizon Press Publishers, Ltd. The articles and short critical pieces were written between 1936 and 1949. Denby is a poet and one of the finest dance critics in history. He makes clear to a reader exactly what has happened on stage—and that is very difficult to do.)

Deutscher, Isaac, *The Prophet Unarmed: Trotsky, 1921–1929.* New York: Vintage Books. (Originally published in 1959 by Oxford University Press. Describes the conditions prevailing in the U.S.S.R. when Isadora Duncan operated her state-supported school there. The three-volume biography, of which this is the second book, is worth reading for reasons having nothing to do with dance.)

di Morini, Claire, "Loie Fuller, The Fairy of Light," in *Dance Index,* March 1942.

Dos Passos, John, *The Big Money.* New York: Houghton Mifflin, 1946. (Part of the trilogy, *U.S.A.,* which, although it seems dated, was a major experiment in American novel-writing. A strongly drawn portrait of the United States during the first third of the century, and a major study in American mythology.)

Doucet, Jerome, Interview with Loie Fuller, in *Revue Illustrée*, November 1, 1903.

Dreier, Katherine S., *Shawn the Dancer*. New York: A. S. Barnes, 1933.

Duncan, Irma, *The Technique of Isadora Duncan*. New York: Dance Horizons, 1970.

——————, *Duncan Dancer*. Middletown, Conn: Wesleyan University Press, 1966.

Duncan, Irma and MacDougall, Allan Ross, *Isadora Duncan's Russian Days*. New York: Covici–Friede, 1929.

Duncan, Isadora, *My Life*. New York: Boni and Liveright, 1927.

Duncan, Isadora, (edited by Sheldon Cheney) *The Art of the Dance*. New York: Theater Arts Books, 1969. (Contains essays and writings by and about Duncan.)

Flemming, Maureen, Interview with Ruth St. Denis, in *The Dancing Times,* December 1934.

Friedman, Edna A., *American Opinions on Dance and Dancing from 1840 to 1940*. Unpublished thesis, New York University, 1940.

Fokine, Michel, *Fokine: Memoirs of a Ballet Master*. Boston: Little, Brown & Co., 1961.

Fuller, Loie, *Fifteen Years of a Dancer's Life*. Boston: Small, Maynard & Co., 1913.

Gamow, George, *One, Two, Three . . . Infinity: Facts and Speculations About Science,* Revised edition. New York: The Viking Press, 1961. (Explains relativity, probability, and other matters so gently that even a dance critic can understand them.)

Gibbs, Angelica, "Profiles: The Absolute Frontier," in *The New Yorker,* December 27, 1947. (A thorough, informative piece about Graham.)

Gilbert, Douglas, *American Vaudeville, Its Life and Times*. New York: Dover Publications, 1963. (First published in 1940 by Whittlesey House. The book makes up in enthusiasm what it lacks in organization, and it is a mine of material.)

Graham, Martha, *The Notebooks of Martha Graham*. New York: Harcourt Brace Jovanovich, 1973.

——————, "Dance, an Interview with Martha Graham," in *Federal Theatre Magazine,* 1933. (No author, no precise date.)

——————, "Martha Graham Speaks," in *Dance Observer,* April 1963, edited by Walter Sorell from a speech Graham gave at The Juilliard School in 1952.

——————, "Says Martha Graham," in *Musical America,* February 1953.

——————, "Martha Graham Talks to Dance and Dancers," in *Dance and Dancers,* February 1963.

Goldner, Nancy, "Dance" in *The Nation.* May 11, 1970. (Essay on Ailey.)

Grauert, Ruth E., et al. *The Dance Theater of Alwin Nikolais,* Souvenir Program for the company, 1968.

Halacy, D. S., Jr., *Computers: The Machines We Think With*. New York: Dell Publishing Co., 1962. (Contains the unfortunate history of Charles Babbage.)

Hastings, Baird, "The Denishawn Era (1914–1931)," in *Dance Index,* June 1942.

Herigel, Eugen, *Zen in the Art of Archery* (translated by R. F. D. Hull). New York: Pantheon Books, 1953.

Higham, Charles, *Ziegfeld*. Chicago: Henry Regnery Co., 1972.

Holmes, Anthony, "On Working With Martha Graham," in *Dance and Dancers*, February 1973.

Horst, Louis, "Pre-Classic Dance Forms." New York: *Dance Horizons*, 1968. (Originally published in 1937 by *The Dance Observer*.)

——————, "Tamiris," in *Dance Observer*, April 1934.

Humphrey, Doris, *The Art of Making Dances* (Edited by Barbara Pollack). New York: Holt, Rinehart and Winston, 1959.

——————, "What Shall We Dance About?" in *Trend: A Quarterly of the Seven Arts*, June/July/August 1932.

Jowitt, Deborah, "Take a Trip With Monk," in *The New York Times*, January 13, 1974.

——————, "Twyla Tharp's New Kick," in *The New York Times Magazine*, January 4, 1976.

Kaprow, Allan, "Calling, A Happening for performers only," in *Tulane Drama Review*, Winter 1965. (This issue of TDR is of great value to anyone interested in the avant-garde theatrical styles of the period.)

Kermode, Frank, "Loie Fuller and the Dance Before Diaghilev," in *Theatre Arts*, September 1962. (A fine piece of work by an eminent scholar.)

Kirby, Michael and Schechner, Richard, "An Interview With John Cage," in *Tulane Drama Review*, Winter 1965.

Kirstein, Lincoln, *Dance: A Short History of Theatrical Dancing*. New York: Dance Horizons, 1969. (Originally published in 1935 by G. P. Putnam's Sons.)

Kisselgoff, Anna, "Paul Taylor Assays Modern Dance," in *The New York Times*, November 28, 1972.

Klosty, James (Ed.), *Merce Cunningham*. New York: Saturday Review Press, 1975. (Contains essays by Carolyn Brown, John Cage, and Paul Taylor, among others, and a fine selection of photographs.)

Lens, Sidney, *Radicalism in America*. New York: Thomas Y. Crowell Co., 1966.

Limón, José, "Dancers Are Musicians Are Dancers," in *The Juilliard Review Annual, 1966–1967*. (A convocation address delivered by Limón on October 5, 1966.)

——————, "Music Is the Strongest Ally to a Dancer's Way of Life," in *Musical America*, February 15, 1955.

Link, Arthur S., *Woodrow Wilson and the Progressive Era, 1910–1917*. New York: Harper & Row, 1954.

Lloyd, Margaret, *The Borzoi Book of Modern Dance*. New York: Alfred A. Knopf, 1949.

——————, "Changing Fashions in Dance," in *The Christian Science Monitor*, February 20, 1960. (About Paul Taylor.)

——————, "Dances About People—For People," in *The Christian Science Monitor*, February 13, 1938. (About Tamiris.)

——————, "The New Martha Graham," in *The Christian Science Monitor*, March 21, 1942 and April 11, 1942.

MacDougall, Allan Ross, "Isadora Duncan and the Artists," in *Dance Index*, March 1946.

Martin, John, *America Dancing*. New York: Dance Horizons, 1968. (Originally published in 1936 by Dodge Publishing Co.)

——————, "Days of Divine Indiscipline," in *Dance Perspectives*, Autumn 1961.

——————, *Introduction to the Dance*. New York: Dance Horizons, 1965. (Originally published in 1939 by W.W. Norton.)

——————, "The Dancer as an Artist," in *The New York Times Magazine*, April 12, 1953. (About Limon.)

——————, "Isadora Duncan and Basic Dance: Project for a Textbook," in *Dance Index*, April 1942.

——————, "A Modern Artist Applies Her Principles to the Broadway Musical," in *The New York Times*, December 1, 1946. (About Tamiris.)

——————, "Victory for Grahamites," in *The New York Times Magazine*, May 7, 1944.

McDonagh, Don, *The Rise and Fall and Rise of Modern Dance*. New York: Outerbridge and Dienstfrey, 1970. (Concentrates on the period that began with Cunningham. Detailed discussions of many dancers of the Judson era.)

——————, *Martha Graham*. New York: Popular Library, 1975. (Originally published in 1973 by Praeger. Contains a valuable chronology of Graham's work compiled by Leighton Kerner and Andrew Wentick with McDonagh's assistance.)

——————, "A Conversation with Gertrude Shurr," in *Ballet Review*, Vol. 4, No. 5, 1973.

McNamara, Brooks, "Vessel: The Scenography of Meredith Monk," in *Drama Review*, March 1972.

Migel, Parmenia, *The Ballerinas: From the Court of Louis XIV to Pavlova*. New York: The Macmillan Co., 1972.

Monk, Meredith, "Comments of a Young Choreographer," in *Dance Magazine*, June 1968.

Morison, Samuel Eliot, *The Oxford History of the American People*. New York: Oxford University Press, 1965.

Morris, Robert, "Notes on Dance," in *Tulane Drama Review*, Winter 1975.

Nelson, Pauline, "An American Dancer," in *The Dance Observer*. (n.d.) (About Graham.)

Nikolais, Alwin, "In the Words of Alwin Nikolais," in *Cue Magazine*, December 27, 1969.

—————————, comments during a symposium, "Composer/Choreographer," in *Dance Perspectives*, Nov. 16, 1963.

Nuchtern, Jean, "Bertram Ross . . . Person and Performer," in *Eddy*, Winter 1974.

Odets, Clifford, *Waiting for Lefty* in *Six Plays by Clifford Odets*. New York: The Modern Library, 1939.

O'Neill, William L., *Everyone Was Brave: The Rise and Fall of Feminism in America*. Chicago: Quadrangle Books, 1969.

Palmer, Stuart, "Doris Humphrey; Mistress of the Group," in *Dance Magazine*, June 1931. (An interview. The magazine prints a transcription of Palmer's questions and Humphrey's answers.)

—————————, "21 Years of Dance In America," in *The Dancing Times*, October 1931.

Pollack, Barbara, "Profile of José Limon," Typescript, an English version of an article that appeared in Spanish in *Visión*, dated March 2, 1956. In the Limon folders of the Dance Collection of the New York Public Library.

Poster, Constance, "Making It New—Meredith Monk and Kenneth King," in *Ballet Review*, Vol. VI, No. 6, 1967.

Rainey, Ada, "The Art of Ruth St. Denis," in *The Theatre Magazine*, April 1913.

Rhodes, Russell, "New York Letter—Shawn and His Men Dancers at Last Reach Broadway," in *The Dancing Times*, April 1938.

Richardson, Anthony and Stangos, Nikos (Eds.), *Concepts of Modern Art*. New York: Harper & Row, 1974.

Roberts, W. Adolphe, "The Fervent Art of Martha Graham," in *The Dance Magazine*, August 1928.

Rose, Barbara, *American Art Since 1900*, revised and expanded edition. New York: Praeger Publishers, 1975. (A well-researched and readable survey.)

"Ruth St. Denis and her Hindoo Dance, 'Radha'," in *The Theatre*, Vol. 6, No. 61, 1906.

St. Denis, Ruth, *An Unfinished Life*. New York: Dance Horizons, 1969. (Originally published in 1939 by Harper & Brothers.)

Schechner, Richard, "Happenings," in *Tulane Drama Review*, Winter 1965.

Schoenberg, Harold, "Choreography, Music, Sets, Etc. by Alwin Nikolais," in *The New York Times Magazine*, December 6, 1970.

Schlundt, Christina L., *The Professional Appearances of Ted Shawn and His Men Dancers; A Chronology and an Index of Dancers 1933–1940*. New York: The New York Public Library, 1967.

—————————, *Tamiris*. New York: The New York Public Library, 1972.

Seroff, Victor, *The Real Isadora*. New York: The Dial Press, 1971. (Loving but thorough.)

Shaw, George Bernard, *Shaw's Dramatic Criticism (1895–98): A Selection* by *John F.*

Matthews. New York: Hill & Wang, 1959. (At times, even wittier than the plays.)

Shawn, Ted, *Every Little Movement; A Book About François Delsarte,* revised and enlarged edition. New York: Dance Horizons, 1963. (Explains the Delsarte system in all its complexity.)

——————, with Gray Poole, *One Thousand and One Night Stands.* New York: Doubleday, 1960.

——————, "The Changes I've Seen," in *Dance Magazine,* June 1972.

Sherburne, E. C., "Fresh Impulse in Theater Is Seen by Helen Tamiris," in *The Christian Science Monitor,* September 1, 1945.

Siegel, Marcia B., *At the Vanishing Point: A Critic Looks at Dance.* New York: Saturday Review Press, 1972. (A collection of reviews from the seasons of 1968 through 1972; especially good are the analyses of modern and avant-garde dance.)

——————, "Far Out Patriarch," in the Brooklyn Academy of Music Program, February 1972. (About Cunningham.)

——————, "José Limón 1908–1972," in *Ballet Review,* Vol. 1. IV, No. 4, 1973.

Sinclair, Andrew, *The Emancipation of the American Woman.* New York: Harper Colophon Books, 1966.

Snell, Michael, "Cunningham and the Critics," in *Ballet Review,* Vol. III, No. 6, 1971.

Sobel, Bernard, *A Pictorial History of Burlesque.* New York: G. P. Putnam's Sons, 1956.

Sorell, Walter (Ed.), *The Dance Has Many Faces,* second edition. New York: Columbia University Press, 1966. (See especially the articles by Cunningham, Nikolais, and Tamiris.)

——————, "Paul Taylor's Stature Grows," in *The Providence Sunday Journal,* January 12, 1964.

——————, "Weidman Returns to the Lexington 'Y' May 4," in *Dance News,* May 1972.

Spitzer, Marian, *The Palace.* New York: Atheneum, 1969. (The Palace Theater, of course.)

Stall, Norma, "Concerning José Limón," in *Saturday Review,* April 16, 1955.

Stanislavski, Konstantin Sergeyevitch (stage name of Konstantin Sergeyevitch Alekseyev), *An Actor Prepares,* translated by Elizabeth Reynolds Hapgood. New York: Theatre Arts Books, 1948.

——————, *My Life in Art,* translated by J. J. Robbins. Boston: Little, Brown & Co., 1924.

Steegmuller, Francis (Ed.), *Your Isadora: The Love Story of Isadora Duncan and Gordon Craig.* New York: Random House and The New York Public Library, 1974. (Letters and diaries, connected by Steegmuller's carefully researched commentary. Very valuable.)

Stone, I. F., *The Truman Era*. New York: Vintage Books, 1973. (Originally published in 1953 by Monthly Review Press. An era depicted in editorials and commentaries by a great liberal journalist.)

———————, *In a Time of Torment*. New York: Vintage Books, 1968. (Stone on the 1960s.)

Sullivan, Mark, *Our Times, 1900–1925*. New York: Charles Scribner's Sons, 1971. (The first volume of the five-volume work was originally published by Scribner's in 1926. Sullivan took on the task of recording everything that affected the life of the average American, from politics to popular music. The book is an invaluable piece of history, and it is also a delight to browse through.)

Tamiris, Helen, "Go On With the Dance," in *The New York Times*, June 27, 1948.

Taylor, Robert Lewis, *W. C. Fields, His Follies and Fortunes*. New York: The New American Library, 1967. (The tribute of one professional to another, great fun to read.)

Terry, Walter, *The Dance in America*, revised edition. New York: Harper & Row, 1971.

———————, *Miss Ruth: The "More Living Life" of Ruth St. Denis*. New York: Dodd, Mead & Co., 1969.

———————, "A New Appraisal of a Historic Modern Dancer," in *The New York Herald Tribune*, August 1, 1948. (About Shawn.)

———————, "Broadway Dance Trends," in *Dance Magazine*, November 1946. (About Tamiris.)

———————, "Open Interviews 5: Helen Tamiris," in *Dance Observer*, May 1971.

Tharp, Twyla, *The Bix Pieces, Part 2*, Typescript, in Tharp files of the Dance Collection, The New York Public Library.

———————, "Questions and Answers," in *Ballet Review*, Vo. IV, No. 1, 1971.

———————, "Twyla, A Woman Creates," in *The Oberlin Review*, January 22, 1971. (An interview; Tharp's remarks are quoted verbatim.)

Todd, Arthur, "Roots of the Blues," in *Dance and Dancers*, November 1961. (An interview with Alvin Ailey.)

Tompkins, Calvin, "Profile; An Appetite for Motion," in *The New Yorker*, May 1968. (Long, detailed piece on Cunningham; a good source.)

Tugal, Pierre, "Martha Graham Is Interviewed by Pierre Tugal," in *The Dancing Times*, October 1950.

Waters, Frank, *Book of the Hopi*. New York: The Viking Press, 1963. (One aspect of the Southwestern American culture that so fascinated Martha Graham.)

Watts, Alan W., *The Way of Zen*. New York: Pantheon Books, 1957.

Wentick, Andrew, "Doris Humphrey Collection," in *The New York Public Library Bulletin*, Autumn 1973.

"When America Learned to Dance" (no author), condensed from *Scribner's Magazine*,

September 1937. (In the files of the general reference section of the New York Library of the Performing Arts.)

Young, Stark, *Immortal Shadows: A Book of Dramatic Criticism.* New York: Hill & Wang, 1948. (Originally published by Charles Scribner's Sons. The book contains reviews written between 1922 and 1947 by a perceptive and literate critic. The final notice in the volume discusses the work of Martha Graham.)

TAPE RECORDINGS

Ailey, Alvin, interviewed by Marian Horosko, 1956, Oral History Archive, Dance Collection, New York Public Library.

Humphrey, Doris, Lecture to the dance workshop at The Juilliard School, 1956, Oral History Archive, Dance Collection, New York Public Library.

St. Denis, Ruth, interviewed by Walter Terry, 1963, Oral History Archive, Dance Collection, New York Public Library.

Shawn, Ted, interviewed by Marian Horosko, Oral History Archive, Dance Collection, New York Public Library.

Shurr, Gertrude, interviewed by Marian Horosko, 1967, Oral History Archive, Dance Collection, New York Public Library.

INTERVIEWS

Several artists were kind enough to permit me to conduct lengthy interviews with them: Carolyn Adams of the Paul Taylor Company, Alvin Ailey, Merce Cunningham, Alwin Nikolais, Paul Taylor, and Twyla Tharp. All interviews were conducted during 1975, except the one with Twyla Tharp which took place in January 1976. The interviews with Cunningham, Nikolais, and Taylor were conducted primarily to gather material for this book. Those with Adams, Ailey, and Tharp were intended to elicit specific information for pieces which have been published elsewhere, but also touched on matters of more general interest, some of which have been incorporated into this book.

ADDITIONAL BIBLIOGRAPHY
PRIME MOVERS, SECOND EDITION

In keeping with the spirit of Joseph Mazo's original research and documentation, this Additional Bibliography contains references culled from the Dance Collection of the New York Public Library. It includes materials published since 1977 (the publication date of the original *Prime Movers*) which the author might have considered "outstanding in their fields" and which relate directly to comments made in the reviews and previews included in the second edition.

BOOKS AND ARTICLES

Acocella, Joan. *Mark Morris*. New York: Farrar Straus Giroux, 1993

Adam, Judy, ed. *Dancers on a Plane/Cage Cunningham Johns*. New York: Alfred A Knopf; London: Thames & Hudson; in association with Anthony d'Offay Gallery, 1990.

Ailey, Alvin. *Revelations: The Autobiography of Alvin Ailey*. Secaucus, NJ: Carol Publishing Group, 1995.

Anderson, Jack. *Art Without Boundaries*. Iowa City: University of Iowa Press, 1997.

——————. "Paul Taylor: Surface and Substance." *Ballet Review* 6, no. 1 (1977); 39 41.

Baker, Rob. "Geometries: the Song and Dance of Laura Dean." *Dance Magazine* (November 1977): 40–44.

Banes, Sally *Terpsichore in Sneakers: Post-Modern Dance*. Boston: Houghton Mifflin Company, 1980. Reprint. Middletown, CT: Wesleyan University Press.

——————. *Writing Dancing in the Age of Postmodernism*. Hanover, NH: University Press of New England, 1994.

Brown, Trisha, et al. "Conversation in Manhattan." *Impulse* (1967): 57–64.

——————. "Three Pieces." *Drama Review* (T65) 19, no. 1(1975): 26–32.

Cohen, Selma Jeanne, ed. *Dance as a Theatre Art*. New York: Dodd, Mead and Co., 1974. Second ed., with a new section by Katy Matheson. Princeton, NJ: Princeton Book Company, 1992.

——————. *Next Week, Swan Lake: Reflections on Dance and Dances*. Middletown, CT: Wesleyan University Press, 1982.

Conklin, J. L. "Alwin Nikolais." *Salome* 32/33 (1983): 50–57.

Croce, Arlene. *Afterimages*. New York: Alfred A. Knopf, 1978.

Cunningham, Merce. *The Dancer and the Dance/Conversations with Jacqueline Lesschaeve*. New York and London: Marion Boyars, 1985. Second (paperback) edition, 1991.

Current, Richard Nelson and Marcia Ewing Current. *Loïe Fuller: Goddess of Light*. Boston, MA: Northeastern University Press, 1997.

Daly, Ann. *Done into Dance: Isadora Duncan in America*. Bloomington: Indiana University Press, 1995.

De Mille, Agnes. *Martha: The Life and Work of Martha Graham*. New York: Random House, 1991.

Dunning, Jennifer. *Alvin Ailey: A Life in Dance*. Reading, MA: Addison-Wesley, 1996.

Fanger, Iris M. "Ralph Lemon: Private Man in the Public Arena." *Dance Magazine* (August 1991): 38-42.

Garafola, Lynn, ed. *José Limón: An Unfinished Memoir*. Middletown, Conn.: Wesleyan University Press; Hanover, NH: University Press of New England, 1999.

Garske, Rolf. "Art Does Not Care What Form It Takes: Interview with Alwin Nikolais." *Ballett International* 13, no. 6–7 (June/July 1990): 23–29.

Graham, Martha. *Blood Memory*. New York: Doubleday, 1991.

Hawkins, Erick. *The Body is a Clear Place and Other Statements on Dance*. Princeton, NJ: Princeton Book Company, 1992.

Highwater, Jamake. *Dance: Rituals of Experience.* Pennington, NJ: Princeton Book Company, 1992.

Horosko, Marian. "Martha Graham at 95." *Dance Magazine* (May 1989): 50–57.

Horosko, Marian, comp. *Martha Graham: The Evolution of Her Dance Theory and Training, 1926–1991.* Pennington, NJ: A Cappella Books, 1991.

Humphrey Centennial Issue. *Dance Research Journal* 28, no. 2 (Fall 1996).

Jamison, Judith, with Howard Kaplan. *Dancing Spirit: An Autobiography.* New York: Doubleday, 1993.

Jones, Bill T., with Peggy Gillespie. *Last Night on Earth.* New York: Pantheon Books, 1995.

Jowitt, Deborah. *Dance Beat: Selected Views and Reviews 1967–1976.* New York: Marcel Dekker, Inc., 1977.

——————. *Time and the Dancing Image.* New York: W. Morrow, 1988.

Kostelanetz, Richard, ed. *Merce Cunningham: Dancing in Space and Time 1944–1992.* Pennington, NJ: A Cappella Books, 1992.

Kriegsman, Sali Ann. *Modern Dance in America: The Bennington Years.* Boston: G. K. Hall, 1981.

Lemon, Ralph. "An Artist's Journey." *Dance/USA Journal* 14, no. 2 (Fall 1996): 11-13.

Levien, Julia. *Duncan Dance: A Guide for Young People Ages Six to Sixteen.* Pennington, NJ: Princeton Book Company, 1994.

Lewis, Daniel. *The Illustrated Dance Technique of José Limón.* New York: Harper & Row, 1984.

Loewenthal, Lillian. *The Search for Isadora: The Legend & Legacy of Isadora Duncan.* Pennington, NJ: Princeton Book Company, 1993.

Louis, Murray. *Inside Dance: Essays.* New York: St. Martin's Press, 1980.

Mason, Francis. "A Conversation with Garth Fagan." *Ballet Review* 23, no. 1 (Spring 1995): 18–28.

Maynard, Olga. *Judith Jamison, Aspects of a Dancer.* Garden City, NY: Doubleday, 1982.

Mazo, Joseph H. Dance reviews and features. *The Record* (Bergen County, New Jersey), 1984–1995.

——————. "Alwin Nikolais: The Nik of Time." *Dance Magazine* (July 1993): 28–31.

Mindlin, Naomi, ed. *Doris Humphrey: A Centennial Issue. Choreography and Dance* (1997).

——————. "José Limón's *The Moor's Pavane.* An Interview with Lucas Hoving." *Dance Research Journal.* New York: Congress on Research in Dance [CORD] 24, no. 1 (Spring 1992): 13–26.

Morris, Gay, ed. *Moving Words: Re-writing Dance.* London; New York: Routledge, 1996.

Norton, M. L. Gordon, ed. *5 Essays on the Dance of Erick Hawkins.* New York: Foundation for Modern Dance, 1983.

Owen, Norton, *A Certain Place: The Jacob's Pillow Story.* Becket, MA: Jacob's Pillow Dance Festival, 1997.

Pollack, Barbara and Charles Humphrey Woodford. *Dance is a Moment: A Portrait of José Limón in Words and Pictures.* Pennington, NJ: Princeton Book Company, A Dance Horizons Book, 1993.

Quasha, Susan and Elizabeth Zimmer, eds. *Body Against Body: The Dance and Other Collaborations of Bill T. Jones & Arnie Zane.* Barrytown, NY: Station Hill Press, 1989.

Sandomir, Larry. *Isadora Duncan: Revolutionary Dancer.* Austin, TX: Raintree Steck-Vaughn, 1995.

Shelton, Suzanne. *Divine Dancer: A Biography of Ruth St. Denis.* Garden City, NY: Doubleday, 1981.

Sherman, Jane. *Denishawn: The Enduring Influence.* Boston: Twayne Pub., 1983.

——————. *The Drama of Denishawn Dance.* Middletown, CT: Wesleyan University Press, 1979.

Siegel, Marcia B. *At the Vanishing Point.* New York: Saturday Review Press, 1972.

——————. *Days on Earth: The Dance of Doris Humphrey.* 1988. Reprint. Durham: Duke University Press, 1993.

——————. *The Shapes of Change/Images of American Dance.* Boston: Houghton Mifflin, 1979.

Sommer, Sally R. "Loïe Fuller's Art of Music and Light." *Dance Chronicle* 4, no. 4 (1982): 389–401.

Spain, Louise, ed. *Dance on Camera: A Guide to Dance Films and Videos.* New York: Neal-Schuman Publishers, Inc. and Lanham, MD and London: The Scarecrow Press, Inc., 1997.

St. Denis, Ruth. *Wisdom Comes Dancing: Selected Writings of Ruth St. Denis on Dance, Spirituality, and the Body.* Edited by Kamae A. Miller. Seattle, WA: PeaceWorks, 1997.

Stodelle, Ernestine. *Deep Song: The Dance Story of Martha Graham.* New York: Schirmer Books; London: Collier Macmillan, 1984.

——————. *The Dance Technique of Doris Humphrey and Its Creative Potential.* Princeton, NJ: Princeton Book Company, Publishers, 1978.

Taylor, Paul. *Private Domain.* New York: Knopf, 1987.

——————. "Another View: Portrait of the artist as Two Young Men." *Dance Magazine* (Jan. 1993): 64–69.

Twyla Tharp. *Push Comes to Shove.* New York: Bantam, 1992.

Tobias, Tobi. "A Conversation with Martha Graham." *Dance Magazine* (March 1984): 62–67.

——————. "Manchild in the Promised Land: Mark Morris." *Dance Magazine* (Dec. 1984): 28–30.

Muriel Topaz, ed. *Alvin Ailey: An American Visionary. Choreography and Dance.* Amsterdam: Harwood Academic Publishers, 1996.

Vaughan, David. "A Conversation with Mark Morris." *Ballet Review* (Summer 1986): 26–36.

——————. "Garth Fagan Dance: Discipline is freedom." *Dance Magazine* (Nov. 1990): 40–43.

——————. *Merce Cunningham: Fifty Years.* Edited by Melissa Harris. New York: Aperture, 1997.

Zollar, Jawole Willa Jo. "Listen: Our History is Shouting at Us." *Update Dance/USA* 8, no. 3 (Nov./Dec. 1990): 16–18.

SELECTED VIDEOGRAPHY

Most videos listed below can be ordered through Princeton Book Company, Publishers at 1–800–220–7149.

Air for the G String. Choreography by Doris Humphrey. Analysis and Coaching by Ernestine Stodelle. 120 minutes, color, 1997. Dance Horizons Video release, Pennington, NJ.

Baryshnikov Dances Sinatra. Starring Mikhail Baryshnikov and members of the ABT. 60 minutes, color, stereo, 1985. Distributed by Kultur, West Long Branch, NJ.

Bill T. Jones: Dancing to the Promised Land. Performed by the Bill T. Jones/Arnie Zane Dance Co. 60 minutes, color, 1994. Distributed by V.I.E.W. Video, New York.

Cage/Cunningham. 95 minutes, color, filmed in 1991. Distributed by Kultur, West Long Branch, NJ.

Charles Weidman: On His Own. Narrated by Alwin Nikolais. 60 minutes, color & b&w, 1990. Dance Horizons Video release, Pennington, NJ.

Dance Black America. Narrated by Geoffrey Holder. 87 minutes, filmed in 1983, color, 1990. Dance Horizons Video release, Pennington, NJ.

The Dance Works of Doris Humphrey: With My Red Fires and New Dance. Choreographed by Doris Humphrey; Performed by the American Dance Festival Company. 60 minutes, filmed in 1972, color, 1989. Dance Horizons Video release, Pennington, NJ.

The Dance Works of Doris Humphrey II: Ritmo Jondo and Day on Earth. Choreographed by Doris Humphrey; Performed by the Limón Dance Company. 40 minutes, color, 1998. Dance Horizons Video release, Hightstown, NJ.

Dancing. Eight-part, multicultural series filmed in locations around the world, first shown on PBS in May 1993. Approximately 60 minutes per tape. Distributed by Kultur, West Long Branch, NJ.

Denishawn: The Birth of Modern Dance. 40 minutes, color/b&w, 1988. Distributed by Kultur, West Long Branch, NJ.

The Doris Humphrey Legacy: Appreciation and Coaching Documentaries. Air for the G. String (90 minutes), *The Call/Breath of Fire* (63 minutes), *The Shakers* (91 minutes), *Two Ecstatic Themes* (90 minutes), *Water Study* (91 minutes). Color, 1998. Dance Horizons Video, Hightstown, NJ.

Doris Humphrey Technique: The Creative Potential. Written, directed, and hosted by Ernestine Stodelle. 45 minutes, color/b&w, 1992. Dance Horizons Video release, Pennington, NJ.

Erick Hawkins' America. Performed by the Erick Hawkins Dance Company. 57 minutes, color, 1992. Dance Horizons Video release, Pennington, NJ.

An Evening with Alvin Ailey. With the Alvin Ailey American Dance Theatre. 108 minutes, color, 1986. Distributed by Kultur, West Long Branch, NJ.

Five Dances by Martha Graham. Performed by Martha Graham Dance Company. 86 minutes, color, 1996. Distributed by Music Video Distributors, Norristown, PA.

Four by Ailey. With the Ailey Ailey American Dance Theatre. 108 minutes, color, 1986. Distributed by Kultur, West Long Branch, NJ.

Griot New York. Choreography by Garth Fagan, featuring Garth Fagan Dance and the Wynton Marsalis Septet. 87 minutes, color, 1995. Distributed by Music Video Distributors, Norristown, PA.

The Hard Nut. Choreography by Mark Morris, performed by Mark Morris Dance Group. 87 minutes, color, 1992. Distributed by Music Video Distributors, Norristown, PA.

Isadora Duncan Dance. Technique and repertory performed by the Isadora Duncan Dance Ensemble directed by Julia Levien and Andrea Mantell Seidel. 60 minutes, color, 1994. Dance Horizons Video release, Pennington, NJ.

José Limón Modern Dance Classics: The Moor's Pavane, The Traitor, The Emperor Jones. (1957) 65 minutes, b&w, first video release 1999. Distributed by Video Artists International, Pleasantville, NY.

Martha Graham Dance Company: WNET/Dance in America. (1976) 90 minutes, color, 1998. Distributed by Warner Elektra, Nonesuch Videos, Bridgeport, NJ.

Martha Graham: The Dancer Revealed. Narrated by Claire Bloom. 60 minutes, color, 1994. Distributed by Kultur, West Long Branch, NJ.

Martha Graham: In Performance. 93 minutes, b&w, first video release 1988. Distributed by Kultur, West Long Branch, NJ.

The Men Who Danced: The Story of Ted Shawn's Male Dancers, 1933–1940. 30 minutes, produced in 1986, color with b&w historical footage, 1990. Dance Horizons Video release, Pennington, NJ.

Murray Louis in Concert: Dance Solos. Choreography by Murray Louis. 45 minutes, filmed 1972–1988, color, 1989. Dance Horizons Video release, Pennington, NJ.

Paul Taylor Dance Company: WNET/Dance in America. (1977) 58 minutes, color, 1998. Distributed by Warner Elektra, Nonesuch Videos, Bridgeport, NJ.

Points in Space. Merce Cunningham Dance Company. 55 minutes, color, VHS HiFi, 1986. Distributed by Kultur, West Long Branch, NJ.

Speaking in Tongues. Choreography by Paul Taylor, performed by the Paul Taylor Company. 54 minutes, color, 1991. Distributed by Music Video Distributors, Norristown, PA.

Three by Martha Graham. With the Martha Graham Dance Company (1965, 1967, 1969). 87 minutes, color, 1996. Distributed by Pyramid Home Video, Santa Monica, CA.

A Tribute to Alvin Ailey. Features the Alvin Ailey American Dance Theatre. 120 minutes, color, 1992. Distributed by Kultur, West Long Branch, NJ.

The World of Alwin Nikolais. Directed and Narrated by Murray Louis, 5 different programs. Color, 1996. Distributed by Murray Louis Studio, New York.

INDEX